Law, Society, Policy series

Series Editor: **Rosie Harding**,
University of Birmingham

Law, Society, Policy offers an outlet for high quality, socio-legal research
monographs and edited collections with the potential for
policy impact.

Also available in the series

Find out more at
bristoluniversitypress.co.uk/law–society–policy

Forthcoming

Observing Justice
Digital Transparency, Openness and Accountability in Criminal Courts
By **Judith Townend** and **Lucy Welsh**

Children's Voices, Family Disputes and Child-Inclusive Mediation
The Right to Be Heard
By **Anne Barlow** and **Jan Ewing**

Adult Social Care Law and Policy
Lessons from the Pandemic
By **Jean McHale** and **Laura Noszlopy**

Sex Worker Rights Activism and the Politics of Rights:
Within and against the Law
By **Katie Cruz**

International advisory board

Lynette Chua, National University of Singapore
Margaret Davies, Flinders University, Australia
Martha Fineman, Emory University, Atlanta, Georgia, USA
Marc Hertogh, University of Groningen, The Netherlands
Fiona Kelly, La Trobe University, Melbourne, Australia
Fiona de Londras, University of Birmingham, UK
Anna Mäki-Petäjä-Leinonen, University of Eastern Finland
Ambreena Manji, Cardiff University, UK
Linda Mulcahy, University of Oxford, UK
Vanessa Munro, University of Warwick, UK
Debra Parkes, University of British Columbia, Canada
Florence Shako, Riara Law School, Riara University, Kenya
Antu Sorainen, University of Helsinki, Finland
Dee Smythe, University of Cape Town, South Africa
Michael Thomson, Leeds University, UK and UTS, Australia
Bridgette Toy-Cronin, University of Otago, New Zealand
Lisa Vanhala, University College London, UK

Find out more at
bristoluniversitypress.co.uk/law-society-policy

EGALITARIAN DIGITAL PRIVACY

Image-based Abuse and Beyond

Tsachi Keren-Paz

First published in Great Britain in 2023 by

Bristol University Press
University of Bristol
1–9 Old Park Hill
Bristol
BS2 8BB
UK
t: +44 (0)117 374 6645
e: bup-info@bristol.ac.uk

Details of international sales and distribution partners are available at bristoluniversitypress.co.uk

British Library Cataloguing in Publication Data
A catalogue record for this book is available from the British Library

ISBN 978-1-5292-1401-7 hardcover
ISBN 978-1-5292-1402-4 ePub
ISBN 978-1-5292-1403-1 ePdf

Cover design: Andrew Corbett
Front cover image: 123rf/gioiak2
Bristol University Press uses environmentally responsible print partners.
Printed and bound in Great Britain by CPI Group (UK) Ltd, Croydon, CR0 4YY

FSC
www.fsc.org
MIX
Paper | Supporting
responsible forestry
FSC® C013604

To Daphne and Danielle

Contents

Acknowledgements

I thank the Leverhulme Trust, University of Sheffield School of Law and Keele University School of Law for financially supporting this research. Alastair Mullis, Roger Brownsword and Anita Bernstein contributed to the early shaping of my thoughts on the topic during the Fellowship bidding process, and Marie-Andrée Jacob, as always, sprinkled some of her magic powder, alongside members from Keele's Faculty Research Office, to make the bid competitive and fundable. Richard Wright, Roderick Bagshaw and Suzanne Ost helped me sharpen and nuance my argument about the applicability of demand-based theory to the viewing of child pornography. At a later stage, Daithí Mac Síthigh, Janice Richardson, Michael Birnhack and Limor Shmerling Magazanik greatly contributed to the shaping of the project at the book proposal stage.

The ideas in this book benefitted from conversations with and feedback from colleagues. John Murphy and Rebecca Moosavian provided me with excellent comments on earlier drafts of the intermediary liability Chapters (2 to 7). (John also did so at unprecedented speed and with an exceptional level of engagement). Paul Davies has done the same for Chapter 8.

I benefitted from presenting early the core ideas of my book at several fora. I would like to thank the participants in the following workshops and conferences: Trinity College of Dublin; QUB, Belfast; University of Galway; Newcastle University; University of Sheffield; Keele University; the LSA meetings in Mexico City, Toronto and Washington DC, SLSA meeting in Leeds, and SLS meeting in London. I would like to extend special thanks to Nikki Godden-Rasul (who has kindled my interest in this topic), John Danaher, Christine Beuermann, Maria Tzanou, Andreas Rühmkorf, Joe Purshouse and Joanna Shapland.

Thanks are due also to Paul Koster and to Richard Pickett. Paul presented me with the idea that multiple instances of consumption by an individual in prostitution markets create a near certainty the individual would purchase sex from a victim of trafficking (following my argument in my previous book on claims against clients of commercial sex). Richard helped me with the calculations presented in Chapter 9.

During the long incubation period for this project, I benefitted from excellent research assistance by many assistants. The most durable and recent has been Katharine Cramond who was most recently joined by Safia Cecchini and Lucy Eastwood. Previously, I greatly benefitted from the assistance of Faiza Ahmed, Emily Prince, Amy Scarrott, Nida Naqvi, Hazel Beddows, Bushra Jalil, James Brown, Yaar Dagan, Gemma Scott and Stella Coyle.

Thanks are also due to the Bristol University Press team, and in particular the series editor Rosie Harding, and to Helen Davies, Becky Taylor and Freya Trand.

Finally, my deepest thanks go to my family: Marie, Daphne and Danielle. The main bulk of the book was written during the trying COVID-19 pandemic, which affected work patterns and involved some home schooling. That I was able to complete the book, while still being there for them (or so they claim) makes me proud and is a testament of their resilience, patience and generosity.

Series Editor's Preface

The Law, Society, Policy series publishes high-quality, socio-legal research monographs and edited collections with the potential for policy impact. Cutting across the traditional divides of legal scholarship, Law, Society, Policy offers an interdisciplinary, policy-engaged approach to socio-legal research which explores law in its social and political contexts with a particular focus on the place of law in everyday life.

The series seeks to take an explicitly society-first view of socio-legal studies, with a focus on the ways that law shapes social life, and the constitutive nature of law and society. International in scope, engaging with domestic, international and global legal and regulatory frameworks, texts in the Law, Society, Policy series engage with the full range of socio-legal topics and themes.

1

Introduction

It was in 2014 when I first became familiar with the term 'revenge pornography' after being invited to a workshop on the topic organized by Nikky Godden-Rasul in Newcastle Law School. This book is the result of my research on this topic, which was supported by a Leverhulme Research Fellowship on the subject (RF-2016-358\8, 'Privacy law, gender justice and end-users' liability: "revenge porn" and beyond'). My point of entry to the debates surrounding what I will term non-consensual intimate images (NCII, more on the terminology to be discussed later) is multifold. First, I have a longstanding interest in defending and developing the role of equality and distributive justice in private law and tort law in particular (Keren-Paz, 2007a). My initial work on these issues focused, in its doctrinal translation, on the tort of negligence. So this project, at a high level of abstraction, is an attempt to develop the argument into the area of privacy law. Second, I have a lingering interest in law, gender and sexuality, and more specifically, in private law responses to gendered harms, often those thought of as an issue of criminal law, rather than of private (mainly tort) law. So having by then just completed the monograph *Sex Trafficking: A Private Law Response* (Keren-Paz, 2013), the time was ripe to move to examining this other pressing, topical and rapidly evolving site of gender-based harm.

Third – and this possibly was the single most important driver of this project – as part of understanding the demand for sexual services as an instance of a mass sexual tort problem, I have developed a theory of liability for the creation of demand for commercial sexual services, which led to some victims of trafficking having been recruited and exploited to satisfy this demand. This – admittedly radical – theory found some support in the USSC decision of *US v Paroline*, which dealt with apportionment of liability of those who viewed images of child pornography to the injury that victim's knowledge about the viewing produced.[1] I was curious to find out,

---

[1] Chapter 8, Part 1.

then, whether viewers, as 'end-users' of NCII ought to be held liable for the significant injuries suffered by victims, and more specifically, whether a demand-based liability has a significant role to play in the NCII context (for the curious readers, the answers are yes and no respectively). The question of viewers' responsibility for (intentional) viewing of NCII was brought to the fore around that time by Jennifer Lawrence – possibly the highest-profile contemporary NCII victim – who commented '[A]nybody who looked at those pictures, you're perpetuating a sexual offense' (Moore, 2014).

Fourth, around that time and as part of another funded research project dealing with the effect of tort liability on innovation in medicine, I got exposed to, and grew interested in, law and technology literature (ES/ N009223/1, 'Liability v innovation: unpacking key connections' 2015–2017; Keren-Paz and Cockburn, 2019). NCII has a clear technological aspect and the contribution of hosts to victims' injury is significant. So this book is as much about platforms' liability for NCII (and a critique of technological neutrality) as it is about viewers', and the research opened my horizons to the vast literature on internet intermediaries' liability for user generated content ('user content') of which NCII is but one example. Fifth, I have a long-lasting interest in the scope of protecting injury to autonomy in private law, tort law and negligence. Soon after my interest in this project was kindled, the High Court rendered its important decision in *Gulati v MGN*, which somewhat reoriented this debate from the law of negligence to the law of privacy (and other torts actionable per se). *Gulati* triggered a thoughtful (yet ultimately unconvincing) critique by Eric Descheemaeker so in Chapter 11, I clarify my position in this debate. Doctrinally, NCII raises questions about the relationship between the interests in privacy and in reputation and the division of labour between the privacy and defamation torts. Clarifying my view on these important issues was my last entry point into this topic.

1. Definition and terminology

NCII involves the unauthorized (1) dissemination and (2) viewing and at times (3) the creation of intimate images. Following others, I argue that NCII is on the spectrum of sexual abuse. To the same extent that a sexual act could be consensual and at times involve an enthusiastically willing participate or instigator and yet at times might involve lack of consent or even participation against one's will, so can the taking, dissemination and viewing of intimate images. The NCII spectrum includes taking (creation) of images of an underlying independent sexual abuse (as of filming a rape), the non-consensual taking of an image of a consensual sexual act or of one's nudity (as in voyeurism, 'creepshots', 'up-skirting' and 'down-blousing'), hacking and sharing of intimate images taken by the claimant and the non-authorized dissemination of images shared consensually with the distributor. What matters is that the *dissemination* (sometimes referred to as the distribution or sharing) of the images is non-consensual and as such undermines the claimant's privacy, sexual autonomy and dignity. A non-consensual taking of the image (when existing) is itself a form of privacy intrusion, which ought to and usually is considered as independent from the wrong involved in disseminating the image.

From a claimant's perspective, there are typically three actors who might be involved in violating her rights. The person who disseminates the intimate image without authorization; I will refer to him as the uploader (and will refer to the uploader and to the viewer as 'him' and to the claimant/victim as 'her' given the gendered aspect of the phenomenon,[2] accepting of course that there are male victims and female perpetrators of NCII). The uploader might be implicated in the unlawful taking of the image or in the commission of any underlying sexual abuse depicted in the image (as in cases of child pornography to which the Online Harms White Paper 2019 and the Online Safety Bill 2021 refer to as child sexual exploitation and abuse images or CSEA).[3] Uploaders' liability for breach of privacy is relatively straightforward (less so in some US jurisdictions) so I will say relatively little on this topic.[4] Viewers who further disseminate the image, or who post offensive comments, or who stalk or harass the victim harm her in a way that is different and more distinctive than those who merely view, possess or host NCII. Those who disseminate further are akin to uploaders and those who act on the information might independently and additionally commit the torts of defamation and/or harassment and in some more rare cases, a follow-up battery.[5] While their scope of liability does raise some interesting questions, these are not cutting edge or foundational, and for time and space constraints would not be addressed here. Nor will I address here the cutting-edge issue of potential liability for deepfakes NCII where (usually) the face of an actual woman is morphed with an intimate image of another and is distributed.[6] I hope to address this issue in future work.

Internet intermediaries, mainly hosts but also search engines and others are another potential defendant and the terrain here is much more contested, given the claim that they should not be considered as publishers of user content. Finally, there is the question whether the mere act of viewing intrudes on the claimant's privacy and if so, whether there should be liability

---

[2] Chapter 6, Part 2.B.
[3] Both instruments use CSEA, but I will refer to the dissemination and viewing of these images as child pornography.
[4] Chapter 8, Part 2.
[5] Chapter 6, Part 2; Chapter 9, Part 2.
[6] Law Commission, 2022: 157,163 (making of a deepfake without sharing it should not be an offence but sharing of a deepfake should); Chesney and Citron, 2019.

for such intrusion. There are four related questions about the scope of viewers' liability: (1) whether they ought to be liable for any initial abuse (if existing) captured in the image; (2) whether they could be liable to claimants whose images they did not view based on a demand-based theory; (3) whether viewers' liability is strict or limited to only those who sought *non-consensual* intimate images; and (4) whether their liability should be limited, and if so how, given that the harm is overdetermined, namely, that the claimant would have suffered identical or nearly identical harm had the particular defendant not viewed the claimant's images.

NCII is a term that was used by Facebook (now Meta) in 2019 in its early transparency reports (Facebook now uses 'intimate images shared without your consent'). The phenomenon is referred to (and this list is not exhaustive) as 'revenge porn' (Mary Franks, 2017 and many others), 'revenge pornography' (Uhl et al, 2018 and many others), 'non-consensual dissemination of intimate images' (NCDII) (Laidlaw and Young, 2020), 'non-consensual sharing of intimate images' (Nova Scotia Act), 'image-based abuse' (IBA) (Henry, Powell and Flynn, 2017), 'image-based sexual abuse' (IBSA) (McGlynn, Rackley and others, for example, McGlynn et al, 2021), 'Technology-Facilitated Sexual Violence' (Henry and Powell, 2018), 'intimate image abuse' (the English Law Commission, 2021, 2022), 'harmful image exploitation', 'distributed intimate visual depiction of an individual' (The US Federal SHIELD Bill on the matter) and 'non-consensual disclosure of private sexual photographs' (the current English NCII provision in S33 of the Criminal Justice and Courts Act 2015). In early drafts of this work I coined the term unauthorized dissemination of nude and intimate images (UDONI), but I have opted for NCII since the latter does not focus on dissemination to the exclusion of viewing, and since, unlike IBSA – which is a very apt term – it is easier to use in sentences focusing on dissemination, hosting or viewing of the images ('viewing IBSA' is a bit awkward and 'viewing IBSA images' is a bit wordy, while 'viewing NCII' is not).[7]

2. Theoretical framework and readership

The book is informed by, and attempts to contribute to, three strands of literature: the first concerns internet intermediary liability for user content of which NCII is but one example. This relates to debates about regulation, criminal law, private law and their relationship, and the extent to which

---

[7] As an aside, IBSA could be mistaken as focusing on the visual capture of an underlying sexual abuse, while its true focus is much broader. It also highlights the (important) nature of NCII as a form of sexual abuse, thus obfuscating its other important dimensions, most notably as a serious breach of privacy.

intermediaries are passive hosts or active authors of the claimant's violation of rights. A related debate is whether to adopt a horizontal model – according to which the scope of hosts' liability or immunity for user content does not depend on the interest undermined by that content – or, as I support, a vertical model according to which the interest in sexual privacy ought to be afforded a stronger protection vis-à-vis intermediaries than other interests, such as reputation and the interest protected by copyright; in fact, sexual privacy is afforded *lesser* protection than that afforded to copyright owners.

The second strand of literature is about privacy and sexual privacy; the third is about private law theory, tort law and the law of remedies. I start from a legal realist, functional, contextual and egalitarian understanding of the law, which accepts that law is a human creation that needs to serve a certain mix of goals and that in this sense is functional; that law has to account for its exercise of power, and ought to take distributive (alongside other) considerations into account, including a commitment to decrease gender inequality; and that, while somewhat political in the broad sense of the term, law has its inner logic and has a craft aspect to it, so it is not the case that anything goes. While I recognize the centrality of 'rights', 'duties' and 'interpersonal justice' to tort law, I claim that policy considerations must be taken into account in developing and evaluating the content of legal rules. These have to do with law's consequences on actual and potential litigants, and beyond, including broad distributive justice considerations (Dagan, 2007; Keren-Paz, 2007a; Hedley, 2009; Priel, 2019). This starting point also entails a dialectic approach to concepts and coherence – a point that will become most evident in the analysis offered to private information as the subject matter of property rights. A degree of local coherence is important, but a contextual approach sensitive to the relevant policy considerations is crucial in order to keep the relevant categories sufficiently narrow and to avoid over conceptualization and excessive deference to the weight that should be given to achieving coherence (Keren-Paz, 2007a, 2013, 2017).[8] Accordingly, the jurisprudential move I defend here – and previously – strives to use the building blocks of private law liability in order to reach socially desirable results by making moves which are considered as legitimate by the relevant community (even if, naturally, contested by some) and even though their outcome might be considered radical or requiring a law reform. In this sense, the outcome ought to be evaluated primarily in terms of justification but also in terms of fit (Dworkin, 1986: 52–3). In particular, while I am not opposed to enacting statutory NCII torts – such a move has several advantages – my conclusion that viewers ought to and can be liable for breach of privacy for viewing NCII and that such liability could be strict, could be

---

[8]   See also Chapter 11, end of Part 2.

achieved (outside of the US with its Federal statutory immunity) by courts applying the misuse of private information common law tort ('privacy tort' or '*Privacy*') or an equivalent. While the E-Commerce Directive (ECD) currently seems to exclude intermediaries' liability for pre-notice user content harm (provided the intermediary is considered as a host and not as a publisher), first principles justify such liability and allow it as a matter of primary liability for breach of privacy. So another jurisprudential move I make is to show how allegiance to first principles about scope of liability for harm allegedly caused directly by a third party ought to lead to a policy reform in terms of internet intermediary liability (which interestingly is to some extent already under way).[9]

The breadth of the jurisprudential and policy ambition of this work comes at a jurisdictional price. This work is neither comparative in the proper sense of the word, nor is focused on one particular jurisdiction; although doctrinally, I draw mainly on English case law. Moreover, as the goals of law – be it private law, tort law, privacy law or regulatory law – are pluralistic, different jurisdictions will give different weight to different considerations in different areas of law. For example, economic analysis of law might be a more dominant analytical lens for American tort laws than for English, but the suggested regulatory framework in England (in the Online Safety Bill and the Online Harms White Paper) clearly takes into account an economic perspective.[10] Economic considerations ought to have some weight in discussing the scope of tort liability, but as the analysis suggests, the role is limited both in terms of the relative weight that ought to be given to efficiency and encouraging competition vis-à-vis other interests such as gender equality and, crucially, in the sense that ultimately economic considerations ought to support strict liability of intermediaries and viewers as the harm NCII cause clearly outweighs any benefits they might bring about.[11]

From this legal realist, functional, contextual and egalitarian starting point I aim to make two contributions. Most immediately, to defend strict liability for sharing, including by hosting, and for viewing NCII. Second, and more broadly, I wish to defend and develop an egalitarian understanding of digital privacy that is sensitive to the technological and gendered aspects of digital privacy and to the way these two aspects interact. The broader insights from this inquiry would hopefully be of interest to students of internet law, law and technology, law, gender and sexuality, law and society and private law theorists beyond the particularities of the NCII case study.

---

[9] Chapter 2, Part 2.

[10] See Chapters 3 and 7.

[11] Chapter 10, Part 4.C. Cf Chapters 3, 6 and 7.

Ultimately, the book aims to make normative/policy-based, theoretical and doctrinal contributions.

3. The main contributions in terms of policy

(1) Hosts should be subject to a filtering obligation so that as long as there is no verifiable consent by a person depicted in an intimate image, the image would not be hosted. Verification could be done, for example, by using multi-factor authentication which is already used in financial and professional contexts (Chapter 7, Part 3.C). (2) Contrary to current regulatory wisdom at both UK and EU levels, a means-based test ought to be rejected, so this filtering duty should be imposed also on smaller hosts (Chapter 7, Part 3.G). (3) Liability for hosting NCII should be strict, rather than being based on a best-efforts or feasibility standard. So hosts should be strictly liable for hosting NCII their filters failed to remove. Facebook's lack of transparency about the incidence of NCII that are not automatically filtered makes it hard to estimate its exposure to that liability and whether it threatens Facebook's financial viability. But regardless, since the harm from NCII is real and serious, and since hosts significantly contribute to the breach of privacy suffered by NCII claimants and the ensuing harm, if Facebook (or any other host) cannot pay the real costs of their enterprise, it is better it does not exist (Chapter 7, Part 3.F). This support for filtering duties and even more so for strict liability goes far beyond existing suggestions in policy debates and in the intermediary liability and the privacy literatures.[12] (4) NCII viewers should be liable for invading the claimant's privacy and their liability should likewise be strict (Chapter 10, Parts 2–3). This recommendation is revolutionary as there is almost no discussion of liability (let alone strict) for viewing NCII.[13]

(5) Since the harm from NCII is exceptionally grave, and since the financial and freedom of expression costs of filtering intimate images are low in comparison to those from other right-infringing user content, there is a case for NCII exceptionalism; so the general filtering obligation should not necessarily extend to other right-infringing content (Chapters 6 and 7). In this sense, the analysis both supports the recent regulatory trend of deviating from the horizontal model – it also vindicates the rather unpopular European Court of Human Rights (ECtHR) *Delfi* decision – but at the same time is critical of the inverted hierarchy of interests, existing in US law and emerging in EU law, according to which intermediaries' exposure to liability to copyright holders is greater than to NCII victims, contrary to the NCII exceptionalism analysis. NCII exceptionalism should also

---

[12] Chapter 2, Parts 2 and 4; Chapter 12, Part 1.
[13] Chapter 9, Part 2.

withstand the critique from the quarters of post-modern and queer critics of 'governance feminism' (Chapter 6, Part 3.F). (6) Contrary to common wisdom that is concerned about giving private actors – intermediaries – the de facto power and the incentive to remove content prior to courts' oversight, access to justice concerns justify imposing such burden on intermediaries. In this regard, the availability of interim injunctions for breach of privacy as opposed to their unavailability in cases of defamation should be translated to the way intermediaries are regulated. Intermediaries should filter content threatening sexual privacy – that is, intimate images not verified as authorized – but should be under no equivalent obligation to filter potentially defamatory material (Chapters 3, Part 4; 5, Part 4.B; and 6, Part 3).

(7) The gap between the regulation of child pornography and of NCII should narrow, as the former is an extreme sub-category of the latter and as both are manifestations of sexual abuse (Chapters 6, Part 3; 8, Part 2; 9, Part 2; and 10, Part 3). (8) NCII should be considered as a form of hate crime (Chapter 6, Part 3). (9) Regardless of the case for hosts' strict liability (or alternatively, for a feasibility standard), post-notice immunity to hosts, as is practised in the US, cannot be justified (Chapter 3). (10) For intimacy beyond nudity – cases often involving issues of cultural difference – a two-prong test of reasonable expectation of privacy should be adopted, similar to the one existing in England and other jurisdictions regarding informed consent. So (unlike the Law Commission's position in its Consultation Paper and Final Report in the criminal context) if the host (or viewer) has a reason to know that the particular claimant depicted in the image is likely to consider the image as intimate, liability (subject to defences) should inhere, even if a reasonable person would not consider the image to be intimate (Chapter 7, Part 3.D).

4. The main theoretical/conceptual contributions

(1) Intimate images should be protected no less vigorously than personal property whether or not they ought to be conceived of as alienable property or as inalienable rights (Chapter 5); accordingly, hosts are akin to sellers of stolen property and viewers to buyers, so both should be strictly liable to NCII claimants (Chapter 4). This insight is revolutionary as even those suggesting treating private information as property shy away from the logical conclusion that recipients of the information should be strictly liable (Sinha, 2019: 605). As part of this analysis, the true features of an inalienable right are discussed and clarified (Chapter 5, Part 2.A). (2) Policy considerations justifying strict liability of merchants selling stolen property apply to an even greater extent to hosts, so at least as long as liability for conversion continues to be strict so too should be the liability for hosting and viewing NCII.

However, even if strict liability for conversion of chattels is too harsh and will be modified, there might still be a strong case for strict liability for hosting or viewing NCII (Chapters 4, Part 5; 5, Part 2.C, D). (3) The viewing of NCII dominantly destroys value (as it harms its victims more than it benefits the viewers) but also misappropriates value from victims to viewers. Under this understanding, strict liability is still justified (Chapter 10, Part 4). (4) Passive recipients of images could and ought to avoid liability if they deleted them promptly. This keeps strict liability in check. Liability for viewing NCII should be more extensive than for possessing them (Chapter 10, Part 3). (5) As a matter of reciprocity, or 'poetic justice', viewers of privacy-infringing user content ought to expect a lesser protection of their privacy in their internet user capacity, for purposes of their identification by internet service providers (Chapter 12, Part 2).

(6) Internet intermediaries actively and significantly contribute to the breach of privacy of NCII claimants and to the ensuing harm and do so for profit (Chapter 3, Parts 3.B–5). First principles about scope of liability in tort in general, and for harm directly caused by third parties in particular, ought to govern the scope of hosts' liability for NCII. These principles are control, fairness and right to an effective remedy (Chapter 3). (7) The nature of NCII as gendered harm provides additional support for NCII exceptionalism (Chapter 6, Part 2.B). (8) US complete immunity of NCII hosts is incompatible with the first principles mentioned earlier and with occupiers of land's affirmative duties (Chapters 2 and 3). (9) Given their business model, means-based limits to affirmative duties in both the areas of occupiers of land and defamation law are inapplicable (Chapter 3). At most, hosts are akin to innocent distributors of defamatory material so should be liable post notice (Chapter 3, Part 2.A). (10) The case for strict liability and for filtering duties (Chapters 6 and 7) is supported but does not depend on accepting the property analysis offered in this book (Chapters 4, Part 5; and 10, Part 4). (11) More generally, the arguments I defend are somewhat modular, so one can reject some while still accepting that the remaining support a significant policy change and constitute a significant conceptual contribution to the understanding of NCII, the appropriate way to respond to them and more broadly to the development of an egalitarian digital privacy framework.

5. The main doctrinal contributions

(1) Analysing the viewing of NCII as an independent intrusion into privacy which ought to lead to liability (Chapter 8, Part 2). This is done with reference to both English law and the intrusion and public disclosure torts in US jurisdictions. (2) Critiquing S230 Communications Decency Act 1996 case law on the conditions for losing hosts' immunity (Chapter 3;

Chapter 2, Parts 3 and 4). (3) Explaining misuse of private information (*Privacy*) as already a stricter form of liability (Chapter 9, Part 3; Chapter 10, Part 2) and as a tort actionable per se, with reference to the debate about the unilateral v bilateral models of the relationship between wrong and harm in tort law and with reference to defamation torts and to injury to autonomy as actionable damage in negligence (Chapter 11, Part 2). (4) Explaining how a fault-based requirement as a condition for *Privacy* liability could look in the context of those coming across NCII while visiting porn websites (Chapter 9, Part 3).

(5) Analysing overlaps between *Privacy* and defamation, and between the protected interests of privacy and reputation (Chapter 11, Part 3). (6) Exploring remoteness in *Privacy* (Chapter 11, Part 4). (7) Exploring the scope of reasonable expectation of privacy (Chapters 7, Part 3.D, 8, Part 2 and 10, Part 3). (8) Exploring the scope of liability for acting in concert and its relationship with primary liability for creation of demand, mainly in the context of child pornography (Chapter 8, Parts 3 and 4; 9, Part 3.B; and 11, Part 5). (9) Explaining the effects of overdetermined causation and of prior and likely future encounter between the viewer and claimant on quantifying and apportioning viewers' liability (Chapters 8, Parts 1 and 3; 11, Parts 4 and 5). (10) Explaining that as the damage from NCII is indivisible, intermediaries in breach of a notice and take down obligation (NTD) might still be liable for pre-notice damage (Chapter 3, Part 4). (11) Exploring the contours of disclosure orders (Norwich Pharmacal Orders) against intermediaries to reveal viewers' identities (Chapter 12, Part 2).

6. Organization

Thematically, the book is divided into Chapters 2 to 7 dealing with intermediaries' liability and Chapters 8 to 12 dealing with viewers' liability. Chapter 2 sets the NCII debate within the broader context of intermediaries' liability for user content. Chapter 3 explains how first principles and analogies to the publication of offline defamatory statements and to liability of the occupiers of land cannot justify immunity beyond notice. Chapter 4 explains that if we conceptualize the right to privacy over intimate images as property, strict liability of hosts follows. Chapter 5 defends the conceptualizing of such right as property and the ensuing strict liability (of hosts and viewers) against two critiques. Chapter 6 makes the case for NCII exceptionalism since the harm from NCII is irreparable, gendered and systemic and since the costs following from holding hosts strictly liable for this harm are lower than the costs in other user content contexts. Chapter 7 complements this analysis by showing that filtering of intimate images is feasible, by criticizing Facebook's practice, by offering a model for effective filtering (backed by strict liability for unfiltered NCII) and by arguing that this model should not be means-based.

Chapter 8 focuses on child pornography with references to US statutory viewers' liability for criminal restitution. It explains that such liability ought to and could be established as a breach of privacy, since viewing child pornography/NCII is in itself intrusive and explains the scope of such liability with reference to remoteness and apportionment. In particular, it explores whether viewers could be liable for any underlying sexual abuse depicted in the image. Chapter 9 argues that viewers seeking NCII ought to be liable for breach of privacy and are likely to be liable under *Privacy*. It also makes the case for fault-based liability for those seeking intimate images surfing porn sites despite the considerable risk that in doing so, they will breach the privacy of claimants whose NCII appears on the site. Chapter 10 explains the existing stricter nature of liability under *Privacy* and argues for strict liability for viewing while delineating an acceptable scope of liability with reference to possession, passive behaviour and reliance. Chapter 11 explores three foundational debates in tort law and the law of remedies: whether liability under *Privacy* for the mere loss of control over the private information is acceptable and whether it ought to accumulate with consequential damages; whether *Privacy* ought to compensate for reputational loss; and liability under *Privacy* for remote losses. It also deals with apportioning viewers' liability. Finally, Chapter 12 asks the question whether viewers' liability is a practicable solution to the problem, focusing on both issues of evidence (identifying viewers) and costs. Chapter 13 concludes.

At a high level of abstraction, the core policy argument in this book is threefold: first, that harm from invading one's sexual privacy is more severe and pernicious than other harms from users' content. As such, it justifies a filtering obligation for hosts backed by strict liability for any remaining images and strict liability of those who view these images; crucially, the same is not necessarily true for other user content such as defamatory speech and breach of copyright. This conclusion is bolstered by the observation that the financial and expression costs following from the filtering and excessive removal of intimate images out of fear of liability are significantly lower than those associated with the removal of other content. These insights are canvassed mainly in Chapters 6 and 7 (the freedom of expression focus is mainly in Chapters 4, Part 4.B, and 7, Parts 3.C–E).

Second, once it is understood that child pornography is a sub-category of NCII, but that the latter involves the same types of harms as the former, the current regulatory gap between the ways the two types of right-violations are treated should be significantly narrowed down. When the difference between civil liability and criminal responsibility is taken into account – under the former, strict liability is less problematic – the regulatory framework applicable to child pornography could be applied to a greater extent to NCII. From the perspective of intermediaries this means an obligation to actively filter such images. From viewers' perspectives, a failure to promptly delete unsolicited NCII should lead to civil liability. These insights are covered mainly in Chapters 6, Part 3; 8, Part 2; 9, Part 2; and 10, Part 3.

Third, hosting and viewing NCII is akin to selling and buying stolen property. Whether the right to privacy ought to be considered as alienable (property) or not, it does not make sense that those who sell and buy it would be in a better position than those who sell and buy personal property. Therefore, an intentional selling or buying of that image should lead to liability, even if the host or viewer is not aware that the intimate image is non-consensual. This is discussed in Chapters 4, 5 and 10, Part 3.

Readers who are mostly interested in the book's policy analysis, to the exclusion of the more theoretical and doctrinal private law discussions, should focus on Chapter 2, Part 4; the introduction to Part 2 of Chapter 3 and in the same chapter, Parts 3, 4, 5.A; Chapter 4, Parts 2, 3, 5.B; Chapter 5, Parts 2.A, 4–5; Chapter 6 (those who are less interested in the normative relevance of the uniqueness of harm covered in Part 3 might wish to focus on Parts 1 and 2); Chapter 7; Chapter 8, Parts 4–5; Chapter 9, Parts 2, 3.A(2), 3.B; Chapter 10, Part 3; Chapter 11, Parts 3–5; and Chapter 12, Parts 1 and 3.

2

Setting the Ground: The Intermediary Liability Debate and Framing Issues

1. Introduction

In this short chapter I set the ground for the argument developed in the next three chapters. Part 2 will introduce the main liability regimes governing internet intermediaries; Part 3 will examine how control and fairness shape the current scope of intermediaries liability in different jurisdictions; Part 4 will situate my argument within existing literature.

2. A primer of intermediary liability

Hosts' and platforms' liability for user-generated content is a contested topic. Hosts are internet intermediaries hosting content created by third parties. They include platforms such as Facebook and Twitter that are usually major social media actors. The two main approaches[1] to the topic are a safe harbour providing the intermediary with immunity subject to an NTD requirement; and complete immunity, allowing intermediaries to self-regulate whether they remove and monitor content. The European safe harbour model is enshrined in the ECD[2] and adopts a horizontal approach: the same NTD model applies to the host's liability regardless of the cause of action, whether it is intellectual property, defamation, breach of privacy or any other tort or criminal offence.

The following caveats and clarifications apply: first, hosts (including platforms) are just one type of internet intermediary. The NTD regime

---

[1] For an overview of possible solutions see Frosio (2017a) and Angelopoulos and Smet (2016).

[2] 2000/31/EC.

applies to hosts in Article 14 of the ECD but not to intermediaries transmitting data (mere conduits, such as internet service providers) and those providing temporary caching services. Second, Article 14 distinguishes between criminal responsibility and civil liability. Criminal responsibility requires actual notice and failure to act expeditiously thereafter. For civil liability it suffices to not be 'aware of facts or circumstances from which the illegal activity or information is apparent' (often referred to as constructive knowledge); but such awareness does not extend to negligent ignorance (Larusdottir, 2010: 484; Riordan, 2016: 403).[3] However, the extent to which platforms that curate and promote user content can enjoy safe harbour, or rather are considered as the creators or publishers of the offending content, is litigated in the Court of Justice of the European Union (CJEU), ECtHR and domestic courts with a general trajectory of increased responsibility for user content.[4]

Third, the safe harbour is relevant to criminal responsibility and to damages but does not preclude injunctions.[5] While Article 15 ECD prohibits member states from imposing *general* monitoring obligations on internet intermediaries (including hosts), Recitals 47 and 48 allow member states to impose specific duties of care to monitor certain content. The borderline between general (prohibited) and specific (permitted) obligations to monitor content is blurred (Ullrich, 2017; Woods 2017; Wang, 2018). The CJEU ruled in 2019 in *Glawischnig-Piesczek v Facebook Ireland Limited*[6] that a stay-down obligation – an obligation to ensure that offending content do not re-appear on the platform after having been removed – is compatible with Article 15's prohibition against a general monitoring obligation; and recent European Commission policy proposals are moving in the direction of expecting increased (seemingly voluntary) proactive monitoring by intermediaries to detect illegal content (European Commission, 2017). Other

---

3   Cf *CG v Facebook Ireland Ltd & Anor* [2016] NICA 54, [60]–[62].
4   In the CJEU see *GS Media BV v Sanoma Media Netherlands BV and Others* C-160/15; EU:C:2016:644; *Stichting Brein v Ziggo BV and XS4All Internet BV*, C-610/15, EU:C:2017:456. For commentary see Rosati, 2017. In the ECtHR the main case is *Delfi AS v Estonia*, App No 64569/09, 16 June 2015, whose contours were defined in *Magyar Tartalomszolgáltatók Egyesülete and Index.hu Zrt v Hungary*, App No 22947/13, 2 February 2016 and *Pihl v Sweden* App No 74742/14, 9 March 2017. The combined effect of this trilogy is that in certain situations (for example, profit motive, hate speech and big circulation of the content) the mere provision of a notice-and-takedown system may be insufficient. For commentary see Brunner, 2016. For a similar trend in national courts see, for example, Cour d'Appel Paris, *UPC et al v Google, Microsoft, Yahoo!, Bouygues et al* [16 March 2016] (FR). For the documenting of a global trend of increased responsibility for user content see Frosio and Mendis, 2020.
5   ECD, Recital 45.
6   Case C-18/18 (3 October 2019).

than notice and stay down, in theory, monitoring duties could encompass a duty of care for reasonable monitoring, a best available technology feasibility standard and a strict liability regime. The merits of such approaches in the NCII context will be discussed throughout the book.

Fourth, the European Commission is moving away from the horizontal model towards a more context- and content-dependent approach with an expectation of more proactive monitoring across different fields but especially hate speech and content harmful to children (European Commission, 2017; Frosio, 2017b). Since April 2019, Article 17(3) of the Copyright Digital Single Market Directive (C-DSM) has explicitly departed from the safe harbour provision for platforms, one of whose main purposes is to give the public access to a large amount of copyright-protected works uploaded by users that it organizes and promotes for profit-making purposes.[7] While nominally, Article 17(8) maintains the prohibition against imposing on such platforms a general monitoring duty, it is suggested that such a de facto obligation was established (Frosio and Mendis, 2020). Finally, the relationship between data protection and intermediaries' liability is unclear, so it might be that hosts, as controllers of personal data, are subject to strict liability and not to the NTD regime. However, the point is unclear both under the Data Protection Directive (Sartor, 2013) and under the new General Data Protection Regulation (GDPR)[8] (Riordan, 2016: 347–8). In particular, there is no clear authority supporting, in the NCII context, liability to pay damages for pre-notice unlawful processing, although this should follow from general principles; more generally, it was argued that the meaning of the obligation imposed by the CJEU in *Google Spain*, and by implication, in Article 17 of the GDPR, at least on controllers such as Google in the context of *lawful* processing, is more akin to a NTD obligation, namely, removal after request (Tzanou, 2020). Furthermore, the recent UKSC decision of *Lloyd v Google* emphasizes that liability to compensate for contraventions of the data protection regime is fault-based.[9] A similar solution to the one I defend in Chapter 4 might possibly be achieved by adopting a broad concept of joint controllership between the intermediary and the uploader.[10]

The ECD's NTD framework is often contrasted with the US alternative model of complete immunity for internet intermediaries (with the exception

---

[7]   Directive 2019/790/EU of the European Parliament and of the Council of 17 April 2019 on copyright and related rights in the Digital Single Market and amending Directives 96/9/EC and 2001/29/EC [2019] OJ L 130/92 (C-DSM Directive), Article 2(6), 17.

[8]   [2016] OJ L 119/1.

[9]   [2021] UKSC 50, [132].

[10] Art 26 GDPR (n13); Case C-210/16 *Wirtschaftsakademie Schleswig-Holstein (Facebook fan page)*, EU:C:2018:388; Case C-40/17 *Fashion ID GmbH & Co. KG*, ECLI:EU:C:2019:629;

of intellectual property infringements and where copyright has a similar NTD safe harbour) set out in S230 of the Communications Decency Act 1996 ('CDA').[11] S230 provides that an internet intermediary ('provider ... of an interactive computer service') and users shall not 'be treated as the publisher or speaker of any information provided by another information content provider' and shall not be held liable on account of good faith removal or blocking ('restricted access') of objectionable material whether or not such material is constitutionally protected. Crucially, and in contrast to the ECD, the immunity precludes injunctive relief against the intermediary; this is the case even where the uploader's liability was established in court (Goldman, 2010). State criminal and civil causes of action (including common law) inconsistent with this provision are precluded but not federal criminal provisions (including child pornography) or intellectual property laws (which are also Federal).[12] On 11 April 2018, the Allow States and Victims to Fight Online Sex Trafficking Act of 2017 ('FOSTA')[13] created a new exception to S230 by removing immunity from websites that unlawfully promote and facilitate prostitution and websites that facilitate traffickers in advertising the sale of unlawful sex acts with sex trafficking victims. As part of a Bill (The SHEILD Act 2021 – Stopping Harmful Image Exploitation and Limiting Distribution) criminalizing the distribution of NCII, a service provider could be responsible 'with regard to content provided by another information content provider' if it 'intentionally solicits, or knowingly and predominantly distributes, content that the provider of the communications service actually knows is in violation of this section'.[14]

In contrast, copyright breaches are subject to an NTD regime under S512 of the Digital Millennium Copyright Act 1998 (DMCA). This regime is based on a notice (with clear requirements on identifying the breaching material), expeditious removal and counter-notice to the content's author who can respond and (under detailed regulation of counter-notice and under the pain of perjury) can insist on reinstating that content (Ahlert et al, 2004, who conclude that the ECD version creates a bigger incentive for unjustified removal).

In the UK, Sections 5 and 10 of the Defamation Act 2013 move partially into greater immunity for intermediaries by providing immunity where the

---

Case C-25/17 *Tietosuojavaltuutettu Jehovan todistajat (Jehovah's witnesses)*, discussed for example, in Ivanova (2020).

[11] 47 USC § 230.

[12] S230(c) 1, 2 and (e).

[13] HR 1865, adding to S230 s (e)(5). For a critical evaluation see Romano (2018).

[14] HR 1620 – Violence Against Women Act Reauthorization Act of 2021, 117th Congress, 1st session s 1413. Currently, (unlike FOSTA) the Bill does not directly amend S230. See the discussion later for the similar solution proposed by Danielle Citron.

uploader's identity is known to the claimant and therefore the latter can sue directly the former. Section 5 conditions loss of immunity, beyond the point of having *notice* and a failure to *take down* the statement according to the procedure set in regulations,[15] in that 'it was not possible for the claimant to identify the person who posted the statement'.[16] Once such identity is revealed, the claimant's only recourse is against the uploader, even though the host failed to remove the defamatory material. S13(1) (a) *allows*, however, courts that give judgement for the claimant to order the operator of a website on which the defamatory statement is posted to remove the statement.

3. Control and fairness in courts' decisions on intermediary liability

I argue in Chapter 3 that control, fairness and access to justice ought to lead us to reject the complete immunity solution. It will be instructive, therefore, to begin by examining how control and fairness already feature in intermediary liability decisions in the US, EU and other jurisdictions.

A. Control

Control, or lack thereof, features as a reason to impose or deny intermediary liability for content both in courts' decisions interpreting the scope of S230 immunity, and outside the US, contemplating the proper scope of liability. Much of the case against intermediaries' liability for user content revolves around the claim that in fact, at least in the absence of knowledge, hosts do not have control over the (allegedly) unlawful content, and therefore should not be liable. Indeed, hosts are specifically contrasted with traditional offline publishers and editors, such as of newspapers, in terms of the former's lack of control over the uploaded content as justification for not imposing liability on them (Laidlaw and Young, 2017: 85). Historically, S230 immunity was justified as a policy motivated intervention to protect hosts from liability in circumstances in which their moderation efforts could be interpreted as demonstrating control, and therefore as giving rise to liability according to established principles, following the decision in *Stratton Oakmont v Prodigy Services*.[17] Courts interpreting S230 take – on the whole – a restrictive approach to what amounts as control sufficient to exclude S230 immunity,

---

[15] The Defamation (Operators of Websites) Regulations 2013, which include a counter-notice procedure. Angelopoulos and Smet (2016: 297) refer (approvingly) to this model as notice-wait-and-take-down.

[16] Defamation Act 2013, s 5(3)(a).

[17] 1995 WL 323710 (NY Sup Ct 1995).

in which ' "all but a handful" of the hundreds of reported decisions on this issue have sided with service providers,' and 'it remain to be seen whether this broad application of S230 immunity is changing' to a trajectory somewhat moving in the direction of limiting this immunity (Brannon, 2019). Crucially, courts held that a service's ability to control the content that others post on its website is not enough, in and of itself, to make the service provider a content developer. In the most classic textbook 'revenge porn' scenario, the defendant intermediary retained its S230 immunity, despite its ability to control the content post notice:[18] An ex-boyfriend posted on Yahoo unauthorized profiles of the claimant containing nude photographs of them both, taken without her knowledge, alongside some kind of open solicitation to engage in sexual intercourse; Yahoo promised to remove the content but failed to do so.

Outside of the US, control features strongly as relevant in determining the scope of intermediary liability, and specifically, in support of NTD liability. The germinal CJEU decision on intermediary liability in *L'Oreal v eBay* hinged on eBay's 'active role of such a kind as to give it knowledge of, or control over, the data relating to those offers for sale' manifested in 'optimising the presentation of the offers for sale in question or promoting those offers.'[19]

The important ECtHR decision of *Delfi*[20] implicitly relies on the defendant's control to justify, in certain circumstances and given the gravity of the harm, liability for hate speech for failing to take measures 'beyond automatic keyword-based filtering or ex-post notice-and-take-down procedures'. Indeed, the requirements that in appropriate circumstances (as in *Delfi*) the defendant is required, in order to avoid liability to 'exercise the full extent of control at its disposal' amounts to a feasibility standard, which is defended in Chapter 6 with respect to serious and irreparable harm, as a fall-back to my preferred strict liability rule.[21] As will be discussed in Chapter 3, Part 4, *Delfi* demonstrates the connection between control and claimants' right to pursue an effective remedy as a reason to keep the intermediary in the liability picture.

In the context of hosting blogs, by operating Blogger.Com, the Court of Appeal in *Tamiz v Google Inc*[22] likened the platform to the provision of a notice board, crucially emphasizing Google's control (terms of use) and its ability to readily remove or block access to any non-complying notice,

---

[18] *Barnes v Yahoo!, Inc*, 570 F.3d 1096 (9th Circuit 2009). See also, Brannon (2019).

[19] C-324/09; *L'Oreal v eBay* C:2011:474 [116].

[20] (n4).

[21] See also n4 and *Max Mosley v Google Inc* 324 0 264/11 (Hamburg District Court, 24 January 2014).

[22] [2013] EWCA Civ 68.

therefore stressing the relevance of the authority of *Byrne v Deane*[23] (the main English authority on offline publication by omission discussed later). This analogy was rightly criticized in *Oriental Press* since unlike the occupier of premises, the provider of a discussion forum is in the business of publishing, or at least facilitating publishing.[24] A similar divide is apparent with respect to search engines. According to Justice Eady in *Metropolitan*, the operator's lack of control over the search terms entered by the user renders the operator to be a mere facilitator, rather than a publisher at common law.[25] But this has been rightly criticized in the Australian decision of *Trkulja v Google Inc [No 5]* – concluding that the operator is a secondary publisher – for ignoring the fact that the search engine algorithm operates precisely as intended by the operators. The operators are not mere passive facilitators (but are rather secondary publishers) since like newsagents in the offline context they have no specific intention to publish defamatory material but do have the intention to publish. After notice, they have both the relevant knowledge and power to remove the publication, so a failure to do so gives rise to an inference of consent.[26]

While the absence of factual control (at least in the absence of knowledge) is used as an argument to deny intermediary liability (of both hosts and search engines), the existence of *potential* control, the right to dictate how its users use its services or the platforms it provides has been used to justify liability. A prime example is Justice Salomdo in *Google Brazil v Dafra*,[27] imposing in effect strict liability for the infringing videos uploaded on YouTube: 'if Google created an "untameable monster," it should be the only one charged with any disastrous consequences generated by the lack of control of the users of its websites'. As discussed earlier, a similar sentiment was expressed by Beach J in *Trkulja:* the search engine algorithm operates precisely as intended by the operators, so Google's claim they had not intended to publish the defamatory material (since they do not have control over the search terms the user enters) and hence are not the publishers has no merit.

Interestingly, Justice Salomdo in *Dafra* quashed Google's 'technical impossibility defence' because lack of technical solutions for fixing a

---

[23] [1937] 1KB 818.

[24] *Oriental Press v Fevaworks Solutions Ltd* [2013] 16 HKCFAR 366.

[25] *Metropolitan International Schools v Google,* [2009] EWHC 1765 (QB) [51].

[26] [2012] VSC 533 [18], [27]. This position was reaffirmed by the High Court of Australia in *Google Inc v Duffy* [2017] SASFC 130 (post notice liability for defamatory hyperlinks; emphasis on control). Cf *Crookes v Newton* [2011] 3 SCR 269 (Canada), which held that hyperlinking does not amount for publishing for purposes of defamation; *Sanoma* (n4) (copyright, knowledge of infringement assumed when links provided for profit).

[27] Special Appeal No 1306157/SP (Superior Court of Justice, Fourth Panel, 24 March 2014).

defective new product does not exempt the manufacturer from liability, or from the obligation of providing a solution. This introduces yet another potential analogy, that of defective product[28] – alternative to occupiers' liability discussed in Chapter 3 and to the seller of stolen chattels discussed in Chapter 4. Moreover, the 'untameable monster' metaphor is reminiscent of strict liability for abnormally dangerous activity, which is established in many US jurisdictions' tort law.[29] This doctrine developed from the English case of *Rylands v Fletcher*,[30] which is currently well understood as a sub-category of nuisance. As such, it is more limited in insisting that the danger escaped from the defendant's land but (like its American progeny) is based on non-reciprocal risk imposed by the defendant on the claimant and hence requires, as a matter of fairness, compensation for the harm even in the absence of fault.[31] Possibly, although I am not going to push this point, the analysis offered in Chapter 6 about the unique, serious and irreparable harm to victims of NCII could be understood as supporting a conclusion that hosting material capable of such serious harms is a type of 'abnormally dangerous activity' for which strict liability is justified (Glassman, 2020).[32] (Note, however, that *pace* Justice Salomdo, this does not apply to copyright-infringing content).

B. Fairness

Courts' decisions duly emphasize the importance of fairness in determining scope of intermediary liability. In its simplest form, fairness refers to the idea that a business model that is based on hosting infringing materials for profit should lead to the intermediary's liability as an author or editor, rather than to its immunity as a host. Certainly, a look at S230 jurisprudence suggests that soliciting illegal content might fail the immunity: the two leading Federal Court of Appeal tests to deny immunity based on loose and narrow interpretations of fairness are the 9th Circuit *Roommates* 'material contribution to unlawfulness of the content';[33] and the 10th Circuit *Accusearch* 'specifically

---

[28] The product safety analogy is unconvincing, but explaining why this is so is too much of a detour for my current purposes.

[29] See Restatement (Third) of Torts § 20(b) (2009).

[30] [1868] UKHL 1.

[31] For the debate whether strict liability is fair, see Chapter 3, n41. Weinrib, 1995 argues that *Rylands* (similar to other pockets of liability in tort law understood to be strict) is in fact fault based.

[32] The American expansion of *Rylands* to abnormally dangerous activity was rejected in England: *Read v Lyons* [1947] AC 156.

[33] *Fair Housing Coun. of San Fernando Valley v Roommates.Com*, LLC, 521 F.3d 1157 (9th Circuit 2008).

encouraging the development of what is offensive about the content', where the website deliberately solicited and advertised unlawful content.[34] Here, care should be taken to distinguish between different intermediaries with different business models. Dedicated 'revenge porn' website operators solicit illegal materials. As such they are complicit with the uploader and are likely to fail S230 immunity as creators or developers of the offending content. Indeed, even Eric Goldman, known for his staunch libertarian support for S230, once speculated that operators of dedicated revenge porn websites such as Texxan.com were not likely to enjoy S230 immunity (Goldman, 2014; and see the discussion later of *Bollaert* and *Backpage*).

However, traditionally, courts took a very restrictive approach as to what is considered 'soliciting' and amounts to 'material contribution' or 'encouragement'. So in a pre-FOSTA case *Jane Doe v Backpage.Com*,[35] immunity was withheld with respect to advertisement of the claimants in the 'Escorts' section, which allegedly contributed to the claimants having been trafficked. Similarly, in *Jones v Dirty World*,[36] the adding by the website operator of the comment 'Why are all high school teachers freaks in the sack' following content alleging the claimant – a cheerleader and a teacher – 'slept with every other Bengal Football player', and a follow-up comment that her ex 'cheated on her with over 50 girls in 4 yrs' did not deprive defendant from S230 immunity as it did not 'develop' the content. In doing so, the court rejected the trial court's tests of (1) intentionally encouraging illegal or actionable third-party postings to which the ISP adds his own comments ratifying or adopting the posts (indeed, such ratification would ordinarily lead to liability under defamation law, as it would deny a claim for neutral rapportage and hence of public interest in publication[37]), or alternatively (2) inviting invidious postings, elaborating on them with comments of their own, and calling upon others to respond in kind. Rather, according to the courts' interpretation of *Roommates* and *Accusearch*, only conditioning publication on content *because* it is unlawful, that is, *selecting for* it, would amount to material contribution, denying immunity.

Note, however, that even by this test – which I view as unduly restrictive – a website operation of NCII should lose their immunity since by definition, a dedicated NCII website selects intimate images for inclusion because of the subject's lack of consent to disseminate the image and hence due to the unlawfulness of the content. Indeed, in *People v Bollaert*,[38] an appellate

---

[34] *FTC v Accusearch Inc*, 570 F.3d 1187 (10th Circuit, 2009).

[35] 817 F.3d 12 (1st Circuit, 2016). For FOSTA see n13.

[36] 755 F.3d 398 (6th Cir. 2014).

[37] In England: S4(3) Defamation Act 2013; *Al-Fagih v HH Saudi Research & Marketing* [2001] EWCA Civ 1634.

[38] (2016) 248 Cal. App. 4th 699.

California decision, an extortionist business model of a revenge porn website was not shielded by S230 immunity so could lead to prosecution: 'Bollaert's design and operation of UGotPosted.com – which required users who wished to use the website to provide content that violated other persons' privacy – does not entitle him to statutory immunity under the CDA.' Goldman (2017) included *Bollmart* in his list of worst S230 decisions for 2016, despite the fact that it is consistent with *Jones'* narrow interpretation of *Roommates* as based on a test of 'selecting for unlawful content' and despite Goldman's concession documented earlier that the operator of a dedicated revenge porn website might not be shielded by S230. In his critique of *Bollaert*, Goldman also notes 'the doctrinal conflict with the *Doe v Backpage* ruling'. Indeed, the decision in *Backpage* (which triggered the change of the law in FOSTA) could be criticized on the ground that it failed to deny immunity in circumstances in which the intermediary selected material for unlawfulness: 'Escort' services are unlawful as a form of prostitution, regardless of the question of whether the claimants were trafficked.

Similarly, in *Vision Security LLC v Xcentric Ventures LLC*[39] the defendant maintained the Ripoff Report website, which allowed competitors, as well as consumers, to post comments. The website operator's business model is based on refusing to remove negative comments, even if the uploader wished to do so, and even when the uploader admits it was false, refusing to upload positive comments and selling its own corporate advocacy program: 'How to make your search engine listings positive'. As the following quote clarifies, the court relied on the defendant's extortionist business model to conclude the operator was not neutral and therefore could not afford itself S230 immunity:

> What interest would a neutral publisher have in maintaining false and harmful content against the wishes of the author unless it advanced its own commercial interests? … Indeed, it is reasonable to infer that the very raison d'être for the website was to commercialize on its ability to sell its program … under this analysis, a service provider is not neutral if it specifically encourages development of what is offensive about the content.

The S230 interpretation is therefore not entirely consistent in terms of the role that fairness or business model serve as a reason to deny immunity. While there is support for the view that at least dedicated revenge porn websites will not be shielded based on fairness and business model considerations (*Bollaert*; *Vision Security*) other case law – including *Backpage* and *Jones* – casts some doubt on such a conclusion.

---

[39]   Case No 2:13-cv-00926-CW-BCW (D Utah, 2015) [7]–[8].

Moving away from the US, the significance of the defendant's business model as to whether it is denied pre-notice immunity is clear. The CJEU, in interpreting the narrower immunity afforded to intermediaries in Europe under the ECD, takes into account profit motive in deciding whether immunity should be given; the profit motive influences the answer to the question of whether the intermediary is under constructive notice (and therefore liable for damages). So most recently in *Sanoma*,[40] dealing with liability for providing infringing hyperlinks, the court held that if those hyperlinks are provided for profit, knowledge of the illegality of the publication on the other website must be presumed. However, posting of hyperlinks without financial gain and knowledge that works have been published illegally would not lead to liability.

The ECtHR in *Delfi*[41] also based its decision that liability of the intermediary did not violate Article 10 guarantee for freedom of expression on the intermediary's economic interest in a number of posts (due to increased advertising) and on the fact that *Defli* did not need to change its business model following the domestic finding of liability (which was for a very low amount of €320). In its most recent internet intermediary decision, *Pihl v Sweden*, the ECtHR based its decision that domestic courts did not infringe Article 8 by holding the host of a defamatory blog not liable also on the fact that the publication was posted on a small blog run by a non-profit association.[42]

Business models or fairness feature in EU member states' domestic decisions too. For example, a Swedish court in the Pirate Bay copyright case *Sony v Neij*,[43] rejected the claim for immunity since the defendant's business model was *substantially* based on infringement. Such a comparison of the proportion of right-infringing out of all activity underlay my argument in the context of sex trafficking that purchasing sex in a market in which some commercial sex providers are forced, and without the ability to ensure that you do not purchase sex from a victim of trafficking is a breach of duty (Keren-Paz, 2013: chapter 7).

4. Situating the argument

Like many debates in life and law, debates over intermediaries' liability for user content raise framing issues. Internet libertarians frame internet

---

[40] (n4).

[41] (n4).

[42] (n4) [31], [35], [37]. Other considerations were the small exposure of the blog and the type of speech, which was defamatory but not hate speech.

[43] Stockholm District Court, Division 5, Unit 52, VERDICT B 13301-06, 17 April 2009.

intermediaries as passive and peripheral to users' speech so draw the conclusion they should surely not be brought into the fray of liability since they should not be viewed as authors, editors or publishers. To take a few examples, Daphne Keller, explaining in the context of the SESTA Bill[44] the difficult choices involved in regulating speech – deterring unlawful activity without unnecessarily suppressing lawful speech – mentions that the 'traditional way to do this is by placing legal responsibility on the speaker or publisher ... Intermediary liability laws shift this, holding OSPs accountable for other people's speech' (Keller, 2017a). Andrew Scott (2016) stated, as part of his opposition to the hinging of intermediary liability on whether the uploader could be sued, that: '[p]ractical difficulties in bringing a claim against one person ... can hardly justify by themselves the extension of joint and several liability to relatively innocent parties'. Similarly, Ryan Turner (2014) noted that: 'the broad definition of "publication" ... facilitates this search for deep pockets'. Eric Goldman (2016), a staunch internet libertarian commented on a failed claim against Facebook '[A]lthough we're sympathetic to how the fake account harmed Caraccioli, he chose the wrong defendant ... Caraccioli just needs to leave Facebook out of it.'

If, however, it is established that based on first principles and proper analogies, the intermediary is implicated in the claimant's right-violation, at least from the moment of notice and failure to act, the onus for arguing that intermediaries nevertheless should enjoy immunity seems to reverse.[45] It is no longer the task of claimants' advocates to explain why an innocent or peripheral party ought to be liable to the claimant. Rather, the onus is on internet libertarians and intermediary apologetics to explain why, contrary to general, foundational principles on scope of liability, platforms and hosts should be excused from liability. Such arguments do exist, and they revolve around free speech (chilling effects) (Friedman and Buono, 2000; Kosseff, 2010); the need to provide a subsidy to intermediaries in order to enjoy a thriving internet industry (Guo, 2008; Goldman, 2012); and the similar fear that liability will be an entry barrier, thus reducing competition (Keller, 2017b). But once the exceptional nature of such claims becomes clear – that they are, in fact, a plea to create an exception

---

[44] The Senate Bill that became FOSTA (n13).
[45] See, for example: (1) critique of S230 immunity (and at times support of NTD): Bartow, 2009; Citron, 2009; Citron and Wittes, 2017 (advocating narrowing immunity only to intermediaries who set up reasonable moderation procedures); (2) support of strict liability or extended monitoring duties: Vedder, 2001: 69–70; Helman and Parchomovsky, 2011; Ullrich 2017. But see Frosio, 2017c: 570–4 (criticizing the direction of travel to stricter obligations); (3) arguments, in the context of S230, that ISPs are best placed to remedy harm resulting from unlawful material, because they retain control over its location: Peterson, 2002; Ottenweller, 2007; Lipton, 2011.

to established liability rules for those sufficiently implicated in breaching the rights of the claimant – it becomes easier to contest the case for immunity both on the merit – on factual and normative grounds alike (Phillipson, 2016)[46] – and on inconsistency grounds: if immunity is so crucial, how is it that US intermediaries thrive despite the NTD safe harbour model for copyright infringements?

It might be useful to map the critique I offer here against complete immunity to hosts onto the existing literature. First, critics of S230 could be broadly classified into two camps: against the legislation itself or against courts' interpretation. Danielle Citron (writing separately and with others) is a leading voice of the former, both in the general context of hate crimes and in the specific context of sexual privacy. And yet, none of the solutions advocated by Citron come close to an NTD regime, which at the very minimum is supported by the first principles examined in Chapter 3, let alone a pre-notice liability, including strict liability, supported by the analysis in Chapters 3 to 7. The most expansive liability regime supported by Citron is immunity based on show of a reasonable response to unlawful uses of their services; crucially the 'immunity would hinge on the reasonableness of providers' ... content moderation practices as a whole – rather than whether specific content was removed or allowed to remain in any specific instance'. Moreover, ISPs 'and social networks with millions of postings a day cannot plausibly respond to complaints of abuse immediately, let alone within a day or two', although 'they may be able to deploy technologies to detect content previously deemed unlawful' (that is, a stay down obligation) and the 'duty of care will evolve as technology improves' (Citron, 2019: 1952–3; Citron and Wittes, 2017).[47] This proposal – especially (1) the examination of the reasonableness of the host's response as a whole and (2) making allowance for the size and means of the host – is similar in spirit to the UK proposed *regulatory* duty of care in the Online Harms White Paper (Department for Digital, Culture, Media & Sport, 2019: 6 Summary; 6.14–6.16) (leading to the Online Safety Bill 2021),[48] although the White Paper emphasizes that the proposal is not intended to affect the existing private law causes of

---

[46] Factually it is unclear whether immunity is or ever was required in order to ensure a continuous thriving platform market. Normatively, it is contested whether this form of subsidy is justified, either in general, or in the NCII context in which such subsidy is likely to be regressive.

[47] Two more limited liability regimes offered are for service providers that (1) 'knowingly and intentionally leave up unambiguously unlawful content that clearly creates a serious harm to others' or (2) 'intentionally solicit or induce illegality or unlawful content' The latter regime is very similar to the emerging courts' interpretation of S230. See Part 3.B and n14 for the Federal SHIELD Bill.

[48] *Online Safety Bill*, 2021, CP 405 S 4(1).

action, which will presumably continue to be governed by the NTD and the evolving notice and stay down standards.

Similarly, in the Canadian context, Laidlaw and Young, who wrote both on intermediary liability in general and on creating a revenge porn tort for Canada, recommend excluding intermediaries from a strict liability injunctive relief tort and waver on whether intermediaries should be liable to damages. Intermediaries should 'generally be immune from liability in NCDII'. 'it may be justifiable for intermediaries to be liable in narrow circumstances where their contribution to the harm is more direct and egregious'. (This seems to echo the 'soliciting' and 'unreasonable management of use' options discussed by Citron earlier.) They conclude that '[A]dditional work is needed to craft a narrow exception to the general rule that internet intermediaries are not responsible for third party NCDII.' Interestingly and crucially, it does not seem that Laidlaw and Young would even support a post-notice liability, despite their insistence that liability (for damages) should hinge on knowledge of the specific images being distributed (Laidlaw and Young, 2020: 157–8, 181–4).[49] In Australia, Suzor et al (2017) ultimately oppose civil or criminal liability for failure to redress NCII and support a copyright-like NTD procedure.

Benjamin Zipursky (2016) – a leading US tort scholar – is a prominent example of the literature prong which is critical of the way S230 was interpreted by the courts. It is interesting to dwell on Zipursky's position, since his methodology in the relevant article is similar to mine – analysing S230 with reference to first principles about tort liability for the actions of third parties – and yet he uncritically accepts congress' intention to limit liability for the failure to remove harmful speech by third parties, despite the fact that such limitation is clearly incompatible with these first principles. For Zipursky (2016: 44) the problem lies merely in cases erroneously extending this immunity to active posting of defamatory materials, contrary to Congress' clear language and intention.[50] My approach is different. First, while the common law's starting point indeed embraces the no duty for omission, both ability or duty to control, which exists at least post notice (as discussed in the next chapter), and profit motive clearly support a duty to remove the unlawful speech. Zipursky (2016: 31) defends S230 as a 'parallel to state Good Samaritan statutes that protect those who voluntarily provide emergency aid' from the 'pathological set of incentives' created by the common law assumption of duty for those volunteering to help

---

[49] Including on 183: Whether defamation's publication by omission 'could apply to a NCDII tort must be addressed'; and see Laidlaw and Young (2019).

[50] Based on *Batzel v Smith*, 333 F.3d 1018 (9th Cir, 2003). For justifying immunity on lack of control see Zipursky (2016: 8, 17).

'strangers'. This is a prime example of problematic framing: ISPs are not really bystanders attempting to save a stranger from a risk created by third parties unrelated to them. Rather, they are largely commercial entities whose business model and mission are to distribute third party's content. Since they are actively implicated in the creation of the risk, they should be liable, and at the very least, should not enjoy complete immunity if they negligently failed to reduce the risk once on notice. Second, even if broad immunity is justified in defamation, given the difficulty in ascertaining whether a prima facie defamatory statement has a relevant defence, no such broad immunity is called for in NCII cases. The first proposition will be defended in the next chapter; the second, in Chapters 6 to 7.

3

First Principles and Occupiers' Liability: The Case against Immunity

1. Introduction

My main goal in this chapter is to establish that any immunity beyond the point of notice – a failure to remove the offending content within a reasonable period of time after notice – cannot be reconciled with first principles for imposing liability in torts for the actions of another and with similar situations in which such a question was raised. The relevant first principles are (1) the defendant's control over the harming activity, (2) fairness – the fact the harm to the claimant was inflicted as part of the defendant's business, that is, within a profit-motive context and (3) not imposing liability on the defendant would undermine the claimant's ability to have an effective remedy for the harm she suffered and therefore undermines the claimant's access to justice. The areas of law establishing liability for post notice failure to avoid the harm from activity directly authored by a third party are: the requirement for publication in defamation law both in the contexts of (1) a secondary publisher and the defence of innocent dissemination; and (2) publication by omission; and the liability of an occupier of land to (3) harms suffered on his land under the tort of negligence; and (4) harms to neighbouring lands under the tort of nuisance. Such liability is possibly conditioned on the burden from intervening being not excessive. I will thus criticize the complete immunity enjoyed by internet service providers for user content according to S230 Communications Decency Act 1996 (CDA), which governs also claims for NCII. S230 leaves claimants who gave notice to the ISP at the mercy of ISP's discretion whether to leave the content or not and protects ISPs from good faith removal of content.

Part 2 will explore the different contexts in which post notice liability is imposed on offline intermediaries for third parties' actions and will explain it as a matter of control and knowledge. Part 3 will turn to the role of the burden in delineating intermediaries' liability. I will argue that (1) the burden hosts have to incur in moderating content is not excessive compared to their available means; I will complement this argument in Chapter 6 by comparing the burden to the harm suffered from NCII, making in effect, a claim to treat NCII differently; and (2) the requirement that the burden be not excessive as a condition for intermediaries' liability ought to be inapplicable to hosts given their profit motive. Part 4 will critique complete immunity and the notice and disclose model – the intermediary as a residual claimant – based on the principle of ensuring effective remedy to those whose substantive rights have been breached.

My other goal is to show that the same first principles can support pre-notice liability. This could be explained based on the understanding that hosts actively contribute to the harm suffered by the claimant rather than merely being a passive actor providing the opportunity for the user to harm the claimant. Pre-notice liability could also be supported by line of cases and doctrines establishing liability (1) in negligence for third party harm in the absence of knowledge; (2) vicariously; and (3) other forms of strict liability based on control and fairness; Part 5 will begin to unpack these doctrines although this task will be completed in Chapter 4.

2. Control and knowledge of offline intermediaries: rejecting post notice immunity

The defendant's control over the harmful or dangerous activity – be that a pre-existing duty to control, an ability to control or an actual control; each alternative is applicable in different contexts – is a stepping stone for assigning legal responsibility in either tort or criminal law. This is true both in general, in deciding whether the defendant is responsible for harm from an activity they directly engaged in,[1] and in particular, for harm directly caused by third parties' activities or by natural forces. In the latter situation, as we shall now see at least in the contexts of publication of defamatory materials, occupiers' liability and nuisance, the defendant's ability to control the harmful acts of third parties who use his property works towards a conclusion that the defendant has authorized or ratified the act, at least after reasonable time has passed from having knowledge of such activity; this conclusion is based on the failure to prevent the continuation of the

---

[1] The doctrines of volition, mental capacity and even the standard but-for causation could be understood as manifestations of the principle that in the absence of control over the situation leading to the claimant's harm, there should not be liability (or criminal responsibility).

harmful activity in circumstances in which the defendant could have done so reasonably easily but failed to. Granted, there is no general duty to act in order to prevent harm from third parties' activities. However, all the established exceptions to this rule have to do with the defendant's control over the situation: special relationship with the victim, or with the third party (sometimes understood in terms of pre-existing duty), which creates an expectation that the defendant will intervene; or the use of a resource of the defendant – over which the defendant has control – as an instrument to harm the claimant. This explains scope of liability determinations in the contexts of duty of care (including the partially overlapping intervening cause question) and vicarious liability.[2]

The first ground to criticize hosts' immunity is that the intermediary has control over what it retains. At least from the moment of notice, the host has the ability to remove the offending content. At times, the host will be the only one with such control, as in media portals to which readers' comments are added. But even when this is not the case, such as a post on, or a page opened in Facebook, the intermediary has the effective control, and almost always the legal right according to terms of use, to remove the offending content. Upon reflection, it is easy to see that several of the exceptions to the no-liability-for-third-parties-acts rule are applicable in cases of hosts. First, as explained in Part 2.B, the virtual space is similar to physical space. Hosts' control over that space should give rise to liability similar to occupiers' liability, which extends to harm caused by known third parties' activities. Related to this, users uploading content are invitees who serve the host's economic interest and the host has control over their behaviour through terms of use. This arguably amounts to a special relationship with the third party (the direct injurer) which justifies liability. Finally, in many cases the victim of the content would also be a user, and as such an invitee. This too might amount to special relationship justifying liability for the third party's harmful content. In what follows, I will show how at least from the moment of notice, the defendant is deemed to have sufficient control and hence be potentially liable for the acts of a third party in the contexts of defamation (by omission, and as a secondary publisher) and occupation of land (negligence and nuisance).

A. Offline defamation

Perhaps the most obvious analogy to hosts' liability for user content is publication of defamation offline and the applicability of the relevant rules to

---

2   See for duty, mainly in the context of occupiers' liability Part 2.B; for vicarious liability and intervening acts Part 5.

internet intermediaries' liability. One basic distinction is between publication by omission and the rules pertaining to secondary publishers, mainly the innocent dissemination defence. Despite some differences between the two rules, which are at times meshed together in judicial decisions,[3] both clearly impose liability (by treating the defendant as a publisher and denying the applicability of the innocent dissemination defence) on defendants who have knowledge (or ability to know) of the defamation and ability to avoid their contribution to its circulation.

At common law, defamation law defines a secondary or subordinate publisher as anyone other than the author, printer[4] or the first or main publisher who has taken only a subordinate part in the dissemination of the publication. Such a person has a defence, despite intentionally participating in the dissemination of the defamatory work if they neither knew nor ought to have known of its defamatory content.[5] Examples include newsagents, vendors and libraries.[6] The original common law defence probably exists in England, alongside the statutory defence of S1 of the Defamation Act 1996. It is clear that once the defendant acquires notice that the publication is defamatory,[7] continuous involvement in dissemination will defeat the defence, from the moment reasonable time has passed to allow action.[8]

Alongside secondary publishers, another line of cases exist, dealing with liability for publication by omission. The typical defendant in these cases is not in the business of assisting with the distribution of a publication; rather it is a property owner, whose property is used by a third party to publish defamatory material. The main authority is *Byrne v Deane*[9] in which the

---

[3] Laidlaw and Young (2017: 8–9) who mention that the main differences between the doctrines are onus, type of required knowledge and moment from which the status as a publisher is established.

[4] A defendant who is only a printer now has the defence of S1(3)(1) DA 1996.

[5] See *Oriental Press v Fevaworks Solutions Ltd* [2013] 16 HKCFAR 366, which applied this rule to hosts (an internet forum provider). Mullis et al (2013: 226) regard *Oriental Press* as more consistent with authority than the CA in *Tamiz v Google Inc*, [2013] EWCA Civ 68 suggesting, in the context of hosts, that in the absence of imputed knowledge, a distributor is not a publisher. For the equivalent US rule see Restatement (Second) of Torts S 581 cmt d (1976); *Lerman v Chuckleberry Publ'g, Inc* 521 F. Supp. 228, 228 (SDNY 1981), rev'd *Lerman v Flynt Distrib. Co, Inc*, 745 F.2d 123 (2d Cir 1984).

[6] See, for example, *Emmens v Pottle* (1886) 16 QBD 354; *Vizetelly v Mudie's Select Library* [1900] 2 QB 170.

[7] See Mullis et al (2013) and Laidlaw and Young (2017) for differences between the common law and the statutory defences.

[8] *Godfrey v Demon Internet Ltd* [2001] QB 201; Mullis et al (2013: 238). Cf *Tamiz* (n5) which reached the same conclusion based on the publication by omission rule. Cf the Australian decisions of *Duffy* and *Trkulja* discussed in Chapter 2.

[9] [1937] 1KB 818.

question was whether alleged defamation (found ultimately not to have defamatory meaning) posted on a golf club billboard could be attributed to the directors of the club, who owned the premises, and where the club rules stated that no notices could be put on the billboard without the consent of the secretary, who was one of the directors. The decision is understood to be based on the idea that from the moment reasonable time passed after notice, the owner is considered as a publisher, if removing the material does not involve considerable difficulty or expense. It was debated in subsequent case law and commentary whether notice and inaction (in the absence of considerable cost) after reasonable time has passed lead by themselves to a status of a publisher[10] or whether these are only indicators for adopting or authorizing the publication.[11] *Byrne* itself gives inconclusive indications as all three judges answered somewhat differently the question, although probably the correct reading is that authorization of the publication is the test and failure to act after notice (which cannot be excused by significant burden) is merely an indication, albeit almost conclusive, of endorsing the statement.

Greer LJ's conclusion seems to accept that knowledge and inaction equal publication:

> by allowing the defamatory statement, if it be defamatory, to rest upon their wall and not to remove it, with the knowledge that they must have had that by not removing it it would be read by people to whom it would convey such meaning as it had, were taking part in the publication of it.[12]

However, previous sentences support an inference of authorization test.[13] Greer gives two reasons for viewing failure to remove upon notice as publication: control, that the secretary 'was entitled to take it down' and lack of significant burden 'when the simplest operation in the world' was not taken, referring to a hypothetical failure to cut a rope by which the poster was hung upon the defendant's garden rail.[14]

For Greene LJ, publication by omission hinges on whether consent to the continuous display of the publication could be inferred from the failure to act upon notice; such an inference could be made where removal (as in *Byrne*) 'was a perfectly simple and easy thing to do involving no trouble

---

[10] *Pritchard v Van Nes*, 2016 BCSC 686, [108].

[11] *Urbanchich v Drummoyne Municipal Council* (1991) *Aust Torts Reports* 81 [193].

[12] *Byrne* (n9) 830.

[13] Id at 829 (defendants 'allowed a defamatory statement to be put up on their walls and to remain on their walls').

[14] Id at 829–30.

whatsoever' but could not be made where removal 'would require very great trouble and expense' as in the example of a defamatory statement carved deeply 'with a mallet and a chisel' on one's stonework which could only be removed 'by taking down the stonework and replacing it with new stonework'. The combination of knowledge with 'having the power of removing it and the right to remove it, and being able to do it without any difficulty at all' lead to a conclusion the defendants 'have elected deliberately to leave' the publication and 'to have consented to its publication to each member who saw it.[15]

Slesser LJ viewed only the secretary as publisher, as the club rules gave her (but not her husband despite being a lessee) control over the removal of unauthorized posts. Slesser did not make any reference to ease (or absence of costs) of removal but rather focused on the secretary's knowledge and control ('dominion over the walls') in reaching a conclusion that 'she did promote and associate herself with the continuance of the publication'.[16] Interestingly, but not surprisingly, Slesser's test of 'adopt and promote' and of 'promote and associate herself with the continuance of the publication' and Greene's test of responsibility for 'continued presence'[17] resonate with continuation and adoption, which are the tests for responsibility in nuisance for third parties' actions (discussed in the next section).

The NTD model obviously much resembles both liability of secondary publishers and of publishing by omission in that duty is triggered by knowledge of the publication (notice) and by the obligation to dissociate the defendant from contributing to the defamation – as deriving from the defendant's control – by avoiding distributing it, in the case of secondary publishers, or by removing it, and avoiding continuously displaying the publication from the defendant's premises, in the case of publication by omission. Possibly, in publication by omission cases, there is no obligation to remove if removal would impose a significant burden on the defendant (Laidlaw and Young, 2017: 7–8). However, for three reasons NTD could be supported by analogy with publication by omission, and even more to the point, the immunity regime of S230 ought to be criticized.

First, the costs of blocking access to online publication after notice is given, ought to be considered as reasonable, even if a reasonable burden limitation is indeed the relevant and appropriate standard. Whether the costs of establishing a pre-notice monitoring regime are excessive or not could

---

[15] Id at 838.

[16] Id at 835.

[17] Id at 838: 'is the proper inference that by not removing the defamatory matter the defendant really made himself responsible for its continued presence in the place where it had been put?'

be debated.[18] But it is hard to argue that removing or blocking access to an online publication once notice has been given involves undue burden.[19] Clearly, such a removal is much more like cutting the rope than replacing the stonework in the *Byrne* examples quoted earlier. This conclusion is bolstered by the following two points: the jurisprudence about occupiers' duty, to be discussed later, clearly ties the level of reasonable effort required to remove the hazard created by a third party with the means of the defendant.[20] This means that for practical purposes, the claims against the most likely hosts should succeed, since, given their size and scope of activity, removal costs are negligible.[21] Moreover, and this is the second point, the relevant burden according to *Byrne* is that of the occupier, not that of third parties (be them the uploader or the audience). This means that the non-pecuniary costs revolving around freedom of expression are irrelevant in deciding whether the burden to remove is so significant as to prevent classifying the defendant as a publisher. This makes sense, since according to *Byrne*, the question is essentially about attributing consent for publication, not one about determining defamatory meaning: once notified, a failure to remove despite ability to do so amounts to endorsement so should lead to the publisher's liability if the publication is defamatory.

Second, *Byrne* is an inconclusive authority on whether the duty to remove is conditioned on the burden being reasonable. Slesser LJ did not mention the extent of the burden at all, Greer LJ simply mentioned that in very low burden cases liability will be imposed and Greene LJ simply contrasted the two extreme sides on the spectrum – situations in which the burden is prohibitive so a failure to remove would not be considered as endorsement and hence publication, and those which involve no burden at all, in which such a failure would clearly amount to endorsement and publication. It is less clear how to classify cases in which burden exists but is not prohibitive.

Third, and most importantly, even if in publication by omission the obligation to remove is conditioned on the burden being reasonable, there is no reason to justify such limitation in cases of online intermediaries. The reason is that in the former context the defendant did not invite the publication, is not in the business of hosting publications and derives no benefit from hosting them. In the latter context the reverse is true. Where a publication is thrusted upon an occupier, it is fairer to resist a conclusion of endorsement and adoption, if removal would require considerable

---

[18] For a conclusion they are not see Chapter 7, Part 3.F–G.

[19] Turner (2014) confuses this, by referring to the costs of monitoring as a reason in support of Defamation Act 2013 S10 notice and disclose immunity.

[20] See Section B. The regulatory framework also takes this into account, See Chapter 7, Part 3.G.

[21] See Part 3.A and cf Chapter 7, Part 3.F–G.

burden. But the same is not true in cases of hosts or of offline secondary publishers. Hosts' business model is to host and assist publications – some potentially unlawful – and do so for profit; whether the profit comes from the uploader, audience or, most frequently, from advertisement is immaterial. It is both the increased foreseeability that during the course of this business some publications will infringe the right of third parties, but particularly the hosts' business model, that make it fair to expose them to liability as publishers, at least if they failed to remove the content expeditiously after notice, and notwithstanding the level of burden involved. The gist of this crucial distinction was captured in *Oriental Press* and endorsed by the editors of *Gately*, although the debate has been somewhat derailed by the question whether publication by omission is limited to posting by trespassers (as interpreted in *Oriental Press*), or not.[22] To my mind, the crucial question is not about trespass but about the business model: since hosts, as opposed to property owners, are in the business of publishing user content and stand to profit from these publications, and since infringing publications are likely to increase their profits,[23] it is fair to view hosts as endorsing the publication and therefore as publishers if they failed to remove it expeditiously after notice, and regardless of the question of 'reasonable burden'. In addition, the causal contribution of the intermediary to the reach of the publication, and therefore to the damage it causes, is more significant online than offline; therefore it will make little sense to carve a more defendant-friendly rule to online intermediaries, than to offline ones. Indeed, as we have seen, the liability of secondary publishers post notice is *not* conditioned on the absence of significant burden from abstaining to disseminate the publication.

Whether the analogy with offline publication is convincing depends on one's view about internet exceptionalism, or technological neutral rules (for a recent neutrality scepticism see Mac Síthigh, 2018). If hosts are indeed like publishers, at least secondary ones, it makes sense to subject them to the same rules applicable to offline publishers. (This is all the more so, where the claimant's interest is either similar, as in an online defamation case, or stronger, as in NCII, a point discussed in Chapters 5 and 6). Indeed this is the view expressed in Mullis et al (2013: 227): 'there is a great deal to be said, absent strong countervailing policy arguments, for bringing internet publications within orthodox common law principles of publication'. If, on the other hand, there is something fundamentally different about online intermediaries, a difference in kind, rather than a difference in extent, perhaps the analogy is misplaced. This is Turner's view (2014: 37): 'The differences between online moderators and hard-copy editors evidences the

---

[22] See n5 and Laidlaw and Young (2017: 8, 22–23).

[23] See Chapter 4, Part 5.B; Chapter 7, n31.

analogical difficulties in applying technology-neutral rules – particularly those developed prior to the creation and use of internet technologies – to online publications'. Courts disagree over finding the correct analogy.[24] Internet intermediaries add to the confusion by inconsistently framing themselves as both mere conduits (who are therefore not obliged to promote others' freedom of expression despite their growing power) and content providers (who are entitled to protection of their freedom of expression). This strategy was not lost on Emma Holten, who launched an activist anti revenge porn campaign named Consent. Holten commented about the ambiguous status of users' relationship with Facebook, and that this ambiguity serves Facebook because it allows them to shield from responsibility: 'Am I their client? Am I in their shop? Because if rights were infringed while I'm in their shop it's their responsibility to show me the security cameras. Or perhaps I'm actually employed by them? Because they give me a service – social network – but I also produce content for them for reward' (Dori, 2018; compare Zuboff, 2019). This ambiguity led Frank Pasquale (2016) to argue that new regulation is needed, one that can balance the rights and responsibilities of such dominant platforms. By analogy, the true multi-layered character of intermediaries – as conduits, content providers and data brokers – justifies a regulatory response holding hosts to account (at least from the moment of notice) for publishing unlawful content.

B. Occupiers liability and nuisance

We have already seen in the previous section that intermediaries' knowledge that publication is defamatory coupled with unreasonable failure to act would lead to liability. The same conclusion is warranted based on an analogy with occupiers' liability in negligence and in nuisance for damage caused by a third party. The analogy is appealing, since at the very least, the host provides space for the activity of the uploader. Indeed, uploaders are invitees. Where a tortious activity by a visitor or a trespasser against third parties takes place on the defendant's premises, the question arises whether the occupier, and not only the third person, is responsible. In both negligence and nuisance the answer is similar and rather clear: the occupier is liable if they know about the hazard or activity and fail to react reasonably. In negligence, the rule (in Britain) could be gleaned from *Smith v Littlewoods*.[25] In *Smith*, liability was not imposed since there was no knowledge of the activity (and foresight was deemed as insufficient). Note that there are two reasons to think that intermediaries' liability for user content should extend beyond the contours

---

[24] See Chapter 2, Part 3.
[25] [1987] UKHL 18. See also *Thomas Graham v Church of Scotland* 1982 SLT (Sh Ct) 26.

of *Smith*. First, there is a distributive justice argument for curtailing liability of property owners. This was the reason to reject mere reasonable foreseeability (as opposed to actual knowledge) of the owner – such a test would impose '[U]nreasonable burden on ordinary households'. Arguably, such concerns are irrelevant to commercial internet intermediaries, some of whom are economic giants (such as Facebook). Such means-based distinction is relevant also to landowner's scope of affirmative duty to respond to natural hazards (like fires): *Goldman v Hargrave*;[26] and to the scope of duty of the lenders' surveyors towards purchasers: *Smith v Bush*[27] where the duty is limited to owners of houses of modest value for dwelling purpose.

Second, *Smith* dealt with scope of liability for trespassers, while providers of content are invitees. It makes sense to have an extended liability for invitees' torts due to the considerations of fairness, collusion and control. Fairness, since the occupier stands to benefit more from an invitee's acts than from a trespasser's. Collusion, since at times the occupier might prefer (for pecuniary or other motives) that the invitee engaged in the conduct infringing the claimant's rights. Indeed, this takes us closer to the realm of authorization, which is a clear ground for liability. Control, since the occupier usually can better control invitees than trespassers in terms of who can enter and what is the expected behaviour on the premises. Of course, at common law, an enhanced duty towards invitees (in comparison to trespassers) as victims is well established.[28] Increased liability *for* invitees' acts is just the flip side of the enhanced duty *towards* them: the closer relationship with invitees is a reason both for enhanced responsibility towards the invitee, but also towards injured third parties from the acts of the invitee.

In nuisance law too, the occupier is liable for third parties' nuisance if, upon acquiring knowledge of the nuisance created by third parties, they neglected to take simple steps to remove it (which is the equivalent of NTD): *Sedleigh-Denfield v O'Callaghan*[29] imposed liability for continuation or adoption of the nuisance. The occupier adopts the nuisance if they use it for their purposes and continue it if they have actual or constructive knowledge of it and neglect to remove it. Note, that the distinction between continuation and adoption hinges on the benefit to the occupier. In the context of hosts, the failure to remove is likely an adoption, given the economic interest in user content, and especially in salacious content. As we can see, the rules in nuisance and negligence are based on the occupiers' control, which exists

---

[26] [1966] 2 All ER 989 (Privy Council).

[27] [1990] 1 AC 831.

[28] *British Railroads Board v Herrington* [1972] AC 877. According to the statutory scheme in England as well, the Occupiers' Liability Acts of 1957 S2 and 1984 S1(4), the duty towards visitors is more extensive than towards a trespasser.

[29] [1940] AC 880.

at least from the moment of knowledge (which could be constructive in nuisance), and probably on the benefits the occupier derives from the third party's activities.[30] Note also, that the nuisance rule applies to trespassers while users are invitees, so there are stronger reasons to hold the intermediary liable for their torts.

One might object that the space in which the publication is made is public and therefore the analogy with duties of private occupiers collapses. It might be that for several purposes and in other contexts such space is public; moreover, it might be desirable to subject major hosts and platforms to some public law duties given their unique nature and the growing importance of digital citizenship in contemporary society. However, the constitutional status of platforms, under US law – litigated mainly under the banner of the 'public forum' doctrine in the first amendment context – remains unclear. Platforms seem to have at most a dual public/private character, rather than being clearly a pure public space (Pasquale, 2016; Peters, 2017: 998; LoPiano, 2018: 549–51). This notwithstanding, the public sphere objection fails for two reasons. First, an occupier of land who is a public body will also be held responsible for an activity of a third party that breaches the claimant's rights if it has knowledge of that activity and ability to prevent it. Second, and more crucially, in terms of the ability to control the activity of the relevant user, currently, website operators, hosts and platforms' owners are more akin to private owners of land. They are under no duty to permit entry to their 'premises', and they regulate access to the 'premises' by a private law contractual terms and conditions framework, rather than by public law duties and powers.

3. Burden, control and fairness

A. Burden

A common argument for immunity revolves around the technical inability to monitor unlawful or offending content. Specifically, there are arguments for either treating online intermediaries differently from offline ones given the significant burden that such a requirement will impose on the defendant, or treating all secondary publishers (at least for purposes of defamation) as mere conduits, hence exempting them even from post-notice liability, so effectively obliterating the innocent dissemination defence (Turner, 2014; Laidlaw and Young, 2017: 87; but Oster, 2015 supports viewing

---

[30] *Sedleigh-Denfield* in fact downplays the relevance of benefit as a reason to impose liability on defendants for third party actions by treating as equivalent grounds for imposing liability adoption, which assumes a benefit, and continuation, which does not. But, of course, a benefit makes the case for duty much stronger.

intermediaries as publishers and the application of a fault-based innocent dissemination defence to intermediaries). If this is the case, arguably the host does not have control over the breaching activity and should therefore not be liable.[31] With technological developments, such as image recognition, the correctness of such claims, at least in NCII context, could be doubted even with respect to monitoring duties. And indeed, this will be the claim I defend in Chapter 7. But be that as it may, technical inability to monitor clearly cannot justify immunity from the moment of notice.[32] Rather, the magnitude of financial costs of operating an NTD system should be compared with the overall profits and costs of the intermediary and with the potential harm from unlawful publications. According to both criteria, there is no reason to support internet exceptionalism, at least in the NCII context. As we have seen in the previous part, the conceptualization most favourable to internet intermediaries is that they are akin to occupiers of land from which a third party harms the claimant. If so, intermediaries should be liable post notice to the claimants at least if the costs of removal are reasonable considering the means of the intermediary. This is clearly the case for post-notice NCII removals. The discussion later and in Chapters 4 and 7 will complement this analysis by referring to the arguments for and against taking the defendants' means into account, based on fairness, active creation of risk, claimants' interests in effective remedy and competition considerations. I will focus here on the financial costs to intermediaries from running a post-notice moderation (or removal) system leaving the discussion of the chilling effect of expression to Chapters 4 and 7. I will first make the point that the costs of moderation ought to be perceived as negligible in comparison to the profits made by the intermediary. I will then reiterate the point gleaned from the discussion of *Byrne v Deane*, that even if the burden is deemed to be significant, a duty to remove post notice might still be required as a matter of fairness.

Surprisingly, data on the relative costs of monitoring compared to the size of the harms from unlawful (or otherwise harmful) content and to the overall profits of intermediaries and platforms is hard to come by. Indeed, the financial costs of monitoring were specifically mentioned as one item that calls for further empirical research in a meta study on online platforms and content moderation (Keller and Leersen, 2020; compare European Commission, 2018a). Frosio, 2020 is 'not aware of empirical studies on costs of online enforcement in UGC platforms'. Many sources mention or rather argue that the financial costs involved in monitoring are significant – be

---

[31] Indeed, both S230's complete immunity, and the ECD's safe harbour prior to notice were premised on the absence of such control. See Chapter 2, Parts 2–4.
[32] Chapter 2, n45.

it under an NTD, 'stay down' or active monitoring (including filtering) models – but hardly ever provide hard facts substantiating these claims (European Commission, 2018b: 397; ICF Consulting Services Limited, 2019: 31; Bjorkegren, 2020). Similar to the methodological controversy around the number of sex trafficking victims, with regard to which it was argued that 'numbers take a life of their own, gaining acceptance through repetition, often with little inquiry into their derivation' (Sanghera, 2004), here too we ought to be cautious not to accept the narrative that these costs are high or prohibitive, in the absence of reliable data and against a background of a very thriving industry.

Take Facebook as an example. While its transparency reports do not reveal a clear picture of its moderation costs (Facebook, 2019), it is estimated that Facebook outsources work to around 15,000 moderators, each being paid around $28,000 annually, so $7,000 quarterly salary would put this cost (105M) at around 2% of its profit for 2018 last quarter (6.9B) (and 0.82% of its revenue (16.9B); Facebook's 2020 annual profit was $32.6B (Isaac, 2019; Newton, 2019; Barrett, 2020; Keller and Leersen, 2020). Of course, Facebook moderation costs significantly exceed the salary costs of moderators (themselves higher than multiplying average salary by number of employees) and include costs of training staff, providing psychological and other support to moderators,[33] setting the policy and, of course, the costs of developing and employing technology in addition to human moderation. Nonetheless, this gives an indication that moderation costs, at least for the big actors, cannot be considered as too high in comparison to either the company's profit (or revenue) or the harm caused from the content.[34]

Traditional standard of care calculations, at least as understood by the law and economics tradition, compare the costs of precaution against the costs of accidents in the margin, and without heed to the parties' (including defendant's) means (Shavell, 2007).[35] If indeed the intermediary's duty is limited to removing an image expeditiously after notice, it might be that the costs of the NTD system would be compared only to the additional (= marginal) harm caused to victims from the delay in removing the image. A related question is whether liability could be apportioned given the fact

---

[33] In response to critiques on inadequate support to moderators, employed largely by contractors, for the significant mental health issues caused by moderation, Facebook stated that they 'take our responsibility to ensure [moderators'] wellbeing incredibly seriously' and 'ensure [partners] provide the support people need, including training, psychological support and technology to limit their exposure to graphic content' (Hern, 2019; see also Newton, 2019).

[34] For the harm see Chapter 6; Chapter 7, Part 3.

[35] *US v Carroll Towing*, 159 F.2d 169 (2d Cir. 1947); It is debated to what extent this indeed reflects how courts determine negligence. See also n37.

that the damage is indivisible. As will be discussed in Part 4, the difficulties in apportioning liability might themselves justify pre notice intermediary liability. For now, I would just like to highlight the unfortunate vicious circle argument against liability caused by a commitment to post notice liability: arguably, the cost involved in setting an NTD monitoring system is too high, since the *additional* harm from a delayed post notice removal is smaller in comparison to this cost (and to the pre-notice harm).[36] However, this ignores the contribution of the intermediary to the significant pre-notice damage caused by use of its platform. For this reason, which is explained further in Part 5 and in Chapter 6, the NTD regime is problematic in itself. Rather, at the very least, if one refuses to accept strict liability as appropriate, a duty of care should be imposed and the costs of setting a proactive filtering system should be compared with the costs of NCII from the moment the image is circulating, rather than from the moment the intermediary failed to remove expeditiously the image after notice. Stephen Giles (2002: 494, 500, 584–5) has meticulously studied English standard of care decisions and found that while decisions are mainly based on balancing, the dominant version is not comparing costs at the margin but rather a duty to invest in precaution as long as the cost is not disproportionate to the expected loss and that judges balance intuitively, qualitatively, verbally, impressionistically and on the basis of tacit assessments of what is fair and socially valuable.[37] Adopting a disproportionate cost test, which is justified given the irreparability of harm,[38] provides even more support to the conclusion that intermediaries ought to be liable for failure to remove NCII, at least after notice.

B. Fairness: business model and complicity

That a third party increases the capacity of the direct tortfeasor to harm the claimant is generally insufficient to hold them liable. For this reason, as a starting point, manufacturers and sellers of alcohol and guns are not responsible for the damage caused to victims by drunken tortfeasors or those who use weapons to commit crimes (Lytton, 2005; AP News, 2019). We have already seen that knowledge can bridge this liability gap. So a seller of gun who knows that the gun is going to be used to kill a victim is likely to be liable to the victim for their damage (Davies, 2011: 356, 362).[39] More

---

[36] This, to an extent is the flip-side of the 'slippery slope/sunk cost' argument against imposing monitoring duties discussed in Chapter 6, n34.

[37] In many, perhaps most, common law jurisdictions, standard determinations are made in a similar way, which can accommodate a variety of considerations, including fairness and equality. See Keren-Paz (2013).

[38] Chapter 6, Part 3.C.

[39] Cf *NCB v Gamble* [1959] 1 Q.B. 11, 23 (Devlin J).

broadly, the fact that the intermediary stands to profit from the illegal activity is a consideration supporting liability for the damage. As we have seen in Chapter 2, Part 3, this is reflected in courts' decisions on the scope of intermediary liability.

The Part 2 discussion about the scope of duty for offline defamation and occupation of land suggests that the effective burden on the intermediary from removal is relevant in determining whether a duty exists to remove the offending material, but this might depend on whether the host stands to benefit from the breaching activity and whether there is any type of collusion between the uploader and the host. This makes sense as a matter of principle. Our duties to avoid harm to others are not absolute, and in negligence law it is well established that the burden of precaution is relevant in deciding whether the defendant is liable to the claimant. As we have seen, since hosts' post-notice liability is based on a logic of authorization, the effective burden is relevant: in the absence of significant burden, the authorization of the breaching activity is straightforward. However, authorization is much harder to establish if the removal involves significant burden. And yet, from the point of principle, the question of benefit is crucial. It is much easier to insist on hosts' liability even if removal (or monitoring) is costly if (and since) they stood to profit from the harming activity than if they just happen to occupy the virtual space in which an unrelated third party injured the claimant.

An alternative way to look at the question of reasonable burden is as follows: if hosts are understood to be active participants in the breach (either due to collusion or given their contribution to the extent of the dissemination and the consequential harm) the extent of the burden to remove should be ignored. In determining liability for intentional torts, unlike in the law of accidents, a cost-benefit calculus is irrelevant; and a breach of privacy underlying an NCII claim is an intentional tort.[40] Moreover, with respect to active creation of risk for purposes of liability in negligence (as distinct from affirmative duties), common wisdom (which I have challenged in Keren-Paz, 2007a: chapter 5) denies the relevance of taking into account the defendant's means in determining his negligence. So, whether the focus is on the benefit the defendant derives from the content or on its active contribution to (1) undermining the claimant's rights or to (2) the extent of the harm suffered, 'burden' becomes significantly less convincing a reason to deny defendant's liability. Another way to put it is that fairness considerations support strict liability — either for non-reciprocal risks or

---

[40]   This distinction was emphasised for purposes of apportionment by Justice Sotomayor in her dissenting opinion in *Paroline v United States*, 572 US 434, 483–4 (2014). The case is discussed in Chapter 8.

when those imposing the risks are likely to benefit from its imposition while those exposed to it are not (or much less so) – this idea is developed later.[41]

In the NCII context the question from fairness is whether hosts which are not dedicated to NCII but which nevertheless host such material should be liable, at least for failure to remove after notice. These hosts could be hosts of dedicated revenge porn website-hosts (that is, a second-order hosts),[42] general porn websites, platforms such as Facebook, Instagram and Snapchat and other online sites (such as Reddit, Tumblr and blogging sites to which NCII was uploaded either by the blogger or by readers) (Uhl et al, 2018; Henry, Flynn and Powell, 2019). *Delfi's* and *Sanoma's* logic could be, and has been (Edwards, 2009)[43] generalized. Note that the news portal, unlike Texxxan, or Accusearch is not a dedicated website to uploading content which is predominantly illegal. Still, the business model of internet 2.0, including of platforms like Facebook and YouTube, is the sale of ads where the user content is shown. As such, hosts have an interest in the uploading of content, and have an even bigger interest in the uploading of content that is likely to attract many users, and hence increase income from selling ads. One way to analyse it is as a matter of fairness: since intermediaries are likely to reap financial benefits from the generation of users' content, it is only fair that they will pay the costs of such activity, where the content harms the claimant. As Chapter 4 further explores there are two versions of the argument: the link between harming activity and profits and the link between harming activity and *increased* profits, giving rise also to the fear of collusion. If indeed infringing content is likely to increase the intermediaries' profits, intermediaries seem to benefit more directly from the infringing content than gun sellers do from illegal use of the sold weapon. The intermediary's position would come close (although would not be identical) to a harm-benefit interaction in which the claimant's harm itself is what brings about the benefit to the defendant (as opposed to the defendant's activity bringing benefit to the defendant with a consequential harm to the claimant). When the harm is inextricably linked with the benefit, there is a stronger fairness case to compensate, as well as corrective justice and possibly efficiency

---

[41] Whether strict liability is fair is debated in tort theory. The two most influential accounts for why this is the case, which inform much of the analysis in this book, are by Fletcher (1972) and by Keating (2000, 2001). For a corrective justice fault-based account of tort law see Weinrib (1995). Cf Beever (2016) (an account of pockets of strict liability in tort law, which is not fairness based).

[42] This was the case of GoDaddy, which hosted Texxan.com. The claim against GoDaddy was rejected and Goldman, 2014 supports this result.

[43] In a more recent edition of the work, Edwards is more equivocal about imposing liability – and specifically proactive monitoring duties – than she was before, although she still seems to think that profit motive could justify liability: Edwards (2018: 253, 259, 286).

justifications (Fuller and Perdue, 1936 [corrective justice]; Keren-Paz, 2014, 2019a [fairness]; Bar-Gill and Porat, 2014 [efficiency]). But see Keating (2019) (doubting the cogency of the fairness argument in the innovative treatments context). From the perspective of control too, at least from the moment of notice (and possibly from the moment of the upload), the intermediary has control over the situation in a way the gun seller does not. Furthermore, the sale of a gun is a one-shot activity (arguably undermining the claimant's interests at some future moment); the dissemination of the image is a continuous undermining of the claimant's interests. These distinctions, in terms of both fairness and control, could thus support liability of internet intermediaries, even if such liability is unwarranted in cases of sale of guns, tobacco and alcohol. Chapter 4 explores the fairness aspect as one justification for hosts' *strict* liability. But surely this argument could justify liability where the intermediary *is aware* that specific content breaches the right of the claimant. Another way to analyse the situation, as Edwards, 2009 suggested, and has underlined the decision in *Sanoma*, is that the financial interest in user content is sufficient to put the intermediary on constructive notice that illegal material is uploaded, which is sufficient for civil liability for damages. This goes some way towards strict liability or duty of care beyond notice and will be discussed later.

4. Right to an effective remedy

So far, I have argued that the main post-notice immunity regime – S230 CDA – cannot be reconciled with first principles of control and fairness. In this part I will argue that it is likewise incompatible with the right, or principle of ensuring effective remedy to those whose substantive rights have been infringed.[44] I will also demonstrate that another post notice immunity

---

[44] The right is enshrined in Article 13 of the European Convention on Human Rights and Art 47 of the EU Charter of Fundamental Freedoms. Usually, the contexts in which this right is litigated are access to court/justice and the choice between remedies (for example, in English domestic context, between damages and injunction *PJS* v *News Group Newspapers* [2016] UKSC 26) [38]–[43]. As I argue in the text, the choice of defendant, against whom an effective remedy is possible, is another, less well-discussed aspect of the right to an effective remedy.

Corrective justice and remedies law theorists debate whether there is a right to a remedy at all. Proponents include John Gardner with his continuity thesis, Sandy Steel and Robert Stevens. Detractors include John Goldberg and Benjamin Zipursky with their civil recourse theory and Stephen Smith. A useful recent summary of the debate is Winterton and Pilkington (2021). Clarifying my position on this important debate is too peripheral for my main argument here: even if there is no right to an effective/ remedy there is an interest that substantive rights will be backed by an effective remedy, and such interest strongly supports intermediaries' liability.

regime – 'notice and disclose', adopted by S 5 of Defamation Act 2013 – which treats the intermediary as a backup defendant where the uploader's identity is unknown – is incompatible with that right to an effective remedy, at least in the NCII context.

Both the complete immunity and the 'notice and disclose' models assume that (1) a successful claim against the uploader alone is sufficient to provide the claimant with an effective remedy and (2) that the intermediary is a peripheral contributor to the claimant's injury. Both assumptions are incorrect. It is clear that NCII claimants prefer removal of the image from the cyberspace over receiving damages (Franks, 2013a; Laidlaw and Young, 2020: 153). Most defamation claimants are similarly motivated by a desire to restore their reputation and have perceived falsities corrected, rather than by a financial motive (Benzanson, 1986: 791; Carroll and Witzleb, 2011: 226). However, depending on the platform's configuration, the intermediary might be the only actor who can remove the offensive publication. While those posting to major social media platforms – such as Twitter, YouTube and Facebook – can delete posts, in other websites it is impossible to do so. One example is the for-profit website Ripoff Report, which publishes complaints about any firm or person (and allows free rebuttals or paid-for arbitration of complaint) and includes 'a well-publicized no-takedown policy' (Goldman, 2010). As Derek Bambauer (2014: 2090) observes '[W]hile the initial revelation of intimate media likely causes some harm, the greater harm comes from the public availability and ongoing sharing of these media.' A cause of action only against the uploader deprives the claimant from the possibility of achieving an effective remedy against the intermediary to remove, or block access to, the offending image. This indeed, featured strongly in *Delfi*, in which the ECtHR rejected the view of the online newspaper as a passive host entitled to pre-notice immunity. The court attached particular weight to the high degree of control that the company exercised over the comments, particularly as once a comment had been posted it was no longer under the original author's control and could only be edited or removed by *Delfi*. The exclusivity of control is an aspect of a right to an effective remedy – without the intermediary's accountability, the claimant is left with a very limited ability to achieve the one remedy most claimants value most – removal of the offending content.

As *Blockowicz v Williams* makes clear, in the US, an injunction enjoining the uploader from further publication is unenforceable against the intermediary.[45] Therefore, Ripoff Report was not required to comply with an injunction against the defendants who posted the defamatory material to remove reports because it had not been named a defendant in the original lawsuit. The

---

[45]   *Blockowicz v Williams* 630 F3d 563,570 (7th Cir. 2010).

problem, of course, cuts deeper than just the (relatively rare) cases in which only the intermediary can take down the content. The problem is that an injunction against the uploader does not put the intermediary under an obligation to remove it, thus denying the claimant the one effective remedy she is after. For this reason, cyberspace libertarians opposed, in their Amici Curia brief in *Garcia v Google*,[46] the circumvention of S230 by relying on copyright law, observing that none of the initial private law claims would provide the claimant with the relief sought: an order requiring all the copies of the film to be taken down.

The Defamation Act 2013 'notice and disclose' model is much less problematic in terms of curtailing the right to an effective remedy due to S 13(1)(a) provision, according to which where a court gives judgement for the claimant in an action for defamation, the court may order the operator of a website on which the defamatory statement is posted to remove the statement. Seemingly, the Act both channels the litigation to the author and at the same time provides an effective remedy. Focusing on the uploader limits the risk of undue removal by the intermediary in order to avoid liability, while the availability of a remedy against the intermediary ensures removal of the offending material from the internet – the real remedy sought by the claimant – if the litigation against the uploader was successful. However, the Act still raises three concerns. First, the remedy against the intermediary is discretionary. While injunctions are usually discretionary, this discretion, if utilized liberally, will undermine the effectiveness of the remedial scheme constructed by the Act. Second, the notice and disclose model provides NCII claimants with inadequate access to justice. According to S 13, removal is limited to a time a judgement is given. While this is consistent with *Bonnard v Perryman*[47] (no interim injunctions in defamation) it is inconsistent with the availability of interim injunctions in privacy claims.[48] So if such a model were to be used in privacy claims, it would at least be needed to ensure that removal is available as an interim remedy,

---

[46] No 12-57302 (9th Cir. May 18, 2015) (en banc). Garcia participated in shooting for a film, supposedly historical Arabian Desert adventure film, whose footage was used by the writer and producer to create an anti-Islamic film. The producer had partially dubbed one of Garcia's lines in order to have her character ask, "Is your Mohammed a child molester?" The film was uploaded to YouTube and Garcia has received death threats. The Ninth Circuit held that Garcia was entitled to a preliminary injunction requiring YouTube to remove the film based on the theory that the film's continued existence on YouTube violated her copyright interest in her performance in the film. In May 2015, in an en banc opinion, the Ninth Circuit reversed the panel's decision, vacating the order for the preliminary injunction.

[47] [1891] 2 Chapter 269 (CA).

[48] *Cream Holdings Ltd v Banerjee* [2004] UKHL 44.

presumably when an interim injunction be given (or would have been given) against the uploader.

Beyond timing, the Defamation Act model necessitates court litigation (against the uploader) in order to receive the sought after remedy (against the intermediaries). While 'notice and disclose' is often hailed exactly since it channels the uploader and claimant to litigate in courts and reduces the quasi-judicial function of private corporations (Turner, 2014; compare Haber, 2016), an often-neglected point is the significant financial cost involved in litigating defamation and privacy. To be sure, the high costs of defamation and privacy litigation and their negative effects on access to justice are generally a well-appreciated problem (though little is done to solve it)[49] but are largely, if not completely, ignored in evaluating the merits of NTD. Alongside the problems involved in letting intermediaries make removal decisions without judicial oversight, the advantage of such a process is that it does not require the claimant to apply for a court injunction. It might also be that channelling claimants to courts in order to remove user content is justified for defamation, but not for NCII claims, for reasons explained more fully in Chapters 4, 6 and 8.

In the context of privacy, any equivalent to S5 Defamation Act will have to grapple with the provisions of data protection. Despite some lack of clarity,[50] it seems that the data protection regime is not subject to ECD's safe harbour provisions. This would mean that the intermediary (which is a controller) is under the obligation to remove the personal data it is unlawfully processing. In other words, an attempt to extend S5 'notice and disclose' approach to privacy claims would seem to be incompatible with the GDPR, which requires remedies, including injunctions, to be available against data processors to prevent unlawful processing. Unlike a platform hosting defamatory material, a host of unlawfully processed personal data is also processing that data, irrespective of whether it has received notice, and is therefore subject to an injunction to prevent its unlawful processing of personal data without the subject's consent. A notice and disclose solution applied to NCII is therefore incompatible with the data protection regime, to the extent that it delays the availability of an injunction against the intermediary until the date in which the court 'gives judgment for the claimant' against the uploader.[51]

---

[49] Indeed, in the UK, as of 6 April 2019, 'success fees' in Privacy and Defamation cases are no longer recoverable, with the effect 'that claimants may have to sacrifice some of their compensation in order to gain access to legal representation'. See Walker (2019) and Chapter 12.

[50] Chapter 2, Part 2.

[51] Defamation Act 2013, s 13.

In addition, excluding the intermediary from the picture of liability where the uploader's identity is known still undermines the claimant's effective remedy where the uploader is insolvent. Of course, that the intermediary is a deep pocket alone is not considered to be a good reason to impose liability on it, when it is truly a peripheral party (Stapleton, 1995; compare Turner, 2014). But my point is precisely that for the reasons mentioned earlier and further explored later the intermediary is not truly a peripheral party. In fact, the agency and solvency points reinforce each other: the uploader might be incapable of meeting the financial obligation to compensate the claimant exactly because the damage significantly increased due to the intermediary's involvement or inaction.[52] The intermediary contributes to the size of the damage in four distinctive ways.[53] An industry whose business model is based on sharing and interconnectedness cannot wash its hands from responsibility to the damage its use causes, at least when the defendant is under notice. It is ironic to absolve the intermediary from liability, since the uploader is identifiable, for damage which but for the intermediary's contribution would have been much smaller (if existing at all). Without the hosts' contribution, the uploader might have been able to pay the smaller 'offline' damage, while unable to pay the bigger 'online' damage.

Moreover, a failure to impose on hosts a proactive duty to monitor/filter NCII is especially unattractive given that (a) the viral nature of disseminating NCII, (b) coupled with hosts' NTD safe harbour, (c) the nature of the harm from NCII as indivisible (d) culminates in serious problems of apportionment of damages. In the absence of a clear regulatory expectation that companies will filter NCII and avoid their initial uploading, victims might not have effective remedy against serious and irreparable damage (depending on whether courts would be willing to apportion liability for post notice harm): by the time the host can become liable for failing to remove 'expeditiously' the image following notice, a significant harm will have already been suffered. On the understanding – explained in Chapter 8 – that the harm from NCII is indivisible, the intermediary's liability should encompass also pre-duty harm: the breach of duty by the uploader (and as I argue, viewers) prior to the breach of the intermediary's duty, and the intermediary's breach of duty (alongside others) caused an indivisible harm. While liability for indivisible harm by concurrent tortfeasors might still be apportioned for policy reasons, no such good policy reasons exist with

---

[52] As discussed in the text's next paragraph, the extent to which this argument is convincing depends on whether the intermediary's obligation to remove the images is post-notice or from the moment the image was posted.

[53] These are discussed in Part 5, as they explain why the intermediary is an active participant in undermining the claimant's rights, so they support pre-notice liability.

respect to *intermediaries* and the default rule of full liability for indivisible harms should apply. Apart from anything else, an attempt to apportion the additional harm from a host's breach of duty – its failure to remove the image (or to ensure it does not reappear, if such a 'stay down' duty indeed exists[54]) will be costly and difficult. So courts could still impose, should they wish to, liability for the victim's entire harm on intermediaries who failed to remove the image after notice. If, however, courts would wish to apportion intermediaries' liability to the estimated additional harm, attributed to the host's post notice breach of duty, and if this additional harm is deemed negligible in comparison to the pre-breach period,[55] effective remedy is undermined: by the end of the litigation against the intermediary, the victim might be left with meagre compensation for the additional harm and possibly with no effective remedy against the uploader of NCII for the significant initial damage. Put differently, the case for intermediary liability is based on intermediaries' active contribution to the creation of the harm, rather than on viewing intermediaries as merely a peripheral actor or a passive forum in which the uploader harms the claimant. This view is aided by the 'black box' lack of transparency regarding the ways intermediaries operate (Pasquale, 2016, Zuboff, 2019; Chapter 7, Part 3.B). Indeed, as we shall see in the next part, the intermediary's active contribution to the claimant's rights violation can justify even pre-notice liability.

5. Pre-notice liability

A. Active contribution to claimant's injury

The control argument could be casted differently, in a way revealing the limitation of the analogy with physical space. The potential reach of NCII distributed online and offline and the respective harm these forms of distribution cause could be compared. Clearly the online distribution is much more extensive (going viral), cheaper, and lasts for longer. The internet intermediary contributes to the extent of the right-violation and the ensuing harm in four distinctive ways. First, the geographical reach of the publication significantly increases in comparison to offline publication. Images (including intimate images) are free from linguistic barriers, and intimate imagery, consensually distributed or otherwise, seems to have universal appeal, at least among men. In addition, the costs of dissemination are zero. Second, cyber publications cross jurisdictional boundaries, therefore claimants might be

---

[54] It seems such a duty emerges. See Chapter 2, n6.

[55] I discuss in Chapter 8 (following Keren-Paz and Wright, 2019) apportionment issues, complicated by the fact the harm is both indivisible and (at least with respect to viewers) overdetermined. Cf, in the context of defamation *Tamiz* (n5) [50].

faced with the difficult tasks of suing, winning and enforcing judgements ex-territorially. American defendants, for example, enjoy broad protection form enforcements of judgements that are incompatible with domestic First Amendment protections according to the 2010 SPEECH Act.[56] In practice, however, due to corporate governance structures, at least the 'big beasts' have solvent subsidiaries in the country in which the claimant resides and suffers the injury, so this becomes less of a problem.[57] Third, online publications are in effect perpetual so can be, at least in theory, accessible forever (subject to the developing right for erasure, which raises its own ex-territorial questions),[58] and to the objection that in practice, as long as the search result does not appear on the first page of Google's search results it is of little significance (Dodge, 2018). Finally, the publication is easily and without cost inter-portable and capable of being copied and has the potential of becoming viral. This means that NCII hosts contribute to the claimant's damage in a very significant way. Rather than merely providing the space in which the 'harmful interaction' – the NCII – occurs, the enabling features they provide contribute materially to the damage.[59] The potential harm from

---

[56] Securing the Protection of Our Enduring and Established Constitutional Heritage (SPEECH) Act 2017, 124 Stat. 2480–2484.

    The following two points should be borne in mind, however: (1) the argument in the text is that claims against intermediaries should be allowed since the remedy against content providers in ineffective, partially due to problems of extra-territoriality; (2) American law is even less hospitable to claims against internet intermediaries by virtue of S230 CDA.

[57] See, for example, *AY v Facebook (Ireland) Ltd* ([2016] NIQB 76. The Department for Digital, Culture, Media & Sport, 2019: 6.10, considers in the White Paper requiring companies that are based outside the UK to appoint a UK or EEA-based nominated representative. However, given concerns raised at the consultation stage there is no such requirement in the draft Bill (Chapter 2, n48).

[58] C-507/17, *Google LLC v CNIL,* 2019 EUR-Lex CELEX No 62017CJ0507 (Sept 24, 2019, CJEU) (right to be forgotten does not apply globally); *Google Inc v Equustek Solutions* [2017] SCC 34 (global application); a Californian court granted an injunction against the enforcement of the order of the Supreme Court of Canada on the grounds that the order undermines US law – S230 of the CDA: *Google LLC v Equustek Solutions Inc,* No 5:17-CV-4207-EJD, 2017 BL 450437 (ND Cal. Dec 14, 2017).

[59] The causal link inquiry, termed also coincidence, denies liability when the defendant's breach of duty merely created the space and time for injury to happen but without increasing its risk. See for example, *Darby v National Trust* [2001] EWCA Civ 189; Keren-Paz (2016). The distinction between mere opportunity and relevant increase of the risk (which involves also a value-judgement about the proper attribution of the risk) is also relevant for duty omission cases, liability for intentional harmful activity by third parties and the connection test in vicarious liability. See for example, Restatement of the Law (Second) Torts S 448 (1965); *Lamb v Camden LBC* [1981] QB 625 (CA); Porat, 2013: 451–2; *Bazley v Curry,* [1999] 2 SCR 534, 559–60 (Per McLachlin J); *Lister v Hesley Hall* [2002] 1 AC 215, [45] (Lord Clyde); *NSW v Lepore,* [2003] HCA 4.[74] (Gleeson CJ); *Prince Alfred College v ADC* [2016] HCA 37 (an opportunity/occasion distinction; criticised by Gray, 2018: 71; *Bellman v Northampton Recruitment* [2018] EWCA Civ 2214,

breach of sexual privacy in a physical space is much more limited than on the internet, in terms of number of invitees (viewers), the duration of the harm and the ease with which the harmful content could be copied and further disseminated. This, and the fact that the host has a business interest in user content and might particularly benefit from harmful content, suggest that liability could be justified not merely based on authorizing the acts of a third person but also on its active contribution to the creation and intensification of the harm. At least where this contribution is accompanied by knowledge and ability to remove the content, a failure to do so should lead to liability. Indeed, as was discussed in Chapter 2, Part 3, the characterization of the defendant news portal as 'active' was a reason for denying the applicability of the safe harbour provisions in *Delfi v Estonia* – the most important ECtHR decision on liability for user content.[60]

B. Control beyond knowledge

So far the claim that control justifies liability was qualified by the requirement that control be accompanied by (or established conditional on) knowledge of the third party's activity. But this could be debated. First, moving away from responsibility to the actions of third parties, control over the interaction leading potentially to harm is advanced as justification for strict liability. Calabresi and Hirschoff's (1972: 1060) classic 'cheapest cost avoider' test – 'which of the parties to the accident is in the best position to make the cost-benefit analysis between accident costs and accident avoidance costs and to act on that decision once it is made' – is clearly about control as the key for imposing (strict) liability. Indeed, a major (if contested) argument in favour of strict liability is that it gives the actor best positioned to reduce the accident costs the incentive to optimally invest in acquisition of information in order to reduce its exposure to liability (Kaplow and Shavell, 1996; compare Ben-Shahar, 1998). In the context of liability for failure to prevent harm from a third party, alongside authorities clearly requiring knowledge as a condition for liability,[61] there are others suggesting that where the harmful intervention by a third party is foreseeable or probable, a negligent failure to prevent such intervention would lead to liability – depending on the relationship between the parties.[62]

---

[22]; Lunney, Nolan and Oliphant, 2017: 867–8; *Morrison v Various Claimants* [2020] UKSC 12, [35].

[60] *Delfi AS v Estonia*, App No 64569/09, 16 June 2015, [94].

[61] Discussed in Part 2 in the contexts of occupiers' liability, continuation or adoption of nuisance and defamation.

[62] *Home Office v Dorset Yacht* [1970] AC 1004 (liability imposed); *Lamb* (n59) (liability denied).

Vicarious liability is another major tort doctrine that in fact imposes liability, this time strict, for the acts of a third party. Control and fairness are two, perhaps *the* two leading justifications for vicarious liability (which is admittedly an embattled terrain in tort theory). The traditional view justifies the imposition of vicarious liability on the employer for torts committed by an employee during the course of employment on the control the former has over the actions of the latter.[63] This is so, even though, by definition, the employer was not negligent in either employing the employee, or in not preventing the specific course of action which led to accident; otherwise, the employer's liability would be direct, not vicarious. It can be seen, then, that even when the employer cannot be said to have created the risk directly, its control over the employee serves as an important justification to hold them liable to the claimant. In the internet intermediary context, not only that same level of control exists, but the host could be said to contribute directly to the claimant's harm in a way the employer liable vicariously usually does not: the injury intensifies due to the properties of platforms in disseminating information, and the uploader's actions are an inappropriate (indeed, usually forbidden) mode of advancing the platform owner's business. Another line of vicarious liability cases exists that belittles the existence of control as a necessary element for imposing vicarious liability. But this line of cases in fact expands liability in circumstances in which fairness – a fair allocation of losses based on the benefit from the risk creating activity – supports liability; it is largely *not* used to deny liability in cases where control is lacking.[64] For these reasons it could be argued that the relationship between the intermediary and the uploader is more similar to that of employer–employee in the vicarious liability context, than to that existing between the defendant and the direct tortfeasor in cases of publication by omission or harm caused by a third party on the defendant's land. Typically, the breaching content serves better the interests of the intermediary than the acts of the third party on the occupier's land would.

Finally, in the area of intentional torts, liability is strict in the sense that lack of knowledge that the intentional act interferes with the rights of the claimant is no defence.[65] Strict liability for intentional torts has been explained

---

[63] *Short v J. & W. Henderson, Ltd* (1945) 79 Ll.L.Rep. 271; *Armes v Nottinghamshire CC* [2017] UKSC 60. Cf Restatement (Second) of Agency § 220(2).

[64] *Catholic Child Welfare Society v The Institute of the Brothers of the Christian Schools* [2012] UKSC 56, [35], [49] (control an 'important' factor, yet not 'touchstone'; *JGE v English Province of our Lady of Charity* [2011] EWHC 287, [35], [38]; *Cox v Ministry of Justice* [2016] UKS [21], [28]; (Deakin, 2012: 558) (control as 'residuary' test). The inconclusiveness of control as a basis for liability was noted early on by Atiyah (1967: 16).

[65] *Hepburn v Chief Constable of Thames Valley Police* [2002] EWCA Civ 1841 [24]; *Marfani v Midland Bank* [1968] 1 WLR 956, 970–1.

in terms of control – scope of responsibility to one's intentional acts (Stevens, 2007: 102) and is relevant for NCII both because breach of privacy is an intentional tort,[66] and because it applies to the innocent undermining of the owner's dominion over the property.[67] On the view, explained in the next two chapters, that private information should be considered as property, hosts ought to be liable for NCII regardless of knowledge, or even fault.

---

[66] See Chapter 9, Part 3.A3; Chapter 10, Part 2.

[67] *Marfani* (n65) ('The duty is absolute. He acts at his Peril').

4

Property and Privacy: The Case for Strict Liability

1. Introduction

Chapter 3 established that S230 Communications Decency Act's (CDA) complete immunity to hosts is incompatible with first principles determining the scope of intermediaries' liability: control, fairness and a claimant's right to an effective remedy. Similarly, complete immunity is incompatible with occupiers' liability and liability of secondary publishers of defamatory statements. This chapter suggests that the analogy with sale of stolen goods is more appropriate than that of occupiers' liability, so that intermediaries' liability for NCII should be strict. It conceptualizes the right to privacy in intimate images as property, defends the applicability of the framework of conflicts over title to chattels to unauthorized dissemination of intimate images and draws the relevant conclusions: whether or not an innocent buyer has better title to the chattel than the original owner, the merchant is always strictly liable to the original owner. Internet intermediaries, as any other merchant selling 'goods' with defective title, ought to be strictly liable to the claimant. I defer the defending of the right to privacy in intimate images as property against several objections and examine possible extensions in Chapter 5. For current purposes, I just wish to clarify that this right should not be confused with copyright, and that it is therefore not limited to the takers of selfies. Rather, the right to control the private information – the claimant's intimate image – should be treated as a property right which could be asserted against (even innocent) third parties, or at least (if deemed inalienable), be protected as if it were, and no less than, a property right. For ease of reading, I will refer to 'intimate images as property' as a shorthand for 'the right to privacy in intimate images as property'. The focus of this, and the next chapter, is hosts' liability; however, Chapter 10, Parts 3 and 4 extend the argument to *viewers'* liability.

The analogy with conflicts over title will highlight three important points. First, that the case for intermediary liability in NCII cases could be mainly defended as derivative to the conclusion that the viewer does not have a legitimate interest in viewing NCII. Therefore, there is no justification for affording the intermediary an immunity, in order to protect viewers' interests. Second, the conclusion that the viewer's interest is inferior to that of the subject of the image (the 'claimant'/ 'victim'/'owner') is reached whether we view the intimate image as property and hence focus on the conditions (if any) under which an innocent buyer can defeat the original owner's title, or whether we resort to traditional balancing exercise between privacy and freedom of expression/information. Accordingly, this chapter will highlight the similarity between security of transactions and freedom of expression as both unconvincing reasons to afford (potential) viewers with access to these images. By implication, the analysis opposes intermediary immunity whose effect is to expropriate the NCII victim's privacy interest and give potential viewers access to the claimant's image.

Third, the case for intermediary liability could alternatively be based on policy considerations explaining why the merchant is always liable in conversion to the original owner, even under legal systems recognizing market overt and even if the thief is identifiable and solvent.[1] This falls back on the principles of control, fairness and effective remedy.

2. Conflicts over title: *nemo dat* versus market overt

This part explains the ramifications, for intermediary liability for NCII, of applying the rules of conflicts over title between the original owner of a chattel and the (possibly innocent) buyer of that chattel. Such an analysis presupposes that intimate images (or, more generally, private information) could be the subject matter of property rights. I will defend the underlying assumption in Chapter 5. Laws regulating conflicts over title adjudicate incompatible title claims to the same asset by remote parties, often both innocent, who lack contractual privity with each other. The scenarios in which such competing claims occur are diverse and include a sale of the same chattel to two prospective buyers and competition between a person having a charge over the chattel and a buyer believing she is buying the chattel free of charge (Mautner, 1991). A prominent scenario in this category is a case in which the chattel is stolen from the original owner and sold to an innocent buyer. As a matter of property law, the title should either be

---

[1] This point is important in rejecting the applicability of the notice-and-disclose model (Defamation Act 2013, s5) to NCII.

given to the original owner or to the innocent buyer.[2] In terms of policy, the competing interests are sanctity of ownership and security of transactions. The latter consideration is especially important where the buyer is buying in a regulated market in the ordinary course of business.

Both civil law and common law systems recognized market overt as an exception to the rule that the original owner retains their title (based on the *nemo dat quod non habet* logic – that one cannot convey greater rights than one has; this is also termed 'the theft rule'). While the exact conditions for operation of market overt vary, they are based on good faith purchase for value from a merchant in the normal course of business. Prior to 1994, in England[3] the common law doctrine of *market overt* allowed a buyer to acquire good title to stolen goods if they were purchased in good faith, without notice of any defect or want of title on the part of the seller and sold in a market that is open, public, and legally constituted by grant, prescription, or statute.[4] In France, the protection to the buyer (which is limited to reimbursement of the price paid) is conditional on buying at a fair, market, public sale or from a merchant selling similar things;[5] in Germany, those buying from a public auction are protected, even if the chattel was stolen;[6] in Israel, the purchaser is protected if the chattel was sold by a person who carries on the sale of property of the kind of the object sold and if the sale was made in the ordinary course of his business and the buyer bought and took possession in good faith.[7] United States jurisdictions (and since 1994, England) adopted the 'theft rule' protecting the rights of original owners of stolen goods in contest with good faith purchasers.[8]

3. Similarities and differences: the intermediaries and the thing sold

Conflicts over title to stolen property typically involve four actors: the original owner, the thief, the seller (who is typically a merchant for purposes

---

[2]   However, a variation of market overt provisions conditions the original owner's right to the chattel in paying the buyer the price the latter paid for the chattel. See for example, Article 2280 of the French Code Civil. Note also, that in theory, a solution of joint ownership exists.

[3]   Sale of Goods (Amendment) Act 1994 (c32) § 1.

[4]   *Clayton v Leroy* [1911] 2 KB 1031.

[5]   Code Civil Article 2280.

[6]   BGB S935(2).

[7]   Sales Law 1968 (Isr) S 34.

[8]   UCC § 1–103 (2011). See Schwartz and Scott (2011) (supporting a "tort type" solution permitting the owner to recover involuntarily transferred goods unless she was negligent in protecting them. If she was negligent, then the buyer can keep the goods).

of the market overt defence) and the buyer. Crucially, in many situations, the merchant will be, or at least might be, innocent in the sense that she is neither aware nor suspects that the item is stolen – after all, the item might have gone through several hands before it got into the merchant's possession. The similarity with NCII is striking: the original owner is the subject of the image that is circulating without her consent; she is the owner in the sense (explained later) that she ought to have at least the right to exclude others from viewing (using) this image without her consent;[9] the thief is the uploader – both intentionally undermine the exclusive control of the owner; the merchant is the host whose platform is used to further disseminate the image; the buyer is the viewer of NCII.

Consider the similarity between the merchant and internet intermediaries: that the merchant is an intermediary goes without saying. Both are a special kind of intermediary; they are repeat players and are in the business of selling items of the type over which a dispute arose.[10] Moreover, the type of dispute is conceptually similar. The innocent buyer in the good faith purchase case is buying an item that the intermediary was not authorized to sell by the original owner. Similarly, the viewer is getting, from the host, access to an image without the owner's consent or authorization. These similarities do not always exist in other intermediary situations. For example, occupiers' liability is a situation in which the intermediary is not necessarily a repeat player: interferences from the land to visitors and neighbours are not necessarily repeated, occur frequently or are part of a commercial activity (to the extent that land occupiers are repeat players, policy considerations indeed support more extensive liability). The occupier is not necessarily in the business of selling anything and indeed what infringed the claimant's right and the type of violation would not usually be the undermining of the claimant's control over their property. Both the merchant and hosts are repeat players; and most hosts, definitely the main ones, are commercial entities. If anything, and turning the focus to distributive justice, the typical internet intermediaries dealing with claims of breach of privacy, infringement of data protections and defamation are stronger than the typical merchant who has to deal with claims by original owners (or buyers). As we shall see, this further justifies their liability to the original owner.

One might object that a passive host is different from a merchant since the latter is at least aware that they are selling something (arguably not knowing only about the defect in title) while the former might not have

---

[9] For the problem of multiple rights over the image see Chapter 5, Part 4.

[10] I qualify this statement later. As we shall see, the fact that the host does not technically sell the image does not weaken the analogy; in fact, it makes the case for intermediary liability even stronger.

actual notice that they are selling the particular infringing item. However, internet intermediaries are not akin to individuals who unbeknown to them store a converted item and hence arguably cannot be considered as convertors. As hosts invite users to upload content on their platform with the intention to make it available to other users for profit, they are materially equivalent to a merchant who is in the business of buying items (which might be stolen, unbeknown to them) and selling them to third parties.[11] It would be odd to exempt from liability a merchant selling stolen goods just because its business model is based on inability to know – if this is indeed the case – what items it is selling. The conclusion that a passive host is still akin to a merchant – and that it uses the image in a way incompatible with the original owner's title – is bolstered by the policy discussion in Part 5, the trends in European intermediary case law narrowing the scope of passive hosting, based, inter-alia, on business model and profit motive (discussed in Chapter 2), and conversion case law highlighting the breadth and strictness of liability under it.[12]

The conflicts in the NCII and stolen chattels contexts are different in several important aspects. Most importantly, the image, as a type of information and unlike a chattel, is a public good that is both non-rivalrous and non-excludable. However, at a deeper level, the conflict seems to be identical. The owner of the intimate image would like to assert her control over it and prevent any unauthorized use by the viewer. In this sense both rivalry and excludability exist: if the owner is given an injunction (in theory against the viewer, in practice against the host) the owner has control over the image. Potential viewers will not be able to view it, so are excluded and the owner's exclusive control prevents such rival use by future viewers. Conversely, if an injunction is denied, potential viewers have access and can make rival use of the image, so the claimant loses her exclusive control over the image in the sense that she cannot prevent (exclude) unauthorized people from viewing and disseminating it (that is, rival use) any further. The similarity with chattels stems from the basic distinction between the copyright and the privacy paradigms. In the former, the owner would like the work/information to be used, but only for remuneration. In the latter, the owner would not like the private information to be accessible to others. The viewing of the private image or information is rival to the right to exclude the viewing – the two cannot exist together – similar to the way in which the third party's use of the owner's car deprives the owner from its use and hence is rival,

---

[11]   Cf the reasoning of Beach J in *Trkulja* discussed in Chapter 2, text to n26.

[12]   *Kuwait Airways v Iraqi Airways* [2002] 2 AC 883, [81]–[82]; *Hollins v Fowler* (1875) LR 7 HL 757.

and unlike the use of copyrighted work by one person which is not rival to its use by another.

4. The viewer's inferior claim ought to deny immunity to the intermediary

A. Immunity as expropriation

In contemporary Anglo-American law, market overt is a forgone alternative to the basic theft rule according to which the original owner has better title to stolen chattel than the good faith purchaser. If intimate images are stolen property, a theft rule equivalent would entail an injunction against any viewer to prevent viewing and further dissemination of the information/ image, including an injunction against the host to prevent further access to the image. The injunction against the host could be justified on realizing both that the host itself is a user[13] and that subjecting it to liability is the best way to prevent the image from being further disseminated and viewed by viewers. As I will argue in this section, since the claimant should clearly prevail in the competition with the viewer, there is no justification to give immunity to the intermediary out of misconceived policy considerations of protecting viewers. This conclusion is unchanged whether the balancing is framed as one between the interests of privacy v freedom of expression (privacy is NOT property), or between sanctity of property and security of transactions (privacy AS property).

Immunity to the host – whether absolute as with S230 CDA, conditioned on the identifiability of the uploader as per S5 of the Defamation Act 2013 or indeed prior to notice according to ECD Article 14's safe harbour – effectively amounts to expropriation, which is illegitimate since it is done without (1) a valid justification; (2) just compensation; and since (3) it is regressive. This is most apparent under S230(c)(1): from the moment the image is uploaded as a user content, neither the host nor other users (=viewers) can be liable for breach of the claimant's privacy, even after notice. Hosts' immunity, therefore, gives the intermediary and the uploader the power (in its Hohfeldian meaning) to 'dispossess' the NCII victim from her privacy 'title' in circumstances in which the remedy against the uploader, if available at all, is ineffective. And it does so for no good reason. Let me explain.

Good faith purchase provisions, similar to public expropriation schemes (such as the Fifth Amendment Taking Clause) involuntarily deprive the owner of her title. To be justified, they need to serve a valid purpose and to provide the owner with adequate compensation. These two

---

[13] Cf Schwartz and Scott (2011: 1338) ('the merchant is effectively a buyer').

requirements are very clear in the context of land expropriation as is well documented, for example, in the US Fifth Amendment Taking Clause jurisprudence. So the taking should serve a public (as opposed to private) interest (eminent domain) and be justified in the sense of being necessary for example, to solve cooperation problems and provide the owner with just compensation (Merrill, 1986; Cohen, 1991). On a closer look, these conditions are satisfied in the context of market overt as well: the priority to the buyer could be justified based on the need to protect security of transactions; this, in turn, is based on evaluation (contested, to be sure) of the buyer's loss; if defeated in the contest over title, as significant as (Mautner, 1991: 120–2) or greater than the original owner's, or on the view that the owner's fault justifies the buyer's priority (Mautner,1991: 121, 128, 48; Schwartz and Scott, 2011). Moreover, the merchant is a repeat player, easily identifiable, and likely to be solvent; therefore, its liability for the value of the converted chattel provides a reasonably effective remedy and 'just compensation' (Dagan, 2002: 15). In the NCII context, as we shall see, there is no good reason to prefer the viewer(s) over the claimant, and damages are not an adequate remedy.

B. Asymmetrical harm

In pursuing the conceptualization further, it is useful to distinguish between viewers who have already gained access to the image and potential viewers who would gain access in the future, should a remedy against the host be denied. Any immunity to the host beyond notice is akin to a refusal to grant an injunction against a merchant intending to sell stolen property to future buyers. Such a position cannot, of course, be supported by any interest in security of transactions since no transaction with future viewers for the 'sale' of the image was conducted.

But it is equally clear that in the competition between the claimant's right to exclude viewers from continuous access to her intimate image and a viewer's right to such continuous access, the claimant's right ought to prevail. I will first establish this conclusion as a matter of traditional data protection and privacy law balancing jurisprudence, and then as a matter of conflicts over titles. In practice, most NCII victims will be satisfied with removing or blocking the image and few would go after the viewers who already had access to the image, even if such an option is viable and practicable (Franks, 2013a; Laidlaw and Young, 2020: 153; compare Keren-Paz, 2013: 54, 143, 257–60; Chapter 12, Part 3). Technologically speaking, blocking or removing such an image by the intermediary will not undermine the access the viewer gained if the image was already downloaded. However, a court in Germany ordered an ex-partner to delete intimate images of the claimant that were in his lawful possession following a breakup despite the absence of any indication of intention to disseminate them (Oltermann, 2014).[14] As this case and the GDPR[15] suggest, and putting to one side issues of practicality, the NCII victim should be able to demand that viewers who possess NCII delete them.

The same conclusion is reached when the matter is looked upon in terms of balancing privacy against freedoms of expression or of information. It is clear that except for very rare circumstances (if any), there is no legitimate public interest in having access to intimate images disseminated without the subject's consent. This means that in terms of balancing, at least according to the European (CoE) and British frameworks, there is nothing to balance, and an injunction against the possessing[16] and further dissemination of the image will be given as a matter of course,[17] although the position is much less clear as to damages.[18] The analysis needs to distinguish between a legitimate public interest in having free access to nude or intimate images, as opposed to having access to the image of the specific claimant. Whatever one's view on the social value of pornography,[19] the debate about speedy removal of NCII is very different from the regulation of pornography. Intimate images (including by amateur uploaders) on the internet are abundant so the denial of access to the claimant's particular images does not really threaten freedom of information, expression or sexual gratification. As for the interest in access to the *claimant's* images, the starting point should be, and is, that there is no legitimate public interest, as opposed to public curiosity, in having access to such images.[20] It is also well established that images are more intrusive than text (Moosavian, 2018),[21] so even where public interest justifies revealing private facts, publishing an intrusive image confirming the newsworthy

---

[14] BGH, Urteil vom 13.10.2015 VI ZR 271/14 https://openjur.de/u/868417.html; the initial decision of Koblenz Regional Court (LG) was affirmed, first by the Higher Regional Court of Koblenz (OLG) and then by the Bundesgerichtshof (Federal Court of Justice) – the highest civil court in the country.

[15] GDPR, Art 7(3) about right to withdraw consent and Art 17 of right to erasure ('to be forgotten').

[16] Cf Urteil (n14).

[17] See *PJS* v *News Group Newspapers* [2016] UKSC 26 [24]; *Von Hannover v Germany* (2005) 40 EHRR 1, [65]; *Couderc and Hachette Filipacchi Associés v France* [2011] ECtHR (Application No 40454/07) [100–101].

[18] The cases id do not deal with claims against viewers or with potential liability for damages.

[19] This is not the place to canvass the huge literature. See for example, Boyle (2014). It relates to empirically contested issues such as possible connections between sex trafficking, prostitution and pornography, and exploitation within the porn industry. See for example, Gauntlett, 1997.

[20] See cases in n17.

[21] *Von Hannover* (n17) [59]; *Reklos v Greece* [2009] ECtHR (Application No 1234/05) [40]; *Murray v Express Newspapers* [2007] EWHC 1908 (Ch) [36]; *Terry v Persons Unknown* [2010] EWHC 119 (QB) [55]; *Campbell v MGN* [2004] UKHL 22 [31].

information would be a breach of privacy,[22] at least in the first instance and as long as the claimant did not contest the veracity of the information.[23] To take a hypothetical example, while there is a clear public interest in revealing the fact that congressman Anthony Weiner sexted a 15-year-old girl a photo of his penis (McAteer, 2017), it is not evident that there is a public interest argument for disseminating this photo, as the contribution of the photo to the legitimate public interest in knowing about such a behaviour is minimal.[24]

Viewed from the perspective of conflicts over title, this is the right decision as far as both security of transactions and balance of convenience are concerned. First, currently in both England and the US the theft rule reigns, so sanctity of property is given a categorical priority over security of transactions. Second, viewers typically would not be able to satisfy the conditions of purchase for *value*, and in some cases would fail the condition of *good faith*. The viewer seldom purchases and pays for the image. The business model of most platforms is based on advertisement rather than payment for the specific image. Websites behind a pay wall offering such images are likely to be either dedicated revenge porn websites or general porn websites. Definitely for the former but arguably for the latter as well, the viewer cannot satisfy good faith without notice status supporting a claim to keep the image (or access to it) since he paid for it.[25] In addition, since (and to the extent that) the payment made is by subscription, rather than for the specific image, it is doubtful whether the *purchase for value* condition is satisfied. Finally, the value needs to be adequate, namely, what is paid has to approximate the market value of the chattel (Maunter, 1991: 111). In *Cnaa'an v USA*, four out of seven Justices held that when the buyer mistakenly believed that the original stolen artwork, sold in the flea market, was a reproduction, adequate value is determined objectively and not based on the reproduction's (lower) market value.[26] By analogy, the value of the NCII image is not the lower market value of a non-NCII image. Arguably, the value of an intimate image should be measured by what the owner would demand to agree to disseminate it or, at the very least, the tort damages that would be awarded for the intrusion; and both would be much higher than what was paid (if at all) to have access to the image.[27]

For all of these reasons, the competition in the NCII context lacks the zero-sum game typifying conflicts over title to chattels. Such equivalence of loss

---

[22] *Theakston v MGN* [2002] EWHC 137 (QB) [78]; *Terry*, id.

[23] Cf *Campbell* (n21) [7] [24].

[24] Cf *Terry* (n21) [43]. For a discussion of public interest in publishing NCII see Chapter 10, Part 3.

[25] See Chapter 9, Part 3.A2.

[26] PD 57(2) 632 (Supreme Court, Israel, 2003).

[27] See Chapter 10, Part 4.C.

might justify the priority of the innocent buyer under a market overt regime. In its absence, clearly the right of the original owner should prevail. Another way to put it is that the stakes in NCII (unlike in title conflicts over chattels) are asymmetrical. The claimant's damage from a rule effectively allowing the image to circulate (by excluding a remedy against the intermediary) is enormous and cannot be adequately compensated by money. The damage to any viewer or potential viewer from not having continuous access to an NCII image, even if he paid for such access, is negligible, at most.

C. Risk taking and victim blaming

1. NCII victim blaming

In the NCII context, there are often victim blaming sentiments suggesting that those who voluntarily shared intimate pictures with their partners cannot complain when these images are disseminated (McGlynn and Rackley, 2017; Skinner-Thompson, 2018),[28] or even that those who take and store intimate photos of themselves do so at their peril (Goldman, 2013 critiqued by Franks, 2013b). A variation of this theme is that victims ought or will adjust their expectations of privacy to reflect the fact that the sharing of personal data becomes more pervasive (Goldman, 2013) (conversely, the decline of Facebook use among youth is explained by privacy concerns [Elyachar, 2018]). As with other cases of 'victim blaming' (usually[29] limited to sexual offences against women), I find them deeply problematic.

To begin with, it is clear doctrinally (at least in England)[30] and is uncontroversial normatively, that the decision with whom, with how many and what type of information to share, and under what conditions is exactly part of one's autonomy that the right to privacy is designed to protect. More specifically, it is clear that a decision to share with some is not a decision to share with all.[31] Moreover, viewed through the lenses of both freedom of sexual expression (McGlynn and Rackley, 2017: 548–9) and creation of information (Kronman, 1978), the approach of 'take-intimate-photos-and-store-them-at-your-peril-lest-they'll-be-hacked' is extremely problematic and counter-productive. A healthy approach to sexuality will refuse to view the voluntary

---

[28] Skinner-Thompson mentions both how the complete secrecy requirement generally curtails privacy protection in US jurisdictions and the regressive distributive effect of the doctrine, including in the NCII context.

[29] But not exclusively. See, for example, the 'Don't Make it Easy For Thieves' campaign by the South Yorkshire Police (2022).

[30] For the different, and problematic US approach, see Skinner-Thompson (2018).

[31] *Prince of Wales v Associated Newspapers* [2006] EWHC 522 (Ch) [42]–[43]. For a different approach (in a different context) by the CJEU see C-543/09 *Deutsche Telekom AG v Bundesrepublik Deutschland 5 May 2011.*

taking, saving and sharing of intimate images as something that should be discouraged. Only a regime that affords robust and effective protection against NCII can be expected to both encourage the voluntary creation and dissemination of such images, while at the same time discourage and prevent unauthorized disseminations which are extremely disempowering, demeaning and harmful.[32]

The problem with the adjust-your-expectation variant, beyond doubts whether its empirical assumption is sound, is that the argument is circular. It is the absence of effective legal remedy to NCII which might cause prospective claimants (and others) to care less about privacy invasions. But as long as double standards about women's sexuality abound,[33] the harm from NCII is not likely to disappear, so any change in attitudes is likely to take a long time and be very speculative. In the meantime, claimants would be left without proper remedy. Alternatively, under the adjust-your-expectation approach, women will indeed create, store and disseminate fewer intimate images than they would have liked to, and this undermines their sexual autonomy and expression. If, on the other hand, the legal system will robustly tackle the problem, including by affording claimants effective remedies against intermediaries, women and men will have much less reason to adjust their expectation of privacy in the digital era. The call for adjusted expectations is therefore nothing more (or less) than a hidden normative argument that we should care less about women's sexual privacy, despite the intolerable costs that NCII imposes on claimants and with the added cost broadcasted widely that, despite (or because of?) the phenomenon's gendered nature,[34] the law does not deem such a serious violation of women's privacy, autonomy and dignity to be worthy of an appropriate response, thus negatively affecting all women, as a group.

---

[32] See Chapter 9, Part 2. For the (unconvincing) contrary concern that a monitoring obligation will chill sexual expression see Chapter 7, Part 3.C.

[33] See, for example, in general Zaikman and Marks (2014). In the cyber context, Citron (2016: 102) mentions how some men have gained popularity and even profits from publicising their sexual encounters with women, whereas women bloggers who have been attacked following similar publication were told they were 'asking for it'.

A shocking example of double standard, victims' blaming and socialization of both can be found in *Miller v Mitchell* 598 F.3d 139 *3rd Cir.* 2010 commented on in Willard (2010: 545–6). Girls who sexted images that were later shared without their consent were required by the District Attorney (DA), as a condition for not being charged with felony child pornography, to attend a five week re-education program on what it means to be a girl in today's society, where they would have to write essays on why what they did was wrong. The boys who transmitted the evidence were not the subject of punishment, with the DA commenting 'high school boys did as high school boys will do and traded the photos among themselves'. Unsurprisingly, the court enjoined prosecuting the girls.

[34] See Chapter 6, Part 2.B.

2. Rejecting entrustment

Interestingly, the law governing conflicts over title does afford stronger protection to owners who did not take the voluntary risk of departing from their property. So, for example, a sale under a voidable title (where the original owner sold the goods but can avoid the contract, due to, for example, misrepresentation) will give the buyer a good title provided he buys in good faith and without notice of the seller's defective title.[35] The rationale is that the original owner agreed to part with the goods (and her title) while the owner of the stolen goods did not, so the conditions for the third party to acquire good title (value, good faith and absence of notice) are less exacting then the conditions required for priority (if at all) where the owner's goods were stolen, which typically include, in addition to this, a purchase from a merchant (usually one who deals in goods of that kind) in the ordinary course of business (Schwartz and Scott, 2011: 1350–3). And of course, under the Anglo-American *nemo dat* rule the buyer is always defeated in the contest with the original owner.

The hacking of intimate images (or even surreptitious taking of such images without the victim's knowledge) is the rough equivalent of stealing, while the unauthorized dissemination of images by someone who duly received them is the rough equivalent of a voidable title sale. Despite this superficial similarity, I would not advocate reduced protection in the latter scenario. The crucial point is the significant difference between the importance of security of transactions in the commercial context, the payment of the goods' value by the buyer and the symmetry of loss borne by the losing party and the absence of these factors in the NCII context. It is not evidently important to secure transactions of intimate images; the recipients of such images are not technically buyers and will not usually pay for them, so they do not give value, and when they do good faith, lack of notice and adequacy of value could be doubted. Most importantly, the losses are asymmetric, and significantly so. From the claimant's perspective, dignity, autonomy, privacy and sexual expression are at stake. From the viewers' perspective, there is no legitimate interest in viewing these specific photos and the interest in viewing or consuming intimate images can be easily satisfied in a way that does not involve such a significant violation of the claimant's interests. Mautner, in his germinal article on allocating priority in conflicts over title posits that the *ex-ante* consideration of allocating the loss to the party better situated to prevent it ought to take precedence over the *ex-post* consideration allocating the loss to the party who will suffer less if losing the contest (Maunter, 1991: 100). But any normative purchase of such an approach must be limited to situations

---

[35] S 23 Sales of Goods Act; U.C.C. § 2-403(1) (2011).

in which the losses are roughly equivalent. Viewed this way, risk taking, or fault, works as a tie breaker, by allocating a roughly equivalent loss to the party better able to prevent the accident. Fault, let alone mere risk taking, cannot justify the imposition of an extreme loss on the original owner when the innocent buyer (if indeed innocent) would suffer a minimal, or no loss at all, from losing access to the image.

D. An effective alternative remedy

The support for good faith purchase laws as appropriately balancing the interests of the parties relies on an under-discussed observation that whoever loses in the conflict can sue the merchant in either conversion or for breach of contract. So, under market overt, the owner can sue the merchant in conversion and receive the value of the chattel stolen (although not a delivery up of the chattel itself). Importantly, under the rules of conversion, the owner can sue anyone, even an innocent third party who takes possession of her goods without her permission. So even if the thief is identifiable and solvent, the owner can sue the merchant. While law and economics scholars debate whether the theft rule or market overt is more efficient,[36] an obvious advantage of market overt is that it works as a loss-spreading mechanism (coupled with incentivizing the merchant to verify whether the goods are stolen, discussed later). Buying from a merchant in the ordinary course of business affords buyers with an insurance against the risk of losing title to the goods. At the same time, it affords the original owner with a repeat player who is likely to be solvent (Dagan, 2002). In the context of ownership over chattels, the availability of damages for the chattel's market value under conversion affords an adequate remedy to the original owner. While inferior to a solution investing the title to the stolen chattel in the owner (which allows the owner to get back possession of the chattel), damages are a good enough alternative remedy helping to justify (alongside the other policy considerations) the lost title of the original owner. Similarly, even under the *nemo dat* rule, the original owner can sue the merchant in conversation and save themselves the trouble of identifying or suing the buyer in possession of their chattel.

There are two important ramifications of these observations in the NCII context. First, affording platforms with immunity is anomalous, since it deprives the claimant from a remedy against the merchant, unlike all other cases of stolen property (whether governed under *nemo dat* or market overt rules). It does so in circumstances in which there is no good reason to prioritize the viewer's interest over the claimant, unlike what is arguably

---

[36] For a summary of the main views in the debate see Schwartz and Scott (2011), n. 10.

the case for buyers of chattels in open markets under a market overt rule, and where, similarly to open markets, the claimant's chances to identify the viewer(s) and recover damages from them are slim. Second, in NCII, and unlike conflicts over chattels, damages alone, recovered from the uploader, platform or viewers, are an inadequate remedy; victims consistently report that the removal of the images is the most important remedy for them, more than being awarded damages. Since the only effective remedy is limiting access to the image, a remedy against hosts and search engines becomes necessary.[37] Therefore, the US solution of denying any remedy against the host is entirely inadequate. Moreover, given that the injury from NCII is serious and irreparable,[38] and that the loss to freedom of expression from removal of such images is minimal, liability of platforms should be strict, as it is for all other merchants selling stolen property. Crucially, hosts' responsibility should extend to monitoring and filtering duties, since unlike cases of stolen chattels, damages against the merchant are an inadequate remedy, so it is imperative to avoid the *initial* dissemination of the image on the platform.

E. Regressive redistribution

The question of whether the redistributive effect of a market overt rule is regressive never featured prominently in policy debates about its desirability.[39] In fact, we do not have a reason to believe that any clear pattern is discernible. A simplistic assumption would be that a redistributive rule is progressive since stolen property is distributed away from the 'haves' at lower prices to the less well off. However, this ignores both the fact that the rich are better able than the poor to invest in fencing their property and the fact that prices in regulated markets are more likely to resemble the market value of non-stolen goods, so those purchasing them are not likely to be especially poor. By contrast, any rule promoting the dissemination of NCII is likely to be regressive, given that most victims are women and most viewers are men. It is also worth highlighting that NCII is a systemic harm with the effect, and in many cases the purpose, of humiliating, marginalizing and silencing women and entrenching patriarchal norms and order.[40] This in itself should be a good reason against a solution – immunity to hosts – that brings about

---

[37] See Chapter 3, Part 4.

[38] See Chapter 6, Part 2.A.

[39] Discussion of the limited role of the ideal of avoiding any preferential treatment of the better-off in the context of takings is provided by Dagan (1999). Mautner's resort (1991) to needs as a secondary criterion to decide the priority in conflicts over title goes also partially towards the relevance of the effects of redistribution, although there is no resort in his theory to socio-economic considerations.

[40] See, for both claims, Chapter 6, Part 2.B.

such a regressive result. In addition, the fact that social media, and more generally user content platforms, are such important agents in maintaining cultural norms (Croucher, 2011) makes it just and appropriate to subject them to liability the motivation and likely effect of which are to reduce the regressive redistribution of social power from women to men.

5. Policies in favour of merchant/intermediary liability

So far, the case against intermediary immunity has been based on the lack of legitimate interest by viewers to have access or 'title' to such images. A focus on the role of the merchant in conflicts over title and the relevant policy considerations only bolsters this conclusion. Both merchants and hosts are repeat players, easily identifiable and commercial actors. The relevant policy considerations are efficiency/control,[41] fairness/business model[42] and loss spreading (Dagan, 2002). These considerations support the liability of merchants (which is indeed the law), regardless of whether the buyer in an open market, the thief, or the thief's transferee could be sued. For this reason, the model of 'notice-and-disclose' for intermediary liability[43] is incompatible with rules governing merchants' liability for selling stolen property.

A. Efficiency

From an *efficiency* perspective, holding the merchant liable is justified, since they have relevant control over the situation; they are in a position to verify the origin of the goods, or at least the identity and contact details of those who sold the stolen item (which will allow the merchant to sue the seller based on title warranty if the merchant is liable in conversion to the owner). Merchants' liability also increases the costs of business by causing them to internalize the costs of stolen goods identified by the owners. This means that merchants with shoddy supply chains (and therefore a higher proportion of stolen goods) will be less able to sell goods cheaply based on depressed purchase costs of the stolen goods. In order to give the appropriate incentive to the merchant, though, it is important to keep them in the frame, even if the thief is identifiable and solvent.

Efficiency considerations apply also to hosts. Their liability could be justified based on their ability to monitor (through both terms of use and

---

[41] See for example, Helman and Parchomovsky (2011); Chapter 2, Part 3, Chapter 3, Parts 2, 3, 5.

[42] See Chapter 2, Part 3; Chapter 3, Part 3.B. Cf Digital Millennium Copyright Act 17 USC §512(1)(B) (1998).

[43] Such model was adopted by the Defamation Act 2013. See Chapter 2, nn15–16.

enforcement) that the content does not violate the rights of others. At the very least, the analogy with merchants suggests that they have the ability, at least, to verify that user content which on its face seriously breaches privacy, if uploaded without the subject's consent, is indeed lawful. The financial costs of monitoring, alongside a chilling effect on expression due to excessive removal of content are mentioned as major policy considerations against intermediary liability. I will deal with these considerations in Chapter 7, but it is instructive to see they did not win the day in other situations in which a merchant sells without authorization the claimant's property.

B. Fairness

There are two versions of *fairness* – both of which are applicable to conflicts over title; the weaker version is simply about the link between the business activity that includes the infringing activity and profits; the stronger is *increased* profits from infringing activity that creates a risk of collusion. The merchant profits from an activity that harms the owner (weaker version); and stolen goods are likely to be cheaper than non-stolen goods and low prices increase the merchant's turnover (stronger version). Alternatively, if the price to the buyer of the stolen good is still the market price (as suggested in 'regressive redistribution' earlier), the merchant profits by having a bigger profit margin as he buys the goods at lower prices, since the goods are potentially stolen. From an efficiency perspective, this gives the merchant an incentive not to inquire as to the origins of cheap goods. The likelihood that the merchant will be sued by the losing party to the conflict over title, therefore, both increases the merchant's incentive to ensure that the goods are not stolen and is fair in the stronger sense of depriving them of an *undeserved* profit or advantage – increased profits due to the fact that the goods are stolen.

Both versions of fairness hold true for hosts. My point is not that NCII is likely to be cheaper 'product' than CII; as documented in Chapter 10, most intimate images are accessible for free and a per-image pricing model almost does not exist. Rather, my point is that intermediaries benefit (indirectly) from hosting intimate images and are likely to benefit disproportionately from hosting NCII due to the increased allure these have to some viewers. Specifically, it has long been acknowledged that pornography has been a driving force in internet development (Baker, 2013; Gilmore, 2016). Moreover, both female nudity and salacious or lewd content (that is, celebrities' nudity, the character of intimate images as unauthorized, and the combination of the two) attract lots of visits, which is good for business (Greenberg, 2014; Pyne, 2015; Bari, 2016; Dori, 2018). That the profits of many hosts are based on advertisements (or data mining) rather than on payments from viewers does not change the economic benefit hosts derive from content likely to be a breach of privacy (Edwards, 2018: 47, 69–71,

85, 87). Note that this should not transform the case for hosts' liability to be a variant of enterprise liability (that is, price as opposed to sanction; for such a case see Keating, 2001). The main responsibility of hosts should be to monitor and block the uploading of NCII,[44] or at least to remove access to NCII upon notice and ensure they do not reappear. However, especially since the injury from breach of privacy is so significant, fairness strongly supports hosts' obligation to compensate the claimant if they breach their monitoring obligation.

C. Loss spreading

A similar point could be made about loss spreading. The merchant is better able to insure or self-insure against the loss from having to pay the value of stolen goods. The owner and buyers might be one-shot players, so for them the loss is significant. For (decent) merchants, the proportion of stolen goods (or more accurately stolen goods identified as such by the original owners) is not that high, so the costs of being liable for the value of the stolen goods they sell is not prohibitive. Loss spreading too supports the liability of internet intermediaries. The harm to viewers from being denied access to NCII is minimal, if anything, either in financial terms or in that of access to information/freedom of expression. But for the subject of the image the harm is very significant. While that harm is not patrimonial, or mainly pecuniary, it is very significant (and irreparable) and deserves a significant award of damages. The uploader, even if identifiable will not always be solvent, so the ability to sue the host for damages is important. Contrary to Turner's complaint (2014: 61; there, in the defamation context), holding the intermediary liable for user content is not an arbitrary or an opportunistic pursuit after a deep pocket; rather, as was explained in Chapter 3, Parts 3.B–5, the intermediary is actively implicated in breaching the claimant's rights, adding significantly to her injury, and doing so for profit.

6. Doctrinal translation

As platforms' immunity from liability to NCII is statutory, accepting the argument defended here means a change to the ECD and to S230 Communications Decency Act to allow liability even prior to notice and, possibly, even to allow an obligation to filter and monitor NCII. The analysis offered explains why such a result is desirable and follows from first principles on intermediary liability for the unauthorized sale of the claimant's property. But the removal of immunity still leaves the question of the cause of action

---

[44] The policy considerations supporting such conclusion are canvassed in Chapters 6 to 7.

under which the intermediary will be liable. As will be discussed in the next chapter, direct application of proprietary torts such as conversion has been offered for biomaterials (Roberts, 2019), sex-trafficking (Keren-Paz, 2013: 142–6), private information (Howden, 2019; Sinha, 2019)[45] and personal data (Ritter and Mayer, 2018; compare Boerding et al, 2018). However, the same result in the NCII context, which I prefer, could be achieved by developing the cause of action of breach of privacy/misuse of private information ('*Privacy*') to impose strict liability, at least on the internet intermediary, but in fact also on viewers,[46] and liability would be imposed regardless of the ability to sue the user who uploaded the intimate image to the platform. Adopting such a solution will also require addressing the relationship between a proprietary privacy right and personal data rights. In short, the considerable overlap existing between privacy and personal data rights makes sense,[47] although it has been recently subject to a convincing critique by Lord Leggatt in *Lloyd v Google*, highlighting the differences between privacy and data protection.[48] To the extent to which the rights with respect to intimate images enshrined under my suggested model do not already exist under the GDPR/DPA[49] they should exist under the personal data regime, in addition to being available under a privacy claim.

---

[45] Crucially, however, Sinha: 605 gravitates towards 'limited modification' of strict liability in the privacy context. See also Chapter 5, Part 4.A.

[46] See Chapter 10. Viewing as intrusion is discussed in Chapter 8, Part 2.

[47] For example of such overlap see *Murray v Big Pictures (UK) Limited* [2008] EWCA Civ 446 [63].

[48] [2021] UKSC 50, [130]–[135].

[49] See Chapter 2, text to n8 on the relationship between the ECD and the DPD/GDPR.

5

Property and Privacy: Objections and Possible Extensions

1. Introduction

In this chapter, I defend the conceptualization of intimate images as property against the 'inalienability' and 'proliferation of property rights' critiques by referring to the 'inalienability paradox': unless inalienable rights are afforded the stronger remedies available to owners, the rights become *more* alienable (Part 2). I then respond to the objection that treating intimate images as property will lead to an undesirable proliferation of quasi/property rights with respect to the same object: reduced alienability, which is the main argument against a proliferation of rights with respect to tradable goods, is in fact exactly the sought-after result for NCII. Finally, the considerations relevant to NCII do not necessarily apply to other contexts such as defamation and copyright. In this sense, the argument defended here lends support to the policy move (documented in Chapter 2) of departing from the EU horizontal approach towards contextual examination of the appropriate scope of intermediary liability. But it also supports a critique of the inverted hierarchy (clearly apparent in US law and emerging in EU law) according to which copyright holders have greater rights against intermediaries than NCII victims, while the reverse rule is much more defensible. Nonetheless, the analysis will suggest that the recent move to a de facto strict liability of (certain) hosts under the recent Copyright–Digital Single Market Directive is consistent with general principles governing the liability of merchants selling stolen property.

2. Privacy, property and inalienability

A. The Inalienability paradox

The usefulness of the analogy with conflicts over title hinges on accepting right to privacy over images (and more broadly private information or data)[1] as a subject matter for property. This of course is disputed,[2] so in what follows I shall clarify my view on this issue, and defend the usefulness of the property framework. The short answer to the question why a property framework is useful is that personal information, including images, could either be treated as property or not. If it should be treated as property, the analogy with conflicts over title clearly shows that the claimant (=the owner) should have priority over both the viewer and the intermediary, so that the image should not be allowed to circulate any further. But if the analogy with property is misplaced, it ought to be so since the interest is inalienable, since what is private by its very nature ought not to be circulated, sold and distributed. But if this is so, the central argument in favour of good faith purchase 'defence' – the need to protect commerce and to ensure security of transactions or, stated somewhat differently, the legitimate interest of the buyer in keeping what he bought in good faith – is simply irrelevant. It follows then, that under non-proprietary understandings of privacy, the balance in the competition between the subject of the information and its recipients should tilt more heavily towards the former. As I have explained in the context of sex trafficking (Keren-Paz, 2013: 142–6), from the fact that a right should be inalienable and therefore, a property framework should be rejected *ex ante*, it does not follow that we should not afford an *ex post* propriety remedy when the inalienable asset was expropriated. In the NCII context, the tension between *ex ante* inalienability and *ex post* affording of proprietary remedy is much less pronounced, since typically the victim is not seeking an account of profits for the misappropriation, but rather removal of the image from the public domain, which clearly supports the nature of the

---

[1] For the difference between private information and big data see Part 4.A.

[2] For a philosophical argument of why we should not conceive of privacy through a property lens see Richardson (2015) especially chapters 4 and 5. See also Roessler, 2015. For a practical opposition to property rights in personal data see Purtova, 2017. For an approach that a broad Lockean theory of property can apply to digital information and that it shares core values with Brandeis' theory about the legal right to privacy see Cloud (2018). See also Judith Jarvis Thomson's observation (1975) that a right to privacy is just a right to property ownership in disguise; and Lessig (2002: 247) (focusing on the rhetorical advantage of framing a claim in privacy as property). For the influence of Lockean property theory on the first US state Supreme Court recognising breach of privacy as a common law tort (which dealt with a right to an image) see Moosavian (2022: chapter 3).

image (information) as inalienable. It should also be noted that private information is not truly inalienable, since the subject can sell it, should she wish to do so. Moreover, in *Douglas v Hello! (No 3)*[3] it was recognized that a right to privacy exists even when the motivation for enforcing it is to increase or maintain the market value of the information.

I turn now to the longer answer to the question of whether intimate images, and possibly other private information should be considered as property. Whether one ought to have a *property* right with respect to a certain subject matter should depend on the consequences of such classification.[4] Contrary to a common understanding under which 'the right to exclude others is a necessary and sufficient condition of identifying the existence of property' (Merrill, 1998: 731), it is the right to alienate (mainly for remuneration) that separates entitlements that we consider inalienable and (only) personal and entitlements which could be alienable and are property. Consider voting: the right is inalienable in that I cannot sell or gift my right to vote, nor waive it in a legally binding way. But undeniably I have a right to exclude others from exercising *my* right to vote. Surely, if I know someone is going to fraudulently use my identity to vote, I should be able to obtain an injunction preventing her from doing so (compare Friedmann, 1989: 16–18). Moreover, as the voting example illustrates, despite being inalienable, illegitimate interference with the right to vote is a tort, for which damages have been and could be awarded.[5] I was not able to find cases in which someone recovered damages for 'converting' the right to vote, as distinguished from 'destroying' it by unlawfully preventing the voter from exercising their right.[6] Nonetheless, it will be quite absurd for a legal system allowing me to recover damages against someone who destroyed (without misappropriating) my right to vote, to deny me a remedy against someone who not only prevented me from voting but also unlawfully misappropriated my vote.[7] This conclusion

---

[3] [2003] EWHC 55.

[4] This, of course, is disputed and follows from my basic legal realist understanding of what law should be understood to be about. See Cohen (1935).

[5] *Ashby v White* (1703) 2 Ld. Raym. 938; *Morgan v Simpson* [1975] QB 151, 161.

[6] Some reports on election fraud mention the criminal equivalent of personation (pretending to be someone else to cast their vote) but it is not always evident whether the person whose identity was used was aware of the personation (see White and Johnston, 2017; Electoral Commission, 2018).

[7] For purposes of quantum, the defendant's motivation (if any) for the interference with the right to vote, and possibly, whether the defendant likely voted as the claimant would have, are likely to be relevant. But since the wrongfulness of denying the claimant from voting ought to be grounded in notions of autonomy and enfranchisement, an award is apposite, even if the fraudster voted as the claimant would have (a question which of course raises evidentiary difficulties).

is bolstered by the fact that the law nearly always treats misappropriation of property as being more serious than mere interference. For example, the former is typically actionable per se (hence no need to show that a trespasser causes damage) whereas the latter (in, say, nuisance law) requires proof of harm.

The availability of damages for the misappropriation (or destruction) of a right that is arguably inalienable – as distinct from a property right – is evident across different areas of tort law: damages for personal injury; *Rookes v Bernard*, under which a profit motive calculated to lead to efficient breaches of duty is an exceptional ground to award exemplary damages in English law;[8] (crucially, by nature, such cynical calculation is more likely to exist in misappropriation than in destruction interferences); damages (under Californian law) in *Moore v Regents of California University*[9] for unauthorized use of biomaterial; and damages for misuse of private information[10] and personal data breaches.[11] With respect to the Californian *Moore* decision, while the majority rejected a property right in biomaterial, it partially relied on the availability of damages for breach of informed consent and fiduciary duty to justify this result.[12] Interestingly, fiduciary duty, as an equitable remedy, lends itself easily to account of profits from the breach of duty, and is itself generally linked strongly with the management of the claimant's property. Similarly, the origin of misuse of private information as an equitable breach of confidence lends itself easily to account of profits for the misappropriation of private information.[13]

In my previous writing, I have stressed that the refusal to protect an inalienable right with at least as strong a remedy as that afforded against

---

8   [1964] AC 1129, 1225–7.

9   51 Cal 3rd 120, 128–32 (1990).

10 *Gulati v MGN Ltd* [2015] EWHC 1482; aff'd [2015] EWCA Civ 1291 (CA).

11 *Vidal-Hall v Google Inc* [2015] EWCA Civ 311.

12 More recent decisions in US jurisdictions accept the possibility of suing in conversion in the biomaterial context. See *Peerenboom v Perlmutter*, No 2013-CA-015257 (Fla. Cir. Ct. Apr. 7, 2017); *Cole v Gene by Gene, Ltd*, No 1:14-cv-00004, 2017 WL 2838256 (D. Alaska 30 June 2017); discussed approvingly by Roberts (2019). In England, sperm was accepted as property for purpose of compensating for its destruction (as distinct from its misappropriation): *Yearworth v North Bristol NHS Trust* [2009] EWCA Civ 37.

13 *Douglas v Hello!* (No 3) [2005] EWCA Civ 595 [249]. But see *Vidal-Hall* (n11) [43], [51] ('Misuse of private information is a civil wrong without any equitable characteristics'; however, implications for available remedies is left as an open question to be decided when the issue arises). *PJS v News Group Newspapers* [2016] UKSC 26, [42] recognized the possibility of awarding a gain-based relief for breach of privacy. However, 'gain-based relief has only rarely been awarded for breach of confidence, and has never been awarded for breach of privacy'. Barnett (2018: 184) supports its award only in exceptional circumstances.

interferences with property is mistaken (Keren-Paz, 2013: 142–6). Such refusal confuses *ex ante* voluntary transfer of the entitlement with *ex post* compensation (or restitution) for its unlawful misappropriation. Across the different contexts in which the status of a certain entitlement as 'property' is debated, the main policy arguments are a dignitarian anti-commodification argument (Seboc, 2003); and the effect on innocent third parties, which relate, in the context of biomaterial, to the fear of stifling medical research,[14] and more generally, to security of receipt.[15] But here lies a paradox: on the commodification rationale, the weaker remedy afforded to the holders of an inalienable right vis-à-vis property owners will make the entitlement *more* alienable, not less. I have stressed this point in the context of denying restitution of profits against those misappropriating an inalienable right (Keren-Paz, 2013: 142–6). But the point is equally valid with regards to the protection afforded to the right against interference from innocent third parties. If we think that a right is so important that it cannot be alienated consensually, how come the remedy against innocent third parties in receipt of the thing misappropriated is more limited in comparison to the remedy available against those in receipt of converted property? By definition we are happy with the alienation of the latter, but not of the former, and yet we protect more vigorously receipt with respect to inalienable right by denying an effective remedy against the third party. The result makes very little sense. One might debate whether strict liability of innocent recipients of property is too harsh or not. But my point is that as long as a legal system imposes strict liability on those interfering with the owner's title, including innocent third parties in receipt of the claimant's property, it will be indefensible to deny at least an equivalent level of protection to those whose inalienable right has been misappropriated.

There is another way to look at this problem: once the entitlement has been misappropriated, it is de facto already commodified and alienated. The remaining question is distributive; namely, who should derive the benefit from the value of the inalienable entitlement, the original owner or the third party. For the reasons explained earlier, the value should be allocated to the original owner, similar to the conclusion reached in the contexts of biomaterial,[16] slavery/trafficking (Keren-Paz, 2013: 145) and personal data (Determann, 2018; Ritter and Mayer, 2018; Roberts, 2019).

---

[14] *Moore* (n9) 143–7.

[15] See the discussion in Part 3 of the related concern about conflicting quasi/property rights to the same subject matter.

[16] *Moore* (n9) 166 (J Mosk, dissenting, citing the Court of Appeal) and n12.

B. Why property?

I will turn now to address three related objections.[17] The first is 'why property'? Arguably, if we conclude, following a weighing of the competing interests, that liability in damages for those who disseminate (or receive) sexual images without the victim's consent should be strict, we end up with a rule which mirrors that adopted by the common law in relation to the liability of those who convert others' property; this is a way of describing a conclusion we have already reached without an appeal to property, or so goes the argument. However, within the legal realist jurisprudence I espouse, intimate images are property since we would like to afford the claimants strong control over them, including strict liability of (at least) those disseminating them; it is not, rather, that strict liability follows because we define these images as property. Resorting to the concept of property and to the conflicts over title framework serves three purposes: (1) ensuring consistency, or coherence – values held in high regard at common law. A careful examination of the policy considerations leads to a conclusion that conceptualizing intimate images as property is analytically correct, leads to desirable results (strict liability of intermediaries) and is principled; (2) ensuring transitivity: since some considerations supporting a market overt solution with respect to chattels (for example, symmetry of harm) do not apply to private images while others do (for example, the insurance function of the intermediary), a solution according to which the internet intermediary is singled out as the only merchant who is not strictly liable for the 'conversion' of the image cannot be justified; I will say more later about transitivity in the context of the inalienability paradox; (3) it could – but does not have to – serve as a doctrinal peg to allow strict liability, by applying directly the tort of conversion; alternatively, it could be used indirectly to reform *Privacy*.[18] Resorting to conflicts over title, therefore, provides justification to a remedy which according to common wisdom and litigation practice is currently unavailable to victims.

C. We need to talk about (the harshness of) conversion

The second challenge is normative: strict liability for conversion is not evidently attractive, so it is disputed whether it should be extended to

---

[17] A fourth challenge will be addressed in Chapter 10, as it more relevant to viewers: that viewing ought to be conceptualized as the destruction of property (privacy), rather than its misappropriation (images) and hence should be governed by negligence, rather than by strict liability.

[18] Chapter 4, Part 6 and see Chapter 10 (discussing the already stricter nature of *Privacy* liability).

intimate images. However: (1) for the reasons discussed earlier, especially in Chapter 4, Part 5, strict liability of commercial intermediaries is clearly justified; (2) broader still, and the following argument applies also to viewers as the recipients of the stolen property, and not only to the intermediaries, one could query the framing of my proposal as an undesirable *extension*. Rather, we could query, whether the exclusion of strict liability with respect to intimate images is unprincipled, paradoxical (by affording weaker remedies against the undermining of stronger interests), and potentially discriminatory, if we accept NCII as a gendered phenomenon.[19] Strict liability for conversion is a well-entrenched rule, despite doubts, expressed both in England and elsewhere, whether it treats some innocent convertors too harshly.[20] The majority in *OBG v Allen*[21] showed reluctance to extend the tort of conversion to a chose in action but it is also not entirely clear that the court felt that strict liability with regards to chattels is too harsh. Rather, the gist of the opinion was that there were good reasons not to extend conversion's strict liability to choses in action in the context of pure economic loss in a commercial context. Similarly, tort and property scholars are split between those insisting that misappropriation is limited to land and chattels, given its link with possession (Cane, 1991: 25–6) and those believing that intangibles can be converted (Green and Randall, 2009: chapter 5; Murphy, 2022). I do not make here a general claim that conversion should be available to all intangible interests and I reserve my judgement on whether the policy considerations on converting a chose of action are similar to that pertaining to conversion of intimate images. To the extent that the *OBG* majority ignores similarities between chattels and intangibles that are relevant for the policy analysis, the argument in this chapter could be read as a critique of that holding. What I do claim is that intimate images that are in practice alienable but are dignitary and are often treated rhetorically as *in*alienable (Allen, 2011)[22] should not receive a lesser protection than that afforded to chattels. Whether this approach is a real or only an apparent 'extension' of conversion's strict liability is beside the point and a sterile debate. What matters is that as long as strict liability is deemed appropriate with respect to lesser and gender-neutral interests (or

---

[19] The normative relevance of both hierarchy of interests and understanding NCII as a gendered harm are explained further in Chapter 6.

[20] See *Kuwait Airways v Iraqi Airways* [2002] 2 AC 88, [80], [103]; In Israel, *Cnaa'an v USA*, PD 57(2) 632 (Supreme Court, Israel, 2003) per Deputy President Levin [11], [43] dissenting.

[21] [2007] UKHL 21.

[22] While the gist of Allen's argument is normative, she also argues that the government does stick us with privacy we do not want and may need to do more of it.

arguably male-dominated interests)[23] it ought to govern also the viewing of intimate images.

Nor is strict liability for conversion limited to jurisdictions – such as England – which do not afford owners with a delivery up (*vindicatio*) of their property from those who had it in their possession. Indeed, Israel, whose property law includes delivery up remedies and market overt, retained the tort of conversion, and excluded the application of market overt where the buyer (still in possession of the artwork) paid the lower market value of a 'kitsch' picture for an original stolen artwork, despite one of the dissenting judges observing that this could expose the buyer to liability under conversion for the market value of the artwork.[24]

More generally, and while exceptions exist, tort theory is split between supporters of corrective justice, which is usually understood to require fault, and supporters of a greater role to distributive justice and strict liability.[25] As I have argued previously, while fairness would tend to justify strict liability, egalitarian commitment might favour fault-based, no-, or strict liability depending on the effect of the legal rule on narrowing or widening gaps in society (Keren-Paz, 2007a). Now this is a big debate and while I tend to support conversion's strict liability, I do not intend to make an intervention here. My point is more about fit and consistency. It is even more so about the way society ought to rank the strength of claimant's legitimate interests and avoid gender-based discrimination. It does not make sense that the protection given to one's car would be more extensive than to one's intimate images. So as long as intentional (though innocent) interference with one's property entails strict liability in general, the same protection ought to be afforded to interests we deem so important that they ought to be inalienable. In addition, NCII is a gendered phenomenon and so is its harm. To exclude strict liability for a type of interference that harms disproportionately women, perpetrated disproportionally by men and harms women significantly more than it does men is discriminatory against women, and in any event unjustified and indefensible from an egalitarian perspective.

This suggests that there are two alternative claims here. One, that intimate images should be treated the same way as chattels. This means that if, due to a legal reform, the tort of conversion is replaced or changes its nature so that an innocent interference does not lead to liability, the same change should apply to the viewing of intimate images. But as long as conversion entails strict liability, so should the viewing of intimate images. The other claim is

---

[23] For economic interests as male-related see for example Bitton (2010).

[24] *Cnaa'an* (n20); The Land Law, 1969 ss 15–20; The Movable Property Law, 1971 s 8; The Sales Law, 1968 s 34; The Tort Ordinance (New Version) ss 52, 53.

[25] Chapter 3, n41.

that even if strict liability is too harsh with respect to chattels, it is not too harsh with respect to intimate images, either because the protected interest in the latter is more important (regardless of gender equality considerations) or because of the nature of perpetration and harm as gendered. Under either account, the following response is not good enough: that strict liability is generally problematic, but since the rule is well entrenched, the least we could do is not to expand it to new territories such as intimate images.

D. Consistency and transitivity

The final objection is that the inalienability paradox is not a paradox at all. Granted, it does not follow from the fact that the law does not respond in the strongest possible terms to a breach that it condones it, even in part. So arguably, that the claims and remedies the law accords to victims do not go as far as they could casts no reflection on the content or stringency of those rights and duties and so, there is simply no paradox involved where inalienable rights receive something less than full protection. However, this misses the point about transitivity: a system that holds merchants selling the victim's stolen car strictly liable, cannot hold hosts liable for less, at least in the absence of convincing policy considerations (which are absent) and at least if it pretends that privacy is as important as cars (if privacy is considered alienable) or more important than cars (if privacy is considered inalienable). Only in a system in which merchants selling stolen cars are not strictly liable, we could have a debate whether hosts ought to also not be strictly liable, or should be nonetheless strictly liable, given the differences (canvassed earlier) between them and other merchants.

3. Competing quasi/proprietary interests

At first blush, the argument that private information should be treated as property faces the objection that it exacerbates the problem of existing competing (quasi) property rights with respect to the same object. So, an intimate image of a woman taken by her ex-partner and disseminated through a platform to a viewer who downloaded the image onto his computer, could give rise to four claims by three individuals: the (1) privacy-based and (2) data protection claims by the subject of the intimate image, (3) the copyright by the taker of the image, and (4) the (weaker) claim by the viewer as the 'owner' of the copy. Standard economic analysis of law opposes multiple property claims with respect to the same object since they decrease efficient use of the object, including by way of its alienation to the high-value user, and create cooperation problems among the multiple owners, as a result of strategic behaviour, sometimes termed the problem of anti-commons (Buchanan and Yoon, 2000; Determann, 2018; Rinehart,

2018; compare Tushnet, 2013).[26] For the following reasons, this concern does not decrease the attractiveness of a property model for NCII. First, the problem of multiple conflicting rights with respect to intimate images remains whether or not privacy (and data) rights are perceived as property or not. As indicated earlier, a right to exclude is at the core of an inalienable right – recall the voting example – so is not unique to property rights.[27] Second, recall the inalienability paradox; it is because unauthorized private information should not be easily circulated that an effective remedy against the platform is needed. Increased platforms' accountability due to application of the property model, including the analogy with conflicts over title is a virtue of the property model, not its vice. The corollary is also important: if *Privacy* or GDPR can affect intermediaries' liability prior to notice without relying on the notion of property, adopting a property model becomes less crucial and is limited to providing a justification which is conceptually sound and consistent with first principles about the proper scope of liability by innocent intermediaries.

Third, the assumption that multiple rights with respect to the same asset are either socially undesirable or inefficient is contested. Beyond the general point that reduced efficiency or tradability is at times a price worth paying for better attainment of other goals,[28] the negative effect (if any) of joint ownership on social welfare depends also on the rules governing management of jointly owned property (Dagan and Heller, 2001: 610).[29] Moreover, it is even unclear whether fragmentation of ownership with respect to data is inefficient so that a clear allocation of a property right over data is mandated as a matter of efficiency: A European Commission technical report found that '[L]egislative intervention to allocate some rights to specific parties might reduce the space for negotiations and may result in less satisfactory arrangements for all parties involved' (Duch-Brown et al, 2017: 32). It concluded (at 47) that '[A]llocating data ownership rights to one or the other party may not be welfare-maximizing either'.

In the NCII context, Derek Bambauer, 2014 suggested investing an additional copyright in the subject of an intimate image independent of

---

[26] *Your Response Ltd v Business Media Ltd* [2014] EWCA Civ 281 [39]–[42].

[27] Determann (2018) seems to disagree, but he targets a property right in data which is additional to existing data subject rights.

[28] In the data-as-property debate the main trade off discussed is with data subjects right to privacy, but also with distributive justice. See for example, Duch-Brown et al (2017), Determann (2018), Boerding et al (2018), Michels and Millard (2019), Birnhack (2020) and Keren-Paz (2020). Equivalent debates across different areas of law (for example, World Trade Organization, competition, tort, consumer protection) are endemic within the critical law and economic scholarship. See for example, Keren-Paz (2007a).

[29] Noting that civil law regimes are superior to the common law's counterpart.

the right of the taker of the photo notwithstanding increased transactions costs for gaining authorization to disseminate the image.[30] So whether the (quasi) property right by the image subject is conceived of as a privacy tort right (as I advocate) or as an additional copyright (as Bambauer and others have suggested), an authorization by, and even paid-for licence from the copyright owner would not trump the right of the image subject: unless the copyright licensee has received the right to disseminate the image from the image subject he should be liable to the latter for breaching her privacy and be subject to the remedies that follow from characterizing this right as proprietary.[31]

4. Possible extensions beyond NCII?

A. Private (sexual) information beyond images

Could the argument defended here be extended to all private information, to private sexual information which is not conveyed by image, or is it limited to intimate images? I will not attempt to answer this question here, and I could see arguments for both sides in the debate. On the one hand, it is generally agreed that images are more intrusive than text.[32] Similarly, the social value of textual expression might be higher than that of images; it might also be harder technically to sort out privacy breaching text from non-breaching text than sorting intimate from non-intimate images (Chapter 7). On the other hand, the analysis of NCII as being sold 'with a defect in title' by the intermediary to the viewer lends itself, it seems, quite comfortably to private information more generally. But even if this is the case, the question of whether private information should be considered as property, as some propose,[33] should be kept separate from the question of whether personal data should,[34] and from the separate question (often meshed together with the former), if so, to whom should it be allocated, the data subject or the data controller?[35] There might be a difference between big data that relates

---

[30] For a more traditional analysis observing the (limited) potential of copyright law in affecting take downs, see for example, Harn Lee (2019) and O'Connell and Bakina (2020).

[31] See Chapter 10, Part 3.E for a discussion of reliance on (deemed) prior consent in commercial contexts.

[32] See Chapter 4, n21.

[33] See Howden (2019), Sinha (2019) and sources in n2.

[34] For insistence on the need for a strict conceptual separation of personal data from personal information see Kanecek (2018). Cf *Lloyd v Google* [2021] UKSC 50, [130]–[135] (on the differences between privacy and data protection regimes).

[35] Many of those opposing ownership in data base their view, at least partially, on the fear that this will undermine data subject rights (mainly to privacy), under the understanding that the property right will be allocated to the data collector/controller, or that power gaps will ensure that ownership will end up in the hands of controllers, to the detriment

to information whose subject is often not even aware exists, gathered and traded, and that is (or its disaggregated parts) usually innocuous and more traditional pieces of private information, including intimate images. Under EU law, personal data is *de facto* owned (and sold) by the controller, subject to the data subject rights enshrined in the GDPR (on alternative understanding, the right is more akin to licensing). In *practice*, data subjects waive most of their rights in return for information and services received from the data controller (Duch-Brown et al, 2017: 16–17; but compare on 'waivability' Prins, 2006). This casts doubt on the (common) understanding of the rights of the data subject as inalienable.[36] Similarly, the right to privacy can be alienated, and in both sexual and other contexts is often sold, as in the entertainment industry.[37]

B. Defamation and copyright

In Chapter 6, I make the case for what I call 'NCII exceptionalism' from a policy perspective: a horizontal approach to intermediary liability is misplaced, since the harm from NCII is more serious than that from infringement of copyright or from defamation, and since the costs from imposing a filtering obligation for NCII are lower. Here, I am concerned with the applicability of the conceptual framework of conflicts over titles to defamation and privacy. The main argument in this chapter is that intimate images (or more broadly private information) should be considered as the claimant's property, so the host should be considered as interfering, by making the image accessible to other users, with the claimant's dominion over the image and hence should be strictly liable. This analysis does not necessarily have to apply to other infringing user content such as defamatory statements and copyright. At some level, the inalienability paradox insight is generalizable: whenever a right is considered inalienable, it should be protected, *ex post*, from interference at least as rigorously as a property right

---

of data subjects. See for example, Determann (2018) and Boerding et al (2018). But see Michels and Millard (2019) ('relying on contractual rights' in the absence of clear property right to digital files allocated to consumers 'may risk suboptimal outcomes for consumers, given imbalances in bargaining power between users and providers of cloud services'). For an argument emphasising the distinctiveness of the 'is that property?' and if so 'to whom should the right be allocated?' questions (in the biomaterial context) see Douglas and Goold (2016).

[36] Duch-Brown et al (2017: 16; the GDPR 'creates inalienable and non- tradable specific rights for natural persons'). Having said this, the rights for erasure (Art 17) and withdrawal of consent (Art 7(3)) complicate this conclusion, although in my opinion do not undermine it: a real inalienable right, such as the right to vote, cannot be legally waived, gifted or sold.

[37] See n3.

would. However, whether reputation ought to be considered as inalienable or as property (Post, 1986), and if so, whether a defamatory statement is a destruction of property or its alienation[38] needs a further analysis before an automatic extension of the argument defended here is made. Similarly, the differences between copyright and a classic property right and the justification of a special regime for copyright are beyond the scope of this chapter. Therefore, from the conclusion that an unauthorized dissemination of an intimate image should trigger the host's liability, it does not necessarily follow that the same, strict liability is warranted in cases of copyright-infringing content. It is instructive to reflect, however, that platforms' de facto strict liability under the C-Digital SM Directive[39] much resembles the solution advocated here (for NCII). Specifically, the fact that this heightened liability is limited to platforms, one of whose main purposes is to give the public, for profit, access to a large amount of copyrighted-protected works uploaded by users, suggests that the policy considerations behind holding a merchant strictly liable to the original owner in conflicts over title situations might apply in the C-DSM context.

5. Conclusion

The analysis offered in this and the previous chapter justifies liability of platforms prior to notice by showing that such strict liability is principled, conceptually sound and consistent with first principles about the proper scope of liability by innocent intermediaries. The suggested model contrasts with both of the two leading regulatory regimes (S230 CDA and ECD Arts 14 and 15) and the bulk of the literature, which largely supports either regime (Chapter 2). If intimate images are understood to be property, it is easy to see why the host should, like any other merchant selling stolen property, be strictly liable to the subject of the image. However compelling the policy considerations behind the good faith for value purchase defence are, they cannot support viewers' right to enjoy access to NCII images, and even less so, a merchant's right. In order to affect the owner's priority over viewers with respect to the image, the intermediary should be subject to an injunction to remove or block access to the image, contrary to US law.

Moreover, understanding NCII as a case of conflicts over title supports strict liability of hosts, rather than merely post-notice liability. Given the following two considerations, hosts should filter and otherwise monitor NCII. First, damages are an inadequate remedy in NCII cases (unlike

---

[38] For the distinction and its limited contribution to concluding whether strict liability for breach of privacy is warranted, see Chapter 10, Part 4.

[39] Chapter 2, n7.

in cases of stolen chattels) since the harm is both irreparable (as will be further established in Chapter 6) and asymmetrical. Second, (as will be further established in Chapters 6 and 7) no significant chilling effect on expression or financial burden on the intermediaries is to be expected. From the policy perspectives of efficiency, fairness and loss spreading as well, intermediaries' immunity is unjustified. While the policy considerations in the contexts of defamation and copyright are different to that of NCII, given the unique harm from the latter, understanding the intermediary as implicated in the unauthorized sale of the claimant's property can support the recent shift to de facto strict liability under the C-DSM.

The inalienability paradox explains why unauthorized dissemination of intimate images should be remedied as property: otherwise, the entitlement that is deemed more important and hence arguably inalienable becomes less protected and more alienable. Nor is the existence of other (quasi) property rights with regards to the image a convincing reason against viewing the privacy right with respect to the images as proprietary.

6

The Policy Debate: Uniqueness of Harm from NCII

1. Introduction

The previous two chapters established the case for strict intermediary liability based on conceptualizing intimate images (or possibly private information) as property. They also established that the policy considerations supporting strict liability of merchant selling stolen property apply to an even greater extent to NCII. This chapter will complement the discussion by pointing to the special policy considerations supporting strict liability for NCII. I defend here a claim for 'NCII exceptionalism' so even if one believes that NTD (or possibly stay down) is an appropriate regime for other content, such as defamation and copyright, strict liability and filtering duties are required and justified for NCII. The case is simple: on the one hand, the harm from NCII is serious and irreparable in a way that the harm from defamation and let alone from copyright is not. Indeed, a glimpse into why this is so was already apparent from the discussion in Chapters 3 to 5, including the right to an effective remedy (Chapter 3, Part 4). On the other hand, the costs of a duty to filter backed by strict liability are much less significant in comparison to cases of copyright and defamation, in terms of both chilling valuable speech and the financial costs of sorting lawful images from unlawful ones. This latter claim will be defended in the next chapter.

Therefore, the argument defended in this (and the next) chapter supports a vertical approach to intermediary liability to user content, which is the direction of travel in EU law and already exists in US law and criticizes the 'inverted hierarchy' entrenched in US law and emerging in EU law, according to which internet intermediaries are more accountable for copyright infringing content than for breach of sexual privacy.

2. Harm from NCII

A. Severe, multifaceted, and irreparable

The harm from NCII is severe and irreparable. NCII seriously impairs normal social functioning both online and offline. As such, it is a life-changing experience affecting long-term broad swathes of interests both online and offline. Online, the effect of (and at times the purpose behind) NCII and the common follow-up abuse and 'slut shaming' is to bar the victim from online existence (Citron, 2016), thus threatening her digital citizenship which in a similar context was described as 'social death' (Kowalski et al, 2008). Consequently, NCII also severely curtails victims' freedom of expression, a point which should be borne in mind in response to claims that a robust remedial and regulatory response is undesirable given its arguable negative effect on users' interests in freedom of expression (Citron and Franks, 2014: 385–6; Citron, 2016; McGlynn and Rackley, 2017; Bates, 2017). Offline, NCII affects the claimant's familial, existing/potential romantic, social and professional relationships, might hinder employment opportunities, might expose her to further offline harassment, stalking, and in situ sexual and other physical abuse by either strangers, or, in conservative societies, by relatives. Extreme cases expose the claimant to risks of serious violence and even death (Bloom, 2014: 240, 244, 245; Kamal and Newman, 2016; Chisala-Tempelhoff and Kirya, 2016; McGlynn et al, 2021: 551–2; Law Commission, 2021: 135). NCII negatively affects the victim's self-confidence/image and her ability to trust others (Bates, 2017).

A survey by the Cyber Civil Rights Initiative (2014) found that 82% of victims (n=361) said they suffered significant impairment in social, occupational, or other important areas of functioning due to being a victim, 93% said they have suffered significant emotional distress, 26% had to create a new identity online, 14% either had quit work or school or were fired from work or kicked from school, 13% have had difficulty getting a job or getting into school, 39% say that this has affected their professional advancement with regard to networking and putting their name out there, 42% have had to explain the situation to professional or academic supervisors, co-workers, or colleagues, 34% said that being a victim has jeopardized their relationships with family and 38% with friends, 13% said they have lost a significant other/partner due to being a victim, 49% said they have been harassed or stalked online by users, and 30% offline (in person or by phone). Research suggests that the harm from NCII is similar to the harm from other types of sexual abuse (Bates, 2017; Sharratt, 2019: 14–15, 19). Davidson et al, in their 2019 rapid evidence assessment of adult online abuse conclude, based on a literature review that '[T]here is wide agreement that the harm caused by revenge porn can be devastating' and 'may be similar to those in other sexual crimes'. Victims, 'may suffer numerous psychological and emotional harms', 'may be subject to online and offline harassment, stalking, and assault', 'may suffer from mental health problems such as anxiety, panic attacks, post-traumatic stress disorder, depression, substance abuse, and suicidal ideation', 'may suffer harms to their employment, careers, and professional reputations' and 'may suffer more intangible/abstract harms such as the violation of personal and bodily integrity, the infringement of dignity and privacy, and inhibition of sexual autonomy and expressions' (Davidson et al, 2019: 59–60, based on studies reviewed in pp 55–59). This is consistent with the view, discussed later, that NCII should be understood as a type of, and on the spectrum of, sexual abuse. Indeed, the seriousness of the harm from NCII, and even its threat is apparent from the fact '[t]here are numerous documented cases of victims of revenge porn committing suicide' (Davidson et al, 2019: 60; and see Kowalski et al, 2008: 49; Cyber Civil Rights Initiative, 2014 [51% of victims contemplating suicide]; BBC News, 2014 [Amanda Todd]; BBC News, 2016 [Tiziana Cantone]; Edwards, 2018b [Damilya Jossipalenya]).

In addition to the breadth of the affected interests, and the significant extent to which these interests are compromised, in the digital environment the harm is also potentially perpetual (see Dodge, 2018 for a discussion and potential qualification). A striking example for this is a victim cited in Sharratt (2019: 15):

> [This has been going on] for nearly 10 years. I originally had around 62 images uploaded online, these images spread very quickly through adult image platforms. To date there have been 8166 URLs displaying my images … I am still living with the consequences of my ex's actions to this day.

There are two distinct points here. First, as any other form of sexual abuse, the harm, other than being serious, is lasting and in many cases is a life-changing experience whose effects can last for many years, or even decades (Kuwert et al, 2014; Thurston et al, 2019; Arnold, 2016: 'For 94 percent of [rape] survivors, [PTSD] symptoms last at least two weeks; for a full half of them, they persist for years, even decades'). Second, as the earlier Sharratt quote indicates, NCII is a continuous or repeated form of violation. This makes the harm more significant for several reasons: it creates a fear that the image might be viewed in the future by prospective intimate partners, employers, children and others; it might lead to further future harm if the images are indeed being seen by these people; it exposes the victim to continuous harassment and stalking from strangers exposed to the images in the future; and it creates a fear that strangers the victim encounters will recognize her (Cyber Civil Rights Initiative, 2014; Davidson et al, 2019; Sharratt, 2019). Tellingly, victims commonly report that any unauthorized viewing is perceived by them as a form of sexual violation, so in a sense it re-enacts the violation ingrained in the initial unauthorized dissemination (or, where applicable, the initial abuse captured in the image). As Sharratt (2019: 14–15) reports:

> Victims also experienced a profound sense of violation, particularly when they considered that hundreds of men might have used their images for sexual arousal. Victims told the helpline: 'I think about all the men that have seen (the images) and it feels like they have had my body over and over again … It feels disgusting'.

In the child pornography context litigated in *Paroline v US* – the viewing of child sexual exploitation and abuse images – the victim, Amy, gave two accounts, which were endorsed by the court, for the reason the trafficking of her images is damaging. One focuses on her fear she would be recognized and therefore humiliated; the other, that each viewing of the images re-enacts the crime.[1] On this understanding, it is easy to appreciate that the harm from NCII is particularly grave since it involves both numerous violations and ones spanning over a very long period of time. Indeed, this led one researcher to speculate – and call for further research to confirm the hypothesis – that '[T]he length of time that a person endures this kind of trauma has a significant effect on how mental health symptoms like PTSD will take hold, suggesting revenge porn victims might also have longer trauma recovery periods than survivors of what therapists call single incident trauma' (Zaleski, 2019).

Digital harms have also extensive geographical reach as the image might be accessed from any place on the globe; and unlike textual expressions of hate crime/bullying or defamation, NCII has no linguistic barriers so its reach is much broader (Chapter 3, Part 5.A). As noted by the Supreme Court in *PJS*, the harm to privacy is irreparable once the image/ information is out and damages are a much lesser effective remedy than in cases of defamation.[2]

---

[1] *Paroline v United States*, 572 US 434 (2014) 440–441 ('… constant fear that someone will … recognize me'; 'the crime has never really stopped and will never really stop … It's like I am being abused over and over and over again'). The court id seems to focus on the latter ('These crimes were compounded by the distribution of images of her abuser's horrific acts, which meant the wrongs inflicted upon her were in effect repeated'). Both recognisability and re-enactment involve long term harm: 'child pornography is "a permanent record" of the depicted child's abuse, and "the harm to the child is exacerbated by [its] circulation"'.

[2] *PJS v News Group Newspapers* [2016] UKSC 26. See also Chapter 3, Part 4's discussion of right to an effective remedy.

B. Gendered, systemic, a form of sexual abuse
1. Gendered

The harm from NCII is gendered and systemic in three distinct ways. First, NCII is perpetrated predominantly by men, with women being predominantly targeted. Second, typically, the harm suffered by women due to the dissemination of their intimate image is more severe than harm suffered by men given the double standards about women's and men's sexuality.[3] Third, the harm is systemic in that NCII's effect (and often, motivation) is to entrench patriarchy, to silence and to marginalize women, and to regulate their sexuality. The harm results from the operation of broad social structures which exceed the actions of a certain and limited number of individuals; and it affects women as a group and not only its direct victims. These aspects of the harm being gendered and systemic make the harm more pernicious, and the stakes in fighting it, higher. Consequently, they call for a greater extent of intermediary liability (and regulatory responsibility). I will defend each of these four claims in order.

In terms of the gendered distribution of victims, an often cited figure suggests a ratio of nine female to one male victim, including the CCRI 2014 report (Cyber Civil Rights Initiative, 2014; Davies, 2015a [eight female complainants to every male]). Davidson et al (2019: 53–4) conclude that '[R]esearch has found that between 60–95% of victims are female' while mentioning dissenting research finding that 'males were more likely both to be a perpetrator *and* a victim of revenge porn'.[4] The American Data and Society Research Institute, 2016 suggests 62.5% of those who were either threatened with or that their image was circulated non-consensually were women. Women under 30 have twice the chance of being a victim compared to men of the same age group and are six times more likely to be a victim in comparison to either women or men over 30. The research showed also that Black people were almost as twice as likely to be victims as White, and LGBs almost six times as heterosexuals. Sharratt's study (2019: 12) analysing responses to Revenge Porn Helpline (and another organization, POSH, focusing on children) found that 73% of cases dealt with by Revenge Porn Helpline were from female callers. A similar percentage (75) for the same Helpline was found in 2015 (Government Equalities Office, 2015); 72.5% of victims reporting cyber harassment to another helpline from 2000 to 2012 were women (Working to Halt Online Abuse, 2014).

---

[3]   Chapter 4, n33.

[4]   The dissenting view is by Walker and Sleath (2017). The four studies that examined gender differences in adult populations found victimisation rates to be higher for males than females.

Now it is possible, that similar to other cases of sexual abuse, men face significant barriers coming forward as victims so tend to under report relative to women. For example, a UK empirical study on NCII, which interviewed 222 UK university students, found that when a victim was described as male they were more likely to be allocated responsibility (or blamed) for the revenge pornography outcome; that both male and female participants showed a tendency to 'minimise perceived harm to male victims of revenge pornography as well as the need for police intervention in cases of male revenge pornography victimisation' (Gavin and Scott, 2019). These barriers may also make it difficult to do the research into this issue in the first place.[5] However, this ignores the real possibility (discussed later) that the harm to men is indeed less significant than it is to women, and since it is perceived as such by the subject, he does not complain, report or seek help. In the context of sex trafficking and prostitution, which I have previously researched, sex positive feminists and advocates often warn against forcing the status of a victim on those perceiving themselves as sex workers (Keren-Paz, 2013: 15, reviewing claims by Laura Agustin and Jo Phoenix). It is possible, that the revisionist view, according to which NCII is not a gendered phenomenon is based on a similar tendency to view as victims men who do not see themselves as victims. In any event, the claim that men under-report their status of NCII victims can account much less (if at all) for findings that women are more likely to be victims when the methodology is based on sampling, and to a lesser extent approaching, internet users and finding the incidence of threats of/NCII within this population, as was the case, for example, in the 2016 American study.

Turning to perpetration, the consensus again is that men are the more likely perpetrators: about twice more likely according to Eaton et al (2017). Both The CCRI 2014 report and Sharratt's 2019 report indicate gendered perpetration.[6] Walker and Sleath's meta study (2017), conspicuous for finding that men are more likely to be victims, finds that men are more likely to be perpetrators. Due to double standards about sexuality, the harm to women from NCII is more significant than to men. Sharratt (2019: 28) concludes that victims of intimate image abuse are disproportionately female and that the impacts of intimate image abuse are highly gendered:

---

[5] See, for example, the problems Dr Nicola Henry experienced in finding men to interview on the topic in this research as reported by Rasker (2019).

[6] Cyber Civil Rights Initiative (2014): 57% of victims said their material was posted by an ex-boyfriend, 6% said it was posted by an ex-girlfriend, 23% said it was posted by an ex-friend, 7% said it was posted by a friend, 7% said it was posted by a family member. Sharratt (2019: 13,16): 'The identity of the [type 1] perpetrator ... could often be narrowed down to a specific male ex-partner ... he [type 2 perpetrator] was almost always a very recent ex-partner'.

On the whole, male sextortion victims carried little shame and self-blame, received a higher proportion of positive police responses and were able to quickly move on from their experiences. On the contrary, female victims (of both types of intimate image abuse) experienced a great deal of shame and self-blame, received a higher proportion of negative police responses, suffered lasting social and emotional impacts and commonly described their experiences as sexually violating.

Davidson et al (2019: 54) summarize the evidence as follows:

> Pina et al (2017) argue that revenge porn is a form of gendered violence predominantly perpetrated against women by men, which negatively affects women more than men. Citron and Franks (2014) also observe that women are more likely to suffer harms as a result of being a victim of revenge porn, due to gender stereotypes, whereas men's sexual activity is generally "*a point of pride*"; thus revenge porn amounts to "*a vicious form of sex discrimination*" (p. 353). Hill (2015) further refers to it as "*a form of "cyber- misogyny*": one online example of gendered hatred, harassment and abuse primarily directed towards women and girls" (p. 117). Similarly, McGlynn and colleagues argue that societal gender disparities, such as sexual double standards, mean that female victims of revenge porn are humiliated, stigmatised and shamed in a way in which men are not (for example, McGlynn & Rackley, 2017a).

These findings are consistent with previous studies highlighting 'the inherently sexually violating nature of intimate image abuse for women' (Sharratt, 2019: 28 based on several studies) and with the finding that following rape, women have a higher risk of developing PTSD than men (Tolin and Foa, 2006).[7]

2. Systemic

The harm is systemic – or systemically gendered – in three important ways. First, NCII regulates victims' sexuality, denies their digital citizenship and curtails their life options.[8] By regulating, silencing and marginalizing victims, and by doing so based on their gender, sexuality and based on a double sexual standard (Zaikman and Marks, 2014; Citron, 2016; Willard,

---

[7] But these findings could be subject to a similar caveat to the one expressed earlier about barriers to men reporting NCII.

[8] See Part 2.A.

2010: 545–6), NCII entrenches patriarchy and is rightly understood as a form of sex-based discrimination (Citron and Franks, 2014: 353).[9] As evidenced by the typical abuse and epithets suffered by NCII victims accompanying or following the initial circulation of the image (Citron, 2016; Davidson et al, 2019). NCII is inherently misogynist (Hill, 2015; Holliday 2015).[10] Similar to other forms of sexual abuse, NCII is also about power and its preservation, not merely about sex.[11] The limited evidence that LGBs and ethnic minorities are more likely to be victims of NCII than heterosexuals and members of ethnic majorities (American Data and Society Research Institute, 2016[12]) only goes to bolster the conclusion that NCII is a systemic and group-based phenomenon.

Second, as instances of patriarchy, discrimination and misogyny, NCII harm is created by many individuals; and more crucially, by social structures and socialization. The harm is created not only by the initial uploader, but also by the intermediary, by secondary distributors, by viewers and by those acting on the information. These include users harassing the victim on and offline, those publishing follow-up defamatory statements, potential employers denying employment based on those images and so on. Broader still, are the structures and agents of patriarchy which socialize men and women to the sexual double standard. Even the pressures operating on girls and young women to share intimate images with their boyfriends is a manifestation of the harm's systemic nature (Lippman and Campbell, 2014).

Third, as a mechanism further entrenching patriarchy, discrimination and misogyny, NCII harms women as a group and not only its direct victims (McGlynn and Rackely, 2017: 546–7). At the immediate level, the fear from NCII might chill women's sexual expression (McGlynn and Rackley, 2017: 546–7; Bates, 2017). Beyond this, by entrenching the patriarchal order, NCII presumably sexualizes and marginalizes all women, by this helping 'to keep them in their place' or as McGlynn and Rackley, 2017 beautifully put it (compare with McGlynn, Rackley and Houghton, 2017):

---

[9] Disseminating *and* viewing NCII are both a form of sexual abuse and a form of sex-based discrimination. See Davidson et al (2019).

[10] The 'purpose [of NCII] is to publicly humiliate' according to Alison Saunders, director of public prosecutions' (Halliday, 2015).

[11] McPhail (2015: 321 [multiple motives including sexual gratification, revenge, recreation, power/control, and attempts to achieve or perform masculinity], 323 [focus on the dual character of rape as political-aggregate and personal-intimate]). The original theoretical claim, that rape is only about power, and not about sex, most associated with Brownmiller (1975), has been widely criticized as inconsistent with evidence. See for example, Palmer (1988) and Shpancer (2016).

[12] But see Davidson et al (2019: 52: 'There is little focus in the literature on victim diversity').

Image-based sexual abuse compromises [also] the dignity ... of all members of the same group (here typically women) ... The ubiquity of image-based sexual abuse sends a message to all women that they are not equal, that they should not get too comfortable, especially online; that it might happen to them. It legitimates the attitudes of those who might not yet have participated directly in the abuse.

It is important to note that the analysis given earlier is agnostic of the motivations of those uploading, distributing and viewing NCII so nothing in the conclusion that the harm is systemic hinges on establishing that NCII is *motivated* by misogyny or patriarchy, or that it can be properly described as a form of hate crime (as I suggest in Part 3). In particular, for my purposes of establishing filtering obligations backed by strict civil liability, it is sufficient to acknowledge that the harm from NCII (beyond being severe and irreparable) is systemic and systemically gendered due to its effect on victims, on women as a group and due to the way it is produced. The harm is more significant when and because the victim is a woman; it is more likely to be suffered because the victim is a woman (and because the perpetrator is a man) and it affects women as a group. NCII's gendered nature is not a coincidence and the phenomenon exists and is harmful due to societal structures. Unsurprisingly, different motives are at stake for uploading, sharing and viewing NCII and these include 'fun/amusement; financial gain; notoriety; bragging; sexual gratification; control; harassment; blackmail/extortion' (Davidson et al, 2019: 54). In a 2017 study 79% of perpetrators self-identified as not intending to hurt the person while 12% did (Eaton et al, 2017).

But such malice or intent to harm or humiliate the victim should be, in criminal law, a consideration in sentencing (or at most a basis for an aggravated offence such as hate crime), rather than a condition for responsibility. More importantly, for civil liability, such an intent could be relevant for aggravated or punitive damages,[13] but ought not be, and is not, relevant for purposes of establishing liability or calculating compensatory damages.[14]

3. Form of sexual abuse

NCII, other than being a grave breach of privacy, is also a phenomenon on the continuum of sexual abuse and such understanding is on the rise (McGlynn and Rackley, 2017; Bates, 2017; Patella-Ray, 2018: 786–91;

---

[13] See Chapter 11, nn9, 10.

[14] See *Paroline* (n1). Compensatory damages are calculated based on the victim's loss, not the tortfeasor's blameworthiness.

Rosenberg and Dancig-Rosenberg, 2021). This is so in terms of perpetration, victim's perception and typical harm. Similar to other instances of sexual abuse, it is a violation of autonomy and dignity in a sexual context, forcing a sexual objectification of the victim. The protected values violated by NCII, argue Rosenberg and Dancig-Rosenberg, 2021 'are similar in nature to those underlying existing sex offenses, namely human dignity, sexual autonomy, and sexual privacy' (compare Sharratt, 2019: 28–9). Victims perceive the acts of dissemination and viewing as violating experiences similar to physical sexual assault: 'victims ... seldom distinguish between digital representations of their body and the body itself and ... often liken non-consensual pornography to sexual assault' (Pattella-Ray, 2018; Sharratt, 2019: 28–9). Actor Jennifer Lawrence famously commented after the 2014 hacking and distribution of her intimate images (the celebrities 'Fappening' case) that '[A]nybody who looked at those pictures, you're perpetuating a sexual offense' (Moore, 2014). Specifically, fear for safety, common to other forms of sexual abuse, is common to NCII victims, more so in female victims (Henry et al, 2017), and the dissemination of the image occasionally leads to further harassment, stalking and sexual assaults (Bloom, 2014; Kamal and Newman, 2016; Chisala-Tempelhoff and Kirya, 2016; Law Commission, 2021; McGlynn et al, 2021). Finally, the mental and reputational injuries suffered by NCII victims are typical to those suffered by victims of other forms of sexual abuse, leading Samantha Bates to recommend that because of these striking similarities, revenge porn should be classified as a sexual offense, treatment strategies for survivors of revenge porn should be similar to effective treatment strategies used for survivors of other forms of sexual victimization, and legislators should consider the similarities between revenge porn and sexual crimes when making legal changes to the status of revenge porn and drafting legislation (Bates, 2017). Indeed, in Israel, NCII was criminalized as part of the Prevention of Sexual Harassment Law 1998, as early as 2014.

Moreover, child pornography images are a specific – indeed extreme – manifestation of NCII (Keren-Paz and Wright, 2019), and a major part of the harm involved in such abuse is the serious and egregious breach of privacy.[15] Once child pornography, whose status as a serious form of sexual abuse is not in doubt, is understood to be a manifestation of NCII, it should be easy to accept that other instances of NCII are also on the spectrum of sexual abuse. That child pornography encompasses instances, typical to NCII, in which no underlying physical abuse occurred bolsters the conclusion that NCII is a form of sexual abuse. These instances, termed pseudo photographs (UK)

---

[15]   See *Paroline* (n1) and in particular Justice Sotomayor at 482–3.

or simulated sexually explicit conduct of a child (US), involve morphing images of an actual child with a sexual content external to that child.

3. NCII exceptionalism: the normative significance of irreparable gendered harm

A. Deprioritizing copyright

The balancing of the competing interests of the claimant, uploader, intermediary and the audience is quite different in the contexts of (sexual) privacy, defamation and copyright. It might be useful to start with some general observations on what separates privacy and defamation as dignitary torts from copyright, then to explain why the interest in privacy is stronger than in reputation (a fact reflected in the case law) and to finish with explaining that for reasons having to do with both irreparability of harm and its gendered nature, the interest in sexual privacy should receive – but does not – the strongest protection. The correct descending order of the need to protect the competing interests is as follows: Sexual privacy, other interests in privacy, reputation and copyright. In fact, both in the US and in the EU copyright holders have a stronger claim against intermediaries than victims of NCII,[16] a state of affairs probably having to do with the lobbying power of the creative industries (Sell, 2003). I accept that the scope of tort liability cannot be determined by the relative strength of the protected interest alone; it ought to and does take into account also the mode of interference by the defendant, the claimant's prior behaviour, and the interests of the defendant, potential defendants and claimants and the public interest (Cane, 1997: chapters 2–4).[17] But none of these other considerations suggests that the current inverted hierarchy is justified. Indeed, the opposite is true. The costs to platforms from complying with filtering obligations are lower for NCII than for defamation and copyright (Chapter 7), nothing in the defendants' (or claimants' prior) behaviour justifies the inverted hierarchy and the public interest, given the nature of NCII as a gendered phenomenon supports NCII exceptionalism.

Privacy and reputation are dignitary interests and as such, not entirely commensurable with money. The focus of dignitary torts – historically trespass to the person (battery, assault and false imprisonment) and to land and to chattels but also defamation and more recently breach of privacy[18] – on

---

[16] Chapter 2, Part 2.

[17] Cf McBride (2019) who seems to adopt a lexical priority of primary over secondary over tertiary interests. The extent to which these particular considerations have been and ought to be taken into account by courts is a matter of debate. One fault line is about the role of public good/policy based considerations including a commitment to distributive justice, as distinct from interpersonal justice considerations.

[18] *Campbell v MGN* [2004] UKHL 22, [50]–[52] (Lord Hoffmann).

protecting one's dignity and autonomy (Abraham and White, 2019; compare Beever, 2015: [22], [28], [42]), led both to these torts being actionable per se,[19] and to that, in the main, they impose strict liability (Abraham and White, 2019: 377).[20] As dignitary, the protected interest in privacy and defamation ought to be afforded stronger protection than the largely commercial interest protected by copyright, especially in the modern ecology in which copyright is allocated to big entertainment corporations as a work for hire, or is otherwise assigned to them, hence seriously weakening any plausible claim to a dignitary interest in copyright-as-personhood.[21] Since the harm from a copyright infringement is merely financial and commercial, it is easily reparable by damages, so there is no justification for a prior restraint in the form of upload filters. Moreover, given the difficulty in deciding whether the use of the work (allegedly protected by copyright) is fair, or otherwise lawful, both the expression costs resulting from the removal of false positives, and the financial costs involved in moderating this content are significant, or at least, much more significant than in NCII cases; financial costs would involve either human moderation alongside automated removal, or developing technology avoiding the removal of false positives.[22]

B. Privacy > Defamation

Turning to the comparison between privacy and defamation, it is well established that 'Damage done by publication of a defamatory statement can be redressed by a public finding at trial that the allegation was false, but an invasion of privacy cannot be cured in a similar way, and for that reason there may never be a trial, whatever damages might be recoverable.'[23] Hence the greater availability of interim injunction for breaches of privacy. The tarnished reputation perhaps is not completely reparable, but a finding that the claimant has been defamed does significantly vindicate her interest. Consistency demands that the logic of 'prevention is better than compensation' that is behind remedying a wrong by an interim injunction

---

[19] This is true for the trespass torts and for libel, in which damages are at large, and seems to be also the position for *Privacy*. See Chapter 11, Part 2. Ibbetson (2001) demonstrates that a history quirk (rather than the importance of the protected interest in itself) accounts for libel being actionable per se. Defamation emerged from the ecclesiastical courts as a common law action on the case for which, originally, harm had always to be proved.

[20] With a focus on American law; and see Chapter 10, Part 2.

[21] For distributive justice-based critiques of copyright which are partially based on these patterns see Netanel (2000: 1884), Farber and McDonnell (2003) and Van Houwelin (2005).

[22] See Taylor (2020) and Chapter 7, Part 3.C,G; Chapter 3, Part 3.A.

[23] *PJS* (n2) [41] (per Mance JSC).

be applied to the availability of a remedy against an intermediary. For reasons explained later, when the injury is irreparable and serious, the intermediary should be subject to an obligation to avoid the upload of the image rather than merely to remove it following a request to do so.

There is also much to be said that conceptually, privacy should be afforded more protection than reputation for two additional reasons: private information is more constitutive of one's personhood than one's reputation; and the property analysis offered in Chapter 4 with respect to appropriation of one's property fits less reputation, which if at all is more destroyed by the defamation than is misappropriated (Chapter 10, Part 4). But space constraints prevent me from defending these propositions in full. I also suspect that most people would care more if an embarrassing information circulating about them is true, than if it is false (which is similar to the point made in *PJS* and quoted in the text). But this is an empirical question which calls for corroboration or refute. While the interest in reputation is dignitary, the costs of excessive removal of allegedly defamatory statements are more similar to copyright's, than to NCII's: given broad defences, the fear from false positives (unjustified removal) is real, with a significant cost to expression and financial cost in sorting lawful from unlawful speech (Angelopoulos and Smet, 2016: 290).[24] For the reasons explained in Part 2, invasions of sexual privacy are likely to cause more severe and more lasting injuries and are hence less reparable than other invasions of privacy.

The discussion later will rely on insights from theories of regulation (supporting at minimum a feasibility standard to reduce the risk of serious personal injury), jurisprudence (the distinction between primary and secondary duties and the ensuing priority that should be given to the avoidance of harm) and tort theory (extending the logic of *quia timet* – anticipatory injunctions – beyond protecting property) to justify a filtering duty based on NCII's irreparable harm.

C. Just regulation

Starting with just regulation, it is useful to employ Gregory Keating's framework (2003a; 2003b; 2012; 2018), developed in the personal injury context to the context of sexual privacy. Keating observes the existence of two regulatory standards in US health and safety law which are more exacting than the cost-benefit analysis: the 'safety' and 'feasibility' tests. Safety-based regulations require risk to be reduced to a point where no

---

[24] Most of the empirical data about false positives and chilling effect, comes, however, from copyright.

'significant risk' of devastating injury remains. Feasibility analysis requires the elimination of significant risks, when they can be eliminated without threatening the long-run health of the activity to which the risks belong (Keating, 2003b: 685). Four characteristics of the harm regulated by these two standards justify, as a matter of fairness, their adoption. 'First, these standards typically apply to toxins and carcinogens which threaten devastating injury – injury which is severe and irreparable. The injuries risked are severe, because they threaten to bring life to a premature close or to impair normal physical functioning seriously.' 'They are irreparable because the harm that these injuries inflict cannot be undone; normal functioning and normal life cannot be restored. Second, the injuries to which these standards apply are avoidable'. 'Third, the category of activity which produces these risks is one which society cannot avoid if it is to reproduce itself and which individual members of society cannot usually avoid if they are to lead decent lives.' 'Fourth, the risks governed by these standards are certain to ripen into some incidence of the harms risked' (Keating, 2003b: 664–645).

While the harms from personal injury and from NCII occur in different contexts and are manifested differently, their similarity is striking. The harm from NCII is severe and irreparable as explained earlier. The harm is avoidable in both senses that filtering systems exist that would minimize the circulation of NCII and that the circulation of NCII, including the timely circulation of intimate images that might be consensual is not required in order to have a functioning and thriving internet, or in order to enhance freedom of expression (including sexual expression) and information. Yet, arguably, the category of activity which produces NCII risks, that is, broadly speaking, social networking, is one which society cannot avoid.[25] The question, rather, is whether it is technologically feasible to have social networking without NCII (or a significant risk thereof). As Chapter 7 demonstrates the answer is yes. Finally, and this again needs to be examined in terms of technological feasibility of privacy by design, the NCII risk is likely to ripen in a socially networking society. The upshot of applying Keating's framework for just regulation to the context of sexual privacy is a support for at least a feasibility standard requiring the elimination of the NCII risk, as far as it is technologically and economically feasible, that is, as

---

[25] This is a contested issue. Historian Yuval Noah Harari (2016: chapter 11) makes the descriptive observation of the 'data religion' whose the foremost duty it imposes is to maximize flow of data by ever growing connection and sharing and the zeal (especially by younger people) to be connected and to share data. In Netflix's The Social Dilemma, 2020 the main theme is how giant tech companies design the platforms to be addictive. Lanier (2018, interviewed in the film) makes a strong normative case to disconnect from social media.

long as such regulation does not threaten the long run health of platforms, social networking and other internet intermediaries. The alternative safety standard would require as a condition for sharing images on platforms a technology that would eliminate a significant risk for the dissemination of NCII, even if such requirement threatens the long-run viability of the activity. Given that filtering is technologically and financially feasible, there is less need to decide between the two standards. However, if forced to choose, I would insist on the safety model. Indeed, my argument in favour of residual strict liability for harm from remaining unfiltered NCII is based on similar considerations. Most individuals who lived satisfying and meaningful social life throughout history did so without virtual social networking, let alone without a massive share of their images, intimate or otherwise. So if the sharing of intimate images cannot be done safely, it ought not be done at all.[26]

D. Theory of rights
1. Primary and secondary duties
Moving from regulation to a theory of rights, the argument advanced here is also based on the priority of avoiding rights' violation (primary duties) in tort law over repairing such violations (secondary duties). As Keating has observed, 'it is better for wrongs not to be done in the first place than it is to attempt to erase their untoward effects once they have been committed' (Keating, 2012: 315; see also Friedmann, 1989: 17–18).[27]

> Primary obligations in tort are obligations not to harm other people in various ways and to respect powers of theirs that confer on them authority over their persons and possessions. To be sure, tort guards these rights with remedial responsibilities of repair, but repair is a second-best form of protection. Tort obligations are discharged most fully when harm is not done and rights are respected in the first instance, not when harm wrongly done is repaired after the fact … Remedying a wrong is a second-best way of respecting a right in the first instance. (Keating, 2012: 318, 320)

---

[26] Cf in the context of playing cricket, Lord Reid's famous statement in *Bolton v Stone* [1951] AC 850 'If cricket cannot be played on a ground without creating a substantial risk, then it should not be played there at all.'

[27] Nor would an economic analysis of law (whose conclusions should not be dispositive on the scope of protection afforded to NCII victims) lead to a different conclusion. As the discussion in this chapter, and in Chapters 4, 7 and 10, Part 4, demonstrates, the harm from viewing NCII far exceeds its benefits.

2. Interim injunctions

Further lessons could be learned from the conditions under which an interim injunction will be given, as well as damages in lieu of injunction. In both cases, a comparison between the losses suffered by the defendant if injunction is granted and by the claimant if it is denied is at the centrepiece of the balancing process. I have already mentioned that the difference between the availability of interim injunctions in privacy and their absence in defamation[28] is based on the greater irreparability of the harm from invasion of privacy. In the law of nuisance, the Supreme Court decision in *Coventry v Lawrence*[29] marks a shift away from the traditional strong pro injunction approach in *Shelfer v City of London Electric Lighting Co*[30] usually understood to regard damages in lieu of injunction as appropriate only 'exceptionally' (Holland, 2014). But even under the more flexible approach understood to be the court's *ratio decidendi*, 'the disproportionate effect on the defendant if an injunction is granted when compared to the loss to the claimant if damages are awarded' is central to deciding whether an injunction will be granted and 'courts may be more ready to grant injunctions to protect the rights of homeowners than they will be to restrain activities which interfere with the occupation of commercial premises' (Holland, 2014: 52).

Lord Sumption even views in lieu damages as the appropriate default while Lord Clark views the *Shelfer* test as dated.[31] But even if this view is warranted with regards to nuisance, the NCII context is very different: first, the interest threatened in nuisance (while arguably not entirely commensurable with money[32]) is less dignitary and more amenable to be compensated by money than lost sexual privacy. Moreover, with proper compensation the claimant is more likely to avoid the negative effects of the nuisance, by for example moving. The costs of such a move are significant and by no means should be overlooked. This indeed is the basis for insisting that injunction is the default remedy. But the NCII victim is much less able to use compensation

---

[28] See respectively *Cream Holdings Ltd v Banerjee* [2004] UKHL 44 (probability of winning the trial test for privacy); *PJS* (n2) (upholding an interim injunction despite the fact the claimant's identity and story of extramarital sexual activities had been widely published online and internationally); *Bonnard v Perryman* [1891] 2 Ch 269 (no injunction in defamation unless it is clear that the alleged libel is untrue); *R (Taveta Investments Ltd) v Financial Reporting Council* [2018] EWHC 1662 (applying *Bonnard*, which over time denied injunction unless it is clear that no viable defence exists, notwithstanding abolishing jury trial by the Defamation Act 2013).

[29] [2014] UKSC 46.

[30] (1895) 1 Ch 287.

[31] *Coventry* (n30) [161], [171].

[32] *Coventry* (n30) [168] (per Mance JSC).

to overcome the significant negative results of NCII. She has no equivalent escape from the cyberspace in which the injury occurred. Second, the power gap in nuisance between the claimant and the defendant is typically smaller than the one between powerful platforms and NCII victims. Indeed, the greater readiness to protect homeowners in the realm of nuisance only goes to bolster the conclusion that the balance in NCII should be strongly tilted in favour of NCII victims. Third, in nuisance (and especially in a right to light cases), the removal of the already built construct is expensive, wasteful and exposes the defendant to potentially strategic behaviour ('extortionate demands') by the claimant (Holland, 2014: 22).[33] While the costs of monitoring and filtering are presumably high (although, as the discussion in Chapter 7 demonstrates, less prohibitive than some would have us believe) imposing them is not wasteful and the problem of strategic behaviour is irrelevant: the investment will prevent severe and irreparable harm to many potential victims.[34] Fourth, in nuisance cases there is a stronger genuine public interest in allowing the infringing activity to continue (for example, interest of employees) than there is in NCII cases. For all of these reasons, the balancing exercise suggests that *Shelfer*'s original test is still appropriate for NCII: the injury is neither small, nor capable of being estimated in money or be adequately compensated by money and an injunction would not be oppressive to the defendant.

3. Anticipatory injunctions

The logic and ethics of the priority of prevention over reparation is best illustrated by the availability, albeit limited, of anticipatory injunctions in tort, mainly in the context of proprietary torts (trespass, nuisance, patent). A *quia timet* is an injunction granted where no actionable wrong has been committed, to prevent the occurrence of an actionable wrong, or to prevent repetition of an actionable wrong (Gee, 2010).[35] Crucially, the graver the likely consequences, the more the court will be reluctant to consider the application as premature. '[T]he degree of probability of future injury is not an absolute standard: what is to be aimed at is justice between the parties, having regard to all the relevant circumstances'.[36] According to such a holistic approach, the significance and irreversibility of the NCII harm should lead to

---

[33] *Jaggard v Sawyer* [1995] 1 WLR 269, 288. A similar concern is behind much of the debate about efficient breach and choosing between alternative measures of 'diminution of value' v 'costs of repair' in both contract and tort law. See Friedmann (1989: 17).

[34] But there is a fear of slippery slope under which courts would increase monitoring expectations once the initial 'sunk' costs of monitoring infrastructure has been developed; discussed by Schellekens (2011).

[35] *Proctor v Bayley* (1889) 42 Ch D. 390, 398.

[36] *Hooper v Rogers* [1975] Ch 43, per Russell LJ.

an injunction even for relatively low individual probabilities. Moreover, the force of extending the logic of *quia timet* injunctions to NCII derives from the nature of NCII as a mass tort. While the probability of non-consensual online dissemination of intimate images of any individual woman is low, the probability of dissemination of such images is very high, and indeed certain.[37] Therefore, given both irreparable and significant harm ensuing from such dissemination and very high probability of a future wrong, issuing an injunction prohibiting the commission of such a wrong is justified. A filtering duty is the equivalent of amalgamated quia timit injunctions sought by potential victims, in circumstances it is certain that in its absence, a few would suffer irreparable and serious harm. Logically, an anticipatory injunction is justified where a quick interim injunction and damages are inadequate. *Vastint Leeds B. V. v Persons Unknown* adopted a two-step test for granting anticipatory injunction: the probability of a future breach and the irreparability of damage. Strong probability was endorsed at the first step; for the second, an important factor is the inadequacy of the alternative remedy of a more-or-less immediate interim injunction coupled by the eventual award of damages.[38]

John Murphy has argued correctly that anticipatory injunctions should be available in negligence to vindicate bodily integrity. Similar to the analysis offered here, Murphy emphasizes the type of the harm and the unacceptability of better protecting one's property than one's bodily integrity as part of the justification for granting anticipatory injunctions in negligence (Murphy, 2007: 510, 518; compare Mooney, 2014: 257). While Murphy is not explicit on this point, I view his argument about the hierarchy of interests as being founded on irreparable harm: where there is no way of restoring the claimant back to their original position, an injunction should be given. I do not, however, endorse Murphy's limitation of granting the injunction only for intentional or careless behaviour. Recall that for the undermining of proprietary interests for which anticipatory injunctions are traditionally available liability is strict. Furthermore, the analysis offered in Chapter 4, viewing intimate images as one's property, can justify the availability of anticipatory injunctions to NCII when in practice, upload filtering obligations substitute anticipatory injunctions, or are their regulatory equivalent in the context of sexual privacy mass torts.[39]

---

[37] Cf Chapter 9, n9 (repeat viewing of porn increases chances of viewing NCII).

[38] [2018] EWHC 2456 (Ch). Other factors include the harm's irreparability and gravity and a greater reluctance to impose a mandatory, as opposed to prohibitory injunction; arguably filtering duty prohibits the defendant from disseminating the claimant's image.

[39] See, for the question whether pre-Copyright-Digital Single Market Directive pre-emptive injunctions can be used against intermediaries for IP infringements, Husovec and Peguera (2015: 14).

E. Gendered harm and broader egalitarian considerations

So far, I have focused on the normative relevance of the harm's seriousness and irreparability as a reason to afford NCII claimants stronger remedies against intermediaries compared with the remedies available to copyright holders and defamed claimants. The fact that the harm from NCII is distinctively gendered, unlike the harm from copyright and defamation, serves as another such justification. I have defended at length the normative relevance of egalitarianism in shaping private law rules in previous work so would refer the interested reader there. In short, a commitment to gender equality, and more generally an egalitarian commitment, requires policy and law makers to take into account the distributive consequences of the regulated activity, for purposes of both private law (that is, the scope of liability and the content of legal rules) (Keren-Paz, 2007a: chapter 5; 2013: chapter 7), and traditional regulation (Prosser, 2006; Adler, 2012; Morgan, 2007; Adler and Posner, 1999). On this understanding, the fact that a more robust regulation (or broader scope of liability) will decrease power gaps between men and women – as a filtering of NCII would – is an independent and important reason to adopt it. The facts that (1) women are more likely to be victims as men; (2) women will typically suffer greater harm from being an NCII victim than men; (3) men are more likely to be perpetrators than women; (4) NCII arguably affects all women by reinforcing patriarchal order and entrenching a norm of shaming sexually liberated women; (5) and is arguably often motivated by misogyny, or at the very least that the choice to disseminate intimate images is not unrelated the victim's (and perpetrator's) gender, are all normatively relevant for a legal system to evaluate the harm as more serious and as justifying its prevention and remedying to a greater extent compared to non-gendered harm of equal measure.

The characteristics of NCII listed earlier are additive: each of them is normatively relevant to support an extended scope of intermediary liability. So even if one is not convinced that claims (4) and (5) are supported by the evidence but that claims (1) to (3) are, or that claim (4) is supported but claim (3) is not, the case for a stronger remedial response is met. It is also important (in the tradition of legal realism which I espouse) to keep the factual categories of the interaction regulated by the relevant legal rule activity sufficiently narrow (Llewellyn, 1931). There might be other subcategories of sexual privacy in which a different gendered pattern exist, for example, kiss and tell cases in which arguably women are more likely to sell a story compromising the privacy of a male celebrity.[40] But a filtering

---

[40] See for example, *A v B* [2002] 2 All ER 545 and Richardson (2012: 148). It is worth noting that courts have been rather quick to protect men's privacy in such situations.

obligation and strict liability for remaining dissemination is discussed in the context of NCII in which the gendered harm is established. Similarly, there is little reason to distinguish between privacy and defamation in the context of NCII as in both cases the harm is likely to be gendered. But in other contexts, there is much less a reason to suspect that the harm from defamation is gendered, at least outside of the context of sexuality. Accordingly, in these other cases there is one less reason to expect a robust remedial response for such defamatory statements, since the absence of a robust response is not problematic distributivity, that is, is not regressive. And of course, there is very little reason to believe that either copyright infringements, or the subsequent harm is gendered.

More broadly and shifting the egalitarian focus from gender to any characteristic potentially identifying the typical parties as strong or weak, in defamation cases, it is hard to generalize and identify the typical claimant as stronger or weaker than the typical defendant. In copyright, due to the routine assignment of the right to industry giants, the typical claimant is much stronger than the typical defendant.[41] Finally, the fact that by definition the intermediary defendant is a likely corporation does not diminish the relevance and strength of the gendered nature of the harm as a reason for a robust response against the intermediary for the following reasons: (1) Even if the typical defendant is gender-neutral, so is random (or heterogenous), as long as the typical claimant is a woman, liability could be supported as a matter of egalitarianism, or of progressive distribution of entitlements (Keren Paz, 2013: chapter 7; Keren-Paz, 2007a: 76–8, 148). (2) The group harm nature of NCII (point 4 in the previous two paragraphs) makes the harm gendered regardless of the defendant's gender. (3) when relevant defendants are assessed as a group: uploaders, intermediaries and viewers, defendants are typically men. This holds true even if intermediary liability is thought of as primary and independent, but it is even more clearly the case if it is understood as secondary accessory liability.[42] (4) intermediaries are a major societal force in maintaining, reproducing and profiting from gendered and patriarchal norms (Croucher, 2011; Lippman and Campbell, 2014); this makes it fair to expect them to pay for the gendered harm they facilitate. This renders unnecessary examining whether the following argument is correct: (5) a 'lifting of the veil' will reveal that those who profit from and control the relevant intermediaries are men.

---

[41] See n21.

[42] For this distinction see Riordan (2016: chapter 5) and Angelopoulos (2020).

F. Policy implications

On accounts of (1) the severity of harm and whether it is ir/reparable, (2) the nature of the harm as not/gendered and (3) the financial and expression costs involved in removing false positives or attempting avoiding such removals clearly there are reasons to prioritize the holders of a right to sexual privacy and to de-prioritize copyright holders. In NCII the harm is irreparable, concentrated, gendered and systemic; the corresponding interest in receiving the information is weak to non-existent; the likelihood of false positives is low so the costs of filtering is likely to be low. The freedom of expression losses from censoring these images is likely to be very low (if existing at all) from the perspective of both the 'speaker' (uploader) and the audience. In contrast, the harm to copyright holders from failure to enforce their right against the intermediaries is mainly economic; as such it justifies less prior restraint in the form of general monitoring duties; while identifying, suing and recovering against those infringing copyright is difficult, leaving the intermediary out of the liability picture undermines less the claimant's rights to an effective remedy. Removal of false positives – valuable speech that should be allowed as fair use or is otherwise not a breach of copyright – is a real possibility, and it involves significant undermining of freedom of expression and public interest. The financial costs of sorting real from false negatives is likely to be significant. In the context of defamation, the balancing is somewhere in between these two poles, but defamation is closer to copyright than to sexual privacy. There is therefore much room to critique both the EU and the US inverted hierarchy which in fact privileges copyright over privacy, instead of the reverse: in the EU by signalling out copyright infringements to pre-notice liability in the Copyright Digital Single Market Directive, while leaving privacy to be regulated under the ECD's NTD regime (although, as indicated in Chapter 2, with an unclear strict liability potential via a data protection route); in the US, signalling out copyright infringements under S512 Digital Millennium Copyright Act's NTD regime while affording complete immunity to privacy breaches under S230 Communications Decency Act (CDA) (although as indicated in Chapter 2, the recent FOSTA amendment to S230 affords some rights to victims of sex trafficking hence partially protecting some aspects of sexual privacy).

The earlier discussion yields at least three policy implications. First, it lends support to critiques of the ECD's horizontal model. In the context of intermediary liability, a question presents itself of whether immunity should be based on a horizontal model or not: whether the scope of immunity should be one and the same regardless of the cause of action (or the interest infringed) or varied. Indeed, some calls for reform in the context of NCII are based on NCII exceptionalism: the idea that the harm from NCII is unique so can justify, exceptionally, a greater extent of intermediary liability for the ensuing harm. So even cyberspace libertarians otherwise lamenting any attempt to reform the overly broad immunity for intermediaries by virtue of S230 CDA are willing to make a specific narrow exception for NCII (Goldman, 2008). From the other side of the spectrum, Citron (2019: 1952–3) has recently suggested a menu of legislative reforms to S230 that vary in the extent to which they limit the scope of immunity, although none of them is strictly limited to NCII. NCII exceptionalism is opposed by queer scholars who apply Gayle Rubin's critique of (radical) feminism's and liberals' anti-sex moral panic (Rubin, 2002; Halley, 2006) to online harms; accordingly, a special rule extending intermediary liability should be resisted, they argue (Karanian, 2019). The previous analysis attempted to defend the moral cogency of NCII exceptionalism. In this sense, despite the fact that prioritizing copyright holders over the subjects of a privacy right is wrongheaded, the break away from horizontal approach, evidenced also in EC's policy documents (European Commission, 2017: 10–12) and, outside of the EU in the ECtHR *Delfi v Estonia*[13] decision (to which I will return shortly) is not. Where the content is likely to cause more harm, or where monitoring is likely to entail lower costs there is more justification to impose liability on intermediaries or to expect more of them as a matter of regulatory standard. Possibly, although this was not gleaned from the previous discussion, in different contexts the extent to which the intermediary contributes to the harm from the content by act or omission, or benefits from the infringing content is also different; this too can justify a different scope of intermediary liability. Indeed, the UK's Online Safety Bill also clearly endorses a vertical approach adjusting the scope of the duty of care to the extent of harm from the content.

Second, in the Online Safety regulatory context, NCII should be levelled up with child pornography (child sexual exploitation and abuse) and terrorism with regards to the active filtering expectation (Department for Digital, Culture, Media & Sport, 2019: 3.12).[44] If at all, there is ground to argue that support for terrorism is harder to filter (more false positives) and that the harm from such content is only probable (by arguably inducing future attacks through propaganda) while the harm from NCII is certain and ingrained in the disseminated content itself. While image child abuse

---

[43] App No 64569/09, 16 June 2015.

[44] The Online Safety Bill, 2021, distinguishes between terrorist and CSEA illegal content (their terminology to child pornography), and other illegal content (including priority illegal content to be determined by the secretary of state). For example, S7(8), 36(2), 41, 44, 64(4). A related complication is that illegal content is defined with reference to criminal offences. So intermediaries would not be under a duty to tackle NCII as illegal where the image's nature as non-consensual, and hence illegal is not evident, even if NCII would be criminalized and be either levelled up with CSEA, or at least defined as priority illegal content.

is undoubtedly at the very serious end of the NCII spectrum (Keren-Paz and Wright, 2019), the White Paper's exclusion of NCII as a serious harm in itself seems misguided and is undermining the proportionate response it claims to adopt. NCII's harm beyond child pornography needs to be acknowledged and appropriately tackled in the framework offered in the White Paper and in the Bill, rather than being excluded or marginalized just because the victim is 18 and above. Catherine Mackinnon (2011: 297–8) has made a similar point in her powerful critique in the context of prostitution of treating differently minor and adult victims. 'If there is nothing wrong with prostitution ... what on earth is wrong with children doing it ... ? And if something is problematic here, how does it change suddenly when she reaches seventeen years and three hundred sixty-six days old?'

The third implication is both a critique of the White Paper (and more generally of hate crimes regulatory framework) and a vindication of *Delfi v Estonia*. The White Paper definition of hate crimes (at 7.16) excludes gender as a hostility to identity ground (protected characteristic), unlike race, religion, sexual orientation, disability or transgender identity;[45] this is typical of hate crime definitions in general. Given the Crown Prosecution Service guideline for a hate crime as '[A]ny criminal offence which is perceived by the victim or any other person, to be motivated by hostility or prejudice, based on a person's [protected characteristic] or perceived [protected characteristic]' (Crown Prosecution Service, 2022), it is hard to see how the typical upload of NCII could not be considered as a hate crime. Clearly, the victim's gender is often central to the motivation to disseminate her intimate image and the double standard about women's sexuality by definition reflects gender prejudice, if not outright hostility.[46] At the very least, instances in which the image is accompanied by offensive language disparaging the victim's sex or sexuality ought to be considered as hate crime (Hill, 2015; Halliday, 2015; Citron, 2016). The data adduced in Part 2.B on perpetrators' motivations (Davidson et al, 2019) is not incompatible with the analysis suggested here: first, there is the question how credible these self-reports are. Second, the relative absence of an intent to hurt the victim as reported by perpetrators is still compatible with prejudice. Lastly, and more importantly, the Crown Prosecution Service guidance focuses on the victim's or any other person's perspective, not the perpetrator's; and the data in Part 2.B indicates that women often, and understandably so, view NCII as based on hostility or prejudice.[47]

---

[45] The Online Safety Bill, 2021 does not refer directly to hate crimes.

[46] See Part 2.B on NCII as a form of gendered violence, gendered hatred, sex discrimination and cyber-misogyny.

[47] Arguably, victims' common perception of NCII as a form of sexual abuse is one such indication (Moore, 2014; Patella-Ray, 2018; Sharratt, 2019).

Delfi, as later developed by *MTE v Hungary*[48] and *Pihl v Sweden*[49] exemplifies a vertical approach to intermediary liability by holding that the scope of intermediary obligation to actively monitor content depends partially on the severity of the ensuing harm. So while hate crime gave rise to proactive monitoring obligation, mere defamation did not. *Delfi* was subject to extensive academic critique from freedom of expression, human rights, intermediary liability and other scholars (Angelopoulos, 2015; Brunner, 2016: 163–74; Georgaki et al, 2016; Polański, 2018) but is vindicated by the analysis offered earlier. First, the departure from a horizontal approach makes perfect sense for the reasons explained earlier. Second, provided that the gendered nature of NCII harm alongside the understanding of NCII as a type of sexual abuse crime leads to its classification as a type of hate crime, *Delfi* supports the lawfulness of pre-notice obligations on intermediaries to filter intimate images as an appropriate balancing of the claimant's Article 8 privacy interest with the defendant's Article 10 expression interest.

---

[48] App No 22947/13, 2 February 2016.
[49] App No 74742/14, 9 March 2017.

7

The Policy Debate: Freedom of Expression and Financial Costs of Filtering

1. Introduction

In this chapter I debunk claims that filtering NCII involves too high costs in terms of either freedom of expression or financial costs, as well as the related claim that such filtering is not technologically feasible. I first focus on Facebook's (now Meta) filtering practice as reflected in its (untransparent) transparency report. I then evaluate this practice to highlight its shortcoming, delineate the contours of an acceptable and practicable NCII filtering backed by (a more controversial) strict liability for harm from remaining NCII. I discuss penumbra definitional issues of intimacy beyond nudity and cultural differences and scope of liability for harms from these images. The approach I take diverges from the recent Law Commission's definition of intimate images (2022), by affording better protection to cultural minorities and taking lessons from medical ethics and law. I also discuss an economy of scales and its potential relevance to smaller intermediaries with a critique of the weight given in recent policy discussions to a means-based test as limiting intermediaries' potential duties to filter content.

2. Existing filtering practice, with a focus on Facebook

As was documented in Chapters 2 to 3, the two main arguments against intermediaries' liability for user content are the financial costs involved in such an obligation – including effects on competition – and a chilling effect on expression given excessive removal of lawful speech (Friedmen and Buono, 2000; Guo, 2008; Kosseff, 2010; Goldman, 2012; Keller, 2017b).

This part is dedicated to examine whether these costs are real or significant for a filtering system of NCII. As the discussion demonstrates, they are not.

In evaluating the financial and expression costs of filtering NCII, it might be useful to start by distinguishing between two versions of a pre-notice liability. One is a best effort – or feasibility – standard (Helman and Parchomovsky, 2011), which is *similar* to the duty of care standard suggested by the government in the Online Harms White Paper and the Online Safety Bill, to the European Commission approach of expecting platforms – albeit voluntarily – to proactively monitor some types of illegal content, and to the C-Digital SM Directive. A feasibility standard would impose liability for any NCII that could have been filtered by the best technology that is or could have been available. This maintains platforms owners' incentive to invest in R&D and to implement the best available technology to eliminate the risk they will be found liable for avoidable NCII. However, there would be no liability for 'unavoidable accidents': accidents that are either too costly to prevent, according to a traditional economic analysis of law cost-benefit analysis or accidents that are impossible to prevent according to a feasibility standard. A strict liability rule would impose liability for any NCII appearing on the platform, thus imposing on the platform both the costs of developing and implementing the filtering system and the costs of compensating victims for any failings of the filtering system.

In what follows I will argue that costs of filtering NCII are affordable; indeed, filtering similar to what I suggest is already conducted by some platforms. I will argue further that the financial costs of liability for 'unavoidable accidents' are hard to estimate, since it is very hard to find the incidence of NCII which cannot be detected automatically. For both claims, I will focus on Facebook – although I will say something on other/smaller platforms towards the end of the chapter – so I will begin with a terminological clarification. Facebook the company rebranded itself as Meta in October 2021, but I will continue using 'Facebook' for both the company and the platform. Its transparency reports, including about removal of contents, apparently refer to both platforms – Facebook and Instagram – but without providing bespoke statistics on each. The reports do not include data on the instant messaging (IM) app WhatsApp (acquired by Facebook in 2014). Unless stated differently, when I refer to Facebook as a platform, this includes also Instagram. I focus on Facebook for the following five reasons: First, Facebook is a major platform, so the way it is regulated, or self-regulates, massively affects the public. Second, it is especially important to get Facebook's regulation right since as one anti-NCII activist observed 'Specialty websites show up in Google searches, but unless you are looking for them no one is going to see you nude ... On Facebook and Instagram you have your family, friends, co-workers, bosses and your real name. Everybody is going to see' (Bowden, cited in Solon, 2019). In this sense, the argument equally applies to other popular platforms to which younger crowds are attracted such as TikTok. Third, Facebook is an especially well-resourced defendant. If it cannot afford the costs of filtering, the argument against adopting a duty to filter becomes stronger (albeit, it is still doomed to fail as it simply shows that the enterprise cannot pay its costs). The reverse is not true; if Facebook can handle the costs of filtering then it might be expected, or willing, to share the technology with other platforms, or the duty might be means-dependent (as is the trend in both UK and EU policy documents), or policymakers might trade-off a competitiveness loss for better protection of victims (that is, the fact that only incumbents can afford effective filtering is not a reason against adopting such a requirement; see Part 3.G).

Fourth, since Facebook started publishing periodical transparency reports (Facebook, 2018–current), and since Facebook is a major actor, it is easier to find figures on Facebook than on smaller platforms – although as we shall see, the task is still difficult. Finally, Facebook poses both a theoretical challenge and a guide for a workable solution due to its no nudity and sexual activity community standard (Meta, 2021),[1] which makes it hard to distinguish between NCII and intimate images disseminated with the subject's authorization. In what follows I will examine the state of the art – which is rapidly moving – of voluntary filtering by Facebook, and more broadly, in the context of child pornography, explain the filtering method of NCII I propose and examine the affordability of such a proposal, including of the strict liability component.

In 2020, Facebook's transparency report mentions in the section on adult nudity the following recent trends: 'Content actioned increased from 30.3 million pieces of content in Q3 2019 to 38.9 million in Q4 2019, primarily driven by a few pieces of violating content that were shared widely in October and November'. The percentage of non-automated removals first reported by users rose from 0.79% in Q1 2020 to 2.1% by Q4 2020. It has most recently been reported at 1.4% in Q1 2021. The equivalent figures for child nudity images (whose prevalence is lower) was 0.5% in Q1 2020 rising to 1.3% by Q4 2020 and now being 1.1% in Q1 2021.

The efficacy of automated filtering seems to improve over time – as was mentioned in a previous transparency report and although the most recent trend belies it – and is probably the result of improvements to AI identifying infringing images appearing for the first time, developments in hashing technologies allowing for detection of near identical images by PhotoDNA

---

[1] 'Adult nudity and sexual activity': 'We restrict the display of nudity or sexual activity because some people in our community may be sensitive to this type of content. Additionally, we default to removing sexual imagery to prevent the sharing of non-consensual or underage content'. See also 'child sexual exploitation, abuse and nudity'.

and the expansion of the pilot, allowing users to send intimate images to a databank for purposes of producing a hash against which copies of the image will be detected and automatically removed. Crucially, the image itself is deleted seven days after its conversion to the indecipherable fingerprint – the hash – reducing the chances of hacking or a leak. The pilot was initially tried in Australia, then expanded to the UK, US, Canada, Pakistan and Taiwan, was planned to launch in additional countries in Europe, the Middle East and Latin America, and 'has now ended, StopNCII.org is now live and will continue to hash private sexual images and prevent these from being shared across partnered sites and platforms' (McIntyre, 2018: 299–300; Davis, 2019; Solon, 2019; Revenge Porn Helpline, 2021). Presumably, as more users send such images, automated removals will further increase.

Hashing technology is being used in the context of child pornography both by the Internet Watch Foundation in its Image Hash list containing in excess of 200,000 unique hashes and recently shared with an American counterpart, and since 2004, in the United States, including by scanning of private emails and files on cloud. IWF uses PhotoDNA, which enables detecting modified variants of the original images (apparently with a low 1 in two billion false positive error) and MD5 hashes detecting exact matches of images (McIntyre, 2018: 299).

Facebook develops its AI to detect NCII beyond nudity or sexually explicit content. Currently, the technology can flag near nudity accompanied by derogatory or shaming text. The flagged post is then sent to a human reviewer for confirmation (Davis, 2019; Salins, 2019). Flagging content as NCII is important since NCII gets priority in queues for content moderation.[2] Note that it is not entirely clear whether the flagging of and priority in moderating NCII is limited to requests for removal, or includes the automated flagging by Facebook's algorithm. So while the transparency report fails to separate removal of NCII from consensual sexually explicit and nudity images, at least the reporting system, and possibly the automatic flagging apparently creates a two-tier system allowing for earlier removal of NCII.

NCII victims still express dissatisfaction with how Facebook handles NCII, commenting particularly on lack of empathy and use of language failing to 'convey the severity of the situation' which 'could be perceived as victim blaming'. While Facebook responds by changing and deleting offensive phrases '[V]ictims and advocates say Facebook needs to do more'.

---

[2] Solon (2019) who mentions that such priority takes place in moderating victims' reports, that Facebook now has a form allowing victims to flag the material as NCII but that Instagram and Messenger do not, and implies that such priority occurs whenever material is flagged as revenge porn, even if automatically: 'Now, anything flagged as revenge porn is treated with a similar level of urgency as content related to self harm.'

Some specific concerns are Instagram's unresponsiveness and that in both Instagram and Messenger victims cannot flag content as NCII so expediated moderation is impossible. A related problem – not unique to Facebook – is that on IM apps victims do not have access to NCII depicting them (Solon, 2019). While messages in IM apps are encrypted end to end, they are stored in a cloud and hence are amenable, in theory at least, for scanning, similar to that done in the US for purposes of detecting child pornography.

3. Evaluation

Is Facebook filtering system robust enough a response to NCII, and can it serve as a general model for filtering NCII across hosts? The crucial unknown figure is the percentage of NCII on Facebook's platform that are not automatically filtered – as they ought to, based on Facebook's anti-nudity/sexually explicit community standard and regardless of their status as NCII – but are rather subject to reporting and are often subsequently removed. While the recent percentage of proactive removal – around 97–99% – is impressive, Facebook's exposure to liability is still significant, due to the sheer volume of images on the platform. Even the lowest percentage of removal following report (0.79% [or 0.90%] in Q1 2020) still leaves around 104,000 images per month.[3] Had all of these images been NCII, strict liability would be punishing indeed. Even under a very low estimation of damage from NCII as averaging $10,000 – the actual average might be at least about five times higher[4] – the liability exposure per quarter would be

---

[3] Solon (2019) mentions that '[E]ach month, Facebook, which owns Instagram, has to assess about half a million reports of revenge porn and "sextortion," a source familiar with the matter said.' The figure in the text that was gleaned from the 2021 transparency report is around a fifth. Possibly, 'reports' might include automate flagging, and the gap with the automated removal figures in the transparency report (around 13M per month, excluding children) explained in that the latter refer to all nudity and sexual activity and not only non-consensual images. However, Solon's article strongly suggests otherwise, by immediately contrasting 'reports' with AI detection: 'The team's goal is not only to quickly remove pictures or videos once they have been reported ... but also to detect the images using artificial intelligence at the moment they are uploaded.' Moreover, the 2022 report both gives a slightly higher figure to the Q1 2021 (0.90, rather than 0.79 in the 2021 report) and adds the caveat that an image processed for reporting and meanwhile being independently flagged is treated as proactively actioned. The exposure for pre-notice liability is therefore higher, as the NCII was detected by users before being removed by Facebook.

[4] *Reid v Price* [2020] EWHC 594 (QB) awarded the (male) victim the £25,000 he requested, where the defence was struck out, indicating that a higher amount, no higher than £60,000, might have been appropriate. In the Max Mosely case, which is in fact, although rarely understood as such, an NCII, £60,000 was awarded. *Mosley v NGN (No 3)* [2008] EWHC 1777 (QB). Reported settlements figures include £37,500 in 2007 to Sienna

$3.12 billion, while Facebook's quarterly profit was $5.89 billion (Facebook, 2020). In the absence of reliable information on the incidence of NCII reported, rather than proactively detected by Facebook, it is hard to know how significant the exposure for undetected NCII is. The following are the points to bear in mind.

A. A proactive and swift action is mandated

Given the serious and irreparable damage from NCII, a proactive and swift action is mandated. Time is of the essence, since by the time an image is circulated a removal is akin to locking the stable's doors after the horses have bolted. This means that Facebook's pilot of use of hashes – commended as a game changer in the child pornography context (McIntyre, 2018: 299) – could be only part of the solution. The main use of hashes is reactive in nature by allowing an effective stay down (ensuring that copies of a removed NCII do not reappear). It is true, that had NCII's potential victims sent all of their intimate images to Facebook's database, hashing could have worked as an effective means of filtering first unauthorized publication of such images. But it would be wrong to burden potential victims with the task of sending intimate images to Facebook – indeed to any entity, be it private or public – as a condition for an effective remedy against NCII. On the level of principle, such a solution is a benign type of victim blaming, now shifting responsibility from Facebook to victims for NCII whose subjects did not send the image to the database as a pre-emptive measure (previously, blame would be attached for creating the image, now it would be attached for not sending it to Facebook); an expectation to send intimate images as a condition for protection is itself intrusive on one's autonomy and privacy; it is not cost-effective as it relies on the proactiveness of millions of individuals; and it still leaves a risk of data leak and the problem of the image appearing on other websites or platforms. Rather, the focus should be on developing technologies and procedures that will automatically and swiftly remove potential NCII even where there is no hash to compare the image against.

The other, and related implication of the need for a timely removal is a need to err on the side of removing false positives, rather than on delayed removal of false negatives. An image flagged by an algorithm as intimate, and hence potentially NCII, should be removed first and then be sent for human inspection for verification of consent (or as being otherwise lawful);

Miller and £42,500 in 2013 to Tulisa Contostavlos (Nicklin and Strong, 2016). Note, that all claimants were celebrities, so might have been awarded higher than otherwise damages. A Denver court awarded a victim $39,000 and juries in US jurisdictions awarded $500,000 and $6.4M awards. (See Rogers, 2014; O'Brien, 2018; Cardi, 2020; see also Chapter 11, n9.)

during the period of (even expediated) human oversight the image might become viral with a serious and irreparable harm. On the other hand, the damage from a delay in reinstating an image which is not NCII is minimal. This has also bearing on the issues of appeal and notice to which I return later. Notice of removal should be sent to the uploader, whenever it is feasible to do so, after the image is removed. And as long as an appeal process for a removal has not been successfully completed the images should stay down. To the extent that the current process requires human moderation once an image has been flagged by the algorithm and before removal,[5] it should be changed. Even if human moderation were currently a condition for removal in cases in which the AI's confidence level is lower than that of human reviewers,[6] it is better to remove first and reinstate later than to delay removal of NCII. Indeed, an interim removal of intimate images before authorization has been verified is one example of the need for more claimant-oriented rules in NCII compared with other content disputes such as defamation and copyright.

B. Facebook's lack of transparency

It is hard to know whether Facebook's system is robust enough and whether strict liability will threaten Facebook's financial viability due to Facebook's lack of transparency. Facebook recognizes the difference between sharing of non/consensual images and that NCII is a more serious problem in both its community standards and in allowing users to flag content as NCII in order to 'fast track' the moderation system. Yet, by collapsing the two categories together, its transparency report obfuscates the crucial information of how many cases of NCII are there, how many of them are removed automatically, how many, after a report, and how long does it take to remove NCII content automatically or after a report. Without this information it is very hard to assess the cogency of claims that filtering is not an effective response (and by implication that there should not be a legal obligation to filter) or that strict liability would be crushing. It is also hard to glean from the transparency report clear figures on the incidence of NCII given the split between adult and child nudity, and the difficulties in deciding whether all child nudity is to be considered as non-consensual (is the parent's consent relevant?). The percentage of automated removal of child nudity is slightly higher than that

---

[5] This is implied by Solon (2019). Facebook's transparency report gives a weak indication of pre-human moderation removal, by distinguishing between content restored following users' appeals and those restored without an appeal. But much more content is restored after an appeal, raising doubt whether the smaller non-appeal restoration represents the entire human oversight of AI removal of images done prior to such an oversight.

[6] As is the case with support of terrorism speech (Bickert and Fishman, 2018).

of adults; it is unclear what can be learned from this fact about the robustness of Facebook's filtering process and whether strict liability can be justified.

It is of course in Facebook's interest to exaggerate the difficulties in effectively upload-filtering NCII in order to dissuade policymakers from imposing a filtering obligation or strict liability for dissemination of NCII on its platform. At the same time, for reputational reasons, it is in Facebook's interest to be perceived as responding quickly and effectively to NCII (and other illegal content) and as devising cutting edge technologies and policies to combat NCII. Both conflicting goals are served by Facebook's lack of transparency. As the excessive costs argument is in essence a kind of defence against a claim that otherwise, platforms should be accountable for the publication of NCII, and as Facebook is in control of the relevant information, any doubt should work against Facebook.

C. Three filtering strategies

Strict liability for failure to filter NCII will require companies to choose one of three strategies. They could, as Facebook does, adopt a community standard of no nude/sexual activity policy, regardless of whether it is consensual or not. This involves a curtailment of sexual expression in that consensual intimate images are removed as a price for ensuring that no NCII is uploaded. There is a good ground to argue that had this been the only course of action available to platforms, the price would have still been worthwhile, given the asymmetry of the harm: the harm from being an NCII victim seems to be much more significant than the harm from the inability to express one's sexuality (for remuneration or otherwise) by sharing one's intimate image online. I concede that some might disagree that the harm is so clearly asymmetrical, and this relates also to the social value of pornography and commercial sex websites[7] and to freedom of occupation of people working in the virtual porn industry. But luckily this is not the choice faced by platforms. Platforms' terms and conditions might allow the sharing of consensual intimate images while banning NCII. Then platforms have a choice between two types of enforcement. They can remove all intimate images unless there is a clear indication that all those depicted in the image are adults consenting to the sharing of the image, and create an appeal mechanism correcting false positives (variation "A"). A variation of this enforcement technique will de facto enable the uploading of intimate images on the platform only after some type of verification of authorization was provided (variation "B"). Indeed, this was already done voluntarily by the Reddit Gonewild community (Suzor et al, 2017: 1095). Alternatively,

---

[7] See Chapter 4, n19.

platforms can develop filters that remove only images that are found to be both intimate and non-consensual.

The latter option seems an inadequate tool to ensure that no NCII are distributed. As such, it is not likely to be used as the sole technique to avoid the sharing of NCII. Mind you, Facebook recently developed an AI attempting to do just that (Davis, 2019; Salins, 2019). But it uses it on top of a filtering system flagging all intimate images, presumably removing all intimate images only after human moderation oversight, and using the additional AI to prioritize the moderation process of NCII. Relying only on AI aiming to detect a likelihood that an intimate image was not authorized will leave too many images unaccompanied by language suggesting the images are unauthorized, and perhaps also images accompanied by a language falsely creating the impression they are consensual ('see how beautiful I look naked') to outwit the algorithm.

Each of the two variations of the 'remove unless authorization is clear' seems adequate, and the choice between them would probably be made based on the empirical question which poses lower financial costs to the platform. Both variations also pose low expression cost. The main difference between them is the moment at which verification of identity and consent is required, before the initial upload, or after removal. Either variation necessitates the creation of a system allowing the platform to verify that the person depicted in the image is indeed the one consenting to the upload. Such technology is already used by IT systems in other contexts, such as multi-factor authentication technologies used to authorize financial transactions with banks or to enter some databases or services (OneLogin, 2022). So the direct financial costs of using such or similar technology alongside AI flagging intimate images is not high and is definitely not crippling. The financial costs of developing the appropriate technology has an anti-competition element, which will be discussed later.

The suggested filtering system – assisted by post-removal human oversight and a notice and appeal procedure – is therefore technologically and economically feasible, at least where direct costs are involved and for established platforms. But what about expression costs? Such a system will create two types of expression costs: delay and forgone expression. The former is caused by the delay in making consensual images available due to either the need to authenticate one's identity when an image is about to be uploaded as a condition for its non-removal (which might involve the need to create some kind of account), or, more significantly, the period of time it takes to restore images which were removed as false positives.

But recall that consensual intimate images are hardly topical; so a delay in making them accessible online is hardly a cost at all. True, any system requiring verification prior to uploading involves some loss of spontaneity, but this loss hardly measures up against the devastating consequences of forced exposure. Besides, loss of spontaneity would not occur when removal is based only on the intimate nature of the image, and when authorization and authentication are relegated to the appeal process. Even without notice of removal to the uploader, the uploader is likely to know that an image they uploaded was removed, so there is little risk consensual intimate images will be removed without a practical possibility of reinstating them. The competing harms to balance are a serious and largely irreparable harm from NCII and a temporary delay in making consensual images available. Not a hard choice really.[8]

Nor is the chilling effect of forgone expression more convincing. It would be reasonable to assume that an intermediary would require not only that all individuals in these images provide their real life identity information that is, name and address but also image information to link themselves verifiably to the visual content. The concern here is of forgone expression due to embarrassment (for example, by tagging the person as promiscuous or 'cheap') or fear that the details of registration will themselves leak, affect the person's reputation or be used to blackmail her. Had such concern been significant, it might also have translated into an indirect financial cost: a reduction of revenue that will threaten the financial viability of the platform.

On balance, the concern is unconvincing. Verifying identity and authorization amounts to a nudge, and it is controversial to count a forgone expression due to a nudge as social cost. At best, we could say that individuals, who might spontaneously agree to their images being uploaded but will refrain from doing so upon reflection or when facing small obstacle, are conflicted about the upload of their intimate images. It might be, then, that the real preferences of this group of people are better served by the suggested procedure. Such a conclusion is supported both by the literature on soft regulation and nudges and, specifically, in the contract and consumer protection domains, by the literature justifying formal requirements for the validity of a contract (most prominently the requirement the contract will be in writing) based on their cautionary function: deterring people from hasty decisions with respect to commitments with potential serious consequences (Kennedy, 1982: 635; Sunstein, 2014). The same logic is apposite here. Intimate images are sensitive information and while their authorized dissemination is to be celebrated, it makes sense to allow people some moments of reflection on whether they would like to do so. Be it as it may, by definition, it cannot be seriously argued that a person who

---

[8] Compare to a similar argument of Keren-Paz (2013: 189) in the context of prostitution of the arguably conflicting interests of non/forced commercial sex providers.

can overcome a nudge but prefers not to, is significantly harmed from not disseminating the image.[9]

Authentication requirements are common in online financial transactions and the managing of digital accounts; these involve private and sensitive information. Few would dispute that sexual information, including (and perhaps in particular) imagery is likewise sensitive. It is therefore both principled and desirable to afford people the same degree of protection with respect to control over, and access to imitate images, as is afforded to their finance, e-mail communication and digital accounts.

One can also doubt how significant the reputational and embarrassment effects of a need to authorize the sharing of the image (and to authenticate one's identity in the process) are. Women who are entirely comfortable with public display of their sexuality or nude images would not be deterred from the need to authorize and authenticate their identity. For women who are more conflicted the argument mentioned earlier applies: it is unclear that the intervention is undesirable, and even if it is, a nudge cannot be considered as imposing serious harm or an intolerable restriction of freedom. Moreover, a woman is not expected to register first, and share intimate images which she would NOT want to share, as a condition to protect herself from NCII. Had this been the case, there might have been weight to the fear of reputational effects from potential leak of the data – such concerns were raised in the context of the debate over the desirability of regulating – by registration of – commercial sex providers (MacKinnon, 2011: 306) and by Facebook's database pilot discussed earlier. Rather, the default remains that an intimate image is filtered out unless the authenticated consent of the person depicted in the image is sought. Therefore, only women (and men) who *concretely* authorize the dissemination of an image will need to go through the process of authenticating their identity, and for these people the reputational/embarrassment costs are likely to be a non-issue.

As was clarified in Chapter 4, Part 4.C, it is the failure to effectively remedy NCII that is likely to impede more sexual expression of women (McGlynn and Rackley, 2017: 546–7). At the very least, the harm from forgone

---

[9] While writing this paragraph I am reflecting that the 'beware the consequences' and 'regret' arguments have been employed by anti-choice activists to support curtailment of abortion rights. I find both such legislation and the supporting arguments extremely unpalatable. But there is a big difference here: the harm for a woman who is pressured to carry pregnancy to term is much more serious than the harm to a woman who is nudged not to release her intimate images. Moreover, a decision about not/having an abortion is time sensitive and irreversible in a way a decision not to upload intimate images is not. So while the harm from not/publishing an intimate image is clearly asymmetrical, the harm from not/having an abortion is not; this makes attempts to steer women towards a certain decision (not aborting) much more problematic.

expression is a price worth paying in order to prevent the significant harm NCII causes. Another advantage of a robust authorization system (induced by a strict liability regime) is that it can enable better continued control over the dissemination of the image: stay down in cases the right-holder withdrew their continuous consent, by this effecting Article 7(3) of GDPR.

Depending on the process by which authentication of identity will be managed, the procedure suggested might be manipulated so that fraudulent authorizations might exist. This is probably true but is hardly an argument against the process suggested. The fact that no system is immune to manipulation does not mean that a more secure system than currently existing ought not to be expected to be installed. Nor does the fact that a fraud-prevention measure fails mean that the losses ought to be borne by the individual rather than by the service provider. Indeed, in the financial sector, losses from fraud are borne by the financial institution, at least in the absence of the customer's negligence, as is the case with unauthorized purchases by credit card.[10]

D. Intimacy beyond nudity

An attempt to regulate intimate images necessitates defining what an intimate image is. An obvious example with which Facebook has to contend is 'near nudes' in which images of scantily dressed women are shared. While such images do not breach Facebook's community standards, they are an instance of NCII when they are shared without the subject's consent. Indeed, Facebook has developed an AI whose aim is to flag such images accompanied by indicators (such as 'a laughing-face emoji along with a phrase like "look at this"') as NCII (Solon, 2019). More generally, defining images as 'intimate' is a difficult issue both theoretically and practically. Theoretically, what is intimate, similar to what is private has both a subjective and an objective element. What is intimate to one is up for grabs for another. That privacy is grounded in autonomy (usually alongside dignity) is largely accepted in both case law[11] and in the privacy scholarship (Benn, 1971; Gavison, 1980; Moreham, 2018a; other accounts resist a reductionist approach of privacy as ingrained only in autonomy, for example, Solove, 2002). If so, the existence of a subjective element is straightforward and is captured in Nicole Moreham's definition of privacy as 'desired inaccess' (Moreham, 2005: 636). The objective element of privacy is captured in the UK by

---

[10] In the UK, The Consumer Credit Act 1974; ss 83,84; in the US, The Fair Credit Billing Act 1974.

[11] *Campbell v MGN* [2004] UKHL 22, [50]–[51]; *Planned Parenthood v Casey* 505 US 833, 851 (1992).

the requirement that the claimant has a *reasonable* expectation of privacy for satisfying the prima facie case of a *Privacy* claim (*Campbell v MGN*;[12] Moreham, 2018b). This too sits well with general principles of tort (and criminal) law protecting manifestations of consent according to an objective meaning, and in the context of informed consent, often adopting a test of material information to the reasonable patient.[13] The objective element has to contend with cultural differences. Three examples will suffice: (1) an image of an Indian woman swimming alongside a male companion in a pool, both fully clothed; (2) an image of a devout Muslim or Jewish woman without a hair cover; (3) an image of a bald woman or man who lost their hair due to chemotherapy.[14] It seems to me uncontroversial that the uploader (who for all practical purposes would always distribute it intentionally) should be liable, and that there should be liability for a failure to remove expeditiously the image post notice. But strict host liability is much more problematic.

A key issue, moving us from the theoretical to the practical, is that it is harder to infer, in the examples given earlier, and unlike in cases of nudity and sexual activity, that the image is intimate, without further information that is not likely to be easily detected by AI (or even by human moderators). As Mark Zuckerberg has put it '[I]t's much easier to build an AI system that can detect a nipple than it is to determine what is linguistically hate speech' (Taylor, 2020). Strict liability might therefore either entail a general removal of images out of the fear that some would be found to be intimate images hosted without consent, despite the fact that most of which are not, or might require expenditure in developing AI better equipped to remove intimate images outside of the nude/sexual activity context. Either way, a major argument for distinguishing NCII from defamation and copyright becomes less convincing in this 'intimacy beyond' context, that the financial and expression costs from filtering are much lower for NCII. In the criminal

---

[12] (n11).

[13] *O'Brien v Cunard SS Co* [1891] 28 NE 266 (apparent consent to vaccination bars a battery claim); *Canterbury v Spence* 464 F 2d 772 (DC Cir, 1972) (first reasonable patient test for informed consent in a US jurisdiction). Even jurisdictions incorporating a subjective limb to the reasonable patient test, include an objective element that the physician is or should be aware that the information was likely deemed significant to the particular patient: *Rogers v Whitaker* (1992) 175 CLR 479, [490] (Australia); *Montgomery v Lanarkshire Health Board* [2015] UKSC 11 [87].

[14] The first example was given by Antigone Davies, Facebook's Head of Global Safety in which the woman asked and was granted the removal of the image: Solon, 2019. The second example is discussed in the literature (for example Hunt, 2011: 199). Hunt would view the image as conceptually private, based on the subject's acute sensitivity, rather than on defining the image as intimate, or based on societal consensus it is private. The third example is a hypothetical presented to me in a pre-consultation stage by the Law commission team for 'Taking, making and sharing intimate images without consent'.

context, similar considerations led the Law Commission (2022: 47, 82, 92) in its final report on sharing and taking offences, to limit intimate images to sexual, nude, partially nude or toileting images, and to exclude images considered intimate by certain religious groups, or to adopt a more subjective test as I will suggest. The Law Commission was of the view that it would be very difficult to prove that the perpetrator had knowledge that the person depicted considers the image as intimate.

The distinction between nudity, for which there should be reasonable expectation of privacy and non-sexual images, for which an expectation of privacy is less obviously reasonable, could be accommodated by adopting a similar test to the British test for informed consent.[15] Such a test would distinguish between images likely to be considered as intimate (and more generally, private) by the *reasonable* person in the claimant's position, and images the platform *is or should reasonably be aware* are considered as intimate by the *particular* claimant. So, an indication that the image in example (2) belongs to a married ultra-orthodox Jewish woman or that the image in example (3) belongs to a person post chemotherapy should create a reasonable expectation of privacy, so should lead to host liability if the image was not authorized. The cancer patient might wish to have the image circulating, but even if such photos are likely to be removed automatically – which is doubtful[16] – they can be reinstated after authentication and consent have been verified. Here too, the stakes are asymmetrical; and imposing the risk about lack of consent on the publisher is consistent with conceptualizing privacy as a dignitary tort (as the analysis in Chapters 9 and 10 demonstrates). As for partial nudity, the considerations are similar to that of nudity:[17] the general cultural norm is that partial nudity is intimate; the social value of circulating images of partial nudity without consent is not high, nor the dissemination of such images is topical; the potential for embracement is significant; and

---

[15] *Montgomery* (n13).

[16] Gauging an image based on wider contextual info is more expensive and more difficult to design (and is less accurate) so might be avoided. In addition, the exposure for liability is likely much smaller even if for the reason that these images are less likely to become viral.

[17] For a similar conclusion (albeit restricting it to circumstances in which reasonable expectation of privacy exists and not in the context of platforms' liability) see Laidlaw and Young (2020: 161–3) (summarising the different approaches in NCII legislation on whether near nudes are covered. For example, The New Zealand definition includes near-nude photos, toileting, dressing and undressing, and upskirting photos, while the US model draft *Intimate Images Act* excludes buttocks and parts of the female breast other than the nipple since it is not uncommon for them to be displayed in public). This was also adopted in the Federal SHIELD/NCII Bill. See Chapter 2, n14. See also Bambauer (2014: 2058, 2093) (defining intimate information to include only sexually explicit conduct, genitals, pubic area or female's nipple or areola) and Law Commission (2022: 54–72).

technologically, identifying near nudity is feasible (and is already done by Facebook). It seems then, that removal unless and until an authenticated authorization is given should also be the solution for near nudes.

Ultimately, a decision regarding the scope of intermediary liability ought to compare the costs of the claimant's damage from the content, the extent to which damages can make good that damage, and the costs of either hosts' liability or of filtering the content. The incidence of truly non-sexualized NCII (as in example (3), but not examples (1) and (2)) might be lower (as they do not cater to a prurient interest in nudity and sexuality); and the average damage from their dissemination might be lower (either because there is more stigma attached to violation of sexual norms or because the image is less likely to be disseminated and viewed widely). If this is true, it might be that strict liability for non-sexualized NCII (and perhaps also for the broader category of 'beyond nudity' NCII such as categories (1) and (2)) is both fair as a matter of enterprise liability and is low enough that would not threaten the financial viability of platforms who would therefore not bother to attempt and filter such images.

As we have seen, 'beyond nudity' intimacy is relevant for determining whether we should expect platforms to filter them (or to be strictly labile if they do not) and Facebook does attempt to filter images beyond nudity, at least in the area of near nudes (Solon, 2019). 'Beyond nudity' intimacy also exacerbates the problem of Facebook's non-transparent reporting of NCII: the prevalence of non-sexual intimate images distributed without consent is unreported by Facebook.

E. Notice and appeal

So far, it transpires that the costs of filtering NCII – both financial and to expression – are affordable. The availability of notice to the uploader that the content (image) had been removed and of an appeal process bolsters this conclusion. The practice of major platforms is to provide an appeal process, although not necessarily to send a notice (Facebook does) when content has been removed (Gebhart, 2019). In the regulatory landscape, requests for removals following notice of copyright infringement in the US, and defamatory material in the UK, already require the host to contact the content provider as a condition for gaining the safe harbour.[18] Many free speech non-governmental organizations and researchers in the area of intermediary liability stress, usually in the context of NTD, the importance of providing notice to the user generating the content removed of the

---

[18] Digital Millennium Copyright Act 1998, 112 STAT. 2860, §512(g)(2), (3); Defamation (Operators of Websites) Regulations 2013, No 3028.

removal, and of providing an appeal procedure; such requirements minimize the expression costs and are supported as a matter of natural and procedural justice (Electronic Frontier Foundation, 2015 [Manila Principles, Articles 5(a)-(c)], 2018 [Santa Clara Principles]; Haber, 2016: 133–4; Angelopoulos and Smet, 2016: 290;[19] Gebhart, 2019; Hoboken and Keller, 2019 [endorsing the Manila Principles]; The C-Digital SM Directive, 2019, Article 17(9)).[20] A notice and appeal system will further curtail unjustified NCII removals. The rare public interest in disseminating an intimate image despite the absence of subject's consent[21] can be vindicated by an appeal process. Presumably, the uploader will need to take the platform to court to establish that public interest exists, since otherwise the platform is not likely to take the risk lest they be sued successfully by the claimant.[22] Given the irreparable harm from publication and risk of error rationale, this result is desirable: the platform should assume the risk of liability if it reinstates an image wrongly believing it was in the public interest to do so.

F. Crushing liability?

As could be recalled, it is hard to estimate whether strict liability would be crushing for Facebook since it is unknown how many NCII are not detected automatically but are rather subject to reporting and subsequent eventual removal. Assuming that this figure is currently sufficiently high to threaten Facebook's financial viability, there are three responses to this concern. First, strict liability will incentivize Facebook to improve its technology and content moderating procedures. Even currently, in the absence of liability threat, and in response to reputational costs only, the efficacy of both the technology and Facebook's overall response to NCII improves, albeit with

---

[19] Angelopoulos and Smet support notice-and-notice for copyright, and notice wait and takedown for defamation, both involving a notice to the author as a condition or in lieu of take down.

[20] The Directive imposes an obligation on platforms to 'put in place an effective and expeditious complaint and redress mechanism' and 'decisions to disable access to or remove uploaded content shall be subject to human review'. For a critique of an earlier draft of the C-DSM on grounds of lack of due process see Frosio (2017d).

[21] Cf Laidlaw and Young, 2020: 173–74 (detailing the public interest defence existing in Canadian provinces NCII statutes, the model US law and the one supported by the authors); Chapter 10, Parts 3.D; 4.D.

[22] Laidlaw and Young (2020: 156–8) suggest to exclude intermediaries from the fast-track tort for removal of an image, based partially on assuming 'that companies like Google and Facebook may resist attempts to find them liable, whereas they would be willing to obey a court order that resulted from a finding of liability against someone else'; they mention at 174 that '[A] declaration by a court that distribution of an image is illegal … will often be sufficient to get an intermediary to take down or de-index the image'.

some fluctuations, as could be gleaned also from Facebook's transparency report (Part 2). The threat of liability will only likely improve Facebook's response. So even if currently the potential exposure of Facebook is unsustainable, it does not mean that this will remain the case.

Moreover, NCII victims will likely entertain different views on whether Facebook is to be blamed or held responsible for their damage. Research suggests that victims are mostly interested in a quick removal of the image (rather than in receiving damages) (Franks, 2013a; compare Benzanson, 1986: 791; Carroll and Witzleb, 2011: 226), so if Facebook will respond quickly to a notice, some, perhaps even many victims will not pursue a claim against Facebook, and the damage of those who would is likely to be lower. In other words, the lack of scholarly consensus of whether strict liability is ethically defensible, is likely to be replicated in NCII victims, so those believing that unless the intermediary is at fault they are not the author of their misfortune will not sue the intermediary, even if they have a right to do so. I made a similar argument in the context of my call to hold those purchasing sexual services from victims of sex trafficking strictly liable, based on the fact that victims have different views on clients' culpability (Keren-Paz, 2013: 54, 143, 257–60; and see Chapter 12, Part 3, on attitudes regarding suing viewers). So especially at the beginning of a legal reform, until (if at all) a strict liability regime will lead to changed attitudes among victims leading them to view Facebook as responsible for the failure to filter the images, the exposure to liability is likely to be much lower than the aggregate harm caused to victims from a failure to filter NCII; it is this latter figure that arguably threatens the financial stability of Facebook. This will leave Facebook time to improve its technology and procedures to ensure that the number of unfiltered NCII and hence the aggregated harm reduces to a sustainable level.

More broadly, there is always an enforcement gap between the extent of right-violation that could lead to a successful claim and the incidence of claims. This gap reflects both access to justice issues and different attitudes towards the attractiveness of litigation as a method of enforcing rights. It would therefore be a mistake to determine the 'sustainability' of intermediary viability based on intermediaries' *theoretical* exposure to liability; rather, what matters is the exposure for *actual* liability which factors in the enforcement gap. In other words, what matters is intermediaries exposure to *damages*, rather than the damage (injury) caused by NCII.

Second, the harm from NCII is significant and real. If eventually Facebook cannot afford to pay damages to NCII victims, there is lots to be said that we are better off without Facebook, since the activity cannot pay its costs.[23]

---

[23] See Chapter 3, Part 5; Chapter 4, Part 5.A; Phillipson, 2016: 136; cf *Pihl v Sweden* App No 74742/14, 9 March 2017. This argument equally applies to smaller actors. See Section

Holding otherwise amounts to expecting victims to subsidize the internet 2.0 business; and it is hard to find a convincing argument for such forced subsidy. Intermediaries significantly increase the harm suffered by victims, a point explained in Chapter 3. The benefits we all derive from platforms allowing user content are significant; but so are the harms produced in the process. If paying for the harms is not affordable, perhaps we are better off without internet 2.0, at least in its current form. It is liability, indeed strict liability that can ensure that the benefits from the industry exceed its costs. Sacrificing claimants' interests for the greater good flies at the face of proper understanding of rights (Dworkin, 1977), and is incompatible with notions of both fairness, requiring that those benefitting from an activity would bear its costs,[24] and efficiency, requiring the internalization of the costs of the activity (Calabresi and Hirschoff, 1972).[25] Morton Horwitz famously explained the very defendant-friendly 19th-century American tort rules as a form of subsidy to entrepreneurship, mainly the rail industry. This had clear regressive effects in blocking the claims of passengers and employees to the benefit of capital owners (Horwitz, 1977: 67–108).[26] Similar regressive effects are apparent in the NCII context. Since the harm is gendered, it is very problematic to afford intermediaries with immunity, especially given the preferential treatment copyright holders receive – a point canvassed in Chapter 6 (the inverted hierarchy problem). More generally, the anti-competition concern is a subsidiary of the utilitarian argument in favour of complete immunity to ISPs, which was used to support S230 and is subject to similar empirical and normative critiques (Guo, 2008; Goldman, 2012).

Finally, those unconvinced by the previous argument can at least support a feasibility standard. Such a standard is less demanding than strict liability but is still more demanding than the European NTD standard. According to such a standard, the intermediaries should be liable if their moderation and filtering practices fell below what is technologically feasible. I have elaborated in Chapter 6 on the differences between feasibility, reasonable care and strict liability standards and on what supports feasibility in the NCII context. A feasibility standard will shield intermediaries from strict liability for currently unavoidable NCII, which might be crushing, while imposing liability for failure to live up to what is feasible at the time the image was circulating. This will create some incentive to improve filtering – out of the

---

G. The current mood music in policy and regulatory debates becomes much more critical to tech giants, and Facebook in particular. See, for example, Chapter 6, n25. This is also reflected in the recent rebranding of Facebook as 'Meta', announced on 28 October 2021.

[24] See Chapter 3, Part 3.B; Chapter 4, Part 5.B.

[25] See Chapter 4, Part 5.A.

[26] Zuboff (2019) makes a similar point that tech giants have been very adept at evading regulation.

fear that claimants might prove that a better filtering was feasible, including by way of showing that other intermediaries developed a better filtering. However, such incentive is clearly reduced in comparison to the one produced by strict liability, under which the threat of liability for 'unavoidable accidents' (accidents not worth preventing) incentivizes defendants to further invest in accident prevention measures. Equivalent debates exist in the context of product strict liability and the 'state of the art' defence (from an American perspective: Berry, 1984; Calabresi and Klevorick, 1985; Kaplow and Shavell, 1996; Ben-Shahar, 1998).[27] The feasibility standard, and variations thereof were offered as possible regulatory solutions to intermediaries' liability (Helman and Parchomovsky, 2011). Feasibility is also tied to the notion of proportionality and the platform owner's means, to which I now turn.

G. Smaller businesses

So far I have argued that upload filtering – backed by strict liability for residual distribution of NCII on the platform – is feasible for internet giants like Facebook. But what about smaller intermediaries? Daphne Keller is among many who expressed concern (in the context of copyright) that a filtering duty stifles competition by preventing entry of new actors due to the prohibitive cost of developing filters that 'are shockingly expensive – YouTube's ContentID' used to filter copyrighted works uploaded in YouTube 'had cost Google $60 million as of several years ago – so only incumbents can afford them. Start-ups forced to build them won't be able to afford it, or will build lousy ones with high error rates' (Keller, 2017b; Spoerri, 2019).[28] In fact, the anti-competitive effect of a duty to filter depends on how large the costs of developing effective technology are (relative to the intermediary's revenue) and whether such technology would be shared by the developer, thus obviating the need to bear the R&D costs. Both the over/under removal problem discussed by Keller and the absolute financial costs of developing filters are less applicable to NCII than to copyright, suggesting that entry barriers are lower. Moreover, there are reasons to believe that effective filtering technology would be shared across the sector. This is the existing practice in the child pornography domain in which hashes are shared; voluntary free licensing to SME and small companies of anti-grooming technology developed by Microsoft was negotiated and is on the verge of

---

[27] *Beshada v Johns-Manville Products Corp.* 447 A.2d 539 (1982).

[28] See also Urban, Karaganis and Schofield (2017, ContendID developing costs were $60M, or 'several times higher'). But recall that in a more recent paper co-authored by Keller and Leersen (2020: 110), the size of the financial costs of monitoring was specifically mentioned as one item which calls for further empirical research.

implementation; there is a policy-regulatory steer towards broadening such collaborative and sharing measures at both the EU and the UK; smaller intermediaries can get a licence for using filtering technology from third parties (such as Audible Magic for copyright); and mandatory licensing from the developers might be available, although, this is unclear (European Commission, 2017; McIntyre, 2018: 299–30; Department for Digital, Culture, Media & Sport, 2019: 8.10, Box 28; Spoerri, 2019: [49]–[52]).

Turning from the empirical to the normative, as was discussed in the previous section, it is not self-evident that it is justified to sacrifice the interests of claimants whose rights were violated by user content, in order to reap the social good the internet 2.0 brings about, even if such trade-off is necessary, which is doubtful. In the regulatory context, the emerging consensus with respect to filtering obligations is that the size of the company and whether it is new to the market are relevant in determining the scope of its duty. So the C-Digital SM Directive creates a best efforts obligation in accordance with high industry standards to ensure the unavailability of specific works for which the rightholders have provided the service providers with the relevant and necessary information (Art 17 (4)(b)); frames compliance determinations to take into account also the size of the service and the costs for service providers of suitable and effective means (17(5)); exempts new and small entrants from pre-notice liability and limits the obligation of such entrants with more than 5 million monthly visitors to prevent further uploads, that is, to a best efforts stay down obligation (17(6)).

Similarly, the Online Harms White Paper will impose a regulatory standard (not an obligation leading to compensation for its breach) of reasonable steps to keep users safe (3.3) adopting a risk-based (5.3–5.6) and proportionate (5.7–5.10) approach, including reach and severity of harm, a reasonable practicable standard (5.7) and regulator's heed to competition, the impacts on small businesses (5.8), a legal obligation on the regulator to support innovation (5.11) and to protect users' rights, particularly to privacy and freedom of expression (5.12). These principles also inform the Online Safety Bill, 2021.[29]

While the commitment to a proportionate response has much to commend it, care should be taken not to over-emphasize the importance of these factors, at least for NCII. First, as the discussion in Chapter 3 demonstrated, a defendant's size and resources are taken into account for failure to reduce a risk the defendants did not create themselves, and where defendants did not

---

[29] The Online Safety Bill, s12(2) (due regard to users' freedom of expression and privacy); S115 (3)(a)(v) (privacy); s29(5)(h) (protecting innovation); S31(1)(a); s58(4A),(4B) (protecting small businesses).

stand to profit from the infringing activity.[30] Given that platforms owners' business model is based on user content and that salacious content is good for business there is much to be said that limitations based on size and profit are inapposite.[31]

Second, a proportionate approach should focus on comparing victims with defendants, rather than comparing smaller with bigger defendants, as resulting from the focus on competition.[32] In my previous research on standard of care I have argued that a defendant's resources should generally be taken into account, where relevant, to decide the extent of their duty. But to be legitimate, such comparison needs to take into account the foreseeable means of typical victims (Keren-Paz, 2003). Both the seriousness of the injury from NCII and its clear regressive distributive pattern serve as a reason to hold even small platforms' owners to a strict liability standard. Put differently, the regressive results from exempting small platforms' owners from extensive duty of care towards NCII victims is more significant than the regressive anti-competition results following from denying a reduced duty to small platform owners (compare, Keren-Paz, 2007a). Earlier, I have advanced the argument that if small businesses' financial viability depends on immunity from serious harm they cause, they better not operate in the market, despite the anti-competition loss. Alternatively, if small businesses need subsidy to further the social interest in competition, the subsidy should come from big businesses (sharing technology) rather than from victims (denying compensation). The White Paper's worthy response is to encourage cross platforms sharing of best practices and new technologies (5.9). Note, however, that this induced collaboration stands in tension with competition whose value underlines the regulatory approach adopted in the White Paper.

Third, the limits of platforms' reach as a duty-limiting factor (endorsed both in the White Paper and the Directive) should also be understood. Disproportionate size of online harms from NCII result from exposure to those in close relationships to the victim: friends, family, significant others, employers and neighbours (Kamal and Newman, 2016; Solon, 2019). If a small platform is likely to similarly reach these inner circle contacts as a big platform would, the regulatory response and the expected standard from the company should be similar, notwithstanding that a bigger platform is likely to reach many more people outside of the victim's inner circle. So not only

---

[30] See, for example, *Byrne v Deane* [2013] EWCA Civ 68; *Sedleigh-Denfield v O'Callaghan* [1940] AC 880.

[31] *Oriental Press v Fevaworks Solutions Ltd* [2013] 16 HKCFAR 366; *Trkulja v Google Inc [No 5]* [2012] VSC 533; *Dow Jones & Co Inc v Gutnick* [2002] 210 CLR 575, [182].

[32] For a similar debate of whether the denial of a right to bereaved relatives should block the claim of professional rescuers see Lords Goff and Griffith (no) and Hoffman (yes, for the majority) in *White v Chief Constable of South Yorkshire* [1998] 3 WLR 1509.

that the relationship between the overall number of viewers and the severity of the claimant's psychological trauma is not linear – a point on which I have co-written (Keren-Paz and Wright, 2019: 263) – but the identity of those exposed to the images matters a lot. I am not aware of empirical studies trying to quantify the relative weight of the harm from (a) the mere intrusion into privacy vs publishing the private information,[33] (b) reputational vs non-reputational harms from publishing private information,[34] (c) publication to people in the victim's inner circle vs to others,[35] and (d) the overall number of strangers viewing the images.[36] Given that the injury from NCII is indivisible, it is doubtful whether such quantification is possible at all (Keren-Paz and Wright, 2019: 202–5 (indivisible harm); 225–30 (equitable apportionment)).[37] What is clear is that, unlike copyright, in which the relationship between financial loss and number of readers of the infringing copy is much more likely to be linear so greater reach is likely to increase the rightholder's loss, the harm from NCII much less depends on reach (Chapter 8, Part 5.B; Chapter 11, Part 5), so limitations of duty based on a more limited reach are much less justified.

---

[33] For a doctrinal discussion see Chapter 8, Part 2, Chapter 11, Part 2.

[34] For a doctrinal discussion see Chapter 11, Part 3.

[35] See Chapter 11, Part 5. Courts do take this into account: In breach of privacy: *Jane Doe 464533 v ND* (2016) 128 OR (3d) 352 (Sup Ct J), [57]; in defamation: *Sadik v Sadik* [2019] EWHC 2717 (QB).

[36] This is taken into account in *Privacy* as each fresh viewing in a new intrusion, a point relevant also for issuing of injunction, despite the fact the information is already in the public domain. See Chapter 8, n12.

[37] For the non-reputational harm from NCII see Laidlaw and Young (2020: 165).

8

The Easy Case for Viewers' Liability: Child Pornography and Apportionment of Liability

1. Introduction

Viewing NCII harms its victims; as was surveyed in Chapter 6, Part 2.B, victims perceive the acts of dissemination and viewing as violating experiences similar to physical sexual assault. This invokes two questions: can viewers be liable to victims and under what conditions, and if so, what should be the scope of liability, for what harms and for how much? In the area of child pornography, US victims have a statutory right for compensation, as part of the criminal process ('criminal restitution' in American parlance) for the pecuniary losses suffered due to their knowledge of the widespread viewing of those images, or as part of a statutory civil cause of action. The first question – of liability for mere viewing – is therefore established, albeit statutorily, for NCII on the extreme end of the scale: cases of child pornography. Following the Supreme Court decision of *Paroline v United States* and the subsequent amendment of the relevant provisions in the 2018 *Amy, Vicky, and Andy Child Pornography Victim Assistance Act (AVAA)*, the second question (scope) was largely settled as using the 'relative role in the causal process' test to apportion the liability of individual viewers.[1]

---

[1]   See 18 USC §§ §2255 (civil remedy), 2259 (mandatory criminal restitution), 2259A (assessments), 2259B (victims' reserve) (2018) and *Paroline v United States,* 572 US 434 (2014) discussed (with a focus on the pre-amended version of §2259) in Keren-Paz and Wright (2019). Despite the fact that the motivation for the 2018 amendment was to strengthen the victim's right to compensation beyond the apportionment test adopted by the majority in *Paroline* of 'relative role in the causal process', eventually, the amended § 2259(b)(2)(B) adopted this test with a 'no less than $3,000' restitution threshold for viewers.

In my previous writing on this topic – with Richard Wright – we focused on the second question. We both commended and critiqued the majority's decision in *Paroline*. Of the three approaches supported by the justices in *Paroline*, we prefer the middle ground solution advanced by the majority (written by Justice Kennedy), of a *sui generis* substantial amount, over the alternatives of no liability due to alleged inability to apportion the individual contribution, the position held by Chief Justice Roberts and justices Scalia and Thomas, and of full liability for the entire injury which might have been caused by thousands if not millions of viewers, advocated by Justice Sotomayor. At the same time, given the nature of the harm as both indivisible and significantly overdetermined, and in fact an instance of a mass tort, we criticized the majority's 'relative role in the causal process' test, which was de facto, and contrary to the court's rhetoric, a manifestation of a proportionate liability test, which is incompatible with the overdetermined character of the injury. Rather, liability should be either a form of conventional award – so a flat amount to all viewers, regardless of their viewing or 'consumption' pattern – or a more individualized damages-at-large approach. Crucially, to reflect the complex nature of the overdetermined injury in situations involving mass sexual abuse, the amount payable by each defendant has to be significantly higher than what would have to be paid under a proportionate liability rule based on relative causal contribution, however such contribution is measured (number of images viewed, amount paid, number of viewers, and so on). The defendant's liability to each of his victims should be set at a level that would be sufficient to compensate, in the particular case or on average (depending on the applicable liability rule), at least for the emotional distress and related pecuniary costs that would have been suffered by the victim solely as a result of the defendant's offence or, preferably, the defendant's offence combined with only a few other offenders' similar offences. It should also compensate for any discrete dignitary and physical losses suffered by the victim as a result of the defendant's conduct. An attempt to award only proportionate award is misguided on both conceptual and policy grounds: overdetermined causation is hard to reconcile with proportionate liability since (by definition) the same injury would have happened but for any individual contribution by each viewer. At the same time, each viewer's actions alone were sufficient to cause substantial emotional distress (caused by victim's knowledge that someone viewed her images) and alongside a much more limited number of viewers, sufficient to produce severe emotional distress. Moreover, any attempt to divide the overall damage by the estimated number of viewers would lead to too small an award, thwarting any of the goals that tort liability might possibly attempt to achieve. This approach was defended in detail in my previous writing on *Paroline* (Keren-Paz and Wright, 2019: 217–18, 223–5), and bears resemblance to my suggested liability rule for the creation of indiscriminate demand by clients of commercial sex providers that contributed to the forced prostitution of women trafficked to partially meet this demand (Keren-Paz, 2013: chapters 6–8, in particular 234, 236–41).

Understanding child pornography as an extreme and complicated instance of NCII gives rise to several lines of inquiry. First, it is easiest to justify viewers' liability for viewing child pornography. So any justified limitations of liability for child pornography are likely to curtail liability for viewing NCII in less egregious circumstances. Crucially, since children cannot consent to the dissemination of the intimate depiction (and of course, to any underlying sexual activity depicted in the image), no lawful viewing of such images is possible (subject to some administration of justice exceptions which do not concern us here). By contrast, the dissemination of an intimate image of an adult does not necessarily raise a privacy issue if the dissemination is consensual. This means it is harder to establish objective fault or intention for the viewing of intimate images proved to be disseminated without consent. This also means that it is easier to justify joint liability of all viewers of the same image based on the theory that all viewers acted in concert (so are joint tortfeasors) in cases of child pornography than in other cases of NCII. (As the later discussion demonstrates, even for child pornography, such a conclusion is contested.)

Second, since the production of the image (involving a real child) is necessarily a serious independent underlying offence, there is a question of whether the viewing contributes factually and should lead to liability for the victim's initial abuse. Other cases of NCII do not necessarily involve an underlying sexual offence depicted in the image or an intrusion of privacy manifested in creating the image (and independent of its dissemination). In addition, whether the production of child pornography and of other NCII is driven by demand is an empirical question needing answering. Third, in the context of sex trafficking, I have argued that contributing to indiscriminate demand could lead to liability to victims trafficked to meet the overall demand even if – and this is crucial – the defendant–client did not have direct sexual contact with the victim–claimant. If the demand for child pornography images indeed drives the initial abuse, there might be a case for civil liability of possessors of child pornography of victims who are not the claimant, provided that factually, the demand might have contributed to a claimant's initial abuse. Beyond these issues, there is the question whether civil liability of viewers (for either child pornography, or other forms of NCII) could be established based on general doctrines and principles of privacy (and perhaps other causes of action) or whether it could only be grounded in statutory provisions for mandatory criminal restitution or civil liability such as 18 USC §§ 2259 and 2255 in the context of child pornography.

The analysis in this chapter will complement that offered in my previous writing by (1) establishing viewers' liability for viewing child pornography under privacy law (as distinct from bespoke statutory provisions); (2) examining whether viewing child pornography could be considered as 'acting in concert' and hence lead to full liability of each viewer to the victim's entire damage from the viewing of their abuse (and possibly also from their initial abuse); (3) arguing that the holding in the US Supreme Court in *Paroline* is compatible with demand-based liability: a viewer could and should be liable for the victim's injury from the initial abuse, as long as the production of the child pornography was also motivated by the prospect of distribution. However, the viewer should not be liable to victims whose images he did not view for harm from either the initial abuse or the circulation of images.

2. The viewing of child pornography as a stand-alone civil breach of privacy

The Supreme Court in *Paroline* took guidance from the principles governing scope of liability in tort law in deciding the scope of liability under the relevant criminal restitution provision. Moreover, Justice Sotomayor, in her dissent, specifically regarded the viewing of child pornography as amounting to the intentional tort of invasion of privacy: 'There is little doubt that the possession of images of a child being sexually abused would amount to an intentional invasion of privacy tort – and an extreme one at that.'[2] Lollar argued (in an article published before the Supreme Court decision in *Paroline* was rendered) that courts' reliance 'on a privacy theory in support of ... compensation orders' is unfounded since 'civil privacy law does not provide a basis for such a remedy'. Lollar's view is based on mistakenly assuming that the relevant privacy tort applicable to viewers is that of 'public disclosure of private facts [which] requires publicity and the "mass communication" of' private, non-newsworthy and highly offensive to a reasonable person information, while viewers 'of child pornography have not typically "made public" the images that they view' (Lollar, 2013).[3] However, Justice Sotomayor's view quoted earlier is based on classifying the possession of child pornography as an intrusion of privacy, a different prong of invasion of privacy that does *not* require publicity as a condition for liability (as made explicit in Comment a of §652B of Restatement (Second) of Torts). Rather, the intrusion upon seclusion tort makes tortious the intentional intrusion 'upon the solitude or seclusion of another or his

---

[2] *Paroline* (n1) 483–4.

[3] Referring to Restatement (Second) of Torts § 652D cmmt a (1977).

private affairs ... if the intrusion would be highly offensive to a reasonable person'. As Comment b to §652B clarifies, the intrusion does not have to be physical and encompasses 'the use of the defendant's senses, with or without mechanical aids, to oversee or overhear the plaintiff's private affairs'. Illustration B specifically covers the clandestine taking 'through a telescope ... of intimate pictures' and Illustration A covers the taking of a photo of the hospitalized claimant over her objection.[4]

While the possessor did not take the image himself, the intentional possession of the image is itself a form of intrusion; this conclusion can be reached based on either an analogy with the criminal offence, or first principles. In terms of analogy, to the same extent the possessor of child pornography is criminally responsible despite the fact he did neither distribute the material nor produce it, civil liability for invasion of privacy is appropriate, at least as long as the act of possession is intentional.[5] As a matter of first principles, knowing possession of intrusively collected private information is itself, or at least could be, an intrusion upon seclusion; arguably, the same conclusion could be reached as to knowingly disseminating and receiving private information even if it was initially obtained without intrusion (as is often the case in NCII cases). Sharing private information with a third party contrary to the claimant's authorization (in the absence of a relevant defence) is intrusive, and knowingly receiving this information is likewise intrusive. This view deconstructs the division of labour between the American intrusion and disclosure torts, a position already gaining support from several privacy scholars, alongside suggestions to soften restrictions of liability under the disclosure tort (Smolla, 2002: 302; Blackman, 2009; Strahilevitz, 2010; Richards and Solove, 2010: 1918–22; Allen, 2010: 1764; Richards, 2011: 382–4). It would mean that every unauthorized dissemination of private information is one kind of intrusion, although the reverse is not true. Some defendants intrude on the claimant's privacy, even if they did not further disseminate the information. A knowing receipt of private information is just one such example of intrusion. While judicial authority for such a view is currently scant, Sotomayor's analysis in *Paroline* supports it, and perhaps interestingly, no other justices disputed this part of

---

[4] Restatement id § 652B.

[5] The analogy is even more convincing in US jurisdictions, in which, contrary to the English position, 'knowing assistance' is a form of accessory liability in tort, further aligning criminal and civil responsibility. See Davies (2015: 216–19; 2016: 19). Note, however, that the argument in the text is based on analogy to the primary, rather than accessory, criminal responsibility of the possessor. In theory, the possessor might be liable in tort as accessory to the primary act of intrusion (or to the primary act of distribution). Whether such liability could be established is in some doubt and will be discussed as part of the discussion in Parts 3–4.

her analysis of the possession of child pornography as an invasion of privacy. It would be an odd result indeed, to say that child pornography, which is accepted as a serious invasion of privacy,[6] allows for no common law (as distinct from statutory *sui generis*) cause of action. By treating separately liability for intentional torts (intrusion) and joint tortfeasorship as reasons for joint and several liability, Justice Sotomayor in *Paroline* seems to imply that liability for knowing possession under an intrusion tort is primary and independent, rather than accessory.[7] One final caveat is in order. In cases of child pornography, the creation of the image is necessarily a form of intrusion, so can support a conclusion that a knowing receipt of such information is also necessarily an intrusion. When the creation of the images is not in itself intrusive (as in many cases of NCII), knowing receipt of the information could still (and I would argue should) be considered as intrusive, but it is less obvious that this view reflects Sotomayor's.

In England, misuse of private information – traditionally more akin to public disclosure of a private fact than to intrusion upon seclusion – has recently been transformed into a tort protecting intrusion per se, even unaccompanied by publication. This is most evident by *Gulati v MGN* in which the Court of Appeal approved the separate award (incidentally, the highest) given by Judge Mann for the hacking into phone of one defendant (Yentob) even when no publication followed, and by the cumulative awards given to other claimants for the intrusion (the hacking) and for the subsequent publication of the information, while specifically rejecting the double counting ground of appeal.[8] This is also evident from other case law of both privacy and breach of confidence.[9] Moreover, liability under *Privacy* of the prospective/publisher of private information known to be obtained by the intrusion of a third party is well established.[10] Therefore,

---

[6]   See, for example, in the context of morphed images *Doe v Boland* 698 F.3d 877 (6th Cir 2012).

[7]   *Paroline* (n1) 482–4.

[8]   *Gulati v MGN Ltd* [2015] EWCA Civ 1291 (CA), [8], [70], [97], [102] upholding *Gulati v MGN Ltd* [2015] EWHC 1482. For support of unification – using *Privacy* to protect from intrusions – see Wragg (2019) and the earlier discussion of the American torts.

[9]   *CTB v NGN* [2011] EWHC 1326 (QB), [23]–[24] (intrusion as justifying injunction against newspapers when information is already in public domain due to social media); *Tchenguiz v Imerman* [2010] EWCA Civ 908, [67]–[69] (knowingly obtaining confidential information as in itself breach of confidence, consistency with *Privacy*); *Catt v Com'r of the Police* [2015] UKSC 9 (systemic retention of info as violating personal autonomy/ article 8).

[10] *Douglas v Hello! (No 3)* [2005] EWCA Civ 595, [11], [12], [259]; cf *The Prince of Wales v Associated Newspapers (No 3)* (CA) [2006] EWCA Civ 1776, [71] in the context of breach of confidence in which the status of the third person who passed the information to the defendant as 'intruder' is in doubt, since she received the information in confidence.

the intentional possessor of child pornography is bound to be liable under privacy since the possession of the images (at least when intentional) will be considered as misuse of private information, regardless of the absence of further dissemination. Indeed, in *Gulati* it was common ground that the defendant is responsible for the intrusion caused by the private investigators, and regardless of not publishing this information,[11] so for intentional possession of information gathered by another's direct intrusion. But whether this liability was accessory or primary is unclear. In addition, it is unclear whether such liability could be extended to child pornography (or other NCII) viewers, who typically do not explicitly request the third party to intrude on the claimant's privacy. Conceptualizing viewing of intimate images – even repeated one – as intrusive in itself was clearly endorsed in *Douglas v Hello! (No 3)*:[12]

> Insofar as a photograph does more than convey information and intrudes on privacy by enabling the viewer to focus on intimate personal detail, *there will be a fresh intrusion of privacy when each additional viewer sees the photograph* and even when one who has seen a previous publication of the photograph, is confronted by a fresh publication of it. To take an example, if a film star were photographed, with the aid of a telephoto lens, lying naked by her private swimming pool, we question whether widespread publication of the photograph by a popular newspaper would provide a defence to a legal challenge to repeated publication on the ground that the information was in the public domain.

Understanding each viewing as intrusive in itself lends itself into holding that the viewer himself is liable for intrusion.[13] Conceptually, there is nothing that limits 'misuse' of private information to only disclosing it, as opposed to obtaining or possessing it, when one should not; or that limits 'intrusion' to exclude the knowing receipt of private information. As was discussed in Chapter 4, an understanding of the mere unauthorized possession of private information as a misuse is consistent with both conceptualizing private information as a subject matter of a property right and the data

---

[11] (n8) [13].

[12] [2005] EWCA Civ 595, [105] (my emphasis). This was echoed in *Contostavlos v Mendahun* [2012] EWHC 850, [25]; and in *PJS v News Group Newspapers* [2016] UKSC 26, [88] (Lord Toulson).

[13] Granted, the court in *Douglas* was concerned with the question whether, and if so when, private information falls into the public domain; the decision lends itself more easily to the proposition that those *sharing* such images can be liable for intrusion – the issue of liability for re-publication.

THE EASY CASE FOR VIEWERS' LIABILITY

protection regime. The latter focuses on possession of personal data – by treating storing of personal data as a form of processing – rather than on the disclosure of such information and the non-possessing obligation was applied by a German court, in the context of intimate images, in requiring a deletion of an intimate photo possessed by an ex-partner in the absence of any concrete concern that the image would be further disseminated.[14]

There are three points to bear in mind here. First, if the previous analysis is correct, it should be applicable to all NCII cases in which possession is intentional, so is not limited to child pornography. If intentional possession of an intimate image taken by a third party without the subject's consent is in itself an invasion of privacy, it is not because the image was of a minor or that its production is a serious criminal offence. Given this, and especially given Sotomayor's observation that there 'is little doubt' that possessing child pornography amounts to the intrusion tort, it is surprising that NCII litigation in the US is based on the public disclosure prong and that it is so difficult to find successful claims against those disseminating the images based on an intrusion theory (online viewers cannot be liable for breach of privacy due to S230 CDA immunity which is extended to users who did not author the content). This is so, especially as is well documented by Skinner-Thompson and others, the narrow confines of the public disclosure tort make it hard for claimants to succeed, by often requiring both complete secrecy of the underlying information, and a disclosure to the public. The former requirement sometimes fails claimants who voluntarily shared the image; the latter, fails some claimants if the disclosure was made to a limited number of people (Lollar, 2013; Skinner-Thompson, 2018: 2069–74). Second, a knowing possession of child pornography might invade the claimant's privacy as a public disclosure of private facts if the possessor can be deemed as a joint tortfeasor with the distributor. Whether this is possible, under either American or English law, will be canvassed in the next part. Finally, at least for the civil side of things, liability should extend to situations in which *viewing* is intentional, even if *possession* as traditionally understood is in doubt – think of a live streaming of an intimate video.[15]

3. Viewers acting in concert? A note on scope of liability

At common law, the starting point for liability in tort is that a tortfeasor contributing to an injury alongside other tortfeasors will be liable to the entire damage (joint and several liability) if the harm is indivisible or if he is a joint

---

[14] BGH, Urteil vom 13.10.2015 VI ZR 271/14 https://openjur.de/u/868417.html.

[15] See Chapter 10, Part 3.

tortfeasor with the others. In my previous writings, I have explained why, despite the fact that the harm from viewing child pornography is indivisible, each viewer's liability should not be full: the harm is overdetermined so a full liability is overkill (Keren-Paz and Wright, 2019: 202–5, 221–30; and in the context of clients' liability for creation of demand which led to trafficking Keren-Paz, 2013: 226–40). Justice Sotomayor reasoned that viewers are acting in concert and for this reason too, liability should be full.[16] But for the same reason that full liability is overkill for indivisible harm caused by concurrent tortfeasors (those acting separately) it is overkill for joint tortfeasors: the overdetermined nature of causation, the fact the harm is produced in a context of a mass tort, so that each contribution is neither necessary nor independently sufficient to produce the entire harm. The ethics behind full liability of those acting in concert works well when the number of those acting in concert in relatively small. In these circumstances, whether liability is based on agreement or inducement, or even (in American jurisdictions, but not in England) on 'knowing assistance', the contribution – provided it is significant enough – makes the imposition of full liability just. But once the contribution is very small, as is the case in mass sexual abuse (or other contexts of mass tortfeasorship) full liability for the entire damage is excessive, although some liability for the entire damage is not.

True, a logic of all or nothing could be applied here: either the contribution is not significant enough to trigger the status of acting in concert at all so no liability for the entire harm should be imposed – at least based on a joint tortfeasorship theory – or, if the contribution is significant enough, liability should be imposed in full, as per the usual rule of liability for acting in concert. However, this binary logic is normatively unattractive. Even assuming that the contribution is significant enough to trigger a claim for liability for *part* of damage – and as we shall see later this assumption is debatable – it does not follow that liability should be full. The fact that so many others contributed to the harm, so that the harm is so overdetermined, makes full liability to be too harsh.

In *Paroline*, Justice Kennedy for the majority concluded that 'this case does not involve a set of wrongdoers acting in concert … for Paroline had no contact with the overwhelming majority of the offenders for whose actions the victim would hold him accountable'.[17] As Justice Sotomayor correctly observed, liability for acting in concert does not necessitate a prearranged plan. As 'possessors like Paroline … act with knowledge of the inevitable harms caused by their combined conduct' and since by 'communally browsing and downloading Internet child pornography,

---

[16] *Paroline* (n1) 482–3.
[17] (n1) 454 referring to Prosser and Keeton §52, at 346.

offenders like Paroline "fuel the process" that allows the industry to flourish' they 'are jointly liable under this standard'. 'Indeed, one expert describes Internet child pornography networks as "an example of a complex criminal conspiracy" … the quintessential concerted action to which joint and several liability attaches'.[18] Scholars debate the accuracy of these claims. The claim that viewing child pornography fuels the process that allows the industry to flourish was argued to lack empirical support, despite being intuitive, at least with respect to *production*: 'child pornography producers also are the consumers of the pornography, so third-party demand for their product does not affect whether it is produced' (Lopez et al, 2012: 31–2). 'The market thesis … is more speculative and ideological than supported by experiential data' (Hamilton, 2012: 1729). However, the later discussion suggests that the picture is more nuanced, so that some production is at least partially motivated by distribution (Part 5.A); and there are findings in the literature that internet users reinforce each other's behaviour, mainly in the sense that joining a paedophile sub-culture results in an escalation of pre-exiting behaviours supported by new sense of community (and in rare cases, 'converting' individuals after having discovered the materials) (Jenkins, 2001: 94, 106–8; Taylor and Quayle, 2003: 132, 144, 186).

The difficulty with the analysis of Justice Sotomayor, is that it proves too much; if correct, it could be applied so that any file sharer in Pirate Bay would be liable for the entire infringement of copyright on the platforms by all users, at least of the same file, since each 'acts to produce injury with full knowledge that others are acting in a similar manner and that his conduct will contribute to produce a single harm', pursues 'the common purpose of trafficking in' copyrighted material (rather than images of child sexual abuse) and acts 'with knowledge of the inevitable harms caused by their combined conduct'. While courts at times accept (and at other times reject) acting in concert theories to impose liability in copyright infringement cases, liability is limited to the facilitating platform, not to all nodes in the network.[19] However, from the fact that Sotomayor's view could be extended to other contexts, it does not follow that it should or necessarily would. Elsewhere, I have argued that recognizing a duty of care with respect to posing indiscriminate demand that led to sex trafficking should not

---

[18] *Paroline* (n1) 482–3 (Justice Sotomayor, dissenting).

[19] In England, compare *CBS Songs Ltd v Amstrad Consumer Electronics Plc* [1988] AC 1013 (no liability for mere facilitation in the absence of common design) with *Dramatico Entertainment Ltd v British Sky Broadcasting Ltd* [2012] EWHC 268 (Ch) and *Football Dataco Ltd v Stan Jones plc* [2013] EWCA Civ 27 (both imposing liability where infringing activity was practically the sole reason for which users entered the websites, unlike the situation in CBS in which significant portion of the recording activity did not involve infringement). See also my discussion later of *Sea Shepherd UK v Fish & Fish Ltd* [2015] UKSC 10.

necessarily be extended to situations in which the demand caused other, less serious losses in other contexts (Keren-Paz, 2013: 158–62).[20] So from the fact that we have good reasons to view possessors of child pornography as acting in concert, it does not follow that we have to view sharers of files infringing copyright as acting in concert. But this ultimately depends on one's view about the importance of coherence in the law, a point on which I have written (Keren-Paz, 2013: 142; 2017: 431–2).

There is another objection to Sotomayor's analysis: if mere 'statistical knowledge' – about others acting in a similar way so that the actor's conduct contributes to producing a single harm – were (or is) sufficient to view tortfeasors as acting in concert, the distinction between joint and concurrent tortfeasors collapses, as the independent contribution to an indivisible harm is in itself traditionally a reason to hold the defendant jointly and severally liable, and in the mass tort context, to hold him for a portion of the entire damage (Keren-Paz and Wright, 2019). Finally, the claim that all possessors, distributors and producers are acting in concert raises difficulties as a matter of statutory interpretation: an aggravating factor leading to enhanced penalties for child pornography is committing 'those offenses in concert with three or more other persons' which (alongside other conditions) amounts to a 'child exploitation enterprise'.[21] If all possessors act in concert by merely operating in the same market, this aggravating factor becomes redundant. This last point, however, is more relevant for the statutory liability for criminal restitution than for civil liability for invasion of privacy.

The doctrinal peg on which the breadth of joint liability for acting in concert could be determined is the 'common' versus 'similar' design. Logically, it is possible to infer that all those participating in a trade of images of a certain victim or of a series including the victim's images have implicitly agreed to participate in the illegal venture of possessing the images. But this inference adds little to the question of scope of liability both because liability for the entire injury is already a possibility (as the injury from knowledge the image is circulating is indivisible), and because this inference does not answer the difficulty of holding a tortfeasor liable to injury which is significantly overdetermined. Moreover, the broader we attempt to cast the liability net, to encompass distribution and production, or for images of victims not viewed by the defendant but rather by other members of the network, it is equally plausible, if not more so, to hold that the design was only similar, rather than common, so that the defendant did not act in concert with others.[22]

---

[20] See also n31 on the normative relevance of the merits of the case.

[21] 18 USC § 2252A(g)(2).

[22] Davies, 2016, in his analysis of English case law observes that '[T]he boundaries of "common design" are still somewhat unclear'; in particular, while de jure, mere knowledge by the accessory that the principal is going to commit an unlawful act is insufficient to

THE EASY CASE FOR VIEWERS' LIABILITY

There is another way to analyse the situation leading to the same conclusion. Sotomayor's analysis bases liability on 'the common purpose of' that is, implicit agreement to 'trafficking in images of child sexual abuse'. If by this she means an agreement to share the images of the specific victim, this is arguably correct, so liability could be based on such tacit agreement. However, liability for the antecedent acts of the production and initial distribution, and to the injury of any victims whose images were not viewed by the defendant (at least if these were not part of a series shared with the defendant) ought to be based on assistance: that the demand for such images – fuelling the process that allows the industry to flourish – is a form of encouragement. One difficulty in supporting liability based on such theory is temporal: the actual encouragement happened after the production and initial distribution took place. Such surmountable causation difficulties are present in any theory of demand-based liability.[23] Beyond this difficulty, the assistance triggering liability for 'knowing assistance' in American jurisdictions should be significant as is clarified by the Restatement:[24]

> The assistance of or participation by the defendant may be so slight that he is not liable for the act of the other. In determining this, the nature of the act encouraged, the amount of assistance given by the defendant, his presence or absence at the time of the tort, his relation to the other and his state of mind are all considered.

A look at these criteria suggests that in the main, a viewer's contribution to the violation of rights by other viewers and participants is likely to be deemed as slight: the degree of assistance is arguably small due to both the indirect and the overdetermined nature of causation; the defendant is absent at the time the breach happened (and in some cases the encouragement act happens after the relevant violation has occurred); and the relationship is tenuous. Certainly, none of the Restatement's Illustrations to knowing assistance (or for that matter, common design) liability are similar to the context of viewing child pornography. The overdetermined character of causation in the context of mass sexual abuse suggests to me that while

---

impose liability, at times 'courts may be prepared to infer a common design simply by virtue of the fact that the accessory knew of the primary tortfeasor's unlawful act'. Davies ties this development with courts' willingness to substitute 'common design' with similarity of design.
[23] I have previously dealt with these difficulties in the context of defending clients' liability for contributing to the trafficking of victims of sex trafficking by posing indiscriminate demand to the purchase of sexual services (Keren-Paz, 2013: chapter 8). For the equivalent discussion in the context of child pornography see Part 5.B.
[24] (n3) § 876(b), comment d.

the contribution *might*, *if at all*, be considered as sufficiently significant for purposes of responsibility for *some* of the overall more remote injuries (of production and dissemination) or of these more remote victims (who were not viewed by the defendant) – whether this is correct will be discussed in the next two parts – it *cannot* justify *full* liability for the entire injury. Indeed, comment d of Clause (b) of § 876 of the Restatement (Second) on Torts, dealing with knowing assistance clarifies that '[I]n determining liability, the factors are the same as those used in determining the existence of legal causation when there has been negligence (see § 442) or recklessness. (See § 501).' It should not come as a surprise then, that for the same reasons leading me to reject full liability in mass tort cases for contributing to an indivisible injury, I reject a solution of full liability based on acting in concert. It is noteworthy that while Justice Sotomayor defended in *Paroline* full liability based on both concurrent liability for indivisible harm and joint liability for concerted action, the majority defended a special less-than-full liability rule based on concurrent liability – and while oscillating on whether the injury is indivisible or not[25] – but denied that possessors of child pornography act in concert. The previous analysis suggests that viewers' status as acting in concert or not should not be determinative of whether liability should be in full. Even if they are, the same good reasons opposing full liability for concurrent tortfeasors are applicable to joint tortfeasors.

In England, there is no stand-alone joint liability for 'knowing assistance'; any such assistance should come as part of a common design.[26] For the reasons explained earlier, it might be that such common design is absent and that there is merely similarity of design; this would depend on whether knowledge is equated with agreement, whose images were traded and whether liability is sought also for the production (so the initial abuse) and distribution of the images.[27] If the common design hurdle is met, liability might still be denied if the assistance is considered to be *de minimis*. In *Sea Shepherd UK v Fish & Fish Ltd*,[28] a 3:2 majority of the Supreme Court deemed the following contribution to be *de minimis*: acquiescence to the use of its name and bank account for raising funds for the tortious activity – destroying illegal nets casted by the claimant – and giving the principal tortfeasor, the Conservation Society, the £1,730 raised, which was a very small proportion of the total costs of the operation. The overall tenor (with Kerr SCJ being the most notable exception) was that it was the defendant's passive role in the fundraising rather than the small amount collected that

---

[25] *Paroline* (n1) 456–7 (suggesting that the harm is indivisible), 461 (doubting whether it is).
[26] *CBS Songs* (n19).
[27] *Paroline* (n1) 479 (Justice Sotomayor, dissenting).
[28] (n19).

was determinative in upholding the trial judge's finding that the contribution was *de minimis*. While above *de minimis* contribution (the English test) seems a lower threshold to cross than significant contribution (the Restatement's test), it is an open question whether possessing child pornography would be considered as above *de minimis* contribution for responsibility for the breaches of duty by other possessors and by distributors and producers (as distinct from liability for the contribution of the defendant's possession *itself* to the harm suffered by the claimant).

Note that liability of one possessor to the acts of others based on acting in concert would be the equivalent of a holding in *Sea Shepherd* (which was never sought) that each individual donor to the operation is a joint tortfeasor with all and each of other donors and (presumably) with the actual tortfeasor (the equivalent of the producer) and with the UK charity defendant (the equivalent of a distributor). There are reasons to doubt whether the court would go that far and perhaps an inference could be drawn from the fact there was no attempt by the claimant to find the identity of individual donors and to hold them to account as joint tortfeasors.[29] If at all, the following two observations from JSCs Kerr, for the majority and Mance, in dissent, suggest that the court would not view possessors as acting in concert with other possessors and with producers and distributors: '[The defendant's] contribution in hard, practical terms was not significant'; 'If the mailshot had yielded nothing or only a tiny sum, I would agree that, despite such authorization, the mere despatch of the mailshot could not be regarded as rendering any actually significant assistance.'[30] On this view, the encouragement that each possessor gives to the illegal action of others is both passive and very small (being overdetermined) so is insignificant enough to implicate the defendant with the illegal activity of other members of the network. Note that this conclusion is not determinative in answering the question whether the contribution to the overall indivisible harm is significant enough to merit liability (at least to part of that harm); the next part will be dedicated to examining this question. Finally, note also that within the realist jurisprudence I espouse, the majority's reluctance to view the defendant (and by extension, the individual donors) as acting in concert might be related to the merits of the case, where the claimant was arguably an illegal poacher while the defendant and the Conservation Society (the principal tortfeasor), environmental activists.[31] In contrast, Justice Sotomayor's expansive view as to the boundaries of action

---

[29] Alternatively, it might be that the claimant thought that going after the donors was not worth the shot and powder or would be a PR disaster.

[30] *Sea Shepherd* (n19) [85] (Kerr); [99] (Mance).

[31] Having said this, while the relevant campaign referred to 'illegal fishing' (*Sea Shepherd* (n19) [10]) the common ground of the litigation (which was limited to the preliminary question of acting in concert) seemed to deny the relevance of that illegality to the question

on concert might have been influenced by the defendant's very unpalatable identity and actions. Analytically, the question whether an underlying tort was or might have been committed by the principal tortfeasor (and if so, how 'excusable' it is) should be kept separate from the question whether the defendant acted in concert. However, the merits of the underlying claim (and of the litigants) might be a factor in courts' determinations about the scope of liability of acting in concert (a descriptive claim)[32] and if they are, this is not regrettable (a normative claim).

★★★

The conclusion from the analysis thus far is that all those who knowingly viewed the victim's child pornography could be liable for an invasion of her privacy so to a significant portion of her overall injury. As an instance of mass sexual abuse and given the overdetermined nature of causation, full liability is too harsh, but liability should be significant and not only proportionate.

This conclusion holds whether or not viewers could be considered as acting in concert, or whether the liability is based on independent (concurrent) breaches of duty causing an indivisible injury. The following three ramifications follow from the fact that viewing child pornography (at least knowingly) is an invasion of privacy, under either the English privacy formulae or the American intrusion upon seclusion tort: First, viewers of child pornography could be successfully sued even in jurisdictions, like England, that do not have a criminal restitution legislation like the one governing the litigation in *Paroline*. Second, if child pornography is captured by the privacy torts, it might be that other types of NCII are captured as well, since child pornography is only one (albeit extreme) instance of NCII. I will return to this point in the next chapter. Third, as a matter of quantum, tort compensation is not limited as criminal restitution is to pecuniary losses,[33] although the extent

---

whether destroying illegal nets is tortious, or whether the Conservation Society could avail itself an illegality defence ([27] (Toulson JSC), [47] (Sumption JSC, dissenting)).

[32] As an aside, in the intermediary liability debate some authors base their opposition to intermediary liability on the assumption that the underlying speech is protected, so should not lead to any liability. See for example, Goldman (2013) ('while I have no love for distasteful content websites, I don't trust my powers to decide what's too distasteful or isn't – and I trust any regulators' ability to evaluate content even less') and Sartor (2013: 12) (fear of censorship in the context of Wikipedia relevant to lack of adequate protection to Freedom of expression, not to the question whether Wikipedia is controller). Some of the debate about *Delfi AS v Estonia*, App No 64569/09 (2015), focused also on whether some of the comments ('go drown yourself') amount to a hate speech.

[33] 8 USC §2259(b)(3). For a discussion (including of a Federal statutory civil suit) see Keren-Paz and Wright (2019: 190–1).

to which liability for invasion of privacy encompasses consequential losses such as loss of employment and romantic opportunities is far from settled.[34]

4. Viewers' liability for the underlying abuse based on the indivisibility of harm

Can viewers be liable for the harm from the initial abuse depicted in the images they viewed? Two theories (or are they three?) could potentially support such liability. First, that the harm suffered by the victim is indivisible. If independent breaches of duty, namely the producer's in making the images and possessors of the images' in viewing them, caused an injury which is indivisible, the liability of each viewer to part of this entire loss could encompass also the injury from the initial abuse. On the specific (and unusual) facts of *Paroline*, the victim (known as Amy) did not claim that the viewer ought to compensate her also for the initial abuse so the court did not decide this point: the loss from the initial abuse was relatively small and following therapy 'her therapist's notes reported that she was "back to normal"'.[35] What led to Amy's breakdown was the subsequent revelation that images of her abuse are trafficked worldwide. The court gave an indication that viewers are not responsible for the initial abuse by mentioning that '[c]omplications may arise in disaggregating losses sustained as a result of the initial physical abuse'.[36] Lower courts subsequently held that the losses caused by the original abuser must be "disaggregated" (removed) from the restitution awarded against later possessors and distributors.[37] But since the injury from being a victim of child pornography is indivisible (Keren-Paz and Wright, 2019: 201–5, 226; for victims of sex trafficking see Keren-Paz, 2013: 226–30), by definition neither it nor the related losses can be disaggregated, although for policy reasons liability can be apportioned.

Not much hangs on giving an answer to this question, and there are good arguments for both sides. To begin with, the solution I support in the contexts of mass sexual abuse – sex trafficking, child pornography, and NCII – is that of apportionment. It is also clear that the responsibility of any viewer for the initial abuse pales in comparison to that of the producer (the same is true for the relative contributions of traffickers who recruited victims and clients whose demand contributed to the recruitment and trafficking of the victim). Ultimately, whether to limit, based on policy,

---

[34] See Chapter 11, Part 4.

[35] *Paroline* (n1) 440.

[36] *Paroline* (n1) 449.

[37] *United States v Galan*, 804 F.3d 1287, 1290–91 (9th Cir. 2015); *United States v Dunn*, 777 F.3d 1171, 1181–82 (10th Cir. 2015); see also *United States v Rogers*, 758 F.3d 37, 39–40 (1st Cir. 2014) (*per curiam*).

the liability of viewers to the estimated part of the injury attributed to the viewing, rather than to the initial abuse, depends on the extent to which the production of the images is fuelled by the demand for such images, which is a contested issue. On the view, endorsed in *Paroline* by both the majority and Sotomayor,[38] that this is the case, there is no good reason to exclude viewers' responsibility for the initial abuse their viewing contributed to its occurrence, as long as the quantum is small in comparison to the overall damage. On the view that production is made mainly for self-consumption, the contribution of the viewers to the initiation of the abuse is minimal, if existing at all, so an attempt to disaggregate the harms from the initial abuse and from the viewing could be justified in principle. But here, too, remains the difficulty of the absence of any reliable yardstick to apportion the overall harm (Keren-Paz and Wright, 2019: 226; Keren-Paz, 2013: 234). What is clear, is that the typical NCII case does not involve an initial abuse but nevertheless the typical harms are significant and similar in nature to the harms from child pornography in the sense that they too are on the spectrum of sexual abuse (Chapter 6, Part 2.B). This means that courts in child pornography cases should not overly discount damages based on the erroneous assumption that a big part of the harm is accounted for by the initial abuse. After all, to begin with, an apportionment is a deviation from the traditional rule of joint and several liability for indivisible harm, and the viewing is not clearly unconnected with the producer's breach of duty. Finally, whatever one's view is on the scope of liability for the initial abuse, this will seldom have bearing on NCII cases beyond child pornography. In these cases, typically, the underlying activity depicted in the image does not involve abuse, so no question arises as to the scope of viewers' liability to the initial abuse, which did not occur.

The liability of possessors of child pornography for the initial abuse could possibly be based on the connection between viewing such images (the demand) and the production of the images which often involves an initial abuse. Doctrinally, this could be either captured as a form of acting in concert – an issue that was largely discussed in Part 2 – or as a form of primary liability, captured by either *Privacy* or negligence. Since a demand-based theory is related to another potential extension – to the trafficking of images of *other* victims – I will deal with it in the next part.

5. Demand-based liability? Three potential extensions

A demand-based theory attempts to hold a defendant to account for indirect harms his behaviour contributed to. While the direct harm was caused by

---

[38] *Paroline* (n1) 439–40, 482–3.

other tortfeasors, the defendant's responsibility is founded on the fact that his own breach of duty caused (in the sense of contributed to) the more direct violation of the victim's rights by third parties. Understood this way, it is easy to see the similarity with the concept of joint tortfeasorship, either as tortfeasors acting in concert, or as the defendant encouraging, and in this sense assisting, the principal tortfeasor.

In Keren-Paz (2013), in the context of sex trafficking, I developed a theory of liability for creation of demand: by posing indiscriminate demand into a market, part of whose supply chains involve women forced into prostitution, the buyers contribute, factually and legally, to these women being trafficked.[39] The demand is indiscriminate in the sense the buyer of commercial sex cannot sort out those forced into prostitution from those who are not. At least if the proportion of those forced is significant enough, such posing of demand should lead to liability. Such liability is not based on notions of accessory liability. Rather, it is based on the tort of negligence. For reasons I explained there, there should be a duty of care, the posing of demand could be considered as a breach of duty, and it was a factual and a legal cause of the injury. The theory has three unique features, one posing a threat of indeterminate liability and two alleviating this fear. The first feature is that a true liability for demand does not entail a direct contact between the victim of sex trafficking and the client. Had the client bought sexual services from the claimant, he could have been liable directly for battery (and as I argue more controversially, in conversion as well [Keren-Paz, 2013: chapter 5]). Nor does the client need to have bought sexual services from any victim. It is sufficient that his (anticipated) purchasing activity contributed to the victim being recruited, sent to the place in which he placed his demand and continuingly being abused there, even if he did not happen to buy sexual services from the claimant (or any other victim).

This poses a challenge of indeterminate liability. What is the relevant market in which the defendant's demand contributed to the claimant having been trafficked? Under certain conditions, the demand in Berlin might have contributed to recruitment of a victim in Moscow and to her exploitation in London, if the trafficker was operating based on a 'general demand' business model. Traffickers might work under either a general demand model or a specific demand model. Under the former, recruitment of victims is done prior to decisions where to exploit them, and based on demand in all potential markets; at a later stage the victim is sent to a site of exploitation based on market research. Therefore, even demand from places in which the victim was not exploited contributes to the victim's trafficking (and if,

---

[39] The discussion in this paragraph (very) briefly summarises Chapters 6 (duty), 7 (breach) and 8 (causation).

contrary to my view, the injury from recruitment and from exploitation could be separated, clients posing demand in places in which the victim was not exploited are also an overdetermined cause of the recruitment). Under a specific demand model, the trafficker responds only to specific market(s) so demand in other markets could not be a cause for either recruitment or exploitation (Keren-Paz, 2013: 205–207).

For reasons I explain in *Sex-Trafficking*, a defeasible and practical solution would be to limit liability in two ways, which are the two other features of the theory. One limitation is spatial and temporal: a defendant would be liable only to victims exploited in the same city(s) in which he bought sexual services in a period ending when the victim's exploitation has ended and starting at the equally long period before recruitment (so if the victim was exploited for six months since recruitment, purchases of sex beginning six months prior to recruitment and ending at the time the exploitation ended would be considered causative). The other limitation has to do with quantum. As the trafficking is the result of demand by thousands, if not millions of people, whose contribution is indirect, and as the theory might lead to liability to numerous victims (even with the spatial and temporal limitations) liability should not be full. But for reasons explained earlier, it should also not be (and cannot be) purely proportionate. In *Sex-Trafficking* I have offered a benchmark of around 4% of the victim's entire damages (Keren-Paz, 2013: 239). In Section A I will examine the applicability of the theory to viewers (1) who viewed the claimant's images – for the initial abuse (under the assumption that this harm could be disaggregated from the harm from viewing); and in Section B to viewers (2) who viewed images of other victims, but not the claimant's, for the claimant's initial abuse; and (3) who viewed images of other victims, but not the claimant's, for the circulation of the images. For each category I will distinguish between the questions 'should such liability exist?' and 'is the holding in *Paroline* compatible with such liability?'.

A. Viewers of claimant: initial abuse

Whether viewers *should* be responsible also for the harm from the initial abuse of their victim (the normative question) depends on answering the factual question whether demand for child pornography causes production.[40]

---

[40] Two caveats are in order. First, resolving the factual controversy is normatively relevant only if the harms from initial abuse and circulation are divisible. Second, the move from factual contribution to (even partial) legal responsibility for the harm is not automatic. But the detailed discussion in *Sex-Trafficking* is applicable here, so to avoid repetition I examine here the extent to which there are differences between the context of sex trafficking and

The evidence is inconclusive. A snapshot of US prosecution of production published in 2012, based mainly on 2010 data, found that about two thirds of producers produced solely for the purposes of self-possession (US Sentencing Commission, 2012: 265). The abuse documented in these images was not, therefore, the result of demand for such images, so a demand-based theory cannot justify viewers' liability for the victim's harm from the initial abuse. Even under Sotomayor's expansive account in *Paroline*, it seems impossible to justify liability when the abuse was not done for the purpose of distributing child pornography, even if it was documented at the time. From a normative perspective, the violation of the right was not done in order to cater to the demand for child pornography, and under our assumption would have occurred even had such demand not existed. From a doctrinal perspective, the viewer can no longer be considered as joint tortfeasor with the abuser, since the viewer and the abuser did not 'act together, with the common end of trafficking in the market for images of child sexual abuse',[41] nor could that harm be even a remote consequence of the viewer's breach of duty, be it invasion (by intrusion) of privacy, or (by analogy with sex trafficking) negligence (Keren-Paz, 2013: chapters 6–8).

But this leaves one third of producers, whose production was at least partially motivated by the demand of others; as Dillof (2017) observes, it may be assumed that the volume of images produced for distribution purposes is bigger than that of self-possessed production; if correct, this means that demand is responsible for more than one third of the material produced in that particular snapshot. Similarly, there is evidence that at least some child pornography offenders produce new child pornography in order to gain access to other child pornography images (US Sentencing Commission, 2012: 96). Viewers of images produced for distribution (but not of images produced solely for self-possession) contributed to the initial abuse so should be liable to part of it. I can see no convincing reason why this should not be left to individual litigation over the point whether the material was produced for distribution or not. This leaves an important policy decision, which I will not attempt to resolve here, who should bear the burden of proof as to whether the production of the particular image was for distribution or not. Even if the burden should remain with the claimant, there would still be cases in which it will be known (due, for example, to a finding of a court convicting a producer) that the image was produced for distribution.

A significant (and probably increasing) proportion of possessors access child pornography through P2P file-sharing sites in which 'individuals

---

child pornography that could justify a different conclusion to those, like myself, who believe that demand-based theory is justified in the context of sex trafficking.

[41] *Paroline* (n1) 479 (Justice Sotomayor, dissenting).

... may be wholly unaware when their data is being accessed' (Dillof, 2017: 1341, 1354). Dillof views this fact as one reason (alongside other, less convincing) to doubt the cogency of market-based harms caused by possession given the absence of a signal about 'the existence of a demand for the production of new child pornography'.[42] However, what matters is that a certain abuse occurred in order (also) to satisfy demand, not that current patters of downstream distribution might or might not contribute to future production with its associated abuse.[43] Therefore, for a successful claim against a viewer for the harm from production it should be sufficient to show that the defendant viewed an image that was produced for distribution, so the fact the image was accessed in a discreet way is immaterial. Similarly, the fact that the distribution of child pornography is in the main (similar to production) not commercially motivated (US Sentencing Commission, 2012: 98–9; Dillof, 2017: 1341), is normatively immaterial. What matters is whether the production and the abuse were done in order to meet demand, not whether the producer or distributor acted out of a profit motive.

Moving to the prediction question, *Paroline* provides some conflicting indications of whether viewers could be liable for the initial abuse. It is fair to say that, at most, the decision might be compatible with a demand-based theory, although this too could be doubted. As was indicated earlier, the suggestion that the harm from the initial abuse should be disaggregated from the harm from viewing indicates that the demand-based theory is rejected. On the other hand, the court stated: 'The demand for child pornography harms children in part because it drives production, which involves child abuse.' Moreover, during oral argument, Justice Breyer suggested that a viewer of images of a victim *other than* Amy 'contributed to her [injuries and losses], too, because it created a market for the entire situation'.[44] This suggests that an extension of liability, to the victim's harms from production

---

[42] Dillof's (2017: 1372) subsequent conclusion that possessors' liability for victims' aggregate harm is justified by rule consequentialism, is similar to my conclusion in this and previous work; more importantly, it significantly qualifies his previous critique of the market-based justification for punishing possession of child pornography.

[43] See Keren-Paz (2013: 208–9, 214–15, 223–5) discussing the temporal difficulties in establishing causation under a demand-based theory, concluding that there could be liability for a harm part of which happened before the defendant's conduct took place. Dillof (2017: 1360) is of the view that '[A]s the term "cause" is generally used, conduct cannot have caused harm that was suffered before the conduct occurred.' In the sex trafficking context, the contribution of demand to the initial exploitation also depends on the traffickers' business model: whether it caters to general, or specific demand(Keren-Paz, 2013: 205–7).

[44] *Paroline* (n1) 439–40; Transcript of Oral Argument, *Paroline v United States*, 572 US 434 (2014) (No 12-8561) at 44–5.

is at least compatible with the court's view; and that the further extension towards victims whose images were not viewed by the defendant might be compatible at least with Justice Breyer's view, and is, of course compatible with Justice Sotomayor's dissent who seemed to adopt a theory of liability based on conspiracy (concerted action).

B. Viewers of other victims: claimant's initial abuse and circulation of images

It is unclear whether the court's analysis in *Paroline* could support liability to a victim for her harm from the initial abuse by those viewing images of other children. If taken seriously, the observation that '[T]he demand ... drives production, which involves child abuse'[45] cannot support a distinction between a viewer of Amy's photos and a viewer of other children as the producer responds to potential viewers, rather than actual ones; Justice Breyer acknowledged this point in oral argument. At the same time, there is nothing in the majority's analysis that explicitly suggests their willingness to impose liability on viewers who did not upload Amy's images; and of course, the holding (*ratio decidendi*) is limited to actual viewers of Amy's images. Moreover, the court's concern with avoiding disproportionate liability[46] might serve as a weak indication that the court would not adopt a demand-based theory against viewers of other victim's images. So while a demand-based liability is still compatible with the holding, and some of the rhetoric, there is no clear or strong indication that the court would recognize it in the future.

There are good reasons not to extend demand-based liability to those who viewed images of other victims for a claimant's harms from both the initial abuse and circulation of images. The reason, in my opinion, does not have to do with the fact that some production was not motivated by the prospect of distribution. As I have argued in the previous section, this is a factual question, so liability could be imposed for production which was (at least partially) motivated by distribution. Rather, the context of child pornography lacks the temporal and spatial built-in limitations that exist in the context of sex trafficking and without which liability is indeterminate and overly broad.

The *prima facie* case for demand-based theory is that in all cases in which production was motivated by distribution, the overall demand for viewing such images, rather than the demand for viewing the claimant's images contributed to both the initial abuse and to the distribution of the images.

---

[45] *Paroline* (n1) 339–40.
[46] *Paroline* (n1) 461.

By viewing other victims' images, the defendant contributed to the claimant's injury from both the initial abuse and the knowledge that her images are circulating. The client buying commercial sex and the viewer of child pornography are similar. The former contributes to the claimant's initial abuse and to her exploitation by others at the site of exploitation even though he did not buy sexual services from the claimant. His contribution is manifested in purchasing sexual services in the site and at the same time the victim was sexually exploited. Similarly, the latter contributes to the claimant's initial abuse and the viewing of her images by others, even though he did not possess, or otherwise viewed Amy's images. His contribution is manifested in downloading images of other victims within the relevant temporal and geographical boundaries. After all, producers of child pornography intent on distributing the images are not likely to know who will view what images, and are likely to work under a general (rather than specific) demand model. This means that in *Paroline*, Amy's abuse was as triggered by those who ended up downloading images of victims other than Amy than those who downloaded Amy's. Logically, once one is willing to go down the road of demand-based liability, it makes little sense to distinguish between viewers based on whether they viewed the specific victim's image, or images of other victims.

Accepting a demand-based theory in the context of child pornography would require the court to come up with temporal and geographical limitations. The constraints suggested in the context of sex trafficking (summarized in the introduction to Part 5) would not necessarily be fitting to the context of child pornography. In terms of spatial limitation, a useful cutting point of liability in the sex trafficking context – to those consuming sex in the city (or cities) in which the victim of trafficking was exploited – is unworkable here. The victim of child pornography is not trafficked, rather her image is, and this image can be viewed simultaneously at very distant destinations. Without an alternative test, any viewer of child pornography around the world should be liable (and on Sotomayor's account, in full) to *all* victims of distribution-motivated production of child pornography *around the world*, for their pecuniary loss (under criminal restitution) from both the initial abuse and the knowledge of the viewing of their images, or if the claim is for invasion of privacy for whatever losses which are compensable under the tort (and which include at least non-pecuniary dignitary losses). This cannot be right.

Similarly, the temporal limitation offered in *Sex-Trafficking* – viewing in the duration of the victim's exploitation (from recruitment until the ordeal is over) and the equally long period preceding the victim's recruitment – is unworkable either. The period in which the victim was abused in order to produce the images might be short, but the images might be circulating for a very long period. So how long after the victim's abuse (and one might ask also how long before) should someone who viewed child pornography containing images of other victims be liable to the claimant?

As this discussion suggests, one might conclude, as I do, that even if one were to accept demand-based theory in the context of sex trafficking, one should resist it in the context of child pornography, since only in the former context one can come up with workable ways to curtail indeterminate liability. Alternatively, supporters of importing demand-base liability from the context of sex trafficking (which is yet to be accepted) to that of child pornography should come up with alternative tests that could limit liability in a way which is both practical and sufficiently principled. I would not attempt to sketch such a test here and will offer only the following observation. Recall that in *Paroline*, viewing Amy's images was considered damaging because of her fear that she would be recognized and therefore humiliated; and because each viewing of the images re-enacts the crime.[47] These accounts also feature in the literature on harms from child pornography (Gewirtz-Myedan et al, 2018) and are similar to victims of other forms of NCII (Cyber Civil Rights Initiative, 2014; Davidson et al, 2019; Sharratt, 2019). The former account can form a basis of a more tailored test: for example, only defendants who are likely to recognize Amy could be considered as the legal cause of her damage. This would leave courts wide discretion in deciding (possibly based on presumptions) which defendants are unlikely to recognize Amy (for example, from other countries, from certain countries, from certain regions in the US and so on). Whatever the merits of such an approach, it is in tension with basing viewers' liability on their contribution to the initial abuse: the demand by viewers unlikely to recognize Amy was as causative to her abuse as the demand by those likely to recognize her.

Both accounts, but the latter more so, raise epistemic difficulties. If the claim's essence is about the fear from being recognized, is the relevant number of viewers who could be the proximate cause of Amy's losses the actual number of potential defendants who could recognize Amy or the number imagined or estimated by Amy? As to the second account, would Amy's humiliation be renewed anytime someone views her images or anytime Amy estimates or imagines someone views them? And is it correct to assume that the humiliation from knowledge that someone views the initial abuse, or takes pleasure from its occurrence is equal to the humiliation felt when the abuse itself took place, as both Amy and the court's rhetoric suggest in adopting the 'crime re-enacted' metaphor?

Thus far, the discussion was based on the assumption that producers of child pornography adhere to a general-demand model, under which they are indiscriminating as to the demand to which they respond in producing

---

[47] Chapter 6, n1.

the images. Academic research, and law enforcement reports do not provide a strong support for the existence of specific demand model of production (Jenkins, 2001; Taylor and Quayle, 2003; Quayle et al, 2006; Fortin, 2011; US Sentencing Commission, 2012; Hessick, 2016; Dillof, 2017). The evidence closest to a specific–demand model is production in order to gain access to images in the particular child pornography community of which the defendant was a member (US Sentencing Commission, 2012: 96). In such cases, arguably, the production catered for demand from all other members of such community but not viewers outside of this community. In such a case, the contribution to the initial abuse is by all members of this community, who are the *potential* viewers of the images, rather than by those who actually viewed the images. Even here, several complications exist. First, the temporal aspect; how far back, before the production, and how far ahead, after the production, would membership in the community trigger liability? The temporal limitation developed in the context of sex trafficking is still inapplicable here. Second, what about harm from knowledge that the image is circulating? Surely, the victim has a reason to fear that members in the community to which the images were distributed would view them. Is this a sufficient reason to hold them liable to the harm from circulation even though they did not happen to view the claimant's images? Finally, research suggests that most members of the relevant communities are inactive in terms of uploading images, or encouraging others to do so (Jenkins, 2001; Fortin, 2011); should they be liable for images they did not view, or should they be considered similar enough to viewers of other victims under a general-demand production model, who should not be liable to the claimant? For all of these reasons, it might be better, on balance, to limit liability in such cases to defendants who viewed the images, rather than cast the net too broadly through a demand-based theory. Such a theory requires dealing with evidentiary and conceptual difficulties regarding scope of liability, remoteness and control mechanism, and, within the private law realm, an expansive (and controversial) use of the torts of privacy or negligence. This conclusion is bolstered, given that the viewers who prompted the producer to produce the images are likely to be liable for the initial abuse and the circulation of the images also as joint tortfeasors who acted in concert by encouraging the production and distribution of the images.

9

Viewers' Liability: Intention and Objective Fault

1. Introduction

One conclusion from the previous chapter is that the viewing of child pornography is a breach of privacy which ought to be captured as such by the relevant privacy torts, is likely to be so captured by the English privacy version and could be captured – albeit with some stretching – by the intrusion tort common in US jurisdictions. Since what makes such viewing a breach of privacy has very little (if anything) to do with the underlying abuse, the same conclusion must be true at least for the intentional viewing of NCII. Part 2 will defend this view with reference to case studies in which viewers look for NCII, while also commenting on the budding policy discussion of whether to criminalize the intentional possession of NCII. Beyond this category questions arise as to (1) whether viewers who took a risk that they might come across NCII should be liable (Part 3) and (2) whether liability for this breach of privacy should be and is strict (Chapter 10). In deciding the former, the degree of risk of undermining the claimant's privacy interests caused by the viewer's behaviour is paramount. The analysis will draw on anecdotal data about the ways NCII are shared and viewed. While comprehensive data on this issue is missing (Henry and Powell, 2018: 202), civil litigation, in the main, does not require this data; rather, the individual behaviour of the defendant-viewer will be sufficient to decide whether liability could be imposed and based on what theory of liability or cause of action; such individual behaviour will often be verifiable to courts.

2. Intentional viewing

Anecdotal evidence abounds that some viewers search for intimate images that were disseminated without the subject's consent. Presumably, the mere fact that the images are disseminated without consent are either a sexual turn-on in itself – a modern variation on the observation in Proverbs 9:17 that '[S]tolen waters are sweet' – or an outlet to misogynistic predilections, so that viewers can revile in the humiliation caused to victims from this indignity (Holten, 2020). Danish activist Emma Holten highlights how the knowledge that her images were non-consensual and her own humiliation were a turn-on for many men who subsequently communicated with her:

> These messages were from men all over the world. Teen boys, university students, nuclear-family dads. The only thing they had in common was that they were all men. They knew it was against my will, that I didn't want to be on those sites. The realisation that my humiliation turned them on felt like a noose around my neck. The absence of consent was erotic, they relished my suffering. It's one thing to be sexualised by people who are attracted to you, but it's quite another thing when the lack of a 'you', when dehumanization, is the main factor.

Holten included in 'Consent' consensual intimate images of herself to both reclaim herself as a sexual subject and to prove that viewers' interest in the initial images was not about nudity but rather about public humiliation, power and control (Dori, 2018). But whatever viewers' motives are, the evidence is robust. First, there are dedicated revenge porn websites.[1] Uhl et al (2018) examined seven non-consensual pornography websites. Some were 'located by utilizing relevant search words on various search engines … [including] "revenge porn," "nude ex," "nude photos of my ex," "places to share nude photos of my ex"'. There is little doubt that the vast majority of those visiting these websites, let alone, after they searched for them, do it with the knowledge that the images included in the websites breach the privacy of those depicted there. Curiously, Uhl et al (2018: 60) mention indications that some images (3%) were posted by the subjects themselves, so are presumably consensual and lawful. But this can mean, at most, that those posting consensually their images in these websites cannot sue viewers of these images; it does not detract from the cause of action of claimants whose images were not distributed consensually. Even if the existence of non-intrusive images on revenge porn websites is known to the average visitor of such websites, which I doubt, inevitably (and by balance of probabilities, also advertently) entering such websites involves viewing images and invading the privacy of those who did not consent (the overwhelming

---

[1] Citron (2019: 1918–19) mentions that in one case the ex-boyfriend posted the victim's photos and videos 'on hundreds of revenge-porn sites' (and also, on porn sites, and adult-finder sites; he also sent her nude photos to her boss).

majority).[2] In addition to dedicated websites, some private online forums are dedicated to NCII such as sharing up-skirt videos, one of which included 4,300 individual threads in a section dedicated to up-skirt videos (Cox, 2018). Citron (2019: 1918) mentions how the intimate images of a woman were uploaded by her boyfriend to a Facebook page called 'Dog Pound,' where members of his fraternity posted videos and images of sexual 'conquests'; and Holten, 2020 mentions 'creepshots': a global phenomenon that entails photographing women without their knowledge or consent, in order to share them in a sexual context online (see also Oliver, 2016). In these examples, viewers have knowledge that the images intrude on the subject's privacy.

As argued in Chapter 8, the viewing of an intimate image is intrusive in itself; so even if liability for breach of privacy requires intention, it should be established for such viewers. This is so, even if – and this is *not* likely to be the case, as explained in Chapter 10 – intention includes subjective awareness that the viewing amounts to a breach of privacy, or is without the subject's consent. Such liability hinges on the viewing itself and not on any further dissemination (sharing) of the image, posting comments on the images which might be considered as defamatory or harassing (Uhl et al, 2018: 60), or any follow-up behaviour that might include stalking or harassment. Similarly, such liability does not hinge on any theory of liability for creation of demand, that is, that the viewing contributed to the initial production or dissemination of the image, which is in itself a breach of duty.

Currently, there is only limited policy and activism push in the direction of holding even culpable viewers of intimate images to account. I have already mentioned that Jennifer Lawrence, perhaps the most famous NCII victim in recent times, likened the viewing of these images to committing a sexual offence; similar sentiments of viewing as violation are commonly expressed by victims (Moore, 2014). The understanding that each viewing is in itself intrusive was clearly endorsed in *Douglas v Hello! (No 3)*.[3] But whether viewers themselves ought to be criminally responsible, or civilly liable for their intrusion, and if so, under what conditions and for how much is hardly discussed. Commentary following Lawrence's NCII tends to doubt or deny the criminal responsibility of viewers, or to view such behaviour as ethically wrong[4] but probably lawful (Steinberg, 2014; Valenti, 2014; Marwick, 2017). A good example is Mackie (2014): 'Thousands of people saw the Jennifer Lawrence pictures. Are they criminally liable? Making,

---

[2]   For some evidentiary difficulties and how to resolve them see Chapter 12, Part 2.

[3]   [2005] EWCA Civ 595.

[4]   See also the academic discussion of the ethics of viewing people suffering (for example, Chouliaraki, 2006). But this deals with a slightly different question as the viewing might not itself be a breach of privacy.

possessing and distributing indecent images of children is prohibited, but accessing pictures of naked adults even doing what adults do is perfectly lawful – unless caught by the offence of voyeurism.' Even Rape, Abuse and International Network (RAINN) stated they are unsure whether viewing would meet the legal definition of sexual assault (Alter, 2014). Similarly, both Danielle Citron and Mary Franks, two leading US academic researchers of NCII, would not go as far as criminalizing viewing (but only distributing), although they are well aware of the harm caused to NCII victims from viewing (Citron and Franks, 2014; Citron 2016; Franks, 2017). Franks in particular makes the comparison with child pornography, only to support criminalizing distribution, not possession (or viewing) itself (Marshall, 2014):

> Everybody was shamelessly passing these celebrity photos around until [gymnast] McKayla Maroney announced that she was underage in her pictures. Suddenly that's child porn. You can go to jail just for looking at child porn, let alone distributing it, so people quit posting her images. If we had a federal criminal law in place that said every time you disclose these images it's a crime, then I think a lot fewer people would have been disclosing them.

From the criminal side of things, the Law Commission Consultation Paper mentions that only three jurisdictions currently criminalize possession of intimate images – New Zealand, Singapore and Tasmania – with only the latter possibly criminalizing possessing an image that was taken with the subject's consent but disseminated without it. The paper provisionally proposes 'that it should not be an offence to possess an intimate image without consent, even when there was never any consent to possession' (Law Commission, 2021: 191–3, 200). While in my response to the consultation I disagreed – when the mental element is satisfied a criminal response is justified for similar reasons that civil liability is – the consultation paper is to be commended for bringing the possibility of viewers' liability into the policy horizon. In their final report (Law Commission, 2022: 169–71) the Law Commission acknowledged they 'understand the strength of argument, and feeling, for criminalising such possession' and while they stick with their initial position and recommend that possession not be criminalized, they qualify that 'Should Parliament choose to criminalize some possession of intimate images without consent, we would recommend that it be limited to cases where there was never any consent to possession.' If other areas of gender-based harms (such as sex trafficking) are any indication, civil liability of perpetrators and even more so, of peripheral parties or enablers, is possible only after their criminal responsibility was established (Keren-Paz, 2013).

Several jurisdictions impose civil liability for NCII, usually as part of *sui generis* legislation that focuses on criminalizing such behaviour;

a non-exhaustive list includes Manitoba, Alberta, Saskatchewan, Nova Scotia, Florida, Texas, North Carolina, Israel and New Zealand.[5] Liability in such statutory torts is almost without exception limited to those disclosing, disseminating or distributing the images. A possible exception is North Carolina whose relevant civil liability provision affords 'any person whose image is disclosed, or used, as described in subsection (b) ... a civil cause of action against any person who discloses or uses the image'.[6] The statute does not define 'use' and uses the term only in the civil liability sub-section which leaves room for the interpretation that this is a deliberate decision to hold viewers who use but do not disclose the image only civilly liable but not criminally responsible. The referred to subsection (b) deals only with disclosure (not use). The civil liability provision is silent on the issue of the mental element, so it is unclear whether the mental element required for criminal conviction is required for civil liability of 'users'.[7]

S6(2) of Nova Scotia's 2017 Unauthorized Distribution of Intimate Images Act is also worth mentioning. While the Act targets distributors, the 'Court may order any person' 'perform such other action as the Court considers just and reasonable', which presumably could apply to viewers to cease possession of such images, 'take down or disable access to an intimate image or cyber-bullying communication' which presumably has mainly hosts in mind, but could perhaps be applied to viewers if take down could be interpreted as including ceasing to possess an image.

3. Risk taking and objective fault

NCII might be posted on general porn sites (not dedicated for non-consensual images), commercial sex sites and adult-finder sites (Dori, 2018; La, 2018; Citron, 2019: 1917–19). Indeed, two of the main porn websites – Pornhub and YouPorn, owned by the same company – set up a dedicated removal request page and YouPorn also co-created, with the Danish Women's Society, an anti-revenge porn awareness-raising video titled 'Ex-girlfriend doesn't know that I shared this!' as part of a new #AskFirst campaign to curb revenge porn (La, 2018). To the extent that porn sites include sub-sections or specific titles indicating that the images are not consensual – as the title discussed – the situation is not really different from that discussed in the

---

[5]   See, for example, *Intimate Images and Cyber-protection Act*, SNS 2017, c. 7 (Nova Scotia).

[6]   G.S. § 14-190.5A. Disclosure of private images. S.L. 2015-250 (North Carolina).

[7]   Indiana's statute imposes liability on those who 'create or obtain' the image; however, it seems that in addition, the defendant needs to disclose the image and to do so with the required mental element. See Indiana Code § 34-21.5-3-1.

previous part. But here I am interested in the consumer of porn who does not have any specific indication that the video or photo he is going to view was posted without consent. If he did view an NCII should he be liable for breach of the subject's privacy?

Two theories could support liability. One, that liability for intrusion of privacy ought to include the taking of unreasonable risk that the defendant's behaviour will intrude on the claimant's privacy. On this theory, surfing porn websites with the ability to know that the incidence of NCII is high enough and that NCII are likely to feature on these websites unduly risks intrusion of the victim's privacy. The other theory is demand-based: that the demand for porn is one driver for the circulation of NCII. If this is true, the viewer is contributing to the initial unlawful dissemination of the images, by this breaching the victim's interest in privacy, regardless of whether the *actual* viewing of the image by the viewer is an independent breach of privacy. Both theories have some resemblance with the theory for clients' liability I developed in the context of sex trafficking (Keren-Paz, 2013). Let me now examine each in detail.

A. Excessive risk of intrusion

On the understanding – examined in Chapter 10 and similar to other intentional torts – that the relevant intention is to view, rather than to view illicit images, any active search for images (or information) that intrudes on the claimant's privacy should lead to liability (in the absence of a relevant defence), however reasonable the search is. So with the exception of passive defendants who inadvertently receive intimate images, intentional viewers are liable regardless of absence of fault. But the position of those looking for intimate images is different as they more clearly took the risk that these images include NCII; depending on how big and how foreseeable the risk is, their behaviour might be unreasonable, and such fault might support liability, even if a stricter form of liability for viewing NCII is deemed too harsh. The analysis needs to distinguish the normative question, that has to do with ethics and morality, from the doctrinal question. The former has to do with deciding (1) whether objective fault should lead to liability, and if so, (2) what level of risk-taking justifies liability; the latter, with the questions (3) is objective fault relevant to breach of privacy determinations; and (4) if not, can liability be imposed in negligence?

1. The normative relevance of objective fault

In a context in which some intimate images are consensual and others are not, searching for intimate images runs the risk of intruding upon the privacy interests of those whose images are distributed non-consensually. The higher the percentage of NCII among all intimate images (or all images, for that matter) the higher the likelihood that an intrusion will occur. One in a million seems a very low risk; 80% is exceedingly high. I would imagine that few people would quarrel with the intuition that a very high percentage of non-consensual material in a given database would justify liability for an intrusion of those whose images were distributed non-consensually and viewed by the defendant, at least if the defendant was aware or ought to have known about the significance of the risk. When the known risk is very high it amounts to subjective recklessness – lack of care whether the specific image viewed is distributed consensually or not – thus satisfying traditional notions of intention.[8] Moreover, under the reasonable assumption that each consumer of porn views multiple intimate images, the chances that he would intrude on a victim's privacy significantly increases. For example, even if the proportion of non-consensual images among all those in a certain porn site is merely 3%, a viewer watching 50 images has roughly 79% chance of viewing one or more non-consensual image(s) (so only 21% chance of not watching any NCII); viewing 100 images increases the chance of viewing one or more NCII to 92%.[9] Such a viewer took a course of action involving high risk he would intrude on someone's privacy, so if he did – if some of the images he viewed were non-consensual – he cannot really complain of being held to account. Even when the percentage of NCII among all images is merely 0.5%, a viewer viewing 100 images stands a nearly 40% chance of viewing NCII.

When the case for liability for invasion of privacy is understood as a matter of excessive risk-taking, it is easy to understand why visiting non-pornographic websites merits a different conclusion. In such websites, occasionally, an intimate image would be available. But the proportion of NCII to all images (or content) available on these websites is so low, that it could not support liability hinging on excessive risk taking. And whatever the merits of strict liability for viewing NCII are, a fault-based theory has to take into account the social value of the regulated activity, so cannot plausibly support the claim that the risk from breaching one's privacy if their image is distributed on a general content website outweighs the benefits of surfing the internet.[10]

---

[8] See, in general, *Three Rivers D.C. v Bank of England* (No 3) [2003] 2 AC 1, [193].

[9] When the proportion of NCII is 5% the chances of viewing at least one NCII or more are around 95% (50 views) and 99.4% (100 views). I used a binomial model for these calculations.

[10] For the considerations in determining fault in the (slightly different) context of a demand for commercial sex see Keren-Paz (2013: chapter 7).

2. How much (risk) is too much?

Reliable data on the percentage of NCII among all images on porn websites is not readily available. We saw earlier that even repeated viewing of images in a database containing as little as 0.5% of NCII involves a significant risk of breaching one's privacy. But whether the percentage of NCII is above or beyond this figure is anyone's guess. The official figures of requests for removal are miniscule in comparison to the overall content: Pornhub's transparency report (2020) mentions 1,081 legal removal requests for content which is either child pornography or non-consensual (in comparison to 650,862 copyright related removals), while the number of videos on the platform at the end of December 2020 ranged between 13 to 4 million. The difference in numbers was due to removal of content from unverified users, following a *New York Times* report revealing a number of inappropriate and illegal videos, including some involving minors. The revelation caused credit companies Visa and Mastercard to cut ties with the company and all related websites (Kristof, 2020; Paul, 2020). Following a subsequent *New Yorker* investigation, finding that pornographic videos of women and girls posted without their consent remained on the site for years, ignoring removal requests, Pornhub's CEO and COO resigned (Bushard, 2022). The Internet Watch Foundation reported only 118 instances of child sexual abuse imagery on Pornhub over almost three years, while, according to Pornhub's transparency report, Pornhub reported 4,171 videos of child sexual abuse to the National Center for Missing and Exploited Children (NCMEC): 'many of these instances were caught by our moderation practices before the content became available for the public'. However, according to the *New York Times* investigation 'if you know what to look for, it's possible to find hundreds of apparent child sexual abuse videos on Pornhub in 30 minutes. Pornhub has recently offered playlists with names including "less than 18," "the best collection of young boys" and "under-age,"'. The investigator 'came across many videos on Pornhub that were recordings of assaults on unconscious women and girls. The rapists would open the eyelids of the victims and touch their eyeballs to show that they were nonresponsive'.

> Pornhub profited this fall from a video of a naked woman being tortured by a gang of men in China. It is monetizing video compilations with titles like 'Screaming Teen,' 'Degraded Teen' and 'Extreme Choking.' Look at a choking video and it may suggest also searching for 'She Can't Breathe.'

'I asked the [NCMEC] ... the number of images, videos and other content related to child sexual exploitation reported to it ... In 2015, it received reports of 6.5 million videos or other files; in 2017, 20.6 million; and in 2019, 69.2 million' (Kristof, 2020).

It is worth bearing in mind the following observations. First, the transparency report – Pornhub's first – does not distinguish between child pornography and NCII, but includes more data on the former. Second, there are reasons to believe that removal requests pertain to only the tip of the iceberg of NCII. Such requests are likely to be made mainly by victims, and many will not be aware that their images appear on Pornhub (Isaacs, 2019). Moreover, unlike child pornography which is relatively easy to detect (with the complication discussed later of young adults role-playing as minors) many uploads of neutral intimate images – those not giving rise to a suspicion that they were disseminated without consent – might in fact be NCII. Pornhub did not configure any way to ensure that those depicted in the images are all consenting adults and has a financial incentive to collude with NCII uploads. The limited data on the prevalence of NCII suggests that the incidence is rather high – 2% of online Americans have had someone actually post an intimate photo of them online without their permission, according to the most reliable study using a nationally representative telephone survey (Data & Society Research Institute, 2016: 4.7)[11] – so it would be surprising if many of those images did not find their way to mainstream porn sites. Third, the gap between the number of removals for alleged copyright infringement and for suspected child pornography or NCII is very significant and surprising, suggesting that we have reasons to doubt Pornhub's official figures. This suspicion is bolstered by the incredible gap between the removals of suspected child pornography on other platforms such as Facebook in comparison to Pornhub (Kristof, 2020). Both the titles of playlists and the evidence of videos depicting unconscious women suggest that the true incidence of NCII (and child pornography) is much higher than is suggested by the removal requests statistics. Indeed, following the *New York Times* report, the two major credit card providers refused to allow payment on Pornhub (leading it to delete content from unverified users, amounting to the majority of content). This amounts to a private judgement that the content on Pornhub – at least as existed prior to the clean-up – was too problematic to consume, which is, I submit, the rough equivalent of a judicial finding that the risk in infringing victim's privacy by viewing images on Pornhub is too high.

Fourth, as the *New York Times'* report clarifies, NCII encompasses not only the non-consensual distribution of consensual intimate activity but also depiction of coerced or non-consensual sexual contact. The assumption that the vast majority of pornographic materials is produced and distributed

---

[11] This, of course, is different from a finding that 2% of all images in a given dataset are non-consensual.

consensually is disputed by anti-porn groups, some of whom are feminist (mainly of the abolitionist strand associated mainly with radical feminism) (Dworkin, 1981; Fight the New Drug, 2020a). The more the production (and distribution) of porn is non-consensual (as in the case of having sex with an unconscious woman) or even coercive – be it commercially produced or amateur – the higher the proportion of privacy-invading images among all images is so the fault-based case for liability strengthens. Relatedly, the more problematic the porn industry is, the less socially valuable is free access to it (or put differently, the less strong is the freedom of expression argument opposing liability for viewing NCII, based on a chilling effect on the porn industry) so the case against liability for viewing NCII based on public interest weakens.

Fifth, any attempt to figure the percentage of NCII, and in particular, those depicting non-consensual sexual contact or intimate images of minors is rendered even more difficult due to the existence of fantasy and role-playing. For example, commercial videos and streams dedicated to teens or to age play must employ young adults and at least disclaim that they do so.[12] Similarly, BDSM (bondage, discipline, sadism and masochism) streams are supposed to depict consensual behaviour and videos depicting rape are hopefully mostly staged (Carotte et al, 2020). While the *New York Times* report does not treat all results of searches looking for minors or violence as truly non-consensual and refers to anecdotes of real abuse, it does not provide any indication of the incidence of NCII. It also mentions correctly the gap between Pornhub's terms and conditions prohibiting the depiction of rape, and the proliferation of such videos on its website. Pornhub are quick to exploit the gap between the real and the imagined by qualifying in their transparency report the no-rape-depiction policy by saying 'Our moderation team carefully evaluates content in order to determine whether what some may consider to be "extreme" fantasies actually violate our Terms of Service and Related Guidelines, or pose a real threat or likelihood of causing serious distress or physical injury to the individuals involved.' So apparently Pornhub does not comply with its own terms and conditions – the transparency report claims that any video is uploaded only after both an algorithm-based and human moderation took place. There is also the question whether the false depiction of rape or non-consensual material is itself harmful so should be banned. But even if we leave these important questions to the side, the *New York Times* report found ample evidence of real NCII and child pornography

---

[12] For example, Pornhub terms of use prohibit to 'post any Content that depicts any person under 18 years of age (or older in any other location in which 18 is not the minimum age of majority) whether real or simulated'. For the gap between the disclaimers and reality see, for example, Vera-Gray et al (2021).

materials, appearing to be as such, leading its author to conclude 'I don't see how good-faith moderators could approve any of these videos'. Advocates of NCII victims and critics of the porn industry such as Kate Isaacs from NotYourPorn mention that porn sites 'know that there is no way we can differentiate fantasy role-play acting, or faked production scenarios, or real abuse'; this allows porn websites to 'hide behind claims of protecting free expression and seemingly stay ignorant on what is consensual and what isn't' (Fight the New Drug, 2020b; Isaacs, 2020; Mohan, 2020).[13] Fight the New Drug featured several publications (2020a, 2020c, 2020d, 2021) documenting NCII on porn sites and the difficulty to distinguish between non/consensual sex in porn production.

Finally, the *New York Times* report might suggest that the risk of coming across NCII is not evenly distributed: 'if you know what to look for, it's possible to find hundreds of apparent child sexual abuse videos on Pornhub in 30 minutes'. So those who search for under-age or non-consensual materials are more likely to find them than those who do not. The former are akin to those browsing images in dedicated revenge porn website, so the argument in Part 2 applies to them. For those not searching for NCII but come across them the question remains whether the proportion of NCII among material not flagged as potentially NCII or child pornography is high enough to merit a fault-based liability for intrusion of privacy, and whether the answer depends on the relevant searches or streams within which the viewer is searching. This bears some resemblance to the question whether liability for contribution to demand leading to sex trafficking could depend on the different segment in which the client bought the sexual services (Keren-Paz, 2013: 210–11).

Vera-Gray et al (2021) examined sexual violence as a sexual script in mainstream online pornography in the UK. 2.2% of the analysable dataset constituted descriptions of image-based sexual abuse in the videos' titles, using 'terms such as "hidden", "spy" and "leaked", but excluded terms such as "ex", 'homemade" and "filmed" as these terms alone do not qualify the representation as being one of image-based sexual abuse' and other instances where 'the non-consent … is ambiguous'. While the authors qualify this finding that they 'do not claim that the titles are describing videos that were *in reality* made and/or distributed without the consent of those featured, though this is likely the case for some' there are reasons to believe that the 2.2% figure of *real* NCII among all images on the website is a conservative estimation: 'the sexual script of image-based sexual abuse on these mainstream porn websites centres largely on the non-consensual *creation*, rather than distribution, of

---

[13] Compare to the critique made by Holten (2020) and Pasquale (2016) of intermediaries' ambiguity about their role.

images.' So, this figure does not include the following: (1) cases in which the creation is consensual but the distribution is not, a fact which is not captured by the coding's focus on voyeurism, which is only one form of NCII; (2) instances in which the non-consensual nature of the creation of the image is likely, based on the title, if ambiguous; (3) the part of BDSM material which was not produced consensually (so, websites' commitment that all BDSM content is produced consensually is taken at face value). For the researchers' purposes, the distinction between real and imagined non-consent is less important, given their observation that some forms of sexual violence would fall foul of the prohibition of simulated extreme pornography (although, imagined NCII scripts of the voyeurism type captured in the research will be lawful, as they do not simulate non-consensual sexual penetration and life-threatening injury) (Vera-Gray et al, 2021: 1251–5). However, the fact that the content accessed might be illegal for other reasons only supports the conclusion that consumption of porn on general porn websites involves too high a risk of violating potential victims' rights and has low social value, hence satisfying fault as a condition for liability for breach of privacy.

I would like to make the following comments. First, it is inconsequential that not all of the images accompanied by titles suggesting they are NCII are really such. What matters is that the proportion of intrusive (non-consensual) content on these websites is high enough to make a viewer's decision to surf these websites unreasonable. Since the dataset in these websites is replete with too many right-violating videos, any victim whose images were viewed by a claimant should be able to sue, not only victims whose video's title is suggestive of a right-violation. Second, and related, the research's findings pertain to first time users; the research was designed to ignore algorithmic adjustments to viewers seeking illegal content. It follows that even a viewer wishing to distance himself from NCII or images involving or simulating sexual violence will be exposed to them on the landing page, thus risking breaching the privacy of all NCII victims appearing there. Third, the 2.2% figure refers to titles suggestive of non-consensual creation of the image, rather than to visual depiction of abusive sexual contact. In total, 12% of the analysable sample of titles described sexual activity that constitutes sexual violence. If some of the other categories of sexual violence are not a simulation, the distribution of these images is yet another form of breach of privacy and of image-based sexual abuse, even though it is counted under another category (save for the fanciful possibility that the victim did not agree to the abusive sexual contact but later agreed to the distribution of its recording).[14] Next, given the apparent appeal of violent

---

[14] See Vera-Gray et al (2021: 1255): Titles such as 'again and again forced' are unlawful as extreme pornography (and possibly obscene), even if simulated and '[I]t is also possible

and non-consensual sex in the porn industry, there is a strong argument for treating titles suggestive of sexual abuse (including NCII) at face value, for the purpose of civil suits. So, someone who views titles suggestive of violence or lack of consent who happens to be sued by the person depicted in the image cannot be heard that it was reasonable for him to believe that this was merely a simulation. Finally, the combination of repeat visits of porn sites and algorithmic matching for tastes significantly increases the risk that a breach of privacy would occur. On the model explored earlier, a 2.2% of NCII (which in fact might be higher), would lead to a 67% of watching at least one NCII after 50 views and 89% after 100 – if these selections are random. However, once a viewer selected a title suggestive of NCII, the algorithm will push similar content whose chance of being NCII is higher than that of a random selection.

3. Fault in breach of privacy

Contrary to Lord Hoffman's dictum in *Wainwright* doubting whether a monetary remedy under Article 8 of the ECHR is payable for 'a merely negligent act',[15] 'the Strasburg Jurisprudence does not lay down lines as clear as this. It is generally unnecessary to establish any particular state of mind in respect of the breach of the convention; the conduct of the parties as a whole, including whether the acts which are alleged to give rise to the violation were deliberate or accidental, may be taken into account in determining the gravity of the interference. The current approach of English law is that what the publisher knew or should have known is one of the circumstances to be considered when determining whether the claimant enjoyed a reasonable expectation of privacy ('*Expectation*') (Warby and Shore, 2016: 484; Warby, Garrick and Strong, 2016: 259).[16] In cases of traditional breach of confidence, an innocent recipient of confidential information may not be liable to pay

---

that some of the material analysed is evidence of real sexual assaults, as well as voyeurism and non-consensual distribution of sexual image offences'.

[15] *Wainwright v Home Office* [2003] UKHL 53, [51]: 'It is one thing to wander carelessly into the wrong hotel bedroom and another to hide in the wardrobe to take photographs'.

[16] *Weller v Associated Newspapers Ltd* [2015] EWCA 1176 (Civ) [37] ('This broad test allows the Court to assess what the publishers knew, and what they ought to have known. It also allows publishers to take account of matters which they did not know, and could not have known about, at the time of publication to show that there was no reasonable expectation of privacy'); *Murray v Big Pictures (UK) Ltd* [2008] EWCA Civ 446 [35] (the test for determining reasonable expectation takes into account 'the absence of consent and whether it was known or could be inferred'); *Imerman v Tchenguiz* (CA) [2010] EWCA Civ 908 [68] ('confidence applies to a defendant who adventitiously, but without authorisation, obtains information in respect of which he must have appreciated that the claimant had an expectation of privacy'); *McKennitt v Ash* [2006] EWCA Civ 1714 [15].

damages[17] although they may be issued an injunction once on notice, subject to defences of bona fide purchase or change of position (Toulson and Phipps, 2006: 3-056–3-064). Crucially for current purpose, the recipient's liability to pay damages depends on what the defendant knew of should have known about the claimant's reasonable expectation of confidentiality, similar to the emerging *Privacy* test, which takes into account the defendant's knowledge, and the circumstances in which he obtained access to the information for purposes of establishing liability (Toulson and Phipps, 2006; Warby and Shore, 2016: 483–4, 486).

It transpires then, that viewers might be liable in privacy under the current state of the law, if they viewed the claimant's NCII image while surfing porn sites, although this is by no means certain. First, as discussed in Chapter 8, the law needs to recognize that the recipient of private information intrudes on the claimant's privacy so in this sense unduly undermines her *Expectation* even though he does not disseminate it further. Second, liability would hinge on a conclusion that the defendant should have known about the claimant's *Expectation*. Given the high risk of breaching one's privacy while surfing porn sites there is much to be said that the defendant should have known that claimants have a reasonable expectation of privacy so should be liable in damages for such victims whose images they viewed. For reasons explained in Chapter 4 and later (in examining strict liability) both the public interest and the good faith purchase for value defences ought not to and would not be available to viewers.

To an extent, the discussion earlier is moot, as the viewer's actions are intentional. Assuming breach of privacy is a 'classic' intentional tort,[18] the relevant intention is to act, rather than to harm or to undermine the claimant's interest;[19] in this sense liability is really strict.[20] Anyone searching for nude images intends to view them, even if he does not intend to intrude on one's privacy (which is not required) or look for NCII. In this sense, Lord Hoffman's conclusion is disputed, on the (correct) understanding that *Privacy* is truly an intentional tort. A person entering mistakenly to the wrong house commits trespass to land – an intentional tort – even if he believes it is their own house, since they intended the entry. There is no reason why mistakenly

---

[17] *Valeo vision SA v Flexible Lamps Ltd* [1995] RPC 205.

[18] This is the position in the US: *Paroline v United States*, 572 US 434, 483–4 (2014); while the Strasburg and English positions might seem different (see n15), they are not. In England, the point was put behind doubt in *Lloyd v Google* [2021] UKSC 50 [133]. See the discussion in the text that immediately follows and Chapter 10, Part 2.

[19] See for example, *Regina v Governor of Her Majesty's Prison Brockhill ex parte Evans* (No 2) [2000] UKHL 48; Stevens, 2007: 100–2.

[20] *Lloyd* (n18) [133]; Varuhas, 2018: 55, 63–5; Chapter 10, Part 2; cf for battery Keren-Paz, 2013: 118–28.

entering the wrong hotel room would not be considered as intentional in the manner leading to liability for breach of privacy. While such innocent entry might amount to de minimis, 'innocently' coming across the claimant's intimate image is nothing but, as it causes significant distress.[21]

4. Role for negligence?

Given my conclusion that the law of privacy can accommodate breaches in which there was no intention to harm, but the risk of infringing one's privacy is significant, there is no need to examine the applicability of the tort of negligence in this context. While negligence was deemed potentially applicable for psychiatric injury following a breach of confidentiality,[22] its general application to NCII raises issues regarding actionable damage, duty of care, and to a lesser extent standard and causation (Keren-Paz, 2013: chapters 6–8; Purhouse and Trispiotis, 2021). But the fact that psychiatric injury and also economic loss are likely results of NCII (Bates, 2017) might suggest that negligence might have a role to play in a civil response to NCII. Given the direct link between the viewing of the NCII and the claimant's harm, some of the difficulties that exist in the context of liability for the creation for demand that led to sex trafficking are inapplicable here: duty and causation seem more straightforward, although issues of overdetermined causes exist. In terms of standard of care, the risk of harm and the social value of defendant's activity clearly indicate a sub-standard behaviour (similar to the conclusion in the sex trafficking context of purchasing sex in a market sufficiently replete with victims of trafficking) (Keren-Paz, 2013: chapter 7).

B. Demand-based liability

Can a viewer be liable not only for the breach of privacy involved in him viewing the claimant's NCII but also for the breach of privacy involved in creating and disseminating the image, and if the image depicted an underlying sexual assault for this assault? And can a viewer of intimate images be liable to claimants whose NCII he did not view, based on the proposition that dissemination (and perhaps creation) of such images was made to meet a demand to which the viewer contributed? We met these questions in discussing child pornography in the previous chapter and I have argued for demand-based liability in the context of sex trafficking.

---

[21] See Chapter 11, Part 2 for the related question whether *Privacy* is actionable per se or requires proof of damage as a constitutive element.

[22] *Swinney v CC of the Northumbria Police* [1996] 3 All ER 449.

For the following reasons I would not support a demand-based liability for viewing NCII, even in contexts, such as surfing porn sites, in which fault could be assumed.

It will be useful to distinguish (as I did in Chapter 8) between liability by a defendant who viewed the image for: (1) the claimant's initial intrusion, which could refer to (1a) the non-consensual dissemination of an image created consensually, (1b) the non-consensual creation of an image and (1c) an underlying sexual abuse captured in an image; (2) the harm NCII victims suffer from viewing, despite the fact the defendant was not one of those who viewed their images; and for (3) any intrusion these victims suffer from the initial creation of the image or any related abuse. Readers will recall that for child pornography, my conclusion was that there should be no demand-based liability of those who did not view the claimant's images. So it goes without saying that the same conclusion should apply to NCII. Not only that the problem of indeterminate liability is applicable here – given the inability to apply spatial and temporal limitations which are applicable in sex trafficking markets – but whether the defendant's viewing contributed to the initial intrusion or dissemination is itself in doubt.

The case for demand-based liability of those who did not view the claimant's images would rest on the proposition that the demand for intimate images in porn websites is what caused the initial dissemination of the image (or the initial abuse, if existing). At a basic level, the non-consensual dissemination of intimate images is by definition demand-based. Whatever possible motive lied behind the non-consensual dissemination, this motive could be achieved only if and to the extent that a third party would view the image: intimidating the claimant or harming her, boasting of the disseminator's sexual prowess, increased esteem and status from peers, misogyny, adoring the subject's beauty. Each motive requires that other people will see the image – otherwise there is no point in disseminating it. Even the threat of dissemination is demand-based in the sense that whatever leverage the person making the threat has, or hopes to have, over the claimant, depends (almost[23]) entirely on what will happen if third parties will view the image. In this sense, then, dissemination is demand-based, and necessarily so. But given other dissemination strategies, including dedicated groups and websites, social platforms, private messaging and emailing people related to the victims, it is very doubtful whether the initial unauthorized

---

[23] A small exception is in rare cases in which a threat to tell a third party that such image exists – without sharing the image itself – will suffice for a leverage. But even here the leverage is demand-based since the information needs to be communicated to third parties, and since the prospect of disseminating the image itself (for example if the claimant denies that such image exists) furthers that leverage.

dissemination was done in order to meet the demand in the porn sites market. So liability would be underinclusive: it is the overall prospect that people would view the image, not only those visiting porn sites which is behind the initial unauthorized dissemination. And the search for images in general, which results with viewing NCII (and arguably, including a search for intimate images outside of porn sites) ought not be considered as unreasonable.

How about liability of those who viewed the claimant's NCII for the initial intrusion involved in disseminating the image and if applicable, its creation and any associated sexual abuse? Here too, I would not support liability since both the causal contribution is in doubt (for the reasons just explained) and fault is also more contested. Unlike prostitution, in which the victim is recruited only to meet demand in the commercial sex market, there is no strong evidence that intimate images are created in order to disseminate them (with or without consent). In some cases they would (as in some cases of voyeurism done for the purpose of dissemination: Cox, 2018; Uhl et al, 2018: 1918; Holten, 2020 – especially 'creepshots'); in other cases it is clearly not the case (as in sexting a boyfriend in which commonly the texter's intention is that the image would not be further disseminated, and the initial disseminator acting in breach of duty did not create the image, although, at times he might have induced the claimant to create and share with him the image); and yet in other cases it would be hard to know whether the creation of the image – even if done without the claimant's consent – was done with the prospect of dissemination in mind. Possibly, the intention to disseminate was formed after the image was created. In this sense, the causation between the demand for images in porn websites, and the creation of NCII is less clear and direct than in the sex trafficking context. True, it is theoretically possible to examine on an individual basis, whether the NCII of any particular victim was created with dissemination in general porn sites in mind. If this were the case, liability of viewers to the initial intrusion or abuse could be justified. But given the difficulty involved in verifying the purpose behind the creation of the image (if applicable), or the dissemination strategy of the uploader, and given that the claimant can sue the uploader for the dissemination and the viewer for intruding her privacy by viewing her image, the benefits of such cause of action seem marginal at best in comparison to the costs and difficulties that such a theory for liability raises.

In conclusion, despite superficial similarity with sex trafficking, NCII do not present a compelling case for demand-based liability. Similar to child pornography, there are no sufficient spatial and temporal limitations to guard against indeterminate liability of those who did not view the claimant's images. Moreover, as the viewing of intimate images of consenting adults is lawful and for many, valuable, the argument that posing demand for such images (which are partially to be met by NCII) is unreasonable is at the very best highly controversial. Finally, the causation between the demand posed by those visiting porn sites – those most likely to satisfy a fault requirement – and the dissemination of the image is much more tenuous than in cases of child pornography.

10

The Power of Property: Strict Liability for Viewing NCII

1. Introduction

Following from the previous chapter, this chapter explains why viewers' liability could and should be strict, rather than be merely fault-based. Building on the discussion in Chapters 4 and 5 it further explains how a property-based understanding of privacy helps justify both strict liability and its proper limits; thus avoiding excessive liability. Hence, this chapter makes three contributions: doctrinal, normative and conceptual. Doctrinally, it explains that (1) the misuse of private information tort (*Privacy*) is already understood as a stricter form of liability; (2) that liability under *Privacy* might be stricter than under breach of confidentiality (from which *Privacy* sprung) and the justifications for this difference; and (3) *Privacy* can therefore accommodate viewers' strict liability for viewing NCII (Part 2). Normatively, it then explains how the concepts of possession, passive behaviour and reliance make viewers' strict liability to be justified and not excessive (Part 3). Theoretically, it inquires how conceptualizing information as property justifies strict, rather than fault-based, liability for viewing, despite the fact that the act of viewing both misappropriates and destroys value (Part 4); it thus complements the analysis offered in Chapters 4 and 5.

2. Current law and the privacy/confidentiality distinction

As we have seen, there is no clear answer to whether liability for *Privacy* is strict, although recently *Lloyd v Google* justified liability for loss of control in *Privacy* (normative damages, or the unilateral model discussed in Chapter 11) based on the nature of *Privacy* as a strict liability tort: 'The privacy tort, like other torts for which damages can be awarded without proof of material damage or distress, is a tort involving strict liability for deliberate acts, not a tort based on want of care.'[1] Varuhas (2018: 63) concludes that liability for *Privacy* 'seems to be towards the stricter end of the spectrum' and while the claimant may need to leap over hurdles which a claimant for trespass to land needs not to, in order to establish the prima facie case for a breach 'this difference does not necessarily demonstrate that liability in misuse of private information is not strict, or at least relatively strict'. Warby and Shore (2016: 486) conclude their discussion of the innocent dissemination defence that it remains to be decided the extent to which ignorance or innocence will afford a defence to a *Privacy* claim and that 'it remains arguable that to escape monetary liability it would be enough, in a confidence case to' 'act in ignorance of the fact that they are causing or contributing to a wrongful disclosure of private facts'. It should be noted, that Warby and Shore have in mind, in discussing *Privacy*, an innocent contribution to the *dissemination* of information, so there is no indication that they appreciate the possibility of strict liability for receipt of private information, although they do focus on such receipt in the context of traditional law of confidentiality.

It is therefore possible, that the current (uncertain) law distinguishes between receipt of traditional confidential information, for which strict liability is less likely (where at least there is some support for denying damages against an innocent recipient of information) and the recipient of private information who might still be liable, if the courts conclude that the claimant still had a reasonable expectation of privacy (*Expectation*), despite the defendant's ignorance or innocence. Still, not only that this conclusion is only a possibility, it also leaves the determination to be the court's discretion, with lack of knowledge operating in the direction that the claimant does not have *Expectation*.[2] The current ambiguous legal position about *Privacy* could be distinguished from what would follow if the property model I defended in Chapter 4 be adopted: accordingly, the viewer as a recipient of 'stolen' property would be strictly liable for the value of that property; importantly, such liability would not be discretionary.

Before examining whether such liability is normatively and conceptually attractive, it would be instructive to reflect on the apparent distinction between liability under traditional claims for breach of confidence and for *Privacy*. One distinction follows the distinction between equitable and common law rights. If information is protected as an equitable property, it makes more sense that a third party will be liable for his interference if he acted unconscionably. Traditionally, liability for both knowing receipt and dishonest assistance is defeated if the third party is innocent. However, if

---

[1]   [2021] UKSC 50 [133].

[2]   See Chapter 9, Part 3, esp. *Weller v Associated Newspapers Ltd* [2015] EWCA 1176 (Civ) [37].

private information, or at least intimate images, are conceived of as the subject of common law property right, similar to personal property or some forms of intellectual property, it makes sense to protect them from the intentional, if innocent act of a third party acting in a way that is incompatible with the owner's claim for dominion over the images.

This different scope of protection fits well with two distinctions between *Privacy* and traditional breach of confidence claims. The first is the nature of information that is commercial in traditional confidentiality cases and personal or dignitary in *Privacy*. The distinction between personal and fungible property suggests it is more important to protect personal property than fungible one (Radin, 1982). One non-obvious application might be that the weaker protection equity affords property, by defeating a claim for damages when the third party is innocent is insufficient, or inappropriate, when the property is personal.[3] On the understanding, discussed in Chapter 6, that classic intentional torts, most notably the trespass torts, but also defamation, protect important dignitary and autonomy interests and vindicate human rights, their strictness ought to apply to *Privacy*. It is therefore unsurprising that liability for defamation is stricter than liability for breach of confidence. Since, as I have argued in Chapter 6, the interest in privacy is stronger than the interest in reputation, liability for breach of privacy should be even more strict that that for defamation.

The second and related reason why liability for breach of privacy ought to be stricter than liability for breach of confidence follows from Lord Hoffman's observation in *Campbell* of the change of focus from the breach of pre-existing relation of trust in confidentiality cases to the nature of information in *Privacy*.[4] Since in breach of confidence the crux of the issue is the unconscionable abuse of trust, it makes sense that unconscionability would be a condition for liability of third parties who received the information, since such liability is derivative to the initial breach of confidence. But as the focus shifted in *Privacy* to the nature of information, and the protection of the claimant's dignity and autonomy, and away from the pre-existing relationship of confidence, the strict nature of the liability with respect to

---

[3]   The reason this application is non-obvious, is that characterising a certain property as fungible suggests that damages for interference with the entitlement (as opposed to an injunction) is more appropriate, since damages can adequately compensate for a commercial loss, rather than for a personal loss. And yet, the traditional law of confidentiality might deny damages against an innocent third party for the fungible loss occurring in a commercial context, while allowing under certain circumstances an injunction. At the same time, a *Privacy* claim might, and I argue ought to, lead to a damages award against the innocent third party for the loss of personal property; but of course, an injunction is also available.

[4]   *Campbell v MGN* [2004] UKHL 22 [51].

the person originally misusing the information can be more easily attached to third parties receiving this private information. Such stricter liability is compatible with other dignitary torts, including defamation and the trespass torts. Specifically, as I have suggested in Chapter 4, strict liability is compatible with the protection to those interfering with the claimant's property. The next two parts will examine this proposition further.

3. Possession, passive behaviour and reliance

A. Possession

In essence, the policy shift I offer in this book is from equitable protection of property to a common law one: As we saw, the law of confidentiality treats (largely commercial) information as equitable property and therefore shields innocent recipients from liability. But if private information, or at least intimate images, are considered a form of common law property, or at least as deserving as strong a protection as if they were property, the liability of those intentionally interfering with the property is well established, either as a matter of trespass (the authorities are clearer with respect to land) or of conversion (Chapter 4). I have already mentioned that the intention has to do with dealing with the property, rather than with knowing that the dealing is unauthorized, or that indeed the property belongs to the claimant. This, in turn, has bearing on the scope of liability of passive defendants. The concept of possession has built-in guarantees against excessive liability, which attenuates the fear from excessive and oppressive liability, by requiring both actual control and an intention to possess: 'an intention to exercise that custody on his own behalf and for his own benefit'.[5] An intention to possess, in general, is an intention to exclusion of all other people, including the owner. As explained in Chapter 4, in the context of images, the rival use by viewers excludes the owner in the sense of denying her right to exclude others, including the defendant, from having access to the image. To satisfy the relevant intention, then, the viewer needs at least to be aware that he was sent an image (or more generally, the item he is considered as possessing) but not its content.[6]

An obvious *starting* point for inspiration is criminal law exemptions from responsibility for possessing child pornography, as the relevant possession is of images. In the UK, S160 of the Criminal Justice Act 1988 criminalizes the possession of an indecent image of a child; defences include 'that he had not himself seen the photograph or pseudo-photograph and did not know, nor had any cause to suspect, it to be indecent' or 'that the photograph or

---

[5] *Mainline Private Hire Ltd v Nolan* [2011] EWCA Civ 189 [1].

[6] *R v Okoro* (No 3) [2018] EWCA Crim 19.

pseudo-photograph was sent to him without any prior request made by him or on his behalf and that he did not keep it for an unreasonable time'.[7] S1 of the Protection of Children Act 1978, criminalizing the taking or making indecent photographs of children, provides a similar defence for a person proving he 'had not himself seen the photographs or pseudo-photographs and did not know, nor had any cause to suspect, them to be indecent'.[8] An equivalent approach to civil liability for viewing NCII would hence protect the real innocent defendants: those who did not view the image, nor had reason to suspect it is intimate (and hence potentially NCII), and those who were entirely passive in the process of viewing the images. It is easy to justify the no liability of members of the first group as they did not breach the claimant's privacy in any meaningful sense: they did not view the image, nor even knew that they could view such images thus potentially breaching the claimant's privacy if the image be non-consensual. It is equally easy to justify liability, which is no longer strict, of a defendant who received NCII and chose to keep it. The same logic lies behind liability beyond notice and failure to take down expeditiously the image applicable to hosts under the ECD; and similar logic is behind the applicability of theft to appropriation of property originally in the accused's lawful possession;[9] and, further afield, behind the possible applicability of constructive trust for money paid under mistake from the moment the recipient is aware of the mistaken payment.[10]

The potential harshness of liability for receipt of images without deleting them might be demonstrated by the case of Robyn Williams, convicted for possessing an indecent image of a child. The image was sent to 17 people on a WhatsApp group by her outraged sister, a social worker (who received the email from her boyfriend). Williams, a black senior Met officer, did not report receipt of the image to the police, who were notified of the image by another recipient, but rather wrote to her sister 'please call'. While Williams was under a duty to report it as a police officer, she was not convicted on the charge of corrupt or improper exercise of police powers for failing to report

---

[7]   S160(2)(b), (c).

[8]   S1(4).

[9]   Theft Act 1969 S3(1).

[10] *Westdeutsche Landesbank Girozentrale v London Islington Borough Council* [1996] AC 669, 716 (Per Lord Brown-Wilkinson); *Fitzalan-Howard (Norfolk) v Hibbert* [2009] EWHC 2855 (QB) [49]. The issue is notoriously unsettled. For an explanation of the case law under which recipient's knowledge is a necessary but insufficient condition for proprietary remedy in mistaken payment cases see Salmons (2015). There are of course important differences: the *in personam* duty to make restitution is strict. The recipient's bad conscience operates (if it does at all) only to affect the strength of the claim against general creditors of the recipient. The similarity is that the legal position of a defendant in physical possession changes once they subsequently acquire relevant knowledge or intention.

it but was subsequently dismissed from her job for gross misconduct. Her appeal against the conviction was dismissed in February 2021 and against her dismissal was successful in June 2021 (Hamilton, 2021). A combination of several factors makes the overall legal response seemingly heavy handed, but makes civil liability in an equivalent NCII case unlikely. First, the absence of sexual interest by the sister who distributed it (indeed, she was outraged by the image) and Williams who received it. Second, Williams' status as police officer made the inaction more serious. As reports on this case did not indicate that any of the other 15 recipients of the image who did not report it to the police were charged with possession, it might be that Williams' status as a police officer was the controlling factor in bringing charges against her (it is, of course, theoretically possible, that all the others deleted the image within a reasonable time and therefore enjoyed the S 160(2)(c) defence that they 'did not keep it for an unreasonable time'. I doubt how likely this scenario is). Third, Williams was naturally hesitant to report her sister and was a decorated police officer. The fact that this led to criminal conviction and consequently to the (temporary) loss of her job seems harsh. Fourth, the stigma involved in a conviction, and the fact she lost her job as a result, seem a disproportionate consequence for her lapse in judgement. Indeed, the fact she was re-instated to her job makes the overall response to this lapse much less problematic. Finally, the swift sacking of Williams who was one of the most senior black female police officers in the country was criticized as an example of the Met's institutional racism (Dodd, 2019).

None of these factors, and their unusual combination, could serve as a reason to oppose imposing liability for *Privacy* on those receiving intimate images and failing to delete them promptly. At the most basic level, the fact that a certain rule might lead to dubious results in rare, hard cases, is not a reason against adopting it, if its application is generally justified. Second, the equivalent of prosecution's discretion whether to indict is the victim's prerogative whether to file a suit. I will deal in Chapter 12 with the broader question of whether NCII victims are likely to sue viewers but it is unlikely to fear that victims would sue a Williams equivalent in a similar type of case. If they would, the broad discretion courts have in balancing *Expectation* and public interest might and ought to lead to no liability – a court might reach a conclusion that retaining the image was supported by the public interest, or (less plausibly) that the victim did not have an *Expectation* vis-à-vis the defendant in such circumstances. Finally, even if there would be liability, its stigmatizing effects are likely to be significantly less than a conviction, and court's discretion about the size of damages might lead to a relatively low award (Chapter 11, Part 2). For example, given victims' account on how they are harmed by NCII – mainly, being recognized and hence humiliated and a sense of violation in their image being viewed by hundreds of men for sexual arousal (Sharratt, 2019: 14–15) – it is likely that the harm from viewing that is not sexually or maliciously motivated, is likely to be much smaller, and therefore justifies a lower award. Doctrinally, this lower quantum could be ingrained in a finding that the dignitary harm is inherently lower or that the invasion of privacy caused less distress; in addition, such a case would not merit the award of aggravated damages.

The technicalities of child pornography prosecution ought not to divert us from the bigger picture: it is possible and desirable to both impose strict liability on those who initially received intimate images that happened to be NCII but exercised choice to keep them (and on those seeking intimate images who happen to come across NCII), while protecting passive defendants who neither viewed the images, nor had a reason to know they received NCII or were sent unsolicited images and deleted them promptly. Such an approach is consistent with (1) other dignitary torts imposing strict liability but insisting on intentional acts, (2) the recognition that the interest of children and non-consenting adults in not having their intimate images viewed is similar, (3) the distinction between criminal responsibility and tort liability, (4) the defences afforded to the viewing of child pornography, and (5) the need to maintain the lesser responsibility of mere viewers in comparison to producers and distributors notwithstanding digital technicalities (discussed later) treating viewers as producers. Luckily, the doctrinal scaffolding of *Expectation* is strong and flexible enough to reach such a result. All is needed is a holding that for *Privacy* liability there needs to be an intentional act, that intention is not about whether the act undermines the claimant's interest (that is, not an intention to view non-consensual images) and that unsolicited images that are not kept do not amount to misuse of private information so there could be no *Expectation* with respect to those whose viewing was non-voluntary.

B. Viewing without possession

The case for excluding liability of those sent unsolicited images, viewed and immediately deleted them might be less evident, but I nonetheless support this result. The defendant in this case has viewed the image, so from the claimant's perspective her privacy was breached. As the concept of intrusion is ingrained in the defendant's unauthorized *access* to the intimate information, rather than in retaining it, there is no justification to hinge liability for intrusion on possession only, to the exclusion of live streaming or other forms of intentional viewing. That viewing, rather than possession is at the heart of the undermining of the claimant's interest in privacy is indeed shared by the Crown Prosecution Service (2020) in the context of (criminal responsibility for) child pornography: '[A] person who has merely viewed an image or video will not have retained any copy of it on their device. Nonetheless, it is submitted that they have "made" an image by causing it to be displayed on that device'. However, if the moral basis for civil strict liability is volition – that one 'acts at his peril', such volition is absent when one is passively sent an image and promptly gets rid of it.

A conceptual complication is that if intention is a constitutive element of possession, one who is being sent an unsolicited image might be considered not to possess it at all, till the moment in which he could make a decision to keep it. In that case, there is simply no category of viewing without possession, and the criminal defence of S160 becomes redundant since the defendant did not possess the image. Whether this is true or not, civil courts could reach the desired result without a need for a statute: no liability for those who were sent unsolicited images, viewed them and promptly deleted them. This could be done by simply concluding that a claimant does not have *Expectation* with regards to recipients of unsolicited images, at least until enough time has passed without the recipient deleting them.

One technological complication is that a viewer who digitally deletes a child pornography on his computer might still be considered as possessing it; although in normal circumstances, deleting images kept on a computer is sufficient to divest oneself of possession of them.[11] Such a common-sense approach should apply to NCII. So if the viewer takes steps to promptly delete the image and does not attempt to access it later, no liability should inhere. A further technological complication is that in the digital environment it is easier to establish the more serious production offence of 'making' a photo than the possession offence in cases of viewing an image on a device that is automatically cached onto its memory. 'Making' was interpreted by the courts to include opening an attachment to an email containing an image; downloading an image from a website onto a computer screen; storing an image in a directory on a computer (which could also be a possession offence, depending on where the image is stored); and accessing a pornographic website in which indecent images appeared by way of automatic 'pop-up' mechanism. For this reason, '[T]he use of section 160 of the CJA 1988 is becoming increasingly rare' (Crown Prosecution Service, 2020). But here too, the same common-sense approach explained earlier suffices.

C. Possession without viewing

The discussion so far demonstrates that viewing an image, even without possession should lead to liability, unless the defendant was passive. But what about possession without viewing? In the area of child pornography, the knowing possession of images could lead to responsibility even if the accused did not view it, provided he knew or had ground to suspect it is

---

[11]   See *R v Porter* [2006] 1 WLR 2633; *R v Leonard* [2012] 2 Cr. App. R. 12. CPS id.

indecent.[12] From a private law perspective, the question of liability is quite finely balanced. The following considerations support liability: (1) Knowing possession puts the victim at risk of future viewing by the defendant or future dissemination with their associated harms. (2) Conceptually, if the right to privacy is ingrained in autonomy and the right to control sensitive private information; and even more so, if the analogy to property is maintained, the mere possession of the images, including the ability to retrieve them, undermines the victim's right to privacy. (3) When the possessor knows the claimant's ('C') identity, the mere knowledge that the defendant ('D') possesses the C's intimate images is humiliating to the victim and therefore harmful. However, this argument might prove too much: it is the knowledge that such images are circulating that is the main source of humiliation, but if the D was passive in receiving them, he cannot be held responsible for this harm, and it is doubtful whether the deletion of the images would change much the harm caused to C from D's knowledge that such images were distributed to him. It is possible that the humiliation is somewhat exacerbated from C's knowledge that D decided not to delete the image, but this additional harm is both speculative and seems small in comparison to the core harm, with respect to which there is a strong case against liability.

The following considerations negate liability for mere possession: (1) To begin with, liability for mere viewing is far reaching and involves casting wide the net of liability. This is especially so where the theory of liability is rather strict. Given that the harm to privacy is mainly from the viewing itself, that any harm from the knowledge that an intimate image exists should usually not be actionable and that the D was passive in finding out that these images exist, liability would be too far-reaching. (2) The overdetermined nature of the harm, and the lower degree of culpability involved in retaining possession of intimate images without viewing them suggests that the harm from this behaviour is either speculative or small to an extent justifying not imposing liability for it.

On balance, I would endorse the following solution. If the defendant is aware that he was sent an intimate image, but had neither indication that the image is non-consensual nor viewed it, he should not be liable. In this case, a strict liability for mere knowing possession of an intimate image without the knowledge or suspicion that the image is a form of an intimate abuse should not lead to liability in circumstances where the main harm is caused by actual viewing rather than by possession. However, where the possessor had a reason to suspect that the image is not only intimate but non-consensual, there should be liability for knowing possession as this behaviour is both more culpable and more harmful. The culpability

---

[12] S160(2)(B) Criminal Justice Act, 1988.

is self-evident; I already made the comparison with knowing possession of stolen property. The harm is also more significant since C's knowledge that D knowingly possesses NCII is likely to create more humiliation and fear. It is more clearly inconsistent with C's right – of which D ought to be aware – to avoid unauthorized uses of the image; and these include also its possession and potential future viewing or dissemination. This result could be achieved thanks to the flexibility of the *Expectation* test. Courts can reach a conclusion that a claimant has an *Expectation* that her images would not be possessed, even without having been viewed, if the defendant had a reason to suspect that these images were distributed without consent while she does not have *Expectation* if the defendant was not aware the intimate images were non-consensual. At the same time, the claimant can have *Expectation* that her NCII would not be viewed by a defendant, even if he was not aware that the images are non-consensual, as viewing undermines to a greater extent the interest in privacy compared to mere possession, and as the right to control the image, especially when understood through a property lens, can justify strict liability, as long as the defendant is not entirely passive.

D. Authorized viewing, unauthorized possession

Similarly, the unauthorized retention of a time-limited image (such as taking a screenshot of an intimate image sent by Snapchat) is an instance in which initial viewing was authorized, but not retention, which entails future unauthorized viewings, potential for blackmail and potential for further unauthorized sharing with third persons. The retention, and any future viewing, should lead to civil liability; this should include also liability of hosts and viewers of such NCII (who were never authorized to host or view the image). Contrary to the Law Commission's position (2022: 117–22), such unauthorized retention should be criminalized as a taking offence (and should also amount to a possession offence by the person making that copy).

★★★

In the area of physical sexual abuse, any sexual contact with a child and a non-consensual sexual contact with an adult leads to criminal responsibility (subject to *mens rea*) and could lead to strict liability under the tort of battery. The starting point for liability for NCII should be the same, namely, that the viewing of NCII of adults is a serious violation of their rights, similar to the violation involved by viewing child pornography (Citron, 2019: 1917).[13]

---

[13] 'The difference in the treatment of perpetrators who target minors and those who target adults is staggering.'

The main difference is one of notice: any intimate image depicting a child is unequivocally illegal. The same is not true for intimate images of adults, which might be consensual. But here there is an important distinction between criminal and private law: while the lack of notice is relevant to criminal law, it might be irrelevant to private law claims, if the interest ought to be protected by strict liability. To the same extent that civil liability for sexual battery ought to be strict, and depending on the jurisdiction might be, so should be the liability for breach of sexual privacy.

E. Reliance on prior publication

In some cases, strict liability might seem harsh due to some reasonable reliance by the viewer that the viewing is lawful. But these cases could be accommodated by interpreting *Expectation* and the public interest defence, which could also include a notion analogous to estoppel. S 33(5) of the Criminal Justice and Courts Act, which deals with disclosure, not viewing, provides a defence to those reasonably believing that the image had been previously disclosed for reward and who had no reason to believe that the previous disclosure for reward was made without the victim's consent. Similarly, the Law Commission Final Report (2022: 300) recommends:

that it should not be an offence to share an intimate image without the consent of the person depicted where:

(1) the intimate image has, or the defendant reasonably believed that the intimate image has, previously been shared in a place (whether offline or online) to which members of the public had access (whether or not by payment of a fee), and
(2) either the person depicted in the image consented to that previous sharing, or the defendant reasonably believed that person depicted in the image consented to that previous sharing,
(3) unless the person depicted subsequently withdrew their consent to the image being publicly available and the defendant knew that they had withdrawn that consent.

Sub-section (3) was added following consultation. So revelations or allegations such as that made by Sharon Stone that she was not warned about explicit shot in Basic Instinct scene (Knight, 2021), or that while shooting the simulated anal rape scene in *The Last Tango in Paris*, Bertolucci 'sprung the butter detail on Schneider at the last minute, because he wanted her onscreen humiliation and rage to be real' and that Schneider 'felt a little raped, both by Marlon and by Bertolucci' (North, 2018) would not lead to viewers' responsibility even if the relevant offences captured viewing, or possession; nor should they lead to civil liability, and this result could be accommodated by either the *Expectation* test or a public interest test. While civil liability could be stricter than criminal responsibility, the relevant issues here are reasonable reliance on presentations of consent and withdrawal of consent initially given in commercial contexts. Possibly, reasonable reliance might limit liability for dissemination or viewing of NCII, but this would also depend on how the GDPR right of withdrawing consent is interpreted by the courts. The private law solution ought not necessarily, but could, emulate the defence in s 33(5) of the Criminal Justice and Courts Act 2015 and the Law Commission's position. Laidlaw and Young (2020: 172) suggested that the ability to 'revoke consent would be limited by any contractual arrangements though it should be possible for someone to breach their contract by revoking consent, subject to paying damages';[14] but it is unclear whether an obligation to pay damages for revocation of consent is justified or is consistent with the data protection regime.

4. Images and information as property: destruction or misappropriation of value?

A. Strict liability for destroying value

As demonstrated in Part 2, the current *Expectation* test could accommodate strict liability and is perceived as a stricter form of liability by some. True, the position defended here expands liability beyond current practice. First, currently, the defendant's knowledge or lack of it *could* be taken into account as *one* consideration whether *Expectation* exists. Second, one can find instances in which lack of knowledge led, or would have probably led to a no *Expectation* finding (Chapter 9, Part A.3). My suggestion is to solidify this discretion in a way that would clarify that at least when intimate images are concerned, defendant's lack of knowledge that the intimate image viewed is non-consensual would not prevent an *Expectation* finding, unless the defendant was passive in coming across them and did not keep them. Conceptualizing intimate images as a type of property, or at least as a subject matter that requires protection that is no less stringent than the one afforded to property supports the conclusion that viewers' liability should be strict. This was the view defended in Chapters 4 and 5, with respect mainly to intermediaries, but in fact also to viewers. In what follows, I examine whether the act of viewing NCII involves a destruction of value, or rather its misappropriation and conclude that it does both, but that even on the

---

[14] For their broader discussion of public interest in publishing NCII see pp 159–60 (a deepake parody of political figure example); 172–3.

understanding of viewing as destruction of property, strict liability, rather than fault should still govern liability for viewing.

Strict liability for viewing NCII might seem harsh given the asymmetry between the harm to the claimant from the breach of her privacy and the benefit to the viewer from viewing the image. In Chapter 4 I explained why this asymmetry ought to entail the priority of the original owner over the innocent buyer in a conflict over title situation. Put differently, the asymmetry seems to justify strict liability for viewing images, which is equivalent to rejecting a market overt solution, according to which the good faith buyer, when other conditions are met, acquires good title to the chattel and hence is not liable to pay damages under the tort of conversion (Ch4, Part 4). I will now evaluate the argument, that the asymmetry, rather, suggests that the subject matter of property was destroyed, rather than appropriated, and hence the relevant paradigm should be negligence, which necessitates fault, rather than conversion which does not. This line of argument, if successful, does not question the conceptualization of intimate images as property, but rather of viewing as appropriation. The logic behind such an argument is that paradigmatically, the value of the thing appropriated remains roughly the same when it is appropriated. Of course, sometimes the market value would be lower than the original owner's use value (one's laptop is a clear example) or of the convertor's (my bottle of water left in the desert and used by a dehydrated hiker). However, in essence, the appropriation does not destroy value but merely redistributes it. Arguably, when one's intimate images are disseminated without consent, one's privacy is destroyed or damaged, rather than being misappropriated, so conversion, with its associated strict liability, is inapplicable.

This reasoning is fallacious. Liability for conversion is strict due to the intentional exercise of dominion over the chattel (as opposed to the lack of that intention when one negligently destroys the property of another), rather than because value is merely redistributed rather than being destroyed or diminished. If I mistake your water bottle as mine and drink its content or dispose of it, value was destroyed, but I am still liable to its value, even though I have nothing to return. Indeed, the intentional destruction of a chattel is a major manifestation of exercising dominion over the chattel which amounts to conversion (rather than a mere interference with the owner's title, which might trigger liability for trespass to chattels). Moreover, a change of position is not a defence to a claim in conversion, so when the converted asset was destroyed by a third party (or by the defendant himself) while at the hands of the defendant convertor, the latter is liable for its value, even in the absence of fault, and in fact in the absence of causation between their breach of the duty and the claimant's loss.[15] Since (and to the extent that)

---

[15] *Kuwait Airways v Iraqi Airways* [2001] 3 WLR 1117 (CA) [606] (subject perhaps to inevitable destruction); cf *Kuwait Airways v Iraqi Airways* [2002] 2 AC 883 (HL), [92]

the viewing is intentional, albeit innocent, it should lead to liability, even if indeed the invasion of privacy should be conceptualized as the destruction of property, rather than its misappropriation.

A second indication that strict liability for conversion does not hinge on symmetry of loss is that stolen property tends to be sold for lower prices than its market value, so conversion, which is paradigmatically about misappropriation, might systematically reduce value and not only redistribute it. Moreover, in situations of conflicts over title, to which the innocent viewing of NCII is analogous, typically, an innocent convertor gave value to purchase the converted chattel, so they lose this value if they have to give up the chattel, even if they do not need to pay damages. Indeed, Mautner's influential observation (1991) that the conflict between the two innocent parties is an accident brings to the fore the understanding that in conflicts over title situations (subject to the possibility of the loser suing the thief, or the merchant) there is a loss that has to be allocated to one of the parties, rather than a reversal of transaction which leaves neither party worse off. For reasons explained in Chapter 4, such loss has to be allocated to the viewer/buyer, rather than to the original owner; and the fact the harm is asymmetrical serves, if at all, only as a further reason why this should be the case. At any rate, the understanding that conversion typically involves a loss to one of the two innocent parties is a further proof that conversion's strict liability cannot hinge on the distinction between redistribution and destruction of value. Finally, damages in conversion also encompass consequential losses; liability for such is likely limited to foreseeable losses when the convertor was innocent and direct losses for those acting in bad faith.[16] For this reason too, the claim that the symmetry between the C's and D's losses is what justifies strict liability in conversion is fallacious. My point is not that the damage from the viewing of NCII is consequential loss (although, if it were, it is foreseeable). Rather, that the innocent convertor's potential liability for foreseeable consequential losses belies the notion that equivalence of harm (or value) is what justifies strict liability for conversion. According to this mistaken notion, the market value of the chattel is the cap for liability, so it is unfair to impose strict liability when the owner's harm is much higher than this value.

('A person who misappropriates another's goods ... takes upon himself the risk of being unable to return the goods to their rightful owner. It matters not that he may be prevented from returning the goods due to unforeseen circumstances beyond his control').

[16] *Kuwait Airways* (HL) (n15) [103].

B. Viewing misappropriates value

The conceptual question remains – and is hard to solve – whether unauthorized viewing is more akin to destruction or rather to appropriation of property, and whether what is appropriated or destroyed is the image itself or the more abstract notion of privacy. Part of the difficulty lies in the fact that viewing NCII is neither purely damaging of value nor purely redistributive. When D unintentionally damages C's car, nothing of value is added to D's balance sheet, nor is there something D can trade. Moreover, D has not received any use value – a subjective benefit or value which has no market value. If D damages C's car out of malice, D receives some kind of non-pecuniary benefit, but still, nothing is added to D's balance sheet, nor can D trade it. In contrast, when D accesses an intimate image (without knowing it is non-consensual), D receives some kind of subjective value: sexual gratification, aesthetic pleasure and so on. Any benefit derived when D negligently damages C's car is derived from the activity that created the risk (presumably driving, perhaps without due care) not from the damage to the car itself.[17] Accessing intimate images is different, since the benefit from accessing C's particular image is inextricably connected with C's harm if the image is non-consensual. The viewer might be innocent, thus unaware that the benefit for himself was received only at the expense of a much bigger harm to C. But this does not alter the conclusion that the benefit is inextricably connected with the harm; nor does the asymmetry of value changes this conclusion. Value was not only destroyed but also redistributed to the viewer. While a pay per image business model is far from common for intimate images, including NCII (and child pornography), the viewer derives value from accessing the images (a value that is not derived from damaging C's car). Moreover, if the viewer pays a subscription for accessing the website or platforms in which intimate images are accessible, what he pays approximates the value he receives from access to intimate images. But even when the access is free, the viewer pays indirectly either by data or by exposure to advertisements: if you are not paying for the product, you are the product.

Depending on whether the image was captured by the viewer or is retrievable by him, the access to the image has also some trade value. True, this value is modest at best since the image could usually be accessed by other means. But by distributing the image further, the viewer does get some benefit, although this value is not necessarily pecuniary. Recall that some child pornography producers started producing in order to have access to new images by way of barter (US Sentencing Commission, 2012: 265). There are obvious differences between inadvertently accessing NCII and

---

[17] For the distinction, and for situations in which the harm itself benefits the defendant see Bar-Gill and Porat (2014).

accessing child pornography, including that the illicit nature of latter reduces the supply of available images and hence creates higher trade value for these images. But the comparison is instructive in showing that while both markets are primarily not financially motivated, images have trade value. If an NCII is accessed knowingly, the use value, and perhaps also the trade value of the image increases, although some of it might still be subjective.

C. Viewing pre-dominantly destroys value

But while accessing NCII (innocently or knowingly) creates some value to the viewer, and in this sense is partially redistributive – since this value is inextricably connected with C's loss – it is undoubtedly smaller than the harm it causes, and in this sense it destructive, and dominantly so. To see that, all we need to accept is that while the value of NCII to those who seek them cannot be lower than the value of intimate images to innocent viewers, the value of the former is still likely to be much lower than the harm to the victim. Recall the evidence that some viewers derive additional satisfaction from viewing NCII because the images are non-consensual (Dori, 2018; Holten, 2020); it follows that these viewers ('seekers') value such images more than they value an equivalent consensual intimate image. And yet, surely even seekers value access to NCII much less than the harm caused to the victim by the unauthorized viewing. Both the Chapter 6 findings about the significance of the harm, and anecdotal damages awards for NCII suggest that the right to privacy is valued in cases of massive dissemination at dozens of thousands of pounds at the very minimum; In *Mosely*, the amount awarded (against the publisher) in 2007 was £60,000 (see also Chapter 7, n4; Chapter 11, nn9–10). While I am not aware of any empirical study examining willingness to pay to have access to NCII, and even granting that any award against viewers should, and is likely to be, lower than the claimant's full damage given that the harm is overdetermined (Chapter 11, Part 5), it is very likely that seekers would be willing to pay much less (if at all) to access NCII – my uneducated guess would be no more than dozens of pounds for any given image, if at all. One indication that this guess is sound is the absence of any known market in which these images are sold, despite the demand for such images and despite the commodification of sex and the prevalent neo-liberal superstructure. Another indication is the relatively prevalent extortionist model applicable in cases in which the operation of dedicated revenge porn (and other reputation destroying websites) is economically motivated;[18] the

---

[18] *People v Bollaert* (2016) 248 Cal. App. 4th 699; Case No 2:13-cv-00926-CW-BCW (D Utah, 2015); Chapter 2, Part 3; Chapter 3, Part 3.B; Cf Digital Millennium Copyright Act 17 USC §512(1)(B) (1998); Chapter 4, Part 5.B.

extortion works precisely since the victim is willing to pay more to remove the image (or the item) than the potential consumers of that image are willing to pay to have (continued) access to it. Finally, even for seekers who put premium on lack of consent, the proliferation of consensual intimate images serves as a (or nearly a) zero-cost substitute; this is a likely significant curb on the willingness to pay significantly for access to NCII. If liability of viewers should be at the minimum at the range of few thousand pounds and their likely willingness to pay is a maximum few dozen pounds (if any), and if willingness to pay approximates the value derived from viewing the NCII, the conclusion that the viewing is dominantly damaging, and only partially redistributive is inescapable.

D. 'Privacy' or 'image'?

The distinction between damaging and appropriating might depend also on the level of abstraction: 'privacy' in the abstract is damaged, rather than appropriated, but images (and more generally information) can be appropriated and (at least to some extent) accumulated and alienated. If I took your car, I have an additional car, but if I took away your privacy, I do not have any additional privacy, I just damaged yours. After all, the defendant's privacy is not enhanced by invading the claimant's privacy. However, what viewers receive from the invasion of privacy both has value, even though it is not an enhanced privacy of their own, and this value is inextricably linked with the harm suffered by the claimant so in this sense is, at least partially, a matter of appropriation, and not only damaging. To see that, I suggest to answer the following questions with relation to the several examples presented in the following list.

1. Is the information private, in the sense that it tells us something about the claimant (who is arguably the owner of the information)?
2. Does the information have value which does not derive solely or mostly from the harm caused to the claimant by the publication?
3. Is this value increased or decreased if the claimant did not consent to the publication?
4. Is the value increased or decreased if the defendant is aware (or erroneously believes) that the claimant did not consent to the publication?

The first three examples are a consensual intimate image, an NCII viewed by an innocent viewer, and an NCII viewed by a 'seeker'. In a case in which an intimate image is consensual (example 1), the information is private in the sense that it is about the claimant (but is not private in the sense that there was no desired inaccess); the viewer derives some (albeit limited) value from access to the image; there is no harm (as the publication is consensual), so by definition the value is independent of the harm; in this scenario, as consent existed, questions 3 and 4 are irrelevant.

Where the intimate image is non-consensual, but the viewer is unaware (example 2), the information is private, and has the same value to the viewer as it had in the previous case. The value is lower than the harm caused from the viewing and it is hard to answer whether it derives solely or mostly from the harm caused by the publication. At a counter-factual level the value is independent from the harm since in theory, it could have been derived without harm had the claimant consented to the publication. Moreover, as the viewer is innocent, the non-consensual nature of the image did not contribute to the value he ascribes to the image. However, at a factual level, the value is inextricably linked with the intrusion of privacy – given the absence of consent, there is no way that the value to the viewer could have been created without the harm to the claimant. In this sense, while largely destructive, the viewing is also a type of innocent misappropriation since the value to viewers was created by the harm to the claimant. Since the viewer was not aware the image is non-consensual no added (or decreased) value exists.

In case of 'seekers' (example 3), the information is private, the value derives in its entirety from the harm to the claimant, as the value from the image would not exist without the intrusion of privacy, and the viewer is aware of this fact. The fact that a non-consensual image was sought (rather than the easily accessible intimate image which is not ear-marked as non-consensual) proves that its value to the viewer is increased due to the fact the image is non-consensual; and (as explained earlier) this higher value is still lower than the harm to the claimant.

Moving away from intimate images to publication of information undermining one's sexual privacy, there will be differing degrees to which the publication is valuable – a point largely captured by the public interest defence. But both in cases of public curiosity without public interest (such as the kiss and tell variety) and of public interest (such as naming a sexual predator) the value of the information is inextricably linked with the harm to the claimant: the reason naming an alleged sexual predator, or a suspect of sexual predation prior to charge is allowed (if this is indeed the case)[19] is that it might alert future potential victims of the predator, thus preventing

---

[19] Recent authorities assert that there is 'a general rule or legitimate starting point' (which does not amount to a legal presumption) that prior to charge, suspects and those arrested as part of criminal investigation enjoy a reasonable expectation of privacy (*Bloomberg LP v ZXC* [2022] UKSC 5); but acknowledge there could be a countervailing legitimate interest to publish one's name as a suspect of sex abuse in the investigation into the matter (which was not established on the facts of that case) *Richard v BBC* [2018] EWHC 1837 (Ch) [248], [252], [317]. The decision in *Richard* was criticized based on the need to encourage other victims of the suspect to come forward (Bennett, 2018). *Bloomberg* dealt

future abuse, encourage other past victims to complain, thus leading to a charge which might otherwise have not been brought due to evidentiary difficulties, and perhaps, deter predatory behaviour by others. All these benefits to the recipients of the information can exist only by undermining the claimant's interest in privacy. The upshot of the discussion is that at least with regards to informational privacy, recipients of information receive some value that derives from the claimant's lost value of her privacy. The following three facts do not alter the conclusion that intrusion into privacy has an element of appropriation, so could justify strict liability (if appropriation were a condition for strict liability, which is not): (1) what is received cannot be properly conceived of as an increased privacy of the defendant; (2) the 'transfer' is wasteful in the sense that the claimant's loss from the lost control over the information is more significant than the recipient's benefit (note that this would not be the case when there is public interest in publishing the information); and (3) in certain circumstances the publication is justified so should not lead to any liability.

★★★

It follows from the previous discussion that strict liability of viewers is much more justified than what might seem to be the case at first glance and that it fits well with current patterns of liability in private law: First, *Expectation* can accommodate strict liability. Second, *Privacy*, as an intentional and dignitary tort is understood to endorse strict (or at least stricter) liability in the sense that intention to act, rather than to violate the claimant's right suffices. Third, understanding private information (or at least intimate images) as property supports strict liability. Fourth, truly passive and innocent viewers can escape liability even under strict liability and even under conceptualization of intimate images as property. Finally, the extent to which strict liability is harsh also depends on how significant the damages will be, and whether in practice such suits against viewers will be filed. Chapters 11 to 12 deal with both questions.

---

with suspicion of corruption, *Richard*, of sexual abuse. In *Bloomberg* too, the publication, which involved a breach of confidentiality, led to liability. See also Moreham, 2019; and Chapter 11, Part 3. In *Flood v Times Newspapers Limited* [2012] UKSC 11 [74],[169], [199], the naming of a suspect in a police corruption case was found to be justified as a matter of public interest in the context of the responsible journalism defence to defamation.

In the wake of the 'Me Too' movement, the potential liability of those naming alleged sexual predators has come to fore. In some cases, victims of alleged sexual predators came forward despite having previously signed non-disclosure agreements (NDAs). See for example, Garrahan and Croft (2018). These cases involve extra layers of complexity in relation to the validity and enforceability of such agreements and ensuing questions about a possible right to restitution for amounts received under the NDA.

11

Scope of Liability for Breaches of Privacy

1. Introduction

This chapter completes the analysis of viewers' liability by discussing the scope of liability in misuse of private information (*Privacy*) both as currently understood by courts and scholars, and as it ought to be. While the discussion focuses on viewers' liability, it is broader than that. It makes references to uploaders and intermediaries and broader still, aspires to make an intervention in current debates about privacy as a tort and the relationship between privacy and reputation, thus contributing to broader debates in tort theory. The direct protection of privacy by a stand-alone tort, as distinct from being protected by the equitable wrong of breach of confidence, is a relatively recent phenomenon in commonwealth jurisdictions. As such, the authority about some fundamental questions is surprisingly scant, and lots of academic discussion reaches its conclusions based on reference to first principles. To my mind, there are three foundational questions about the scope of liability for breach of privacy, relevant to determining whether the typical harms suffered by NCII are capable of being compensated by a *Privacy* claim (or a comparative equivalent): The first, whether *Privacy* ought to compensate for the mere diminishing of control, for distress (and other consequential losses) or for both. This has bearing on debates in tort law and the law of remedies on the extent to which injury to autonomy ought to be an actionable damage in its own right (Part 2). The second, whether *Privacy*, or rather only defamation, ought to compensate for reputation loss. This relates to broader debates about the division of labour between different areas of law and claimant's election; coherence, the relevance of dated authorities and law's expressive potential (Part 3). The third, whether some types of consequential losses such as loss of employment, loss of dependency due to a break of marriage and losses from follow-up physical attacks or from suicide are too remote (Part 4). A fourth question, which is unique to *viewers'* liability, concerns apportionment of liability for overdetermined harm to which many viewers contributed (Part 5).

2. Compensating diminution of control, distress or both?

First, there is the question whether damages ought to be available for the breach of the right itself – the mere undermining of the claimant's control over the private information – and if so, whether such damages ought to accumulate to consequential damages (mainly for distress) or are alternative to them. In England, the authority of *Gulati v MGN* is that 'normative' damages can be given, and that in appropriate cases they can (and have) accumulate(d) with damages for distress.[1] The question is theoretically interesting and important but in the context of NCII has very limited practical bearing: since significant distress will almost always inevitably be present – indeed, often there will be some form of post-traumatic stress disorder – substantial damages will be available even if one were to eschew the role of normative damages. Conversely, since the award of damages for the breach itself is in practice subsidiary, it is unlikely to be awarded in NCII claims (against uploaders, viewers and intermediaries alike). As was best demonstrated by Eric Descheemaeker, such award is subsidiary in the sense it is given only when award for distress uncharacteristically would be much lower than what is deemed appropriate given the seriousness of the breach (Descheemaeker, 2018: 143, 153–4).

The academic terrain is split between those supporting an award for the loss of control itself – two prominent voices are Nicole Moreham (2018a) and Jason Varuhas (2018) – and those who oppose them, at least in accumulation to damages for distress – the most powerful claim against is presented by Descheemaeker (2018) with Robert Stevens (2018) also opposing them. Moreham's main point is that normative damages sit well with the harm model (what Descheemaeker calls a bipolar model) since the breach undermines the claimant's autonomy and dignity (irrespective of any distress and other consequences it might causes) and that protecting these values is the *raison d'être* of *Privacy* (and the corresponding ECtHR Article 8 jurisprudence). Descheemaeker's view is that the diminution of

---

[1]   [2015] EWHC 1482. In *Lloyd* v *Google* [2021] UKSC 50, the UKSC refused to extend this holding to breaches of data protection since personal data rights are not necessarily based on establishing reasonable expectation of privacy [130] and since liability for *Privacy* is strict, while liability for contraventions of data protection is fault-based [132]–[133]. The court ([114]–[123]) also relied on statutory interpretation of S13 of the Data Protection Act 1998.

control is an alternative way to think of the harm manifested in distress; that compensating both is double counting, as it is impossible to think of the seriousness of an invasion irrespective of its consequences, especially as no one is suggesting a conventional award for the mere undermining of control; that it is also incoherent with the rest of tort law, which opted for the bipolar model compensating the claimant for the harmful consequences from the wrong, and not for the wrong itself, and that resolving this question relates to another: whether the damages are individual or standardized; if the latter, the difference between the unipolar and bipolar models become very small; in practice, despite the opening position of the bipolar model being individual quantification, there is some measure of partial standardization.

The positions of both Moreham and Descheemaeker are well argued and have lots of appeal to them; my own position is (perhaps counter-intuitively) somewhere in between. Descheemaeker is correct about the risk of double counting, the relevance of the choice between individual and standardized awards and the practice under which there is already some standardization of awards, despite the starting point of individualized awards. In this respect, it is useful to note the following: in the area of non-pecuniary losses for personal injuries, English courts traditionally adopted (at least facially, and subject to the caveats mentioned by Descheemaeker) an individual approach to pain and suffering but a standardized approach – mainly objective but in fact hybrid – to loss of amenities of life.[2] Moreover, the area of compensating for injury to autonomy – on which I have written in the past and on which Israeli courts (and scholars) developed rich jurisprudence (Keren-Paz, 2007b; 2017; 2018; 2019b; Jacob, 2012)[3] – has to grapple with similar quantification questions. It is notable that in *Rees v Darlington MH NHST*,[4] the clearest – some would say the only[5] – and controversial example of recognizing injury to autonomy as actionable damage in negligence, the House of Lords opted for the ultimate standardize award of a conventional (flat) award for interfering with the claimant's reproductive autonomy. As I have argued, a conventional award is appropriate in cases in which the

---

[2] For the objective aspect see *H West & Son Ltd v Shephard* [1964] AC 326, 349; *Wise v Kaye* [1962] 1 QB 638; *Lim Poh Choo v Camden and Insligton AHA* [1980] AC 174.

[3] *Daaka v Carmel Hospital* 53(4) PD 526 (Supreme Court, Israel, 1999); CA 10085/08 *Tnuva v Raabi* (No 2) (Supreme Court, 4.12.2011); CA 8037/06 *Barzilaay v Prinir Ltd* (Supreme Court, Israel, 4.9.2014); CA 1303/09 *Kadosh v Bikur Holim Hospital* (Supreme Court, Israel, 5.3.2012);CA 4576/08 *Ben-Zvi v Hiss* (7.7. 2011, Supreme Court); *Ma'a'daney Aviv Osolovsky Ltd v The Chief Rabbinate Council, PD 56 249*, 276 (2002, SC, Israel).

[4] [2003] UKHL 52.

[5] Other cases are a matter of interpretation; for mine, according to which other cases recognize the right, albeit inconsistently see Keren-Paz (2018).

claimant was deprived only from the opportunity to refuse consent to the treatment but would have consented had she been asked; I termed these cases type 1 injury to autonomy.[6] But where consent would have been refused, type 2 cases such as *Rees*, the approach should be individual. Breaches of privacy, including NCII are a clear type 2 casas, in which the claimant was 'moved' without her consent to a subjectively inferior state of affairs, and therefore a conventional award is misplaced. Israeli courts also specifically grappled with the question (with inconsistent authority) whether damages for injury to autonomy accumulate to damages for the bodily injury caused by the failure to secure the claimant's consent (in cases she would have refused treatment) or are swallowed by the latter.[7]

I am less certain than Descheemaeker that it is impossible to quantify the seriousness of an invasion without resort to consequences, real or potential. He might be right about that, but I think further inquiry is needed. This goes in part hand in hand with Moreham's approach viewing the diminution of autonomy and dignity as a consequence of the invasion, which is likely to have its own gradation, and yet could be distinct from the distress caused by the invasion. Whether such an evaluation could be made without reference to the typical distress likely to be caused from the invasion is yet another question to which the answer might be debated. Many considerations familiar to reasonable expectation of privacy inquiry intuitively lend themselves to examining potential consequences but might be meaningful without resort to consequences.[8] These include the mode of intrusion (tapping a phone seems more intrusive than eavesdropping to a conversation in the gym's changing rooms); the type of information (information about one's health, seems more intrusive than about one's taste in wines); the level of intrusion (medical information on a chronic, acute or sensitive condition such as cancer, dementia, infertility, abortion, impotence or STD is more invasive than information about having a cold, breaking a leg or receiving the flu jab); the mode of dissemination (disseminating the information to many, or to those who know the claimant is more intrusive than disseminating it to few and who do not know her); the duration of the intrusion or the likely circulation of the information (tapping a phone for a year seems more intrusive than tapping it for one day) and so on.

---

[6] Examples include *Chester v Afshar* [2004] UKHL 41 and *Daaka* (n3).

[7] For discussion with conclusion that the dominant view seems to exclude accumulation see Keren-Paz (2018: n91 and accompanying text).

[8] Varuhas (2018: 72) makes a similar point, focusing on assessing the degree of intrusion with reference to *Expectation* considerations. Similarly, Moreham (2018a) justifies compensation for the mere loss of dignity and autonomy with refence to the reasons behind protecting privacy in the first place.

Finally, I am less certain than Descheemaeker that adopting a hybrid model of damages is indeed undesirable, incoherent or would lead to double counting. Damages for the diminution of control would be awarded as a matter of course, and could be accompanied by additional damages for consequences, if additional damage is pleaded, proven, and not too remote. The normal 'normative' award would reflect privacy's intrinsic value, which is not based on proof of the claimant's subjective distress, although it might refer to the typical distress likely to follow from the intrusion. The size of this award would depend on the criteria listed earlier, so would change according to the context in which the intrusion has occurred. Whether the viewer acted deliberately (for example, knowing that the image is non-consensual), negligently (taking an unreasonable risk that the image might be non-consensual) or innocently, would feature in determinations of how serious the invasion is, and could also feature specifically in awards of aggravated damages and punitive damages (as it has, occasionally, in decisions against uploaders and those intruding by taking unauthorized intimate images;[9] in England the availability of exemplary damages for *Privacy* is an open question[10]). Such an award would serve compensatory,

---

9 For some Canadian cases see three BC 'peeping tom' cases: *Malcolm v Fleming* [2000] BCJ No 2400 (BC SC) (35k punitive); *M (LA) v I (JE)* 2008 BCSC 1147 (20K general, 5K loss of income opportunity, 35 punitive); *TKL v TMP* 2016 BCSC 789 (85K general); and two Ontario default judgements in unauthorized dissemination cases: *Jane Doe 464533 v ND* (2016) 128 OR (3d) 352 (Sup Ct J) (50K general, 25K aggravated, 25K punitive; this was the maximal amount recoverable under this simplified procedure; the default judgement was set aside but no report exists on how the case was resolved and whether a full hearing took place; it is still considered as the case which recognized public disclosure of private facts torts in Ontario); *Jane Doe 72511 v N.M.,* [2018] O.J. No 5741 (same split of damages and heavy reliance on *Jane Doe 464533*). All these cases are discussed by Berryman (2018); *ES v Shillington* 2021 ABQB 739 (Alberta court recognizes in a default judgement a public disclosure of private facts awarding the claimants 155K: 80K general, 25K aggravated, 50K punitive). In US jurisdictions 'punitive damages awards are fairly common in nonconsensual pornography dissemination cases' (Goldman and Jin, 2018: 283, 303); although the study suffers from some methodological limitations. For aggravated damages in general see for example, Tibury (2018).

10 Eady J in *Mosley v NGN (No 3)* [2008] EWHC 1777 (QB) [197] ruled they are not available; but this was doubted by Mance SCJ and by Toulson SCJ (dissenting) in *PJS v News Group Newspapers* [2016] UKSC 26 [42], [92]. If NCII is to be understood as a type of sexual abuse, surely punitive damages should be available (if they are available at all in tort claims in a certain jurisdiction). But in England, on the authority of *Rookes v Bernard* [1964] AC 1129 (HL), their award in cases of sexual abuse (including NCII) is doubtful, as tortfeasors' behaviour does not seem to fit into any of the three categories including category B: calculated behaviour to make a profit in excess of the compensation payable to the claimant. The conclusion which applies to viewers will usually apply to the distributor of NCII, although possibly a different conclusion might be reached as to platforms.

vindicatory and deterrent purposes. If the claimant could show that she suffered exceptional distress beyond the typical one, she would be able to receive an additional award: if the behaviour was intentional as a direct consequence,[11] and if not, if the additional distress (or other consequences) is foreseeable;[12] the regular rules regarding eggshell skull claimants should be applicable for non-deliberate behaviour,[13] a point captured correctly by Mann J in *Gulati* in his reference to thin-skinned claimants.[14] Such a test enjoys the best of both worlds. In standard cases it leads to standardization of awards, horizontal equality (that is, between claimants), predictability and reduction of litigation costs. In the standard case, provided the basic award is sufficiently high, there is no need to litigate the hard-to-verify question of the claimant's subjective distress. Rather, the focus would be on the parameters which make the invasion to privacy a serious one (and the likely distress, significant). The important point is that a measure of standardization would avoid double counting whether the court's focus is on the diminution of the claimant's control over her private information or on the likely distress from the intrusion (but not both); consistency will be enhanced as the court would be able to draw support from previously decided cases. On the other hand, the possibility to add in appropriate cases compensation for exceptional distress will increase flexibility and the ability to respond appropriately to exceptional circumstances.

I turn to Descheemaeker's concern about lack of coherence. First, his own observations reduce the significance of the charge from incoherence: that under a standardized award model the difference between the unipolar and bipolar models reduces if not disappears; and that in practice there are elements of standardization in compensating both pecuniary and non-pecuniary losses. Second, as he hints, but does not fully unpack, the hybrid model applies in defamation law. Courts award damages at large and in addition, in appropriate cases, special damages (Part 3). Damages at large are very similar to awarding damages for the diminution of the right itself, as the damage is presumed. Defamation law has a long pedigree and is a central area of tort law; so the adoption of hybrid model is neither new to tort law nor a niche. What is more, it is quite similar to breach of privacy as both are dignitary torts, so coherence might in fact support applying this

---

[11] Stevens (2018: 112) with a direct reference to NCII as an example; *Kuwait Airways v Iraqi Airways* [2001] 3 WLR 1117 (CA) [103].

[12] *Kuwait* (n11).

[13] *Smith v Leech Brain & Co* [1962] 2 QB 405.

[14] *Gulati* (n1) [229]: 'A thinner-skinned individual may be caused more upset, and therefore receive more compensation, than a thicker-skinned individual who is the subject of the same intrusion. Mr Nicklin accepted that, in relation to distress, the "egg-shell skull" principle applied.'

model also to breach of privacy. Finally, the adoption of an objective measure for quantum (standardization of awards), or at least a hybrid model of both individual and standardized (objective) elements is more widespread than is even acknowledged by Descheemaeker; it includes also the hybrid model for loss of amenity, which has an objective element and a standardized starting point, but also allows courts to adjust awards to take account of the special features of the claimant's case (Tettenborn, 2021: 27, paras 57–9).[15] Similarly, liability for breaches on informed consent is also a hybrid of objective and subjective factors (Chapter 7, Part 3.D)[16] and this *might* translate also to the quantification stage. With the examples discussed by Descheemaeker himself (2018: 156–8), which include property damage, personal injury, false imprisonment and defamation, we might have reached the point in which the exceptions have swallowed the supposed rule so that the mixing of subjective and objective tests is indeed the norm within tort law, rather than an incoherent aberration of privacy law.

3. Reputation

A. Privacy *damages should compensate for reputational loss*

The relationship between the interests in privacy and in reputation, and between the torts of *Privacy* and defamation raise interesting questions that are of theoretical and practical importance (Yatar, 2003; Tomlinson, 2010; Hartshorne, 2012; Witzleb, 2014; Barendt, 2015; Cheer, 2016; Parkes, 2016; Mangan, 2017; Rolph, 2017; Bennett and Wragg, 2018; Moreham, 2019; Jinana, 2020). While implicated by NCII, these are not unique to this context and are indeed a bit peripheral to the questions whether to impose liability on viewers, intermediaries and distributors of NCII and to what extent. The position of English courts is basically sound: when the published information is both private and defamatory the claimant can sue for *Privacy*;[17] specifically, *Privacy* covers false private information.[18] It is currently unsettled whether *Privacy* damages also compensate for lost reputation.[19] At the same

---

[15] *H West & Son Ltd v Shephard* [1964] AC 326, 365.

[16] For my similar critique of a claim that resort to subjective values at the liability stage, in the context of compensating injury to autonomy, brings incoherence to tort law see Keren-Paz (2017).

[17] *Hannon News Group Newspapers Ltd* [2015] EMLR; *Khuja v Times Newspapers Ltd* [2017] UKSC 49 [21], [34].

[18] *McKennitt v Ash* [2006] EWCA Civ 1714 [86].

[19] Yes: *Richard v BBC* [2018] EWHC 1837 (Ch) [334]–[346], [350], [409]–[430]. Supporters include Bennett (2018) and (implicitly) Descheemaeker (2018); detractors include Wragg (Bennett and Wragg, 2018) and Stevens (2018: 113). No: *Sicri v Associated Newspapers* [2020] EWHC 3541 (QB) [163]. Only if the defendant is given the opportunity and fails to defend as true any statements that give rise to the privacy action and subject to

time, there are instances in which the dominant element of (commercial) reputation in the claim was relied upon, alongside other reasons, to deny the issuing of an interim injunction;[20] and there is some doubt whether established defences from the defamation realm are applicable to *Privacy*.[21]

The typical experience of an NCII victim is that both interests in privacy and in reputation are undermined, and often, as in cases of doxing – revealing the user's identity, which might include address – also freedom from harassment (Davidson et al, 2019: 46). It is useful to distinguish between the core case of non-consensual dissemination of an intimate image and a typical experience of victims under which the initial dissemination is accompanied by derogatory comments. The core case involves reputation loss because in a society in which double standards about sexuality exist, people tend to think less of women whose intimate images are distributed. The typical losses suffered by victims, which include loss of social, professional, and romantic relationships and opportunities are a manifestation of this truism. To the extent that the disseminated image for itself creates an innuendo, or is accompanied by text suggesting that the claimant agreed to the dissemination of the image, agreed for the image to appear on pornographic websites, agreed for the image to be taken when this is not the case, or agreed to provide sexual services on a commercial basis or on demand, the publication is not true and hence could also lead to liability in defamation (although the claimant has an interest to pursue the claim in privacy in order to be able to receive an interim injunction). Moreover, victims' typical experience involves a follow up communication which is defamatory, harassing, or both. So a follow-up comment that the claimant is a whore is both an invasion of her privacy – recall that false private information is a breach of privacy under both the English and (some) American case law[22] – and defamatory. The initial image in itself, and the follow-up comment in itself are both a breach of privacy and defamatory, and undoubtedly, the combined

---

the possible award of solatium for the claimant's distress and upset caused by their belief that the allegations are false: *Bloomberg LP* v *ZXC* [2019] EWHC 979 (QB) [150]–[151]. The Supreme Court in *Bloomberg LP* v *ZXC* [2022] UKSC 5 [79], in which the award was not subject to appeal, opined: 'We have reservations about the extent to which quantification of damages for the tort of misuse of private information should be affected by the approach adopted in cases of defamation, [as was done in *Sicri* and *ZXC*, but not in *Richard*, TKP] but it is not appropriate to address this in this judgment'.

20 *Terry v Persons Unknown* [2010] EWHC 119 [95], [96], [123].

21 *Mosely* (n10) [140]–[143] (responsible journalism). The Restatement (Second) of Torts §§ 652F,G (1965) applies defamation's defences of absolute and qualified privileges *mutatis mutandis* to the privacy torts.

22 *McKennitt* (n18); Restatement (n21) § 652E; *Peoples Bank & Trust Co. v Globe Int'l, Inc* 786 F. Supp. 791, 792 (D. Ark. 1992); but see *Jews for Jesus, Inc v Rapp*, 997 So. 2d 1098 (Fla. 2008) (no false light claim exists in Florida).

experience involves the undermining of both interests. Viewers, as distinct from distributors (including intermediaries if they are to be considered as publishers) do not commit a tort of defamation by reading the publication, although, on the analysis offered in this book, they do commit a breach of privacy. But on the view, which I support, that damages for breach of privacy compensate also for the claimant's reputational loss, this interest is protected also vis-à-vis viewers. Any other view risks leaving NCII victims without proper remedy, even against the uploader. As the core harm from NCII is plausibly reputational (due to double standards about sexuality) and derives mainly from the claimant's nude image, which is arguably a true fact (and not from any accompanying innuendos) there is a risk it would not be recoverable under defamation, so it ought to be recoverable in *Privacy*. Sexual privacy harms are significant and are inextricably linked with reputation so ought to be compensated in full. When a publication is not about a private matter, truth is a defence to otherwise defamatory statement. But where the information is private, reputational loss from its publication ought to be recoverable in *Privacy* regardless of whether the information is true or false. Of course, if the amount recoverable in *Privacy* under diminution of control or distress is high enough to cover reputational losses, there is no need for a separate head of damages for reputation loss – otherwise there will be a double counting problem.

The *Richard* decision suggests that reputation can be protected both via an award of general damages and via an award of special damages for damage consequential on the breach of privacy if foreseeable.[23] While care should be taken to avoid double counting, this approach is conceptually sound. In defamation, general damages are at large, so are presumed, and do not require special pleading and proof. This makes them very similar to the unipolar model adopted in *Gulati* according to which compensation is given for the undermining of the right itself. Indeed, if injury to reputation is presumed in defamation, and if *Privacy* compensates also for reputational loss, taking into account reputational loss as part of general damages for breach of privacy is straightforward. In libel, concrete consequential losses can be awarded as special damages in addition to general damages[24] and in slander, which is not actionable per se, special damages are the gist of the claim; awarding additional damages in *Privacy* for consequences of reputational loss is therefore principled: it sits well both with the award of special damages in libel and with the award of consequential losses in privacy (to be discussed later),

---

[23] *Richard* (n19). The quantification of special damages was left for a later proceeding [454].

[24] See for example, *ReachLocal UK Ltd v Jamie Bennett* [2014] EWHC 3405 (QB), refuting Campbell's prediction (2011: 197) 'that liability for special damages for defamation will, at some point, be queried in the English courts'.

be they reputational or other. The main issue is to avoid double counting and, as was and will be further discussed, the test for remoteness will be either directness or foreseeability and should be directness for intentional wrongdoers and foreseeability for innocent ones.

B. Right thinking people

Two further related comments are needed: about the gap between right thinking and real people and its relevance to NCII claims; and about the changing mores, their implication to the authority of old cases and the harmonization of privacy and defamation. I have already referred to the question, raised in the Law Commission Consultation Paper, whether the reasonable expectation of privacy test should take into account the claimant's membership in minority group whose values are more conservative (Chapter 7, Part 3.D). The broader question, familiar in the area of defamatory meaning, is whether a defendant should be liable for a statement that actually lowers the claimant's reputation in the eyes of ordinary members of society, but ought not do so in the eyes of right thinking members.[25] The issue is important and also has a cardinal temporal aspect: sexual mores are changing, generally in the direction of greater acceptance of extra marital sex. This raises two questions: first, whether, if we oppose the double standard about women's sexuality, we ought to conclude that damages for reputational loss in the NCII context should not be awarded, since right thinking people should not think less of a woman whose intimate images are circulating. This in essence is the critique of sex positive post-modern feminists of singling out NCII (and more generally sex-related harms) as uniquely harmful so as requiring a special, serious and possibly an exceptional response (Chapter 6, Part 3.F). However, it would be unfair to deprive a claimant of remedy for reputational damage actually suffered, just because people are not as elevated as judges, society, thinkers or activists would like them to be. This visits the sins of the audience's prejudices on the claimant, or, from a different perspective, uses the claimant as a means to achieve a symbolic or educational end, thus being problematic both deontologically and distributively (Keren-Paz, 2007a: 152–4; Keren-Paz and Wright, 2019: 212). I suspect that those opposing compensating claimants in false attribution as gay cases do so partially, since they falsely attribute bigotry to these claimants: as if the claimant going to court means

---

[25] *Byrne v Deane* [1937] 1KB 818; *John v MGN* [1997] QB 586; *Shah v Akram* [1981] LS Gaz R 814. In the last 30 years or so, with the advancement of LGBT rights, courts are split on whether falsely referring to the claimant as gay is capable of being defamatory, with many commentators arguing it ought not. See for example, Bennett (2016).

that *he* thinks that being gay is wrong; and since the claimant is a bigot, he should not get a remedy. But this might often not be the case. Reputation is a relational concept, and it is not the claimant's fault that others think less of him because they think he is gay. A claimant might sincerely be against any discrimination based on sexual orientation but still suffer reputational loss if was labelled as gay, since his social circle is less accepting than he is. So even though ideally, and getting back to the NCII context, we would like to do away with double standard about men and women's sexuality, and even if (and I am less sure of that), in an ideal world there is no reason for anyone to feel shame about their intimate images, this should not serve as a reason to deny remedy from actual claimants whose lives are ruined due to the publication of intimate images (or defamatory statements). To a large extent, courts do take into account the gap between the ideal of right-thinking people and the reality of actual people with all their biases, although perhaps they should do so even to a greater extent.[26]

In fact, compensating for reputational loss in *Privacy* when the embarrassing fact was private could provide an elegant way to reduce the tension between the demands of justice to the claimant and the need to express the appropriate symbolic messages. If, for example, a person being falsely referred to as gay could get compensation since sexual orientation is a private fact, he could get an award that would compensate him *de facto* for reputational loss (alongside other losses), without the expressive cost involved in acknowledging that being referred to as gay is likely to reduce one's reputation in the eyes of right-thinking members of society, or the cost of doing away with the established test for defamatory meaning. What is more, understanding sexual orientation as a private matter allows compensation in cases of outing where the claimant is gay but did not wish this fact to become public knowledge.[27] In some cases, they might have suffered reputational consequences as a result, which could be remedied while again sidestepping the 'right-thinking members' test. The same is true in the NCII context, in which the injury is conceptualized in terms of depriving the claimant of her sexual autonomy with no need to rely on the right-thinking members test in order to compensate the claimant for her reputational loss. In any event, in the NCII context, there is a consensus that the harm is serious and is worthy of criminal and civil responses. This is demonstrated by both the passing of legislation (mainly criminalizing the dissemination of NCII) and the courts' developing of the common law (by recognizing a public disclosure tort) in order to respond to NCII.[28]

---

[26] See *John* (n25) (eating disorder considered as defamatory). The fact that many courts still consider being gay as capable of being defamatory is yet another indication.

[27] *BVC v EWF* [2019] EWHC 2506 (QB) [246].

[28] See, for example, *ES* (n9) and *Intimate Images and Cyber-protection Act*, SNS 2017, c. 7 (Nova Scotia).

C. Dated mores

The second and derivative question is whether old defamation authorities that are ingrained in older, largely defunct notions of morality are still good law given developments in privacy law.[29] This is one aspect of the harmonization question of these two partially overlapping areas of law. An example of a dubious authority based on dated sexual mores is Scrutton LJ's obiter dictum in *Watt v Longsdon*[30] on the scope of qualified privilege:

> It cannot, on the one hand, be the duty even of a friend to communicate all the gossip the friend hears at men's clubs or women's bridge parties to one of the spouses affected. On the other hand, most men would hold that it was the moral duty of a doctor who attended his sister in law, and believed her to be suffering from a miscarriage, for which an absent husband could not be responsible, to communicate that fact to his wife and the husband.

A doctor daring these days to communicate such information to the patient's husband, and probably to patient's sister (the physician's wife) as well, is likely to face both fitness to practise disciplinary proceedings by the GMC[31] and civil liability for breach of medical confidentiality and possibly also for *Privacy*. It is well established that an adulterer has a reasonable expectation of privacy.[32] The more difficult question is whether the cheated upon partner's interest in receiving the information could justify privileging the defendant who tipped the husband off so that the former would not be liable for breaching the claimant's privacy. Similar to Eady J's analysis in *Mosley*,[33] the twin questions are whether English law ought to (and does, this is currently an open question) recognize qualified privilege for *Privacy*, and if so, whether in any given case tipping off the husband is privileged. I think that qualified privilege should be accepted and that as a starting point, a cheated partner has

---

[29] I have discussed a similar question in the context of claims by commercial sex providers against clients in Keren-Paz (2013: 53).

[30] [1930] 1 KB 130, 150. The case is still considered as an important authority on the general issue of scope of qualified privilege. In fact, the quote is still cited in a contemporary leading tort TCM: Lunney, Nolan and Oliphant, 2017: 765. In contrast, the abolition of words imputing unchastity or adultery to any woman or girl as a slander per se (S 14(1) of the Defamation Act 2013) is less relevant for NCII purposes: what was abolished is not the award of general damages for imputing unchastity to women but only the award of general damages for slanders, which was always an exception.

[31] Cf for example, *NMC v Wardle*, FPC 20–22 May 2019.

[32] For example, *CC v AB* [2006] EWHC 3083 (QB); *CTB v NGN* [2011] EWHC 3083 (QB); Warby, Garrick and Strong, 2016: 225.

[33] (n10).

a legitimate interest in receiving information about their partner's affair. But whether any third party has a corresponding duty to convey this information ought to, and would probably depend on the circumstances in which the third party (the defendant in a *Privacy* claim brought by the cheating party) found out about the affair and their relationship with both the partner and the claimant. While Eady J in *CC v AB* correctly observes that the cuckolded husband might have a special interest in *making* a limited communication about the affair (but denies the husband's interest in communicating to the media about the affair),[34] the analysis does not guide us in deciding who might have a corresponding moral or social duty to inform the husband about the affair (a point that was not raised in that litigation).

What is crystal clear to me is that courts would *not* afford a doctor – family member of the patient or not – a privilege to compromise his patient's interest in confidentiality pertaining to both medical and sexual matters and divulge the information to the husband whose interests conflict with those of the patient (if indeed she was having an extra-marital affair). The gendered language used by Scrutton L – 'most men would hold' – is somewhat telling, and a feature of its time. Most people some 90 years later would hold the opposite view. The importance of the interest in medical confidentiality was affirmed recently by the end-result in *ABC v St George's Healthcare & Others* in which the failure to disclose to the pregnant claimant that she might be a carrier of Huntington's disease, thus undermining her reproductive autonomy, was not considered a breach of duty of care owed to her, given her father's interest in medical confidentiality.[35] In the NCII context, according to both older, traditional sexual morality and the new, the unauthorized dissemination of intimate images is inexcusable, so the general question of harmonizing defamation and privacy law and better aligning liability based on changing sexual mores is of less importance for purposes of determining the liability of uploaders, intermediaries and viewers.

4. Remoteness: pecuniary losses, attacks and suicide

In the sister area of liability for viewing NCII, that of US criminal restitution for viewing child pornography, compensation is *limited* to pecuniary losses.

---

[34] *CC* (n32) [19], [35]. I reserve my judgement on whether this aspect of the decision is too harsh towards the defendant. In general, the court seemed to be quite unsympathetic to the defendant and wrongly so. Be that as it may, the distinction between limited dissemination that is permitted and a broader dissemination that is forbidden is the heart of qualified (and absolute) privilege.

[35] [2020] EWHC 455 (QB). The claim was initially struck out on the ground that a duty could not exist as a matter of law in [2015] EWHC 1394 (QB) but the striking out was quashed in [2017] EWCA Civ 336.

In *Paroline*, these future losses were calculated to be nearly $3 million in lost income and almost $500,000 in treatment and counselling costs.[36] So while the court grappled with complex apportionment and scope of liability issues, accepting that tort law would be a useful guiding starting point, compensation for the medical expenses resulting from the trauma and for the consequent loss of income capacity are mainstream in criminal restitution cases. Surprisingly, pecuniary losses are seldom awarded, or even pleaded in privacy cases, although there is a consensus they should be available based on first principles.[37] In *M (LA)*,[38] a British Columbia decision (in which liability for breach of privacy is statutory), the plaintiff was awarded $5,000 for loss of earning capacity due the depression from which she suffered after having found out her boyfriend clandestinely took videos of her and her infant child in the bathroom over a long period of time. In *Richard*, a non-NCII case, the claimant was awarded costs of 'reasonable and justifiable attempt, targeted at a foreseeable event' to mitigate his reputation loss with respect to potential follow-up publications and for a loss of a book advance that was consequential on his reputation loss; the court adopted a foreseeability test for remoteness, although no argument was made that the test should be directness of loss.[39] Both Jason Varuhas and Robert Stevens suggest that at least intentional wrongdoers would be liable for direct and natural consequences (even if not reasonably foreseeable); according to Varuhas, this rule might apply 'arguably more generally', namely to all those liable under these torts, so would capture also innocent viewers (Varuhas, 2018: 73–4; Stevens, 2018: 112[40]). The distinction between deliberate and innocent tortfeasors is supported (in the context of conversion) by the decision in *Kuwait*.[41] In *Richard* there is a suggestion that foreseeable yet indirect losses

---

[36] *Paroline v United States*, 572 US 434 (2014) 441.

[37] Nicklin and Strong, 2016: 598 (courts have yet to consider claims for loss of employment, dealing or endorsements; this pecuniary loss is akin to special damages in libel); Descheemaeker, 2015: 281–2 (pecuniary loss tends to be noticeably absent but could potentially arise in a privacy case as a consequential loss and would be recovered under the usual conditions; this is so given the negative effect on reputation; in a real sense this is a quasi-defamation action; in pure privacy cases it is difficult to imagine economic loss consequential on the release of information). Cf *Swinney v CC of the Northumbria Police* [1996] 3 All ER 449, in which claim in negligence for revealing of the identity of informers, who received threats and suffered psychiatric injury withstood a strike out motion. Note that as a pre-HRA case, the question whether *Privacy* could be claimed was not raised.

[38] (n9) [24], [39].

[39] *Richard* (n19) [409]–[430].

[40] According to Stevens, in cases of deliberate wrongdoing such as the posting of compromising photos of an ex on the internet, all direct (non-coincidental) consequential loss should be recoverable, regardless of whether it was reasonably foreseen or not.

[41] *Kuwait* (n11) [103].

are recoverable; this is contrary to common wisdom as uttered in *Kuwait* that where the tests do not yield the same result 'the foreseeability test is likely to be the more restrictive'.[42]

Loss of earning capacity could and does follow NCII not only from depression, but also due to reputational loss (recall Richard's book advance): current employers might fire, or future employers avoid hiring, a claimant whose intimate images are circulating, and in theory, if the claimant is a celebrity, endorsements may be lost (Chapter 6, Part 2.A; Descheemaeker, 2015: 281–2; Nicklin and Strong, 2016: 598).[43] There is a fine point here: if the employer fires the claimant because he thinks less of her but not because he fears reputational damage to the business given the continuous circulation of the images, there is no factual causation between viewing by other viewers and the loss of job. In that case, while the uploader of the photo and the one(s) bringing the image to the attention of the employer are factually and legally responsible for the economic loss as a direct consequence of the wrong, other viewers are not responsible for this loss. But in the normal course of events, the decision to fire the victim will be based, at least partially, on the employer's fear of reputational loss from employing her, or of her reduced productivity given the fact her images are circulating and could be potentially viewed by customers and co-workers. In such a case, there is factual causation between the viewers' viewing and the decision to fire the claimant, so liability should be established for this economic loss. Similar to my conclusion in the context of clients' liability to victims of sex trafficking, and for similar reasons, liability should inhere even if the viewing took place *after* the claimant was fired (Keren-Paz, 2013: 207– 09, 223–41; Keren-Paz and Wright, 2019: 204–5): the prospect of future viewing by unidentifiable potential clients is what largely behind the decision to fire the claimant. I posit that the economic loss from losing one's job is direct – it might even be considered as reasonably foreseeable – even if the decision to fire the claimant is discriminatory or otherwise unlawful. The question whether the viewer was innocent is relevant here, as the applicable test might be that of reasonable foreseeability, and the conclusion under this

---

[42] *Richard* (n19) [423]; *Kuwait* (n11) [100].

[43] Cf *Mason v Huddersfield Giants* [2013] EWHQ 2869 (QB). The claimant, a rugby player, was unfairly dismissed by his employer, following a tweet from his account, sent unbeknown to him by his girlfriend, of a teammate's anus the latter took with the claimant's phone when all players were heavily drunk. In a follow-up tweet, the claimant clarified it was not his anus but did not name anyone. The club cited as a reason for dismissal reputational concerns about family values, but there was no NCII angle to the case. The dismissal was considered unfair as the claimant followed instructions to remove the tweet, did not do anything deliberately and at best 'omitted to … remove promptly a tweet he had not posted of a photograph he had not taken'.

test might well be that a discriminatory decision to fire the claimant is too remote a consequence of the initial wrong – in that case the claimant might be able to sue successfully only the employer.

Beyond NCII, there is another sexual privacy scenario that in theory can cause consequential financial loss: the collapse of a marriage (or other forms of long-term relationships involving financial dependency) due to disclosure about infidelity. Successful (and even unsuccessful) claims in such circumstances are hard to find, presumably given the prevalence of a defence around the use of such information for purposes of legal proceedings (Law Commission, 2021: 330–3). But in theory, the defendant releasing the information causing the claimant's partner to divorce the claimant might have acted independently of the partner. I was not able to find any authority indicating that in such cases the financial loss is recoverable, and it is an open question whether damages would be awarded in such a case. It seems that this loss is as direct (and as foreseeable) as the one involving loss of employment (with respect to which authority is equally scant). Possibly, one or more of the following three intuitions are at work here to block such claims: (1) the modern recoil from recognizing a quasi-proprietary right with regard to one's spouse's sexual services (and hence the demise of claims for loss of consortium and alienation of affection); (2) (perhaps alternatively) a lingering notion that the adulterer is at fault so should not be remedied for their losses; (3) the related idea that recognizing such a claim undermines the law's coherence as the claim against the defendant attempts to undo the financial consequences of the divorce so as if undermines its justification. But while such logic still blocks tort claims to undo the results of criminal conviction,[44] liability for transferred loss is recognized in other civil contexts.[45] In a hypothetical case[46] in which an intimate photo of the claimant with another man caused her husband to divorce her, the decision to divorce is presumably ingrained in the husband's knowledge about the infidelity, not in the mere circulation of the wife's intimate images. While this has limited relevance for the cause of action against the disseminator of the image, as the information that the claimant had an affair is presumably private,[47] it might be relevant for the scope of liability of the viewer: presumably his viewing was not the factual cause of the divorce, although this conclusion could be subject to debate in some circumstances.

---

[44] *Gray v Thames Trains Ltd* [2009] UKHL 33.

[45] *White v Jones* [1995] UKHL 5.

[46] The Cyber Civil Rights Initiative survey, 2009 found that 13% of victims said they have lost a significant other/partner due to being a victim.

[47] See nn30–3.

The dissemination of intimate images might subject victims to physical violence either by stalkers or, in conservative cultures, by family members due to notions of 'family honour' (Chapter 6, Part 2.A). These consequences are a direct result of the publication of the information so should lead to liability of the uploader. The older authority of *Swinney*, dealing with potential liability of the police for psychiatric injury following failure to hold the identity of an informer confidential, leading to threats, is a weak indication that such a consequence is not too remote, even on negligence's narrower foreseeability and intervening causes tests.[48] But the question remains whether a viewer's viewing is the factual and legal cause of the injury. The two scenarios might call for different conclusions: the stalker who attacked the claimant did not seem to have done so due to the images having been viewed by others, so viewers should not be liable to that injury. Note, however, that since much of the harm from the physical attack might overlap with the harm from victim's knowledge of the viewing – in other words, due to the fact that the harm from NCII is indivisible – to that extent, viewers' liability is unaffected. So if for example, the loss of income capacity is the same, with or without the attack, the viewer remains liable, although, for the reasons having to do with apportionment, discussed in the next part, viewers' liability will be in any event limited.

A different conclusion is due in cases of 'honour' attacks. Here it seems that in the eyes of the attacker the main reason for the attack is exactly the fact the intimate image was viewed by many and is potentially viewable by many more. In other words, it is not only the fact that someone disseminated the image or that the victim voluntarily shared it with someone or allowed the intimate image to be taken that caused the attack. It is possible, that even cases in which an image was taken and disseminated without the victim's knowledge would cause an attack. In that case, it is both the viewing and the dissemination that are the cause of the attack, so intentional viewers ought to be responsible for the consequence. This is a site in which the culpability of the viewer might be normatively relevant. There is much to be said that such physical attack is direct but not reasonably foreseeable (since it is based on an intentional and culpable intervention by a third party). Hence, while a deliberate viewer ought to be liable for this consequence (even if his liability ought to be limited, as explained later), an innocent viewer ought not be.

It is not uncommon for some NCII victims to die by suicide or to attempt it (Chapter 6, Part 2.A). This consequence is direct so should lead to liability

---

[48] *Swinney* (n37). The indication is weak both because the decision was a motion to strike out and because its focus was on the possibility to establish duty of care, not on the issue of remoteness.

of the uploader and at least of deliberate viewers. It is beyond doubt that the actual and potential viewing of the image by many viewers is a main source of distress to victims so is factually related to the suicide. The personal injury case law views suicide as a potentially reasonably foreseeable result of the initial breach of duty.[49] This suggests that even non-deliberate viewers might be held liable for that consequence. However, one can rightly doubt whether this result is appropriate. In practice, under the solution defended later of a limited amount payable by each viewer, resolving the question becomes less acute as no single viewer would be held liable in full for the consequence of the lost life. Moreover, courts could take into account in deciding the amount payable by each viewer, whether they were deliberate; if so, a higher amount will reflect also the deliberate viewer's contribution to the suicide. The conclusion that at least deliberate viewers ought to be liable for the victim's suicide should not be opposed on the ground that privacy is not a post humus interest.[50] It is one thing to believe that the estate ought not to have a right to sue someone for publishing private (or defamatory) information post humus. It is another, to deny an otherwise valid claim for breach of privacy which affected the victim so profoundly that she took her life. Any other conclusion would lead to a reduction of liability due to the more severe consequences of the tort; a position which makes little sense and under which the victim's suicide becomes a factor mitigating the defendant's liability.

5. Apportionment in mass torts (again)

Liability of viewers, in the main, is for the harm from viewing itself.[51] In this sense viewers are not peripheral to the main harm, as arguably those buying sexual services from a non-victim in a market whose supply involves victims are, and as viewers of child pornography are for the initial abuse depicted in the images. So the reason to support a limited scope of liability of viewers is not that they are peripheral, but rather that they are many. In addition, for innocent viewers – those who did not seek NCII – liability might seem harsh, so a limit on liability is important.

---

49 *Corr v IBC Vehicles Ltd* [2008] UKHL 13; *Pigney v Pointer's Transport Services* [1957] 1 WLR 1121.

50 Privacy is traditionally understood as a personal right and as such does not survive death, although the picture is complicated (for example, medical confidentiality seems to survive) and changing (some statutory inroads in some jurisdictions in the context of digital assets). See in general, *Jaggi v Switzerland* (2008) 47 EHRR 30; Edwards and Harbinja, 2013; Banta, 2016; Davey, 2020.

51 The limited exception is liability of seekers for unlawful taking of the image and for any underlying abuse if these were made with dissemination in mind.

In recent years, I have dealt extensively with mass sexual torts and implications for scope of liability, first in the context of sex trafficking and then in the context of child pornography. A summary of my position with some extensions of the original analysis is found in Chapter 8 so it would be redundant to rehearse the arguments here (Keren-Paz, 2013: chapter 8; Keren-Paz and Wright, 2019; Chapter 8, except for Part 2). I would just like to highlight the following: The harm from viewing is overdetermined but less so than when buying sexual services that led to a victim being trafficked. In the latter case, the harm would be practically the same if any small group of buyers which includes the defendant would have abstained. Only when many would have abstained this might have made a difference, so the contribution of each individual client is small indeed. In viewing NCII, each viewer's actions alone were sufficient to cause substantial emotional distress and alongside a much more limited number of viewers, sufficient to produce severe emotional distress. The amount to be paid should therefore reflect this fact. The harm from knowledge about viewing is indivisible but for policy reasons could be apportioned (Keren-Paz and Wright, 2019; Keren-Paz, 2013). The fact that both seekers and innocent viewers, with different levels of fault ought to be liable suggests that an individual approach to liability should be applied. Seekers should be liable for direct and natural consequences (including suicide) and for invasions of privacy and sexual abuse done in order to disseminate the images; awards of both aggravated and punitive (exemplary) damages should be available. Innocent viewers should be liable for foreseeable consequences with no aggravated and exemplary damages available and should not be liable for underlying infringements of privacy (Part 2). For either type of viewer, liability should not be full. As the harm is indivisible and to a large extent continuous, liability could be imposed also for harms occurring prior to viewing (Chapter 8, Parts 3, 5.A, 5.B). Viewers' liability should be *sui generis*; several but not purely proportionate. This means that the claimant can sue several viewers and accumulate the awards awarded against each, at least as long she does not receive more than her overall damage (Keren-Paz, 2013: 216–19, 230–4, 236–40; Keren-Paz and Wright, 2019; Chapter 8, Part 3). I am not sure how useful it is to suggest a benchmark for an award against viewers, but perhaps an award in the range of 10% of the entire damage might be appropriate against seekers, especially if the quantum of the entire damage is assessed on the low side (Keren-Paz, 2013: 239; Keren-Paz and Wright, 2019: 228–9).[52] This could be adjusted down for innocent viewers or if the total quantum of damages is very high. The fact that the damages are at large provides courts with flexibility so they can take into account the mass tort

---

[52] For level of awards see n9 and Chapter 7, n4.

aspect of viewing NCII and the circumstances in which the viewing took place to achieve a just result that leaves claimants with a significant award without being oppressive to viewers.

An area that probably calls for development is calibrating the size of damages to the extent the viewer's identity is likely to harm the claimant or to cause her distress (Gewirtz-Meydan et al, 2018).[53] First, remote viewers who are less likely to encounter the claimant are likely to cause less distress and harm. Second, distress and harm are more likely when the viewer and claimant already know each other. So seekers who view images of a classmate, roommate, workmate and the like, should be liable to (arguably significantly) higher damages. Less intuitively, even innocent viewers who know the claimant should pay higher damages (recall that passive viewers would not be liable) since their viewing causes more harm.

---

[53] Cf *Paroline* (n36).

12

Is Suing Viewers Practicable?

1. Introduction

Is suing viewers practicable?[1] Both academic writing and policy discussions of NCII largely focus on both the uploaders of these images and on criminal responses to the phenomenon, although exceptions obviously exist.[2] While the civil liability of intermediaries is discussed, and considered as the new NCII frontline (Rackley et al, 2021), liability of viewers of images is indeed a cutting-edge idea that might, or not, become a future frontline. There is a general consensus that civil action against uploaders is relatively straightforward – a practitioner cited by Rackley et al refers to these cases as 'nearly all slam-dunk cases' – although, as we have seen, the picture in the US is less straightforward (Lollar, 2013; Skinner-Thompson, 2018). At the same time, the consensus is that the practical potential of claims against uploaders is limited due to the high costs of litigation and the prospect that many uploaders would be judgement-proof (Goldman and Jin, 2018: n290; Rackley et al, 2021).[3] In particular, the Law Commission Consultation Paper concludes 'that civil remedies are costly, time-consuming and may not be effective or accessible to most or all victims. Seeking redress through the

---

[1] For my discussion of similar difficulties involved in suing clients buying sexual services from victims of sex trafficking see Keren-Paz (2013: chapter 9).

[2] For the mainstream focus see for example, sources in Chapter 6, Part 2.A; and Law Commission (2021). For few exceptions see Brown (2018, exemplifying a fairly 'out there' scholarship contemplating a civil response, mainly tort based, against distributors of NCII); Suzor et al (2017); Department for Digital, Culture, Media & Sport (2019, online harms White Paper); Citron (2019); and Rackley et al (2021). None of these sources supports viewers' liability, or intermediaries' strict liability and some (like Suzor, the White Paper and to some extent Rackley et al) support a response which is focused on neither criminal nor civil liability.

[3] Other obstacles are the fear that the suit would draw further attention, which is significant where anonymity is not granted.

civil courts may require a victim to risk their financial security. It can be an ineffective tool' (Law Commission, 2021: 398). The verdict by Rackley et al (2021) is less damning: after explaining the unaffordability of civil litigation to most victims, the authors mention that 'the civil law has teeth and – if it bites – can leave perpetrators, and (in some cases) those who enable them, liable for substantive damages'. Echoing the argument I have made for the role of private law in remedying sex trafficking (Keren-Paz, 2013), the authors mention the empowering potential of private law, in that claimants have control of the process in civil litigation and by allowing more opportunity for recognition. Ultimately, however, recognizing that 'the sticking point, of course, is money', the authors suggest to focus energy in suing hosts, which if would prove successful, would dramatically change the technological landscape. In US jurisdictions, a study of judicial resolution, both criminal and civil, of NCII dissemination between the years 1984 and 2016 found 89 such cases of which only 18 civil enforcement cases (some of which lumped together distinct claims against different defendants) in which damages were awarded; of the 89 cases 11 relied also on invasion of privacy, 7 on public disclosure of private facts and 2 on false light or defamation. The authors mention that the actual number of cases litigated during the period that cannot be captured might be higher; however, this is likely to affect more *sui generis* state laws than common law claims (Goldman and Jin, 2018). At any rate, both the volume of cases and the number of successful claims seem to be very low. In Part 2, I will discuss the evidentiary hurdle faced by claimants of identifying viewers, which is unique to claims against viewers; then, in Part 3, I will deal with the issue of financial costs, in which I will summarize the findings relevant to uploaders and explain the potential differences from claims against viewers.

2. Evidence

Suing viewers involves two evidentiary difficulties: identifying those who viewed the claimant's images and identifying the images viewed by a defendant if the relevant website contained the images of numerous individuals. Technologically, it is possible to monitor traffic into a certain website, webpage or image, that is, to track the fact that certain individuals visited a certain website or viewed a particular image; but first, potential claimants need to know that their image is in circulation. In the context of child pornography, sophisticated technology and far-reaching investigative powers and resources are used in order to reveal the identity of viewers; but child pornography involves high level criminality, attempts of users to hide their identity and corresponding significant enforcement action by law enforcement, the ISP industry and charities (Cox, 2015; Peersman et al, 2016).[4] In the US, child pornography victims are notified when their images are captured. NCII users will not benefit from this extensive (and expensive) law enforcement activity: The possession of NCII is not currently criminalized, and even if it would, much less resources would be put into identifying viewers as their behaviour is likely to be deemed much less culpable in comparison to viewers of child pornography.

Once a claimant is aware that her image is circulating, she can request courts to order the ISP and operators of websites hosting her images to reveal the identity of those who viewed them. The flip side of the perceived reduced culpability of viewers of NCII (Franks, 2017: 1253–4)[5] is that they – at least many of them – are less likely to use technologies and channels, such as dark web and VPN (virtual private network) to hide their identity. So similar to users infringing ISP and other rights, viewers' identity is both likely to be known to the ISP and be available to the claimant – following a judicial order against the intermediary[6] – who can then pursue a legal suit against the viewers. In England, these orders are termed Norwich Pharmacal Order ('NPO'). For purposes of an NPO, the claimant needs to show an actionable wrong by the person whose details the claimant seeks the defendant to disclose, that the defendant is mixed up in those wrongs (even though defendant is innocent), that the claimant intends to seek redress against the alleged wrongdoer and that disclosure is necessary and proportionate to the third party's privacy and personal data fundamental rights. The following points should be borne in mind:

1. Thus far, orders were sought against the equivalent of distributors; for example, those posting defamatory statements, and sharing copyrighted materials. However, if the analysis in this and previous chapters is sound, viewing intimate images itself is a form of wrongdoing, and hence the logic that the disclosure of the viewers' personal data is necessary and proportionate as the only way to pursue claims against them would hold. One might dispute my claim that viewing ought to be considered as an intrusion which should lead to tort liability. But if one accepts that unauthorized viewing is a civil wrong, disclosing the identity of the

---

[4] S60A of the Investigatory Powers Act 2016 allows public authorities to request evidence of visits to illegal website which must be maintained by ISPs.

[5] 'Williams's reaction reflects the widespread contemporary view that looking at a woman's naked body without her consent is both normal and justified.'

[6] In the UK: *Golden Eye (International) Ltd & Anor v Telefonica UK Ltd* [2012] EWHC 723; *Rugby Football Union v Viagogo* [2011] EWCA Civ 1585, aff'd 2012 UKSC 55; in the CJEU: C-275/06 *Productores de Música de España (Promusicae) v Telefónica de España SAU* [2008] 2 CMLR 465.

wrongdoer is necessary in order to sue him. Interestingly, in *Viagogo*, the Court of Appeal endorsed the Rugby Football Union's (RFU) claim that the buyer of a ticket in the black market is also a wrongdoer. While the RFU sought to disclose only the identity of sellers and those advertising the sale of the tickets, nothing in the court's analysis suggests that an order against the buyers would have been resisted had the RFU sought it.[7] The viewer of NCII is akin to a buyer of a ticket in the black market in that both receive something contrary to the claimant's authorization. The court's property-based analysis – accepting that a buyer of a ticket in the black market trespasses if he enters the stadium with the ticket, and declining to decide on the RFU's 'much more problematic proposition' that the buyer in a black market converts the ticket – sits well with the analysis offered in Chapter 4 of privacy invasion as a property invasion.

2. NPOs are given in cases involving commercial interests (*Viagogo*), defamation and IP infringements. Given the more serious interests threatened by NCII, a proportionality analysis ought and is likely to lead to disclosing the details of NCII viewers. Moreover, as the main balancing exercise for NPO is between the claimant's interests and the user's privacy and data protection interests, there is much to be said that when the alleged wrongdoing is manifested in a serious undermining of the claimant's privacy, relatively little weight should be given to the user's privacy interest militating against disclosing his identity. This 'poetic justice' logic is behind claims such as that victims of sex trafficking should be allowed to sue innocent clients in conversion since the latter treated the former as property (Keren-Paz, 2010), that restitution of proceeds from a conscious wrongdoer (so not allowing deduction for costs in producing the net profit) is consistent with corrective justice since it denies the defendant a protected interest in his own property, a right he denied the claimant (Weinrib, 2000), and that that society should be intolerant towards the intolerant (Nehushtan, 2007). More generally, this logic is behind the role of reciprocity in tort theory (Fletcher, 1972) and in justifying qualified privilege (in order to protect a defendant's legitimate interest) as a defence to defamation and breach of privacy claims.[8] Some UK and ECtHR authorities go in a similar direction, emphasizing the sexual privacy interests of victims as reason for rejecting privacy-based claims of suspects in the context of gathering evidence against them. In *Sutherland v HM Advocate*,[9] in

---

[7] *Viagogo* id [1], [19]–[20].

[8] *Watt* [1930] 1 KB 130, 147; *CC v AB* [2006] EWHC 3083 (QB); *Mosley v NGN (No 3)* [2008] EWHC 1777 (QB).

[9] [2020] UKSC 32 [43].

the context of 'paedophile hunters' the Supreme Court concluded that Article 8(1) was not engaged by the decoy divulging the evidence to the police based, inter alia on that:

> The actions of the appellant were aimed at the destruction or limitation of the rights and freedoms of a child under article 8 which are the subject of positive obligations owed to children by the state under that provision, in a context in which those positive obligations outweighed any legitimate interest the appellant could have under article 8(1) to protection for his actions.

The court relied on *KU v Finland* in which the domestic failure to force, based on domestic privacy laws, an ISP to identify a user who placed as advert suggesting that the 12-year-old applicant was looking for an intimate relationship, amounted to violation of the applicant's right to respect of his private life.[10] While *Sutherland* emphasizes the rights of children and the fact the prohibited behaviour is criminalized – points that distinguish the liability of viewers of NCII from that in *Sutherland* – the court also emphasizes as a reason that Article 8 was not engaged that the evidence was gathered by a private citizen, rather than by the state. This, and ECtHR authority that the state might be in breach of its positive obligation to victims in not affording an effective criminal response to serious violations of sexual autonomy, even though civil remedy is available,[11] suggest that the state might have a positive obligation to enable an effective civil response against viewers of NCII, at least if viewing is considered as an actionable wrong, and at least against intentional viewers, so that an NPO is likely to be given to reveal viewers' identity.

3. The disclosure is sought against those who committed 'actionable wrong' against the claimant. It follows then that whatever the scope accepted by courts of viewers' liability, it should lead to disclosure of details of potential wrongdoers falling within this scope. So for example, if contrary to my view, courts (or the legislature) would decide that only those knowingly or recklessly viewing NCII should be civilly liable, the court ought to accept NPO requests against those visiting dedicated websites. If the standard is that of negligence,

---

[10] [2009] 48 EHRR 52. But see *Benedik v Slovenia* CE:ECHR:2018:0424JUD006235714 in which there was an interference with the right of respect for private life in relation to a police investigation into the downloading and copying of child pornography by the applicant via the internet.

[11] *X and Y v The Netherlands* (1986) 8 EHRR 235 [27].

arguably the court ought to give an order against those visiting general porn websites in which the claimant's image appeared (Chapter 9, Part 3.A.2, 3). If liability is strict, an order should be given against all those who actively surfed websites in which such image appeared. Should NCII become a statutory tort, specific disclosure provisions could encompass viewers, similar to Nova Scotia's Act, which currently targets distributors: the 'Court may order any person' to 'provide to the applicant any information in the possession of the person that may help identify a person who may have used an Internet Protocol address, website, electronic username or account, electronic mail address or other unique identifier that may have been used to distribute an intimate image without consent'.[12] This could be amended to 'distribute or view'.

4. The NPO applicant needs to have a genuine intention to seek redress against the person whose details are sought. For this reason, the NPO request was rejected in *Golden Eye (No 2)*.[13] This is not likely to be a hurdle to claims against viewers. It is not very likely that claims against viewers will be recognized while claims against intermediaries would not and if claims against intermediaries be recognized, the likely demand for claims against viewers will be likely small. But even if an alternative defendant exists, and is deeper pocketed, as long as the viewer committed an actionable wrong, a claimant is likely to be deemed to have a genuine intention to seek redress against the viewer if she bothers to take the trouble and expense involved in seeking an NPO.[14] Indeed, if the claimant has an available claim against the intermediary and yet she seeks the details of viewers who committed an actionable wrong against her in viewing the images, it seems that the conclusion she has a genuine intention to seek redress against the viewer(s) only strengthens. The claimant in *Golden Eye (No 2)* presented a consistent failure to sue any of those alleged wrongdoers whose details were disclosed in previous NPOs. This is not likely to be the case of NCII victims seeking NPO. Nor is the fact that the claimant is likely to choose carefully which viewers out of all those viewing her images she will sue likely to be considered as negating a genuine intention to seek redress according to the relevant cases: 'I accept the Applicants' submission that they cannot be expected to sue everyone and that it is not necessarily abusive for them to seek a

---

[12] See, for example, *Intimate Images and Cyber-protection Act*, SNS 2017, c. 7 (Nova Scotia).

[13] *Golden Eye International v Virgin Media and Persons Unknown* [2019] EWHC 1827 (Ch).

[14] Cf *Viagogo* (n6) [23].

sum by way of settlement which is higher than that which would be awarded by a Court'.[15]

5. An NPO is predicated on the assumption that the intermediary is innocent yet is sufficiently mixed-up with the third party's wrongdoing so has to disclose the latter's identity. It is beyond doubt that similar to the other contexts in which intermediaries were asked to disclose the identity of wrongdoers, they will be considered as sufficiently mixed-up with the user for the purposes of the NPO test. The bulk of the argument presented in Chapters 2 to 7 was that the intermediaries are not really innocent but rather have themselves committed an actionable wrong against the claimant. If this view be accepted, the practical motivation to go after the viewers will significantly diminish. However, legally speaking, the fact that the intermediary is not innocent, only strengthens the claim for disclosure: if the intermediary supported the tort or acted to obstruct justice, then disclosure is prima facie appropriate.[16]

6. The necessity and proportionality analysis revolves around whether the claimant has alternative means of identifying viewers. Since she typically would not, the court will likely give an order to disclose. While the Supreme Court in *Viagago* disapproved of the Court of Appeal's presumption of proportionality in ordering disclosure where no alternative way to identify the wrongdoer exists, in *practice* such presumption might be operative and it does not seem that NCII viewers will form part of the 'limited instances' in which data subjects' rights will be so strong as to outweigh the claimant's interest in disclosure.[17]

I turn now to the second evidentiary problem. Consider a defendant who visited a dedicated revenge porn website whose landing page includes the claimant's image. Should he be liable for invading the claimant's privacy? If liability for NCII is going to hinge on viewing (as distinct from possessing) an image, should a visitor of such a website be considered as having viewed (and hence breached the privacy) of all victims whose images were available on that website, or only those he has actually viewed? To begin with, the history of clicked images could be retrieved from the ISP and the website operator. When there is no indication of clicks, session replay scripts, which are commonly used, record user's keystrokes, mouse movements, and scrolling behaviour, along with the entire contents of the pages they visit, and send them to third-party servers (Englehardt, 2019; Ravenscraft, 2020). Such scripts, if available, could enable the court to determine whether the

---

[15] *Golden Eye (no 2)* (n13) [59]–[60]; cf *Viagogo* id [24].

[16] *Totalise v Motley Fool Ltd* [2001] EWCA Civ 1897.

[17] *Viagago* (SC) (n6) [46]; cf Riordan, 2016: 87.

visitor viewed the claimant's images. Finally, some legal presumptions could be developed, for example that all images in the website, or at least those observable on the landing page would be considered as viewed by the visitor.

3. Costs

The costs of litigating against the uploader are prohibitive, and are even more so where information is sought from the intermediary in order to be able to identify the uploader. Chrissy Chambers crowdfunded her claim with an estimated cost of £22,000 to begin proceedings (Marshall, 2016).[18] The costs of obtaining an NPO against a platform in the NCII context are estimated to be in the range of £50,000–£60,000 (Law Commission, 2021: 398). These costs are typically incurred in order to identify one uploader, so are likely to be higher, although presumably, not linearly, if disclosure of details of numerous viewers is sought.

As a general observation, the practicability of claims against viewers seems to be possibly greater than that of claims against uploaders and lower than that of claims against intermediaries. The costs hurdle is general to claims against all potential defendants. For early litigators against viewers, the risk of liability for the defendant's costs should the claim fail is an added hurdle, although, to be fair, claims against uploaders are still a rarity despite the availability of no win no fee agreements and a practitioner's observation that most of these cases are 'slam-dunk'. This reveals a general access to justice shortcoming which is important and highly problematic but whose detailed analysis is beyond the scope of the present work. In terms of costs, the paucity of claims against uploaders despite the soundness of the cause of action (beyond lack of awareness (Rackley et al, 2021)) might be the result of the estimation that the uploader is judgement-proof. In this sense, a claim or claims against viewers might increase victims' access to justice since there are many more potential defendants to choose from, since the claimant can pick viewers who are more likely to be solvent, and since, assuming liability is limited to a substantial amount that still falls significantly short from full compensation, there will be many more solvent defendants within reach.

The solution of *sui generis* liability of viewers I support (liability to a significant amount which is neither full, nor proportionate or purely several) (Chapter 11, Part 5) decreases the practicability of the cause of action against viewers. It requires the claimant to conduct several litigations against numerous viewers in order to receive adequate compensation. However,

---

[18] Chambers has settled her claim, as did the claimant in *AY v Facebook (Ireland) Ltd* ([2016] NIQB 76 after Facebook's motion to strike out the claim has failed (see Kleeman, 2018; Irish News, 2018).

this is both mandated by the demands of justice (avoiding excessive viewers' liability) and with proper apportionment would hopefully still leave the claimant with acceptable measure of compensation even if just one, or few viewer(s) is sued successfully. Granted, the experience of US victims of child pornography in receiving (supposedly) mandatory criminal restitution has not been great. The big impact of the 2018 AVAA – the Federal post-*Paroline* legislation discussed in Chapter 8 – was not necessarily a change in prevalence of victims seeking restitution as much as it was a change in the minimum awards of victims already seeking restitution; The Act set a $3,000 floor for criminal restitution against any individual convicted viewer. But not all victims whose viewers are prosecuted seek restitution – although most of those identified by the victim notification system do. In 2020, restitution was ordered in 570/1023 of child pornography sentencing cases (which include possession, but also production and distribution); the mean award was $17,615, the median, $9,000 (US Sentencing Commission, 2020). The big problem, however, remains one of collecting the restitution orders made:

> While most of the victims in the [victim notification system] have likely received some amount of restitution over the years, it is a small fraction of their total losses. We have received restitution checks for 15 cents. The vast majority of restitution orders are never paid and if they are paid they are not paid in full. (Mabie, 2021)

> At one point the collection rate for my clients was 7%. I now make more of a point to negotiate the payment itself in addition to amount of the order. I think we are up to 12%. My office also has received checks for as little as 1 cent. (Hepburn, 2021)

It is anyone's guess whether enforcement of awards ordered in civil trials against viewers of NCII would be more effective. Presumably, the control a claimant has over whom to sue combined with the fact that presumably viewers of NCII come from a heterogenic socio-economic background (but isn't that true for viewers of child pornography?) would increase the chance that damages be collected. In addition, convicted offenders of child pornography are more likely to be incarcerated so might be less pressed to pay restitution orders than viewers of NCII who will not be incarcerated. Given the additional cost involved in identifying NCII viewers, the more significant the liability of each individual viewer, the more viable the claim is. As previously explained, the amount owed by each viewer should be significant (Chapter 11, Part 5; Chapter 8, Part 1).

The question whether claims against viewers are practicable is itself largely academic and (regardless) should not be dispositive of deciding whether to recognize such claims: if intermediaries would be held liable for hosting these images suing viewers becomes unnecessary in order to receive compensation. However, if some claimants wish to sue viewers, they should be able to do so, if this cause of action is otherwise conceptually sound and just. The fact that such cause of action would not be an effective regulatory tool is neither here nor there; some compensation is better than nothing, and access to justice hurdles regarding otherwise meritorious claims should be alleviated, rather than serve as a justification to deny the cause of action (Keren-Paz, 2013: chapter 9, in the similar context of claims against buyers of sex from victims of sex trafficking). Furthermore, claimants' motivations might be other than seeking effective financial relief. In *M (LA)*, the claimant's motivation in suing civilly was to hold the defendant to account, in the absence of a criminal avenue[19] – a point that is pertinently relevant to claims against viewers who might equally not be criminally responsible. Similar motivations seem to exist also in the field of sex trafficking. In *AT v Dulghieru*, the claimants sued their traffickers who were already incarcerated and had already unsatisfied confiscation orders made against them, totalling approximately £786,000.[20]

Finally, if and when such cause of action be established, it is possible that access to justice in this area would be improved. The costs of suing viewers would presumably be lower if the possession (or viewing) of NCII were to form a statutory tort (or, if intentional, a criminal offence). As Chapter 9, Part 2, demonstrated, currently, there is only limited policy and activism push in the direction of holding even culpable viewers of intimate images to account. This book suggests that viewers ought to be accountable to victims of NCII and that *Privacy* civil strict liability is a good start, which can and ought to be adopted by courts. Unlike S230 Communications Decency Act, Article 14 ECD's safe harbour is inapplicable to users so viewers' liability (outside of the US) does not require any legislative change.

---

[19]   *M (LA) v I (JE)* 2008 BCSC 1147 [17], [23].
[20]   [2009] EWHC 225 (QB).

13

Conclusion

I have attempted in this book to expand the very substantial and growing literature, and policy discussions, around intimate image abuse, by focussing on issues around civil law, platform and viewers' liability. The book advances the field by engaging with ways to tackle these forms of abuse beyond the criminal law (the dominant and familiar approach).

Policy-wise, the book highlights several important points. The harm from intimate image abuse is the product of deep societal currents; it is systemic and gendered. Crucially, it is produced by many, not only by those who upload or actively distribute these images. As such, the response should target both internet intermediaries and viewers. Intermediaries are not merely the providers of passive and neutral fora in which such abuses occur. Rather, by hosting these images (and also by aggregating, although this has not been the focus of my argument), they both actively contribute to the claimant's right-violation and to the ensuing harm, and do so for profit; their business model relies on user generated content and they disproportionately benefit from illegal (and especially salacious) content. Therefore, not only should they not enjoy post-notice immunity (as the US regulation grants them) but they should actively filter such images and should be strictly liable for any remaining non-consensual intimate images they host. In reality, hosts sell the claimant's images without the claimant's consent. As long as the sellers of chattels – 'normal' stolen property – are strictly liable to the original owner, as is currently overwhelmingly the case, so should hosts. But even if we have reasons to think that strict liability of sellers of chattels is too harsh, there are reasons to believe, as explained in the book, that strict liability of hosts is still justified. Based on the inalienability paradox, I have concluded that whether we should treat intimate images (or more broadly private information) as the subject of property right, as is currently at least the de facto situation, or as too precious to be sold voluntarily (and hence as inalienable), the seller of such images – and indeed the buyer – cannot be in a better position of the one who sells or buys stolen chattels without the owner's authorization.

Nor should general strict liability of hosts for users' content violating other rights follow. Intimate image abuse is different from many other types of violation: it is a dignitary harm which leads to severe and largely irreparable harm, it is gendered, and it is a type of a sexual abuse. It is also easier to filter and as such the financial and freedom of expression costs involved in its removal are significantly lower than the costs involved in cases of defamation and copyright. So the analysis offered in this book criticizes both the US and the EU main regulatory frameworks: the US's (and increasingly so the EU's) for favouring the wrong type of interest – copyright; the EU's for traditionally adopting the horizontal approach according to which intermediaries' extent of liability does not depend on the type of violation ingrained in the users' content. Having said so, the argument defended in this book could support the policy move of de facto strict liability of some big profit-based hosts to copyright violations of users in the Copyright Digital Single Market Directive. But in that case, a requirement to actively filter intimate images becomes even more justified and necessary.

Nor is the slack cut to smaller platforms by EU and UK regulation justified, at least as far as NCII is concerned. The active contribution, profit motive and significance of harm all point to the conclusion that if a platform cannot pay its costs, and if a regulated market cannot ensure the sharing of technology effectively filtering such images, the platform should be out of business, despite any possible loss to market competition. In cases of sexual privacy, the harm is disproportionately caused by viewers who know or who are likely to know the claimant. As long as these people are likely to view the images hosted by a small platform, there is no justification to distinguish small from big platforms.

The harm to claimants from NCII is caused mainly by the viewing of these images. Viewers' contribution to the right-violation and the harm caused to the claimant requires that they too be held to account. The understanding of viewing NCII as the equivalent of buying stolen property (for which civil liability is largely strict) leads to a conclusion that viewers' liability should be strict. Moreover, understanding the viewing of child pornography as a specific (and extreme) case of NCII suggests that the stark difference between a zealous regulatory response to the former and a very lax response to the latter does not make sense. The defences to criminal responsibility in the child pornography context could be adopted as safeguards to avoid over-broad civil strict liability in the context of NCII. The similarity between the child pornography and the NCII contexts also demonstrates the usefulness of the property-based regulatory approach to viewing NCII, as the criminal responsibility for viewing child pornography is governed by the concept of possession which has a clear property lineage. While I have not pushed the point in the book, criminal responsibility for intentional viewing of NCII could be justified along these lines.

Even if strict viewers' civil liability is deemed too harsh, there is still a case for a fault-based liability: those who seek intimate images in commercial porn websites take a significant risk that some of the images they view are non-consensual. Therefore, they should be liable to claimants whose NCII they viewed on the website. Obviously, those who seek NCII, on any platform, because they are non-consensual, or otherwise know the images are non-consensual should be liable for breach of the claimant's privacy.

The harm from viewing NCII is over-determined – so most of it cannot be pinned down to any individual viewing. On this understanding, NCII is an instance of mass torts, in which many defendants are involved in the right-violation and the ensuing harm. For reasons explained in the book, the liability of each individual viewer should be to a significant amount, but not to the claimant's entire loss.

Alongside the policy contributions, the book makes contributions to private law theory and doctrine, mainly in the areas of tort, remedies, and privacy law. These are summarized in the introduction and will not be repeated here. From the perspectives of both policy and theory – mainly jurisprudence and private law theory – the book defends an approach underlying also my previous work: that private law is an appropriate regulatory tool to problems most often thought of only or mainly through a criminal law prism; that it has an empowering potential – it allows claimants to decide whether they view themselves as victims, and if so, who is responsible for the right-violation and under what theory (in other words, private law is instrumental in the naming, blaming, claiming process); that it expands the potential pool of those who could and should be responsible to the relevant right-violations (in our case, also platforms and viewers, not only uploaders and distributors); and that it could be used either alongside criminal responsibility (or other regulatory responses) or in lieu of such responsibility. So for example, even if the recent Law Commission's recommendation (2022: 171) not to criminalize possession of NCII be adopted, there is still room to impose civil liability for viewing or possessing these images. The social cost of intimate image abuse is heavy. Private law strict liability for breach of privacy imposed on hosts and viewers, alongside an upload filtering requirement, can help carry this burden, if not significantly reduce this cost.

References

Abraham, Kenneth and White, Edward. (2019). The Puzzle of the Dignitary Torts. *Cornell Law Review*, 104(2): 317–80.

Adler, Matthew. (2012). *Well-Being and Fair Distribution: Beyond Cost-Benefit Analysis*, Oxford: Oxford University Press.

Adler Matthew and Posner, Eric. (1999). Rethinking Cost-Benefit Analysis. *Yale Law Journal*, 109(2): 165–248.

Ahlert, Christian, Marsden, Chris and Yung, Chester. (2004). How Liberty Disappeared from Cyberspace: The Mystery Shopper Tests Internet Content Self-Regulation. *Academia*, [Online] 1 January. Available from: https://www.academia.edu/686683/How_Liberty_Disappeared_from_Cyberspace_The_Mystery_Shopper_Tests_Internet_Content_Self-Regulation [Accessed 22 July 2022].

Allen, Anita. (2010). Privacy Torts: Unreliable Remedies for LGBT Plaintiffs. *California Law Review*, 98(6): 1711–64.

Allen, Anita. (2011). *Unpopular Privacy: What Must We Hide?* Oxford: Oxford University Press.

Alter, Charlotte. (2014). Clicking on Jennifer Lawrence's Nude Photos Is Sleazy, but Is It Really Sexual Assault? *Time*, [Online] 2 September. Available from: https://time.com/3258898/jennifer-lawrence-kate-upton-naked-photos-icloud-hacking/ [Accessed 22 July 2022].

Angelopopulos, Christina. (2015). Delfi v Estonia: ISPs and the Freedom to Impart Information. *The IPKAT*, [Blog] 24 June. Available from: http://ipkitten.blogspot.nl/2015/06/delfi-v-estonia-isps-and-freedom-to.html [Accessed 22 July 2022].

Angelopoulos, Christina. (2020). Primary and Accessory Liability in EU Copyright Law, in Rosati, Elenora (ed) *The Routledge Handbook of European Copyright Law*, Abingdon: Routledge, 193–214.

Angelopoulos, Christina and Smet, Stijn. (2016). Notice-and-Fair-Balance: How to Reach a Compromise Between Fundamental Rights in European Intermediary Liability. *Journal of Media Law*, 8(2): 266–301.

AP News. (2019). Sandy Hook Lawsuit against Gun-Maker Set for Trial in 2021. *AP News*, [Online] 11 December. Available from: https://apnews.com/7105329aaf8f039abab83c2836c288af [Accessed 22 July 2022].

Arnold, Carrie. (2016). Life after Rape: The Sexual Assault Issue No One's Talking About. *Women's Health*, [Online] 13 September. Available from: https://www.womenshealthmag.com/life/a19899018/ptsd-after-rape/ [Accessed 22 July 2022].

Atiyah, Patrick. (1967). *Vicarious Liability in the Law of Torts*, London: Butterworths.

Baker, Berenice. (2013). The Internet Wouldn't Exist without Porn. *New Statesman*, [Online] 17 June. Available from: https://www.newstatesman.com/politics/2013/06/internet-wouldn-t-exist-without-porn [Accessed 22 July 2022].

Bambauer, Derek. (2014). Exposed. *Minnesota Law Review*, 98(6): 2025–102.

Banta, Natalie. (2016). Death and Privacy in the Digital Age. *North Carolina Law Review*, 94: 927–90.

Bar-Gill, Oren and Porat, Ariel. (2014). Harm-Benefit Interactions. *American Law and Economics Review*, 16(1): 86–116.

Barendt, Eric. (2015). An Overlap of Defamation and Privacy? *Journal of Media Law*, 7(1): 85–91.

Bari, Shahidha. (2016). Female Nudity Is Powerful – But Not Necessarily Empowering. *Aeon*, [Online] 12 September. Available from: www.aeon.co/ideas/female-nudity-is-powerful-but-not-necessarily-empowering [Accessed 22 July 2022].

Barnett, Katy. (2018). Gain-Based Relief for Breach of Privacy, in Varuhas, Jason and Moreham, Nicole (eds) *Remedies for Breach of Privacy*, Oxford: Hart, 183–204.

Barrett, Paul. (2020). Who Moderates the Social Media Giants? A Call to End Outsourcing. *NYU Stern Center for Business and Human Rights*. [Online] Available from: https://www.stern.nyu.edu/experience-stern/faculty-research/who-moderates-social-media-giants-call-end-outsourcing [Accessed 30 September 2022].

Bartow, Ann. (2009). Internet Defamation as Profit Center: The Monetization of Online Harassment. *Harvard Journal of Law & Gender*, 32(2): 102–47.

Bates, Samantha. (2017). Revenge Porn and Mental Health: A Qualitative Analysis of the Mental Health Effects of Revenge Porn on Female Survivors. *Feminist Criminology*, 12(1): 22–42.

BBC. (2014). Man Charged in Netherlands in Amanda Todd Suicide Case. *BBC News*, [Online] 18 April. Available from: https://www.bbc.co.uk/news/world-europe-27076991 [Accessed 22 July 2022].

BBC. (2016). Tiziana Cantone: Suicide Following Years of Humiliation Online Stuns Italy. *BBC News*, [Online] 16 September. Available from: https://www.bbc.co.uk/news/world-europe-37380704 [Accessed 22 July 2022].

Beever, Allan. (2015). What Does Tort Law Protect? *Singapore Academy of Law Journal*, Special Issue: 626–42.

Beever, Allan. (2016). *A Theory of Tort Liability*. London: Hart.

Ben-Shahar, Omri. (1998). Should Products Liability Be Based on Hindsight? *Journal of Law, Economics, and Organization*, 14(2): 325–57.

Benn, I. Stanley. (1971). Privacy, Freedom, and Respect for Persons, in Pennock, J. Ronald and Chapman, John W. (eds) *Nomos XIII: Privacy*, New York: Atherton Press, 1–26.

Bennett, Theodore. (2016). Not so Straight-Talking: How Defamation Law Should Treat Imputations of Homosexuality. *University of Queensland Law Journal*, 35(2): 313–30.

Bennett, Thomas. (2018). Why Sir Cliff Richard's Case Was Rightly Decided: Part 2: The Public Interest Balance. *INFORRM*, [Online] 2 August. Available from: https://inforrm.org/2018/08/02/why-sir-cliff-richards-case-was-rightly-decided-part-2-the-public-interest-balance-thomas-bennett/ [Accessed 22 July 2022].

Bennett, Thomas and Wragg, Paul. (2018). Was Richard v BBC Correctly Decided? *Communications Law*, 23(3): 151–65.

Benzanson, Randall. (1986). The Libel Suit in Retrospect: What Plaintiffs Want and What Plaintiffs Get, the Symposium: New Perspectives in the Law of Defamation. *California Law Review*, 74(3): 789–808.

Berry, Andrew. (1984). Beshada v Johns-Manville Products Corp: Revolution-Or-Aberration-In Products Liability Law. *Fordham Law Review*, 52(5): 786–803.

Berryman, Jeff. (2018). Remedies for Breach of Privacy in Canada, in Varuhas, Jason and Moreham, Nicole (eds) *Remedies for Breach of Privacy*, Oxford: Hart, 323–48.

Bickert, Monika and Fishman, Brian. (2018). Hard Questions: What Are We Doing to Stay Ahead of Terrorists? *Facebook Newsroom*, [Online] 8 November. Available from: https://about.fb.com/news/2018/11/staying-ahead-of-terrorists/ [Accessed 22 July 2022].

Birnhack, Michael. (2020). Personalized Privacy. *Tel Aviv University Law Review*, 42(2): 381–404.

Bitton, Yifat. (2010). Liability of Bias: A Comparative Study of Gender-Related Interests in Negligence Law. *Annual Survey of International & Comparative Law*, 16(1): 63–128.

Bjorkegren, Alex. (2020). DCMS. Email correspondence to Tsachi Keren-Paz, 12 Feb.

Blackman, Josh. (2009). Omniveillance, Google, Privacy in Public, and the Right to Your Digital Identity: A Tort for Recording and Disseminating an Individual's Image Over the Internet. *Santa Clara Law Review*, 49(2): 313–92.

Bloom, Sarah. (2014). No Vengeance for Revenge Porn Victims: Unravelling Why This Latest Female-Centric, Intimate-Partner Offense Is Still Legal, and Why We Should Criminalize It. *Fordham Urban Law Journal*, 42(1): 234–89.

Boerding, Andreas, Culik, Nicolai, Doepke, Christian and Hoeren, Thomas. (2018). Data Ownership: A Property Rights Approach from a European Perspective. *Journal of Civil Law Studies*, 11(2): 323–70.

Boyle, Karen. (2014). Feminism and Pornography, in Evans, Mary, Hemmings, Clare, Henry, Marsha, Johnstone, Hazel, Madhok, Sumi, Plomien, Ania and Wearing, Sadie (eds) *The SAGE Handbook of Feminist Theory*, London: SAGE, 215–29.

Brannon, Valerie. (2019). *Liability for Content Hosts: An Overview of the Communications Decency Act's Section 230.* Congressional Research Service.

Brown, Jonathan. (2018). 'Revenge Porn' and the Actio Iniuriarum: Using 'Old Law' to Solve 'New Problems'. *Legal Studies*, 38(3): 396–410.

Brownmiller, Susan. (1975). *Against Our Will: Men, Women, and Rape*, New York: Simon & Schuster.

Brunner, Lisl. (2016). The Liability of an Online Intermediary for Third Party Content: The Watchdog Becomes the Monitor: Intermediary Liability after *Delfi v Estonia. Human Rights Law Review*, 16: 163–74.

Buchanan, James and Yoon, Yong. (2000). Symmetric Tragedies: Commons and Anti-Commons. *Journal of Law and Economics*, 43(1): 1–14.

Bushard, Brian. (2022). Pornhub CEO And COO Resign amid Blowback over Nonconsensual Videos of Minors. *Forbes*, [Online] 21 June. Available from: https://www.forbes.com/sites/brianbushard/2022/06/21/pornhub-ceo-and-coo-resign-amid-blowback-over-nonconsensual-videos-of-minors/ [Accessed 22 July 2022].

Calabresi, Guido and Hirschoff, Jon. (1972). Toward a Test of Strict Liability in Tort. *Yale Law Journal*, 81(6): 1055–85.

Calabresi, Guido. and Klevorick, Alvin. (1985). Four Tests for Liability in Torts. *Journal of Legal Studies*, 14(3): 585–627.

Campbell, John. (2011). An Anomaly: Special Damages for Libel. *Journal of Media Law*, 3(2): 193–8.

Cane, Peter. (1991). *Tort Law and Economic Interests*, Oxford: Oxford University Press.

Cane, Peter. (1997). *The Anatomy of Tort Law*, London: Hart.

Cardi, Julia. (2020). Denver Judge Awards Damages in Civil Revenge Porn Lawsuit. *Law Week Colorado*, [Online] 26 August. Available from: https://lawweekcolorado.com/2020/08/denver-judge-awards-damages-in-civil-revenge-porn-lawsuit/ [Accessed 22 July 2022].

Carotte, Elise, Davis, Angela and Lim, Megan. (2020). Sexual Behaviours and Violence in Pornography: Systematic Review and Narrative Synthesis of Video Content Analyses. *Journal of Medical Internet Research*, 22(5): e16702.

Carroll, Robyn and Witzleb, Normann. (2011). 'It's Not Just about the Money' Enhancing the Vindicatory Effect of Private Law Remedies. *Monash University Law Review*, 37(1): 216–40.

Cheer, Ursula. (2016). Divining the Dignity Torts: A Possible Future for Defamation and Privacy, in Kenyon, Andrew. (ed) *Comparative Defamation and Privacy Law*, Cambridge: Cambridge University Press, 309–30.

Chesney, Robert and Citron, Danielle. (2019). Deep Fakes: A Looming Challenge for Privacy, Democracy, and National Security. *California Law Review*, 107: 1753–820.

Chisala-Tempelhoff, Sarai and Twesiime Kirya, Monica. (2016). Gender, Law and Revenge Porn in Sub-Saharan Africa: A Review of Malawi and Uganda. *Palgrave Communications* 2: 16069.

Chouliaraki, Lillie. (2006). *The Spectatorship of Suffering*, London: SAGE.

Citron, Danielle. (2009). Cyber Civil Rights. *Boston University Law Review*, 89(1): 61–125.

Citron, Danielle. (2016). *Hate Crimes in Cyberspace*, Cambridge: Harvard University Press.

Citron, Danielle. (2019). Sexual Privacy. *Yale Law Journal*, 128(7): 1870–961.

Citron, Danielle and Franks, Mary Ann. (2014). Criminalizing Revenge Porn. *Wake Forest Law Review*, 49(2): 345–92.

Citron, Danielle and Wittes, Benjamin. (2017). The Internet Will Not Break: Denying Bad Samaritans Section 230. Immunity *Fordham Law Review*, 86(2): 401–23.

Cloud, Morgan. (2018). Property Is Privacy: Locke and Brandeis in the Twenty-First Century. *American Criminal Law Review*, 55(1): 37–75.

Cohen, Felix. (1935). Transcendental Nonsense and the Functional Approach. *Columbia Law Review*, 35(6): 809–49.

Cohen, Lloyd. (1991). Holdouts and Free Riders. *Journal of Legal Studies*, 20(2): 351–62.

Cox, Joseph. (2015). How the FBI Located Suspected Admins of the Dark Web's Largest Child Porn Site. *Vice*, [Online] 2 March. Available from: https://www.vice.com/en/article/jpgm7d/how-the-fbi-identified-suspects-behind-the-dark-webs-largest-child-porn-site-playpen [Accessed 22 July 2022].

Cox, Joseph. (2018). Inside the Private Forums Where Men Illegally Trade Upskirt Photos. *Vice*, [Online] 8 May. Available from: https://www.vice.com/en/article/gykxvm/upskirt-creepshot-site-the-candid-forum?utm_source=mbtwitter [Accessed 22 July 2022].

Croucher, Stephen. (2011). Social Networking and Cultural Adaptation: A Theoretical Model. *Journal of International & Intercultural Communication*, 4(4): 259–64.

Crown Prosecution Service. (2020). Indecent and Prohibited Images of Children. *CPS*, [Online]. Available from: https://www.cps.gov.uk/legal-guidance/indecent-and-prohibited-images-children [Accessed 22 July 2022].

Crown Prosecution Service (2022). Hate Crime. *CPS*, [Online]. Available from: https://www.cps.gov.uk/hate-crime [Accessed 22 July 2022].

Cyber Civil Rights Initiative. (2014). End Revenge Porn. *Cyber Civil Rights*, [Online]. Available from: https://www.cybercivilrights.org/wp-content/uploads/2014/12/RPStatistics.pdf [Accessed 22 July 2022].

Dagan, Hanoch. (1999). Takings and Distributive Justice. *Virginia Law Review*, 85(5): 741–804.

Dagan, Hanoch. (2002). Market Overt as Insurance, in Lerner, Shalom and Lewinsohn-Zamir, Daphna. (eds) *Essays in Honour of Joshua Weisman*, Jerusalem: Harry and Michael Sacher Institute for Legislative Research and Comparative Law, 15–42.

Dagan, Hanoch. (2007). The Realist Conception of Law. *University of Toronto Law Journal*, 57(3): 607–60.

Dagan, Hanoch and Heller, Michael. (2001). The Liberal Commons. *Yale Law Journal*, 110(4): 549–624.

Data & Society Research Institute. (2016). Nonconsensual Image Sharing: One in 25 Americans Has Been a Victim of "Revenge Porn". *Data Society*, [Online] 13 December. Available from: https://datasociety.net/pubs/oh/Nonconsensual_Image_Sharing_2016.pdf [Accessed 22 July 2022].

Davey, Tina. (2020). Until Death Do Us Part: Post-Mortem Privacy Rights for the Ante-Mortem Person. University of East Anglia: Doctoral Thesis.

Davidson, Julia, Livingstone, Sonia, Jenkins, Sam, Gekoski, Anna, Choak, Clare, Ike, Tarela et al (2019). Adult Online Hate, Harassment and Abuse. *UK Council for Internet Safety*, [Online] June. Available from: https://assets.publishing.service.gov.uk/government/uploads/system/uploads/attachment_data/file/811450/Adult_Online_Harms_Report_2019.pdf [Accessed 22 July 2022].

Davies, Caroline. (2015a). Revenge Porn Cases Increase Considerably, Police Figures Reveal. *The Guardian*, [Online] 15 July. Available from: www.theguardian.com/technology/2015/jul/15/revenge-porn-cases-increase-police-figures-reveal [Accessed 22 July 2022].

Davies, Paul. (2011). Accessory Liability for Assisting Torts *Cambridge Law Journal*, 70(2): 353–80.

Davies, Paul. (2015). *Accessory Liability*. Oxford: Hart.

Davies, Paul. (2016). Accessory Liability in Tort. *Law Quarterly Review*, 132: 15–19.

Davis, Antigone. (2019). Detecting Non-Consensual Intimate Images and Supporting Victims. *Facebook*, [Online] 15 March. Available from: https://about.fb.com/news/2019/03/detecting-non-consensual-intimate-images/ [Accessed 22 July 2022].

Deakin, Simon. (2012). *Markesinis & Deakin on Tort Law*, 7th edn. Oxford: Oxford University Press.

Department for Digital, Culture, Media & Sport. (2019). *Online Harms White Paper* (CP 57). Available from: https://assets.publishing.service.gov.uk/government/uploads/system/uploads/attachment_data/file/973939/Online_Harms_White_Paper_V2.pdf [Accessed 22 July 2022].

Descheemaeker, Eric. (2015). The Harms of Privacy. *Journal of Media Law*, 7(2): 278–306.

Descheemaeker, Eric. (2018). Claimant-Focused Damages in the Law of Privacy, in Varuhas, Jason and Moreham, Nicole (eds) *Remedies for Breach of Privacy*, Oxford: Hart, 143–63.

Determann, Lothar. (2018). No One Owns Data. *Hastings Law Journal*, 70(1): 1–44.

Dillof, Anthony. (2017). Possession, Child Pornography, and Proportionality: Criminal Liability for Aggregate Harm Offenses. *Florida State University Law* Review, 44(4): 1331–54.

Dodd, Vikram. (2019). Targeting of Supt Robyn Williams 'Example of Met Institutional Racism'. *The Guardian*, [Online] 26 November. Available from: https://www.theguardian.com/uk-news/2019/nov/26/police-officer-robyn-williams-sentenced-unpaid-work-possessing-child-abuse-video [Accessed 22 July 2022].

Dodge, Alexa. (2018). Cyber Harm, 'Real' Harm, Emotional Harm: Legal Conceptions of the Harm Caused by Non-Consensual Intimate Image Sharing. American Law and Society Association, 9 June, Toronto.

Dori, Roni. (2018). I'm Going to Be a Revenge Porn Victim for the Rest of My Life. *Haaretz*, [Online] 4 January. Available from: https://www.haaretz.com/world-news/europe/2018-01-17/ty-article-magazine/.premium/im-going-to-be-a-revenge-porn-victim-for-the-rest-of-my-life/0000017f-e540-d7b2-a77f-e7474d740000 [Accessed 22 July 2022].

Douglas, Simon and Goold, Imogen. (2016). Property in Human Biomaterials: A New Methodology. *Cambridge Law Journal*, 75(3): 478–504.

Duch-Brown, Nestor, Martens, Bertin and Mueller-Langer, Frank. (2017). *The Economies of Ownership, Access and Trade in Digital Data*. Seville: European Commission.

Dworkin, Andrea. (1981). *Pornography: Men Possessing Women*. London: The Women's Press.

Dworkin, Ronald. (1977). *Taking Rights Seriously*. Cambridge: Harvard University Press.

Dworkin, Ronald. (1986). *Law's Empire*. London: Fontana Press.

Eaton, Asia, Jacobs, Holly and Ruvalcaba, Yanet. (2017). Nationwide Online Study of Nonconsensual Porn Victimization and Perpetration: A Summary Report. *CCRI*, [Online] June. Available from: https://www.cybercivilrig hts.org/wp-content/uploads/2017/06/CCRI-2017-Research-Report.pdf [Accessed 22 July 2022].

Edwards, Lillian. (2009). The Rise and Fall of Intermediary Liability Online, in Edwards, L. and Waelde, C. (eds) *Law and the Internet*, 3rd edn. London: Hart, 47–88.

Edwards, Lillian. (2018). With Great Power Comes Great Responsibility? The Rise of Platform Liability, in Edwards, L. (ed) *Law, Policy and Internet*, London: Bloomsbury. 253–90.

Edwards, Lilian and Harbinja, Edina. (2013). Protecting Post-Mortem Privacy: Reconsidering the Privacy Interests of the Deceased in a Digital World. *Cardozo Arts & Entertainment Law*, 32(1): 83–130.

Edwards, Valerie. (2018b). Student Whose Girlfriend Killed Herself after He Threatened Her with Revenge Porn Could Face Trial. *NZ Herald*, [Online] 11 June. Available from: https://www.nzherald.co.nz/world/news/article.cfm?c_id=2&objectid=12068489 [Accessed 22 July 2022].

Electoral Commission. (2018). Analysis of Cases of Alleged Electoral Fraud in the UK in 2017: Summary of Data Recorded by Police Forces 2018. Available from: https://www.electoralcommission.org.uk/__data/assets/pdf_file/0006/239973/Fraud-allegations-data-report-2017.pdf [Accessed 22 July 2022].

Electronic Frontier Foundation. (2015). Manila Principles on Intermediary Liability. *Manila Principles*, [Online]. Available from: https://www.manil aprinciples.org [Accessed 22 July 2022].

Electronic Frontier Foundation. (2018). The Santa Clara Principles on Transparency and Accountability in Content Moderation. *Santa Clara Principles*, [Online]. Available from: https://santaclaraprinciples.org [Accessed 22 July 2022].

Elyachar, Jacob. (2018). Young Social Media Users Ignore Facebook, Embrace WhatsApp as Primary News Source. *Tech Times*, [Online] 14 June. Available from: www.techtimes.com/articles/230255/20180614/young-social-media-users-ignore-facebook-embrace-whatsapp-as-prim ary-news-source.htm [Accessed 22 July 2022].

Englehardt, Steven. (2019). No Boundaries: Exfiltration of Personal Data by Session-Replay Scripts. *Freedom to Tinker*, [Online] 15 November. Available from: https://freedom-to-tinker.com/2017/11/15/no-boundaries-exfiltrat ion-of-personal-data-by-session-replay-scripts/ [Accessed 22 July 2022].

European Commission. (2017). *Tackling Illegal Content Online: Towards an Enhanced Responsibility of Online Platforms*, Brussels: European Commission.

European Commission. (2018a). *Overview of the Legal Framework of Notice-and-Action Procedures in Member States SMART 2016/0039 – Final Report*, Brussels: Directorate-General for Communication Network, Content and Technology.

European Commission. (2018b). *Proposal for a Regulation of the European Parliament and of the Council on Preventing the Dissemination of Terrorist Content Online*, Brussels: Directorate-General for Migration and Home Affairs.

Facebook. (2018–current). Transparency Reports. *Facebook*, [Online]. Available from: https://transparency.facebook.com [Accessed 22 July 2022].

Facebook. (2019). 2019 Community Standards Report. *Facebook*, [Online]. Available from: https://transparency.facebook.com/community-standards-enforcement [Accessed 22 July 2022].

Facebook. (2020). Facebook Reports First Quarter 2020 Results. *Facebook*, [Online] 29 April. Available from: https://investor.fb.com/investor-news/press-release-details/2020/Facebook-Reports-First-Quarter-2020-Results/default.aspx [Accessed 22 July 2022].

Farber, Daniel and McDonnell, Brett. (2003). Why (and How): Fairness Matters at the IP/Antitrust Interface. *Minnesota Law Review*, 87: 1817–70.

Fight the New Drug. (2020a). Can the Line between Consent and Coercion Get Blurred during Porn Production? *Fight the New Drug*, [Online] 15 July. Available from: https://fightthenewdrug.org/consent-and-coercion-blurred-in-porn-production/ [Accessed 22 July 2022].

Fight the New Drug. (2020b). Pornhub Reportedly Refused to Remove Videos of This Minor's Sexual Assault – until She Posed as Her Own Lawyer. *Fight the New Drug*, [Online] 14 July. Available from: https://fightthenewdrug.org/pornhub-refused-to-remove-videos-of-this-minors-sexual-assault/ (link no longer accessible) [Accessed 22 July 2022].

Fight the New Drug. (2020c). Are Porn Sites Protecting Victims of Nonconsensual Content? We Investigated, Here's What We Found. *Fight the New Drug*, [Online] 14 July. Available from: https://fightthenewdrug.org/what-porn-sites-could-be-doing-to-protect-victims/ [Accessed 22 July 2022].

Fight the New Drug. (2020d). Their Private Videos Were Nonconsensually Uploaded to Pornhub, and Now These Women Are Fighting Back. *Fight the New Drug*, [Online] 10 April. Available from: https://fightthenewdrug.org/their-private-photos-were-shared-non-consensually-to-pornhub-and-now-these-women-are-fighting-back/ [Accessed 22 July 2022].

Fight the New Drug. (2021). 7 Cases of Nonconsensual Porn and Rape Tapes Pornhub Doesn't Want Consumers to Know About. *Fight the New Drug*, [Online] 3 February. Available from: https://fightthenewdrug.org/pornhub-reportedly-profits-from-nonconsensual-videos/ [Accessed 22 July 2022].

Fletcher, George. (1972). Fairness and Utility in Tort Theory. *Harvard Law Review*, 85(3): 537–73.

Fortin, Francis. (2011). Usenet Newsgroups, Child Pornography and the Role of Participants. *The International Centre for Comp. Criminology*, Panel Presentation at the Third Annual Illicit Networks Workshop (3 October).

Franks, Mary Ann. (2013a). Why We Need a Federal Criminal Law Response to Revenge Porn. *Concurring Opinions*, [Online] 15 February. Available from: http:// www.concurringopinions.com/archives/2013/02/why-we-need-a-federal -criminal-law-response-to-revenge-porn.html (link no longer accessible) [Accessed 22 July 2022].

Franks, Mary Ann. (2013b). Adventures in Victim Blaming: Revenge Porn Edition. *Concurring Opinions*, [Online] 1 February. Available from: www.concurringopinions.com/archives/2013/02/adventures-in-victim-blaming-revenge-porn-edition.html (link no longer accessible) [Accessed 22 July 2022].

Franks, Marie Ann. (2017). Revenge Porn Reform: A View from the Front Lines. *Florida Law Review*, 69(5): 1251–338.

Friedman, Jonathan and Buono, Francis. (2000). Limiting Tort Liability for Online Third-Party Content under Section 230 of the Communications Act. *Federal Communications Law Journal*, 52(3): 647–66.

Friedmann, Daniel. (1989). The Efficient Breach Fallacy. *Journal of Legal Studies*, 18(1): 1–24.

Frosio, Giancarlo. (2017a). Internet Intermediary Liability: WILMap, Theory and Trends. *International Journal of Learning Technology*, 13(1): 16–38.

Frosio, Giancarlo. (2017b). Death of 'No Monitoring Obligations': A Story of Untameable Monsters. *Journal of Intellectual Property, Information Technology and Electronic Commerce*, 8(3): 199–215.

Frosio, Giancarlo. (2017c). From Horizontal to Vertical: An Intermediary Liability Earthquake in Europe. *Journal of Intellectual Property Law & Practice* 12(7): 565–75.

Frosio, Giancarlo. (2017d). Reforming Intermediary Liability in the Platform Economy: A European Digital Single Market Strategy. *Northwestern Law Review*, 112: 19–46.

Frosio, Giancarlo. (2020). Email correspondence to Tsachi Keren-Paz, 8 February.

Frosio, Giancarlo and Mendis, S. (2020). Monitoring and Filtering: European Reform or Global Trend? in Frosio, Giancarlo. (ed) *The Oxford Handbook of Online Intermediary Liability*, Oxford: Oxford University Press, 544–65.

Fuller, Lon and Perdue, William. (1936). The Reliance Interest in Contract Damages. *Yale Law Journal*, 46(3): 373–420.

Garrahan, Matthew and Croft, Jane. (2018). Philip Green Case Brings NDAs Back into the Spotlight. *Financial Times*, [Online] 26 October. Available from: https://www.ft.com/content/fa225f02-d873-11e8-ab8e-6be0dcf18713 [Accessed 22 July 2022].

Gauntlett, David. (1997). Ten Things Wrong with the Effects Model, in Dickinson, Roger, Harindranath, Ramaswami and Linné, Olga (eds) *Approaches to Audiences: A Reader*, London: Arnold, 120–30.

Gavin, Jeff and Scott, Adrian. (2019). Attributions of Victim Responsibility in Revenge Pornography. *Journal of Aggression, Conflict and Peace Research*, 11(4): 263–72.

Gavison, Ruth. (1980). Privacy and the Limits of Law. *Yale Law Journal*, 89(3): 421–71.

Gebhart, Gennie. (2019). Who Has Your Back? Censorship Edition 2019. *Electronic Frontiers Foundation*, [Online] 12 June. Available from: https://www.eff.org/wp/who-has-your-back-2019#provides-meaningful-notice [Accessed 22 July 2022].

Gee, Steven. (2010). *Commercial Injunctions*, 6th edn. London: Sweet & Maxwell.

Georgaki, Konstania. Rollo, Alessandro and Giakoumakis, Emmanuel. (2016). Escaping the Slippery Slope: Freedom of Expression and Cyberspace Regulation after the Delfi Case. *CUSPE Communications*, [Online]. Available from: https://doi.org/10.17863/CAM.25630 [Accessed 22 July 2022].

Gewirtz-Meydan, Ateret, Walsh, Wendy, Wolak, Janis and Finkelhor, David. (2018). The Complex Experience of Child Pornography Survivors. *Child Abuse and Neglect*, 80: 238–48.

Gilles, Stephen. (2002). The Emergence of Cost-Benefit Balancing in English Negligence Law. *University of Chicago-Kent Law Review*, 77(2): 489–586.

Gilmore, Lauren. (2016). Porn Pioneers: How Adult Entertainment Boosts Technology. *The Next Web*, [Online] 30 August. Available from: https://thenextweb.com/news/porn-pioneers-adult-entertainment-boosts-technology [Accessed 22 July 2022].

Glassman, Jordan. (2020). Too Dangerous to Exist: Holding Compromised Internet Platforms Strictly Liable under the Doctrine of Abnormally Dangerous Activities. *North Carolina Journal of Law and Technology*, 22(2): 293–333.

Goldman, Eric. (2008). The Sex Tape Problem ... and a Possible Legislative Solution? *Technology & Marketing Law*, [Blog] 11 July. Available from: https://blog.ericgoldman.org/archives/2008/07/the_sex_tape_pr.htm [Accessed 22 July 2022].

Goldman, Eric. (2010). Ripoff Report Isn't Bound by Injunction against User Post–Blockowicz v Williams. *Technology & Marketing Law*, [Blog] 28 December. Available from: www.blog.ericgoldman.org/archives/2010/12/ripoff_report_d.htm [Accessed 22 July 2022].

Goldman, Eric. (2012). Online User Account Termination and 47 USC § 230(c)(2). *UC Irvine Law Review*, 2(2): 659–674.

Goldman, Eric. (2013). What Should We Do about Revenge Porn Sites Like Texxxan? *Forbes*, [Online] 28 January. Available from: www.forbes.com/sites/ericgoldman/2013/01/28/what-should-we-do-about-revenge-porn-sites-like-texxxan/#5cf7fe2c7eff [Accessed 22 July 2022].

Goldman, Eric. (2014). Revenge Porn Is Bad, But It's Not GoDaddy's Fault. *Forbes*, [Online] 10 April. Available from: https://www.forbes.com/sites/ericgoldman/2014/04/10/revenge-porn-is-bad-but-its-not-godaddys-fault/#61ca3d243f6e [Accessed 22 July 2022].

Goldman, Eric. (2016). Facebook Isn't Liable for Fake User Account Containing Non-Consensual Pornography. *Forbes*, [Online] 8 March. Available from: www.forbes.com/sites/ericgoldman/2016/03/08/facebook-isnt-liable-for-fake-user-account-containing-non-consensual-pornography/#33a30d7a79b2 [Accessed 22 July 2022].

Goldman, Eric. (2017). Ten Worst Section 230 Rulings of 2016 (Plus the Five Best). *Technology & Marketing Law Blog*, [Blog] 4 January. Available from: https://blog.ericgoldman.org/archives/2017/01/ten-worst-section-230-rulings-of-2016-plus-the-five-best.htm [Accessed 22 July 2022].

Goldman, Eric and Jin, Angie. (2018). Judicial Resolution of Nonconsensual Pornography Dissemination Cases. *I/S: A Journal of Law and Policy for the Information Society*, 14(2): 283–352.

Government Equalities Office. (2015). Hundreds of Victims of Revenge Porn Seek Support from Helpline. *Government Equalities Office*, [Online] 23 August. Available from: https://www.gov.uk/government/news/hundreds-of-victims-of-revenge-porn-seek-support-from-helpline [Accessed 22 July 2022].

Gray, Anthony. (2018). *Vicarious Liability: Critique and Reform*, Oxford: Hart.

Green, Sarah and Randall, John. (2009). *The Tort of Conversion*, Oxford: Hart.

Greenberg, Andy. (2014). Hacked Celeb Pics Made Reddit Enough Cash to Run Its Servers for a Month. *Wired*, [Online] 10 September. Available from: https://www.wired.com/2014/09/celeb-pics-reddit-gold/ [Accessed 22 July 2022].

Guo, Richard. (2008). Stranger Danger and the Online Social Network. *Berkley Tech Law Journal*, 23(1): 617–44.

Haber, Eldar. (2016). Privatization of the Judiciary. *Seattle University Law Review*, 40(1): 115–72.

Halley, Janet. (2006). *Split Decisions: How and Why to Take a Break from Feminism*, New Jersey: Princeton University Press.

Halliday, Josh. (2015). Revenge Porn: 175 Cases Reported to Police in Six Months. *The Guardian*, [Online] 11 October. Available from: https://www.theguardian.com/uk-news/2015/oct/11/revenge-porn-175-cases-reported-to-police-in-six-months [Accessed 22 July 2022].

Hamilton, Fiona. (2021). Police Officer Robyn Williams Sacked over Child Abuse Video Wins Her Job Back. *The Times*, [Online] 17 June. Available from: https://www.thetimes.co.uk/article/police-officer-sacked-over-child-abuse-video-wins-her-job-back-after-appeal-g7g0dhrfp [Accessed 22 July 2022].

Hamilton, Melissa. (2012). The Child Pornography Crusade and Its Net-Widening Effect. *Cardozo Law Review*, 33(4): 1679–1729.

Harari, Yuval Noah. (2016). *Homo Deus: A Brief History of Tomorrow*, London: Penguin.

Harn Lee, Yin. (2019). Delivering (Up). A Copyright-Based Remedy for Revenge Porn. *Journal of International Property Law & Practice*, 14(2): 99–111.

Hartshorne, John. (2012). An Appropriate Remedy for the Publication of False Private Information. *Journal of Media Law*, 4(1): 93–116.

Hedley, Steve. (2009). Looking Outward or Looking Inward? Obligations Scholarship in the Early 21st Century, in Robertson, Andrew and Tang, Hang Wu. (eds) *The Goals of Private Law*, London: Hart, 193–214.

Helman, Lital and Parchomovsky, Gideon. (2011). The Best Available Technology Standard. *Columbia Law Review*, 111(6): 1194–242.

Henry, Nicola and Powell, Anastasia. (2018). Technology-Facilitated Sexual Violence: A Literature Review of Empirical Research. *Trauma, Violence & Abuse*, 19(2): 195–208.

Henry, Nicola, Powell, Anastasia and Flynn, Asher. (2017). Not Just 'Revenge Pornography': Australians Experiences of Image-Based Abuse: A Summary Report. *RMIT University*, [Online] May. Available from: https://researchmgt.monash.edu/ws/portalfiles/portal/214045352/revenge_porn_report_2017.pdf [Accessed 22 July 2022].

Henry, Nicola, Flynn, Asher and Powell, Anastasia. (2019). *Responding to Revenge Pornography: Prevalence, Nature and Impacts*, Melbourne: Criminology Research Advisory Council.

Hepburn, Carol L. (2021). Savage Lawyers, Seattle. Email correspondence to Tsachi Keren-Paz, 8 September.

Hern, Alex. (2019). Revealed: Catastrophic Effects of Working as a Facebook Moderator. *The Guardian*, [Online] 17 September. Available from: https://www.theguardian.com/technology/2019/sep/17/revealed-catastrophic-effects-working-facebook-moderator [Accessed 22 July 2022].

Hessick, Carissa B. (ed) (2016). *Refining Child Pornography Law*, Ann Arbor: University of Michigan Press.

Hill, Rachel. (2015). Cyber-Misogyny: Should Revenge Porn Be Regulated in Scotland and if So How? *SCRIPT-ed*, 12(2): 117–40.

Hoboken, Joris and Keller, Daphne. (2019). Design Principles for Intermediary Liability Laws. *Transatlantic Working Group*, [Online] 8 October. Available from: https://www.ivir.nl/publicaties/download/Inte rmediary_liability_Oct_2019.pdf [Accessed 22 July 2022].

Holland, David. (2014). Remedies after Coventry v Lawrence: Shelfer Shelved? *Landmark Chambers*, [Online]. Available from: https://www.landm arkchambers.co.uk/wp-content/uploads/2018/07/DMH-CovLawrence. pdf. [Accessed 22 July 2022].

Holten, Emma. (2020). Consent. *Frikson*, [Online] 14 June. Available from: https://friktionmagasin.dk/consent-86fe7b14282f [Accessed 22 July 2022].

Horwitz, Morton. (1977). *The Transformation of American Law 1780–1860*, Cambridge: Harvard University Press.

Howden, Spence. (2019). Text Messages Are Property: Why You Don't Own Your Text Messages, but It'd Be a Lot Cooler if You Did. *Washington and Lee Law Review*, 76(2): 1074–126.

Hunt, Chris. (2011). Conceptualizing Privacy and Elucidating Its Importance: Foundational Considerations for the Development of Canada's Fledgling Privacy Tort. *Queen's Law Journal*, 37(1): 167–99.

Husovec, Marti and Peguera, Miquel. (2015). Much Ado about Little: Privately Litigated Internet Disconnection Injunctions. *International Review of Intellectual Property and Competition Law*, 46(1): 10–37.

Ibbetson, David. (2001). *A Historical Introduction to the Law of Obligations*, Oxford: Oxford University Press.

ICF Consulting Services Limited. (2019). *Research into Online Platforms Operating Models and Management of Online Harms*, London: Department for Digital, Culture, Media & Sport.

Irish News. (2018). Facebook in Legal Settlement over Naked Picture of Northern Ireland Girl (14). *Irish News*, [Online] 9 January. Available from: www.irishnews.com/news/northernirelandnews/2018/01/09/ news/facebook-in-legal-settlement-over-naked-picture-of-northern-irel and-girl-14--1228484/ [Accessed 22 July 2022].

Isaac, Mike. (2019). Facebook's Profits and Revenue Climb as It Gains More Users. *New York Times*, [Online] 30 January. Available from: https://www. nytimes.com/2019/01/30/technology/facebook-earnings-revenue-profit. html [Accessed 22 July 2022].

Isaacs, Kate. (2019). Pornhub: The Ongoing Revenge Porn Investigation. *Open Access Government*, [Online] 29 October. Available from: https:// www.openaccessgovernment.org/revenge-porn-investigation/76810/ [Accessed 22 July 2022].

Isaacs, Kate. (2020). Pornhub Needs to Change – or Shut Down. *The Guardian*, [Online] 9 March. Available from: https://www.theguardian.com/global-development/2020/mar/09/pornhub-needs-to-change-or-shut-down [Accessed 22 July 2022].

Ivanova, Yordanka. (2020). Data Controller, Processor, or Joint Controller: Towards Reaching GDPR Compliance in a Data- and Technology Driven World, in Tzanou, Maria. (ed) *Personal Data Protection and Legal Developments in the European Union*, Hershey: IGI Global, 61–84.

Jacob, Assaf. (2012). *Daaka's* Ache and the Evolution of 'Harm to Plaintiff's Autonomy'. *Hebrew University Law Review*, 42: 5–85.

Jenkins, Phillip. (2001). *Beyond Tolerance: Child Pornography on the Internet*, New York: New York University Press.

Jinana, Haider. (2020). The English Torts of Defamation and (False) Privacy: Analysing the Impact of the Overlap on Defences, Interim Injunctions and Damages. Keele: PhD Dissertation.

Kamal, Mudasir and Newman, William. (2016). Revenge Pornography: Mental Health Implications and Related Legislation. *Journal of the American Academy of Psychiatry and the Law*, 44(3): 359–67.

Kanecek, Vaclav. (2018). Ownership of Personal Data in the Internet of Things. *Computer Law & Security Review*, 34(5): 1039–52.

Kaplow, Louis and Shavell, Steven. (1996). Accuracy in the Assessment of Damages. *Journal of Law and Economics*, 39(1): 191–210.

Karanian, Lara. (2019). Stripped of Dignity? Humiliation, Privacy and the Punishment of Revenge Porn. *LSA Annual Conference*, 31 May, Toronto.

Keating, Gregory. (2000). Distributive and Corrective Justice in the Tort Law of Accidents. *Southern California Law Review*, 74(1): 193–224.

Keating, Gregory. (2001). The Theory of Enterprise Liability and Common Law Strict Liability. *Vanderbilt Law Review*, 54(3): 1285–336.

Keating, Gregory. (2003a). Irreparable Injury and Extraordinary Precaution: The Safety and Feasibility Norms in American Accident Law. *Theoretical Inquiries in Law*, 4(1): 1–88.

Keating, Gregory. (2003b). Pressing Precaution beyond the Point of Cost-Justification. *Vanderbilt Law Review*, 56(3): 653–750.

Keating, Gregory. (2012). The Priority of Respect over Repair. *Legal Theory*, 18(3): 293–338.

Keating, Gregory. (2018). Principles of Risk Imposition and the Priority of Avoiding Harm. *Revus*, 36: 1–30.

Keating, Gregory. (2019). Justice for Guinea Pigs. *Law Innovation and Technology*, 11(1): 75–92.

Keller, Daphne. (2017a). SESTA and the Teachings of Intermediary Liability. *SSRN*, [Online] 2 November. Available from: www.ssrn.com/abstract= 3121296 [Accessed 22 July 2022].

Keller, Daphne. (2017b). Problems with Filters in the European Commission's Platforms Proposal. *CIS Blog*, [Blog] 5 October. Available from: http://cyberlaw.stanford.edu/blog/2017/10/problems-filters-european-commissions-platforms-proposal [Accessed 22 July 2022].

Keller, Daphne and Leersen, Paddy. (2020). Facts and Where to Find Them: Empirical Research on Internet Platforms and Content Moderation, in Persily, Nathaniel and Tucker, Joshua. (eds) *Social Media and Democracy: The State of the Field and Prospects for Reform*, Cambridge: Cambridge University Press, 220–51.

Kennedy, Duncan. (1982). Distributive and Paternalist Motives in Contract and Tort Law, with Special Reference to Compulsory Terms and Unequal Bargaining Power. *Maryland Law Review*, 41(4): 563–635.

Keren-Paz, Tsachi. (2003). Egalitarianism as Justification: Why and How Should Egalitarian Considerations Reshape the Standard of Care in Negligence Law. *Theoretical Inquiries in Law*, 4(1): 1–60.

Keren-Paz, Tsachi. (2007a). *Torts, Egalitarianism and Distributive Justice*, Farnham: Ashgate.

Keren-Paz, Tsachi. (2007b). Compensating Injury to Autonomy: Normative Evaluation, Recent Developments and Future Tendencies. *Colman Law Review* 22: 187–266.

Keren-Paz, Tsachi. (2010). Poetic Justice: Why Sex-Slaves Should Be Allowed to Sue Ignorant Clients in Conversion. *Law & Philosophy*, 29: 307–36.

Keren-Paz, Tsachi. (2013). *Sex Trafficking: A Private Law Response*, Abingdon: Routledge.

Keren-Paz, Tsachi. (2014). Injuries from Unforeseeable Risks which Advance Medical Knowledge: Restitution-Based Justification for Strict Liability. *Journal of European Tort Law*, 5(3): 275–309.

Keren-Paz, Tsachi. (2016). Liability for Consequences, Duty of Care and the Limited Relevance of Specific Reliance: New Insights on *Bhamra v Dubb*. *Journal of Professional Negligence*, 32(1): 48–65.

Keren-Paz, Tsachi. (2017). Compensating Injury to Autonomy: A Conceptual and Normative Analysis, in Barker, Kit, Fairweather, Karen and Grantham, Ross. (eds) *Private Law in the Twenty-First Century*, Oxford: Hart, 411–37.

Keren-Paz, Tsachi. (2018). Compensating Injury to Autonomy in English Negligence Law: Inconsistent Recognition. *Medical Law Review*, 26(4): 585–609.

Keren-Paz, Tsachi. (2019a). No-fault (strict): Liability for Injuries from Innovative Treatments: Fairness or also Efficiency? *Law, Innovation and Technology*, 11(4): 55–74.

Keren-Paz, Tsachi. (2019b). Gender Injustice in Compensating Injury to Autonomy in English and Singaporean Negligence Law. *Feminist Legal Studies*, 27(1): 33–56.

Keren-Paz, Tsachi. (2020). The Uncreditworthy's Tale: Personalized Default Rules and the Problem of Tracking. *Tel Aviv University Law Review*, 42(2): 421–46.

Keren-Paz, Tsachi and Cockburn, Tina. (eds) (2019). Regulating Innovative Treatments: Information, Risk Allocation and Redress. *Law, Innovation and Technology*, Special Issue, 11(1): 1–174.

Keren-Paz, Tsachi and Wright, Richard. (2019). Liability for Mass Sexual Abuse. *American Criminal Law Review*, 56(1): 185–234.

Kleeman, Jenny. (2018). YouTube Star Wins Damages in Landmark UK 'Revenge Porn' Case. *The Guardian*, [Online] 17 January. Available from: www.theguardian.com/technology/2018/jan/17/youtube-star-chrissy-chambers-wins-damages-in-landmark-uk-revenge-porn-case [Accessed 22 July 2022].

Knight, Lewis. (2021). Sharon Stone Says She Was Not Warned about Explicit Shot in Basic Instinct Scene. *The Mirror*, [Online] 18 March. Available from: https://www.mirror.co.uk/3am/celebrity-news/sharon-stone-says-not-warned-23756519 [Accessed 22 July 2022].

Kosseff, Jeff. (2010). Defending Section 230: The Value of Intermediary Immunity. *Journal of Technology Law and Policy*, 15(2): 123–58.

Kowalski, Robin, Limber, Susan and Agatson, Patricia. (2008). *Cyberbullying: Bullying in the Digital Age*, Oxford: Oxford University Press.

Kristof, Nicholas. (2020). The Children of Pornhub. *New York Times*, [Online] 4 December. Available from: https://www.nytimes.com/2020/12/04/opinion/sunday/pornhub-rape-trafficking.html [Accessed 22 July 2022].

Kronman, Anthony. (1978). Mistake, Disclosure, Information, and the Law of Contracts. *Journal of Legal Studies*, 7(1): 1–34.

Kuwert, Phillipp, Glaesmer, Heide, Eichhorn, Svenja, Grundke, Elena, Pietrzak, Robert H. and Freyberger, Harald J. et al (2014). Long-Term Effects of Conflict-Related Sexual Violence Compared with Non-Sexual War Trauma in Female World War II Survivors: A Matched Pairs Study. *Archives of Sexual Behaviour* 43(6): 1059–64.

La, Lynn. (2018). YouPorn's Cringey Revenge Porn Video Is a Step in the Right Direction. *CNET*, [Online] 27 March. Available from: https://www.cnet.com/news/revenge-porn-youporn-reporting-tool/# .

Laidlaw, Emily and Young, Hilary. (2017). *Internet Intermediary Liability in Defamation: Proposals for Statutory Reform*, Ontario: Law Commission of Ontario.

Laidlaw, Emily and Young, Hilary. (2019). Internet Intermediary Liability in Defamation. *Osgoode Hall Law Journal*, 56(1): 153–202.

Laidlaw, Emily and Young, Hilary. (2020). Creating a Revenge Porn Tort for Canada. *Supreme Court Law Review*, 96(2): 147–87.

Lanier, Jaron. (2018). *Ten Arguments for Deleting your Social Media Accounts Right Now*, New York: Random House.

Larusdottir, Jónína Sigrún. (2010). Liability of Intermediaries for Copyright Infringement in the Case of Hosting on the Internet. *Stockholm Institute for Scandinavian Law*, 472–88.

Law Commission. (2021). *Intimate Image Abuse: Consultation Paper* (CP 253), London: Stationary Office.

Law Commission. (2022). *Intimate Image Abuse: A Final Report* (Law Com No 407), London: Stationary Office.

Lessig, Larry. (2002). Privacy as Property. *Social Research*, 69(1): 247–69.

Lippman, Julia and Campbell, Scott. (2014). Damned if You Do, Damned if You Don't … if You're a Girl: Relational and Normative Contexts of Adolescent Sexting in the United States. *Journal of Children and Media*, 8(4): 371–86.

Lipton, Jacqueline. (2011). Combating Cyber-Victimization. *Berkeley Tech Law Review*, 26(2): 1104–54.

Llewellyn, Karl. (1931). Some Realism about Realism: Responding to Dean Pound. *Harvard Law Review*, 44(8): 1222–64.

Lollar, E Cortney. (2013). Child Pornography and the Restitution Revolution. *The Journal of Criminal Law and Criminology*, 103(2): 343–83.

Lopez, Tess, Allenbaugh, Mark and Ellis, Alan. (2012). Trends and Practice Tips for Representing Child Pornography Offenders at Sentencing. *Criminal Justice*, 27(3): 31–2.

LoPiano, James. (2018). Public For a Purpose: Analyzing Viewpoint Discrimination on the President's Twitter Account. *Fordham Intellectual Property, Media & Entertainment Law Journal*, 28(3): 511–70.

Lunney, Mark, Nolan, Donal and Oliphant, Ken. (2017). *Tort Law*, 6th edn. Oxford: Oxford University Press.

Lytton, Timothy. (ed) (2005). *Suing the Gun Industry*, Ann Arbor: University of Michigan Press.

Mabie, Margaret E. (2021). Email correspondence to Tsachi Keren-Paz, 8 September.

Mackie, Jeannie. (2014). Jennifer Lawrence's Nude Photo Leak Was a Scandal, but Legally Speaking It Was Not a Sex Crime. *The Independent*, [Online] 10 October. Available from: https://www.independent.co.uk/voices/comment/jennifer-lawrence-s-nude-photo-leak-was-scandal-legally-speaking-it-was-not-sex-crime-9786886.html [Accessed 22 July 2022].

Mackinnon, Catharine. (2011). Trafficking, Prostitution, and Inequality. *Harvard Civil Rights Civil Liberties Law Review*, 46(2): 271–310.

Mangan, David. (2017). *The Relationship between Defamation, Breach of Privacy and Other Legal Claims Involving Offensive Internet Content*, Toronto: Law Commission of Ontario.

Marshall, Jojo. (2014). Why We All Need to Worry about Revenge Porn. *Elle*, [Online] 24 September. Available from: https://www.elle.com/life-love/sex-relationships/news/a15497/what-is-revenge-porn/ [Accessed 22 July 2022].

Marshall, Tom. (2016). YouTube Star in £22,000 Crowdfunding Bid to Finance Revenge Porn Legal Battle. *The Evening Standard*, [Online] 28 February. Available from: https://www.standard.co.uk/news/crime/yout ube-star-in-ps22-000-crowdfunding-bid-to-finance-revenge-porn-claim-a3190901.html [Accessed 22 July 2022].

Marwick, Alice. (2017). Scandal or Sex Crime? Gendered Privacy and the Celebrity Nude Photo Leaks. *Ethics and Information Technology*, 19: 177–91.

Mautner, Menachem. (1991). The Eternal Triangles of the Law: Toward a Theory of Priorities in Conflicts Involving Remote Parties. *Michigan Law Review*, 90(1): 95–154.

McAteer, Oliver. (2017). Anthony Weiner Jailed for Sexting Underage Girl Photos of his Penis. *Metro*, [Online] 25 September. Available from: www.metro.co.uk/2017/09/25/anthony-weiner-jailed-for-sexting-underage-girl-photos-of-his-penis-6954415/ [Accessed 22 July 2022].

McBride, Nicolas. (2019). *The Humanity of Private Law: Explanation*, London: Hart.

McGlynn, Clare and Rackley, Erica. (2017). Image-Based Sexual Abuse. *OJLS*, 37(3): 534–61.

McGlynn, Clare, Rackley, Erica and Houghton, Ruth. (2017). Beyond 'Revenge Porn': The Continuum of Image-Based Sexual Abuse. *Feminist Legal Studies*, 25: 25–46.

McGlynn, Clare, Johnson, Kelly, Rackley, Erika, Henry, Nicola, Gavey, Nicola and Flynn, Asher et al (2021). It's Torture for the Soul': The Harms of Image-Based Sexual Abuse. *Social & Legal Studies*, 30(4): 541–62.

McIntyre, T.J. (2018). Internet Censorship in the United Kingdom: National Schemes and European Norms, in Edwards, Lillian (ed) *Law, Policy and the Internet*, 3rd edn. London: Hart, 291–331.

McPhail, Beverly. (2015). Feminist Framework Plus: Knitting Feminist Theories of Rape Etiology into a Comprehensive Model. *Trauma, Violence, & Abuse*, 17(3): 314–29.

Merrill, Thomas. (1986). The Economics of Public Use. *Cornell Law Review* 72(1): 61–116.

Merrill, Thomas. (1998). Property and the Right to Exclude. *Nebraska Law Review*, 77(4): 730–55.

Meta. (2021). Facebook Community Standards; Part III Objectionable Content; Adult Nudity and Sexual Activity. *Meta*, [Online]. Available from https://www.facebook.com/communitystandards/adult_nudity_sexual_activity [Accessed 22 July 2022].

Michels, Johan and Millard, Christopher. (2019). Mind the Gap: The Status of Digital Files under Property Law. *Queen Mary School of Law Legal Studies Research Paper No 317/2019*, [Online]. Available from: https://ssrn.com/abstract=3387400 [Accessed 22 July 2022].

Mohan, Megha. (2020). I was Raped at 14, and the Video Ended Up on a Porn Site. *BBC*, [Online] 10 February. Available from: https://www.bbc.co.uk/news/stories-51391981 [Accessed 22 July 2022].

Mooney, Annabelle (2014). Restoring Trust: Plachimada, the Human Trust and Anticipatory Negligence as Restorative Justice. *International Journal for the Semiotics of Law*, 27(2): 243–61.

Moore, Caitlin. (2014). Jennifer Lawrence on Hacked Photos: Anybody Who Looked at Those Pictures, You're Perpetuating a Sexual Offence. *Washington Post*, [Online] 7 October. Available from: https://www.washingtonpost.com/news/arts-and-entertainment/wp/2014/10/07/jennifer-lawrence-on-hacked-photos-anybody-who-looked-at-those-pictures-youre-perpetuating-a-sexual-offense/ [Accessed 22 July 2022].

Moosavian, Rebecca. (2018). 'Stealing Souls'? Article 8 and Photographic Intrusion. *Northern Ireland Law Quarterly*, 69(4): 531–58.

Moosavian, Rebecca. (2022). Pavesich v New England Insurance Co (1905), in Wragg, P. and Coe, P. (eds) *Landmark Cases in Privacy*, Oxford: Hart, chapter 3.

Moreham, Nicole. (2005). Privacy in the Common Law: A Doctrinal and Theoretical Analysis. *Law Quarterly Review*, 121: 628–36.

Moreham, Nicole. (2018a). Compensating for Loss of Dignity and Autonomy, in Varuhas, Jason and Moreham, Nicole (eds) *Remedies for Breach of Privacy*, Oxford: Hart, 125–42.

Moreham, Nicole. (2018b). Unpacking the Reasonable Expectation of Privacy Test. *Law Quarterly Review*, 134: 651–74.

Moreham, Nicole (2019). Privacy, Reputation and Alleged Wrongdoing: Why Police Investigations Should Not Be Regarded as Private. *Journal of Media Law*, 11(2): 142–62.

Morgan, Bronwen. (2007). *The Intersection of Rights and Regulation*. Farnham: Ashgate.

Mullis, Alistair, Parkes, Richard and Busuttil, Godwin. (eds) (2013). *Gately on Libel and Slander*, 12th edn. London: Sweet & Maxwell.

Murphy, John. (2007). Rethinking Injunctions in Tort Law. *Oxford Journal of Legal Studies*, 27(3): 509–36.

Murphy, John. (2022). *The Province and Politics of the Economic Torts*, Oxford: Hart.

Nehushtan, Yossi. (2007). The Limits of Tolerance: A Substantive-Liberal Perspective. *Ratio Juris*, 20(2): 230–57.

Netanel, Neil W. (2000). Market Hierarchy and Copyright in Our System of Free Expression. *Vanderbilt Law Review*, 53(6): 1879–932.

Newton, Casey. (2019). The Trauma Floor. *The Verge*, [Online] 25 February. Available from: https://www.theverge.com/2019/2/25/18229714/cogniz ant-facebook-content-moderator-interviews-trauma-working-conditions-arizona. [Accessed 22 July 2022].

Nicklin, Matthew and Strong, Chloe. (2016). Remedies and Sanctions, in Moreham, Nicole and Warby, Mark (eds) *Tugendhat and Christie: The Law of Privacy and The Media*, 3rd edn. Oxford: Oxford University Press, 555–619.

North, Anna. (2018). The Disturbing Story Behind the Rape Scene in Bernardo Bertolucci's Last Tango in Paris, explained. *Vox*, [Online] 26 November. Available from: https://www.vox.com/2018/11/26/18112 531/bernardo-bertolucci-maria-schneider-last-tango-in-paris [Accessed 22 July 2022].

O'Brien, Ashley Sara. (2018). Woman Awarded $6.45 Million in Revenge Porn Case. *CNN* [Online] 9 April. Available from: https://money.cnn. com/2018/04/09/technology/revenge-porn-judgment/index.html [Accessed 22 July 2022].

O'Connell, Aislin and Bakina, Ksenia. (2020). Using IP Rights to Protect Human Rights: Copyright for Revenge Porn Removal. *Legal Studies*, 40(3): 442–57.

Oliver, Kelly. (2016). Rape as Spectator Sport and Creepshot Entertainment: Social Media and the Valorization of Lack of Consent. *American Studies Journal*, [Online]. Available from: http://www.asjournal. org/61-2016/rape-spectator-sport-creepshot-entertainment-social-media-valorization-lack-consent/ [Accessed 22 July 2022].

Oltermann, Phillip. (2014). Revenge Porn Victims Receive Boost from German Court Ruling. *The Guardian*, [Online] 22 May. Available from: www.theguardian.com/technology/2014/may/22/revenge-porn-victims-boost-german-court-ruling [Accessed 22 July 2022].

OneLogin. (2022). What Is Multi-Factor Authentication (MFA)? *OneLogin*, [Online]. Available from: https://www.onelogin.com/learn/what-is-mfa [Accessed 22 July 2022].

Oster, Jan. (2015). Communication, Defamation and Liability of Intermediaries. *Legal Studies*, 35(2): 348–68.

Ottenweller, Cara. (2007). Cyberbullying: The Interactive Playground Cries for a Clarification of the Communications Decency Act. *Valparaiso University Law Review*, 41(3): 1285–334.

Palmer, Craig. (1988). Twelve Reasons Why Rape Is Not Sexually Motivated: A Skeptical Examination. *The Journal of Sex Research*, 25(4): 512–30.

Parkes, Richard. (2016). Privacy, Defamation and False Facts, in Moreham, Nicole and Warby, Mark. (eds) *Tugendhat and Christie: The Law of Privacy and The Media*, 3rd edn. Oxford: Oxford University Press, 349–85.

Pasquale, Frank. (2016). Platform Neutrality: Enhancing Freedom of Expression in Spheres of Private Power. *Theoretical Inquiries in Law*, 17(2): 487–514.

Pattella-Ray, P.J. (2018). Beyond Privacy: Bodily Integrity as an Alternative Framework for Understanding Non-Consensual Pornography. *Information, Communication and Society*, 21(5): 786–91.

Paul, Kari. (2020). Pornhub Removes Millions of Videos after Investigation Finds Child Abuse Content. *The Guardian*, [Online] 14 December. Available from: https://www.theguardian.com/technology/2020/dec/14/pornhub-purge-removes-unverified-videos-investigation-child-abuse [Accessed 22 July 2022].

Peersman, Claudia, Schulze, Christian, Rashid, Awais, Brennan, Margaret and Fischer, Carl. (2016). iCOP: Live Forensics to Reveal Previously Unknown Criminal Media on P2P networks. *Digital Investigation*, 18: 50–64.

Peters, Jonathan. (2017). The Sovereigns of Cyberspace and State Action: The First Amendment's Application – or Lack Thereof – to Third-Party Platforms. *Berkeley Technology Law Journal*, 32(2): 989–1026.

Peterson, Devon. (2002). Child Pornography on the Internet: The Effect of Section 230 of the Communications Decency Act of 1996 on Tort Recovery for Victims against Internet Service Providers. *University of Hawaii Law Review*, 24(2): 763–96.

Phillipson, Gavin. (2016). Press Freedom, Public Interest and Privacy, in Kenyon, Andrew (ed) *Comparative Defamation and Privacy Law*, Cambridge: Cambridge University Press, 136–63.

Polański, Przemysław Paul. (2018). Rethinking the Notion of Hosting in the Aftermath of Delfi: Shifting from Liability to Responsibility? *Computer Law & Security Review*, 34(4): 870–80.

Porat, Ariel. (2013). *Torts*, Vol 1, Tel Aviv: Nevo.

Pornhub. (2020). 2020 Pornhub Transparency Report. *Pornhub*, [Online]. https://help.pornhub.com/hc/en-us/articles/1260803955549-Transparency-Report [Accessed 22 July 2022].

Post, Robert. (1986). The Social Foundation of Defamation Law: Reputation and the Constitution. *California Law Review*, 74(3): 742–94.

Priel, Dan. (2019). Two Forms of Formalism, in Robertson, Andrew and Goudkamp, James (eds) *Form and Substance in the Law of Obligations*, Oxford: Bloomsbury, 165–94.

Prins, Corien. (2006). When Personal Data, Behaviour and Virtual Identities Become a Commodity: Would a Property Rights Approach Matter? *SCRIPT-ed*, 3(4): 270–303.

Prosser, Tony. (2006). Regulation and Social Solidarity. *Journal of Law and Society*, 33(3): 364–87.

Purshouse Craig and Trispiotis, Illias. (2021). Is Conversion Therapy Tortious? *Legal Studies*, 42(1): 23–41.

Purtova, Nadezhda. (2017). Do Property Rights in Personal Data Make Sense after the Big Data Turn? Individual Control and Transparency. *Journal of Law & Economics Regulation*, 10(2): 64–78.

Pyne, Saikat. (2015). This Is How Porn Sites Make Money. *Business Insider*, [Online] 7 August. Available from: www.businessinsider.in/this-is-how-porn-sitesmake-money/articleshow/48385361.cms [Accessed 22 July 2022].

Quayle, Ethel, Erooga, Marcus, Wright, Louise, Taylor, Max and Harbinson, Dawn. (2006). *Only Pictures? Therapeutic Work with Internet Sex Offenders*, Lyme Regis: Russell House Publishing.

Rackley, Erica, McGlynn, Clare, Johnson, Kelly, Henry, Nicola, Gavey, Nicola and Flynn, Asher et al (2021). Seeking Justice and Redress for Victim-Survivors of Image-Based Sexual Abuse. *Feminist Legal Studies*, 29: 293–322.

Radin, Margaret. (1982). Property and Personhood. *Stanford Law Review*, 34(5): 957–1016.

Rasker, Rachel. (2019). The Typical Victim of Revenge Porn Probably Isn't Who You Think It Is. *ABC Life*, [Online] 2 September. Available from: https://www.abc.net.au/life/the-typical-victim-of-revenge-porn-isnt-who-you-think-it-is/11240576 [Accessed 22 July 2022].

Ravenscraft, Eric. (2020). Almost Every Website You Visit Records Exactly How Your Mouse Moves. *One Zero*, [Online] 5 February. Available from: https://onezero.medium.com/almost-every-website-you-visit-records-exactly-how-your-mouse-moves-4134cb1cc7a0 [Accessed 22 July 2022].

Revenge Porn Helpline. (2021). Not without My Consent: The Facebook Pilot. *Revenge Porn Helpline*, [Online]. Available from: https://revengepornhelpline.org.uk/information-and-advice/reporting-content/facebook-pilot/ [Accessed 22 July 2022].

Richards, M. Neil. (2011). The Limits of Tort Privacy. *Journal of Telecommunications and High Technology Law*, 9: 382–84.

Richards, M. Neil and Solove, J. Daniel. (2010). Prosser's Privacy Law: A Mixed Legacy. *California Law Review*, 98(6): 1918–22.

Richardson, Janice. (2012). If I Cannot Have Her Everybody Can: Sexual Disclosure and Privacy Law, in Richardson, Janice and Rackley, Erika (eds) *Feminist Perspectives on Tort Law*, Abingdon: Routledge, 145–62.

Richardson, Janice. (2015). *Law and the Philosophy of Privacy*, Abingdon: Routledge.

Rinehart, Will. (2018). The Law & Economics of Owning Your Data. *American Action Forum*, [Online] 10 April. Available from: https://www. americanactionforum.org/insight/law-economics-owning-data/ [Accessed 22 July 2022].

Riordan, Jianni. (2016). *The Liability of Internet Intermediaries*. Oxford: Oxford University Press.

Ritter, Jeffrey and Mayer, Anna. (2018). Regulating Data as Property: A New Construct for Moving Forward. *Duke Law & Technology Review*, 16: 220–77.

Roberts, Jessica. (2019). Genetic Conversion *SSRN*, [Online] 15 March. Available from: https://ssrn.com/abstract=3357566 [Accessed 22 July 2022].

Roessler, Beate. (2015). Should Personal Data Be a Tradable Good? On the Moral Limits of Markets in Privacy, in Roessler, Beate and Mokrosinska, Dorota (eds) *Social Dimension of Privacy: Interdisciplinary Perspectives*, Cambridge: Cambridge University Press, 141–61.

Rogers, Brian. (2014). Jury Awards $500,000 in Revenge Porn Lawsuit. *Houston Chronicle*, [Online] 21 February. Available from: https://www. houstonchronicle.com/news/houston-texas/houston/article/Jury-awards-500-000-in-revenge-porn-lawsuit-5257436.php [Accessed 22 July 2022].

Rolph, David. (2017). The Interaction between Defamation and Privacy, in Barker, Kit, Fairweather, Karen and Grantham, Ross (eds) *Private Law in the Twenty-First Century*, Oxford: Hart, 463–78.

Romano, Aja. (2018). A New Law Intended to Curb Sex Trafficking Threatens the Future of the Internet as We Know It. *VOX*, [Online] 18 April. Available from: www.vox.com/culture/2018/4/13/17172762/fosta-sesta-backpage-230-internet-freedom [Accessed 22 July 2022].

Rosati, Eleonora. (2017). The CJEU *Pirate Bay* Judgment and Its Impact on the Liability of Online Platforms. *EIPR*, 39(12): 1–17.

Rosenberg, Roni and Dancig-Rosenberg, Hadar. (2021). Reconceptualizing Revenge Porn. *Arizona Law Review*, 63(1): 199–228.

Rubin, Gayle. (2002). Thinking Sex: Notes for a Radical Theory of the Politics of Sexuality, in Plummer, Ken (ed) *Sexualities: Critical Concepts in Sociology*, Abingdon: Routledge, 143–78.

Salins, Sara. (2019). Facebook Says It Made an A.I. Tool That Can Detect Revenge Porn Before It's Reported. *CNBC*, [Online] 15 March. Available from: https://www.cnbc.com/2019/03/15/facebook-ai-tool-detects-revenge-porn-before-its-reported.html [Accessed 22 July 2022].

Salmons, David. (2015). The Availability of Proprietary Restitution in Cases of Mistaken Payments. *Cambridge Law Journal*, 74(3): 534–67.

Sanghera, Jyoti. (2004). *Churning Out Numbers: Trafficking and Statistics*, Office of The High Commissioner for Human Rights, Working Paper No 16.

Sartor, Giovanni. (2013). Providers Liabilities in the New EU Data Protection Regulation: A Threat to Internet Freedoms? *International Data Privacy Law*, 3(1): 3–12.

Schellekens, Maurice. (2011). Liability of Internet Intermediaries: A Slippery Slope? *SCRIPT-ed*, 8(2): 154–74.

Schwartz, Alan and Scott, Robert. (2011). Rethinking the Laws of Good Faith Purchase. *Columbia Law Review*, 111(6): 1332–84.

Scott, Andrew. (2016). *Reform of Defamation Law in Northern Ireland: Recommendations to the Department of Finance*, Belfast: Northern Ireland Law Commission.

Seboc, Anthony. (2003). Reparations, Unjust Enrichment and the Importance of Knowing the Difference between the Two. *NYU Annual Survey of American Law*, 58(4): 651–8.

Sell, Susan. (2003). *Private Power, Public Law: The Globalization of Intellectual Property Rights*, Cambridge: Cambridge University Press.

Sharratt, Elena. (2019). Intimate Image Abuse in Adults and Under 18s. *SWGFL*, [Online]. Available from: https://swgfl.org.uk/assets/documents/intimate-image-abuse-in-adults-and-under-18s.pdf [Accessed 22 July 2022].

Shavell, Steven. (2007). *Economic Analysis of Accident Law*, rev edn. Cambridge: Harvard University Press.

Shpancer, Noam. (2016). Rape Is Not (Only) about Power; It's (Also) about Sex. *Psychology Today*, [Online] 1 February. Available from: https://www.psychologytoday.com/gb/blog/insight-therapy/201602/rape-is-not-only-about-power-it-s-also-about-sex [Accessed 22 July 2022].

Sinha, Alex. (2019). A Real-Property Model of Privacy. *DePaul Law Review*, 68(3): 567–614.

Síthigh, M Daithí. (2018). *Medium Law*, Abingdon: Routledge.

Skinner-Thompson, Scott. (2018). Privacy's Double Standards. *Washington Law Review*, 93(4): 2051–106.

Smolla, A Rodney. (2002). Accounting for the Slow Growth of American Privacy Law. *Nova Law Review*, 27(2): 289–302.

Solon, Olivia. (2019). Inside Facebook's Efforts to Stop Revenge Porn Before It Spreads. *NBC News*, [Online] 19 November. Available from: https://www.nbcnews.com/tech/social-media/inside-facebook-s-efforts-stop-revenge-porn-it-spreads-n1083631 [Accessed 22 July 2022].

Solove, Daniel. (2002). Conceptualizing privacy. *California Law Review*, 90(4): 1087–155.

South Yorkshire Police. (2022). Don't Make I Easy for Thieves. *South Yorkshire Police*, [Online] 4 March. Available from: https://www.southyorks.police.uk/find-out/crime-prevention-advice/dont-make-it-easy-for-thieves/ [Accessed 22 July 2022].

Spoerri, Thomas. (2019). On Upload-Filters and Other Competitive Advantages for Big Tech Companies under Article 17 of the Directive on Copyright in the Digital Single Market. *Journal of Intellectual Property, Information Technology and Electronic Commerce Law*, 10(2): 173–86.

Stapleton, Jane. (1995). Duty of Care: Peripheral Parties and Alternative Opportunities for Deterrence. *Law Quarterly Review*, 111(2): 301–45.

Steinberg, Joseph. (2014). Can You Be Arrested – or Sued – for Viewing or Sharing Nude Celebrity Photos? Here Are Some Relevant Laws. *Forbes*, [Online] September 24. Available from: https://www.forbes.com/sites/josephsteinberg/2014/09/24/can-you-be-arrested-or-sued-for-viewing-or-sharing-nude-celebrity-photos-here-are-some-relevant-laws-2/?sh=2c60718560cc [Accessed 22 July 2022].

Stevens, Robert. (2007). *Torts and Rights*, Oxford: Oxford University Press.

Stevens, Robert. (2018). Damages for Wrongdoing in the Absence of Loss, in Varuhas, Jason and Moreham, Nicole (eds) *Remedies for Breach of Privacy*, Oxford: Hart, 97–124.

Strahilevitz, Lior. (2010). Reunifying Privacy Law. *California Law Review*, 98(6): 2007–48.

Sunstein, Cass. (2014). Nudging: A Very Short Guide. *Journal of Consumer Policy*, 37(4): 583–8.

Suzor, Nicolas, Seignior, Bryony and Singleton, Jennifer. (2017). Non-Consensual Porn and the Responsibilities of Online Intermediaries. *Melbourne University Law Review*, 40(3): 1057–97.

Taylor, Josh. (2020). Not Just Nipples: How Facebook's AI Struggles to Detect Misinformation. *The Guardian*, [Online] 16 June. Available from: https://www.theguardian.com/technology/2020/jun/17/not-just-nipples-how-facebooks-ai-struggles-to-detect-misinformation [Accessed 22 July 2022].

Taylor, Max and Quayle, Ethel. (2003). *Child Pornography: An Internet Crime*. Abingdon: Brunner-Routledge.

Tettenborn Andrew. (ed) (2021). *Clerk & Lindsell on Torts*, 23rd edn. London: Sweet & Maxwell.

Thomson, Judith Jarvis. (1975). The Right to Privacy. *Philosophy & Public Affairs*, 4(4): 295–314.

Thurston, Rebecca C, Chang, Yuefang, Matthews, Karen A., Von Känel, Roland and Koenenm Karestan. (2019). Association of Sexual Harassment and Sexual Assault with Midlife Women's Mental and Physical Health. *JAMA Internal Medicine*, 179(1): 48–53.

Tibury, Michael. (2018). Aggravated Damages. *Current Legal Problems*, 71(1): 215–44.

Tolin, David and Foa, Edna. (2006). Sex Differences in Trauma and Posttraumatic Stress Disorder: A Quantitative Review of 25 Years of Research. *Psychological Bulletin*, 132(6): 959–92.

Tomlinson, Hugh. (2010). Defamation and False Privacy, Some Thoughts. *INFORRM*, [Online] 14 December. Available from: https://inforrm.org/2010/12/14/opinion-defamation-and-false-privacy-hugh-tomlinson-qc/ [Accessed 22 July 2022].

Toulson, Roger and Phipps, Charles. (2006). *Confidentiality*, 2nd edn. London: Sweet & Maxwell.

Turner, Ryan. (2014). Internet Defamation Law and Publication by Omission: A Multi-Jurisdictional Analysis. *University of New South Wales Law Journal*, 37(1): 34–62.

Tushnet, Rebecca. (2013). Performance Anxiety: Copyright Embodied and Dis-embodied. *Journal of the Copyright Society of the USA*, 60(2): 209–48.

Tzanou, Maria. (2020). The Unexpected Consequences of the EU Right to Be Forgotten: Internet Search Engines as Fundamental Rights Adjudicators, in Tzanou, Maria (ed) *Personal Data Protection and Legal Developments in the European Union*, Hershey: IGI Global, 279–301.

Uhl, Carolyn A., Rhyner, Katlin J., Terrance, Cheryl and Lugo, Noël. (2018). An Examination of Nonconsensual Pornography Websites. *Feminism & Psychology*, 28(1): 50–68.

Ullrich, Carsten. (2017). Standards for Duty of Care? Debating Intermediary Liability from a Sectoral Perspective. *Journal of Intellectual Property, Information Technology and Electronic Commerce Law*, 8(2): 111–27.

Urban, M. Jennifer, Karaganis, Joe and Schofield, L. Brianna. (2017). Notice and Takedown: Online Service Provider and Rightsholder Accounts of Everyday Practice. *Journal of the Copyright Society of the USA*, 64(3): 371–410.

US Sentencing Commission. (2012). Federal Child Pornography Offences. *USSC*, [Online]. Available from: https://www.ussc.gov/sites/default/files/pdf/news/congressional-testimony-and-reports/sex-offense-topics/201212-federal-child-pornography-offenses/Full_Report_to_Congress.pdf [Accessed 22 July 2022].

US Sentencing Commission. (2020). 2020 Annual Report and Sourcebook of Federal Sentencing Statistics. *USSC*, [Online]. Available from: https://www.ussc.gov/sites/default/files/pdf/research-and-publications/annual-reports-and-sourcebooks/2020/2020-Annual-Report-and-Sourcebook.pdf [Accessed 22 July 2022].

Valenti, Jessica. (2014). What's Wrong with Checking Out Stolen Nude Photos of Celebrities. *The Atlantic*, [Online] 1 September. Available from: https://www.theatlantic.com/entertainment/archive/2014/09/leaked-photos-nude-celebrities-abuse/379434/ [Accessed 22 July 2022].

Van Houweling, Molly S. (2005). Distributive Values in Copyright. *Texas Law Review*, 83(6): 1535–80.

Varuhas, Jason. (2018). Varieties of Damages for Breach of Privacy, in Varuhas, Jason and Moreham, Nicole (eds) *Remedies for Breach of Privacy*, Oxford: Hart, 55–95.

Vedder, Anton. (2001). Accountability of Internet Access and Service Providers: Strict Liability Entering Ethics? *Ethics and Information Technology*, 3(1): 67–74.

Vera-Gray, Fiona, McGlynn, Clare, Kureshi, Ibad and Butterby, Kate. (2021). Sexual Violence as a Sexual Script in Mainstream Online Pornography. *The British Journal of Criminology*, 61(5): 1243–60.

Walker, Dominic. (2019). Costs Reforms for Privacy and Defamation Cases Come into Force Next Week. *JMW*, [Online] 26 March. Available from: https://www.jmw.co.uk/services-for-you/media-law/blog/costs-reforms-privacy-and-defamation-cases-come-force-next-week [Accessed 22 July 2022].

Walker, Kate and Sleath, Emma. (2017). A Systematic Review of the Current Knowledge Regarding Revenge Pornography and Non-Consensual Sharing of Sexually Explicit Media. *Aggression and Violent Behaviour*, 36: 9–24.

Wang, Jie. (2018). *Regulating Hosting ISPs Responsibilities for Copyright Infringement*, Singapore: Springer.

Warby, Mark and Shore, Victoria. (2016) Justifications and Defences, in Moreham, Nicole and Warby, Mark (eds) *Tugendhat and Christie: The Law of Privacy and The Media*, 3rd edn. Oxford: Oxford University Press, 471–551.

Warby, Mark, Garrick, Adèle and Strong, Chloe. (2016). Misuse of Private Information, in Moreham, Nicole and Warby, Mark. (eds) *Tugendhat and Christie: The Law of Privacy and The Media*, 3rd edn. Oxford: Oxford University Press, 211–68.

Weinrib, Ernest. (1995). *The Idea of Private Law*, Oxford: Oxford University Press.

Weinrib, Ernest. (2000). Restitutionary Damages as Corrective Justice. *Theoretical Enquiries in Law*, 1(1): 1–38.

White, Isobel and Johnston, Neil. (2017). *Electoral Fraud since 2010*, House of Commons Library Briefing Paper Number 6255). Available from: researchbriefings.files.parliament.uk/documents/SN06255/SN06255.pdf.

Willard, Nancy. (2010). Sexting and Youth: Achieving a Rational Response. *Journal of Social Sciences*, 6(4): 542–62.

Winterton, David and Pilkington, Timothy. (2021). Examining the Structure of Remedial Law. *Modern Law Review*, 84(5): 1137–58.

Witzleb, Normann. (2014). Interim Injunction for Invasions of Privacy: Challenging the Rule in Bonnard v. Perryman? in Witzleb, Normann, Lindsay, David, Paterson, Moira and Rodrick, Sharon. (eds) *Emerging Challenges in Privacy Law*, Cambridge: Cambridge University Press, 407–40.

Woods, Lorna. (2017). When Is Facebook Liable for Illegal Content under the E-Commerce Directive? CG v Facebook in the Northern Ireland Courts. *EU Law Analysis*, [Blog] 19 January. Available from: www.eulawanalysis.blogspot.com/2017/01/when-is-facebook-liable-for-illegal.html [Accessed 22 July 2022].

Working to Halt Online Abuse. (2014). Comparison Statistics 2000–2012. *Halt Abuse*, [Online]. Available from: http://www.haltabuse.org/resources/stats/Cumulative2000-2012.pdf [Accessed 22 July 2022].

Wragg, Paul. (2019). Recognising a Privacy-Invasion Tort: The Conceptual Unity of Informational and Intrusion Claims. *Cambridge Law Journal*, 78(2): 409–37.

Yatar, Eric. (2003). Defamation, Privacy, and the Changing Social Status of Homosexuality: Re-Thinking Supreme Court Gay Rights Jurisprudence. *Tulane Journal of Law and Sexuality*, 12: 119–58.

Zaikman, Yuliana and Marks, Michael. (2014). Ambivalent Sexism and the Sexual Double Standard. *Sex Roles*, 71(9): 333–44.

Zaleski, Kristen. (2019). The Long Trauma of Revenge Porn. *OUP Blog*, [Blog] 22 September. Available from: https://blog.oup.com/2019/09/the-long-trauma-of-revenge-porn/ [Accessed 22 July 2022].

Zipursky, Benjamin. (2016). The Monsanto Lecture: Online Defamation, Legal Concepts, and the Good Samaritan. *Valparaiso University Law Review*, 51(1): 1–56.

Zuboff, Shoshana. (2019). *The Age of Surveillance Capitalism*, London: Profile Books.

Index

References to footnotes show both the page number and the note number (14n4).